Lone Star Legacy

A Texas Cookbook

Austin Junior Forum

The objective of Austin Junior Forum is to create a greater interest among young women in civic, educational and philanthropic fields. Profits from the sale of *Lone Star Legacy* will be returned to the community through Austin Junior Forum projects.

Library of Congress No. 81-69340
ISBN 0-9607152-0-7

Additional copies may be obtained at the cost of $14.95 per book, plus $2.00 postage and handling. Texas residents add $.93 sales tax between 1-1-87 and 8-31-87; after 8-31-87 add $.77 sales tax. Send to:
Austin Junior Forum Publications
P.O. Box 26628
Austin, Texas 78755-0628

Photography by Mike Flahive
Austin, Texas

First Printing December 1981, 10,000
Second Printing March 1982, 10,000
Third Printing May 1982, 10,000
Fourth Printing September 1982, 30,000
Fifth Printing November 1983, 30,000
Sixth Printing May 1985, 30,000
Seventh Printing November 1986, 30,000

Printed by Hart Graphics, Inc.
8000 Shoal Creek Blvd.
Austin, Texas 78758

Foreword

From the majestic peaks of the Davis mountains in the west, across the rolling plains to the pine forests in the east and the sun-kissed shores of Padre Island on the Gulf of Mexico, Texas offers a panorama of cultures, lifestyles and experiences. Its history is both colorful and legendary. For three centuries, Texas was governed and influenced by foreign rule, and then our hearty pioneers proclaimed their desire to be free, regardless of the cost. Thus was born the Republic of Texas, an independent nation for nearly a decade before joining the United States of America.

From this beginning, Texas has emerged as not merely a state, but a state of mind. In its people are combined the stamina of European immigrants, the warm-hearted friendliness of the early Anglo settlers, the gracious elegance of old Mexico, and the relaxed hospitality of the South.

This unique lifestyle is reflected in the cuisine, as well. Whether the meal is a casual backyard barbecue or a formal seated dinner, the unmistakable flavor of Texas abounds. Blessed with a vast array of fresh seafood, prime beef, crisp vegetables and succulent fruit, our menus mirror the natural resources of this land. Complemented by the addition of native herbs and spices, Texas cooking is in a class by itself.

We have prepared this cookbook as a tribute to our state. Within its pages, you will find a collection of recipes, both old and new. Many have been passed down to us from past generations, others were graciously shared by present friends. All are meant to bring you closer to the true essence of Texas and its people.

In the spirit of the name, Texas, a Caddo Indian word for *friendship*, we offer you a gift prepared with love, our *Lone Star Legacy*.

The Cookbook Committee sincerely appreciates the enthusiastic participation of the club membership in testing and compiling the recipes for this book.

Original Cookbook Committee

Mrs. Dudley Baker, Chairman

Mrs. Larry Hall, Co-Chairman

Mrs. Don Bradford

Mrs. Ron Garrick

Mrs. Larry Lerche

Mrs. Ken Moyer

Mrs. Jim Rado

Mrs. Jim Schultz

Mrs. Denman Smith

Mrs. Charles Tupa

1986-87 Cookbook Committee

Mrs. Terry Arndt, Chairman

Mrs. Dudley Baker

Mrs. John Biggar

Mrs. Tom Blair

Mrs. Joe Bowles

Mrs. Ron Bruney

Mrs. Reece Goodman

Mrs. Paul Holcomb

Mrs. Richard Mizner

Mrs. Larry Nau

Mrs. Craig Smith

Mrs. Denman Smith

Mrs. Robert Vossman

Contents

Since the first ship entered the Gulf of Mexico and the excited cry was heard, "Land ho!", this coast line has welcomed the settler to new security, the refugee to new freedom, and the adventurer to new excitement. Much history has been made along the shores of our Gulf coast. Today, it is a mecca for fishermen, both for fun and profit. An enormous fishing industry brings fresh shrimp, oysters, crab and other exotic varieties of fish into port daily. The Gulf coast has also become synonymous with winter recreation, offering almost year-round tropical weather along its southern shores. Padre Island is now a National Seashore and boasts of hotels and condominiums to equal those along the nation's east coast. Many frost-bitten dwellers of the Midwest travel to Texas during the winter months to enjoy the warmth and sunshine prevalent here. The proximity of South Padre to the borders of old Mexico lure the more adventurous tourists, as well, and they are usually equally delighted with the shopping and entertainment found there.

Appetizers and Beverages pictured: Margarita, Dudley's Bloody Mary, Mimosa, Beer Boiled Shrimp, Spinach Dip in Rye Bread and Caviar Mold.

Appetizers and Beverages

Ken's Picadillo Dip

½   pound hot bulk sausage
1   pound ground beef
1   teaspoon salt
Pepper to taste
1   can (16 ounces) tomatoes, cut up
3   green onions, chopped
1   jar (2½ ounces) chopped pimientos

¼ to ½ cup almond slices
1   clove garlic, finely chopped
1   can (6 ounces) tomato paste
2   jalapeños, seeded and chopped
½ to ¾ cup golden raisins
¼   teaspoon oregano

Mix meats together by hand. Put into a large pan and barely cover with water. Add salt and pepper. Stir meat until well blended. Simmer covered for 30 minutes. Add remaining ingredients and cook 15 minutes longer. Serve hot in a chafing dish with chips. Freezes well. For a change of pace, substitute cashews for almonds.

Mrs. Ken Moyer (Bonnie)

Picadillo Dip Con Papas

5   pounds lean ground beef
1   tablespoon salt
1   tablespoon pepper
3   teaspoons cumin, divided
1   medium green pepper, diced
1   medium onion, diced

4   medium tomatoes, peeled and diced
5   small potatoes, peeled and diced
1½ tablespoons salt
1   teaspoon pepper
4   ounces slivered almonds

Combine meats, one tablespoon salt, one tablespoon pepper, and two teaspoons cumin. Cook over medium heat until meat is done. Drain excess fat. Add vegetables and stir well. Sprinkle with remaining salt, pepper, cumin, and almonds; blend well. Cover and cook over low heat until the potatoes are done. About 50 servings. *This dip is hearty enough to serve as a taco filler.*

Mrs. Jim Rado (Vicki)

Beef Picadillo Dip

1   pound ground beef
1   small onion, chopped
¾   cup chopped pimiento
¾   cup slivered almonds,
    toasted
1   teaspoon salt
1   teaspoon pepper
2   cloves garlic, minced
½   teaspoon oregano
½   cup water

1   can (4 ounces) chopped ripe
    olives
1   can (4 ounces) mushrooms,
    drained and chopped
1   can (10 ounces) Ro-Tel
    tomatoes and green chilies
1   pound grated Velveeta
    cheese
1   cup golden raisins, optional

Brown ground beef; drain grease, and add remaining ingredients. Simmer 2 hours. Serve with tortilla chips.

Mrs. Ed L. Mears (Kate)

Mexican Sausage Dip

1   pound bulk sausage
11 ounces cream cheese

1   can (10 ounces) Ro-Tel
    tomatoes and green chilies

Fry sausage until brown. Pour off grease. Add cream cheese and Ro-Tel tomatoes. Heat thoroughly. Serve with chips.

Mrs. Bill Butler (Stephanie)

Jiffy Chili Cheese Dip

1   can (19 ounces) chili
    without beans
1   can (16 ounces) refried
    beans

1   can Cheddar cheese soup

Mix all ingredients; heat thoroughly. Serve dip warm in a chafing dish with corn chips and tortilla chips.

Mrs. James Hurlbut (Marsha)

 Mexico's green chile has a place of honor in most Texas kitchens. This spicy vegetable adds zest to almost any dish.

Hot Sausage and Cheese Dip

1   **pound hot bulk sausage**
1   **pound ground beef**
1   **onion, chopped**
1   **can (4 ounces) mushrooms, drained, chopped**

1   **can cream of mushroom soup**
2   **pounds Velveeta cheese**

Sauté sausage, beef and onion; drain grease. Add remaining ingredients and heat slowly until cheese is melted. Serve hot with tortilla chips.

Mrs. Larry Keith (Virginia)

Hot Seafood Dip

1   **stick butter**
8   **ounces cream cheese**

1   **can (6½ ounces) crab meat, or 1 can (6½ ounces) minced clams, or 2 cans (3¾ ounces each) smoked oysters**
Tabasco, optional

Melt butter slowly; add cream cheese and stir until melted. Combine mixture well with a hand mixer or wire whip. Add seafood; reheat adding Tabasco if desired, or thinning with milk if needed. Serve in a chafing dish with bread cubes for dippers.

Mrs. Denman Smith (Sandra)

Hot Crab Meat Dip

8   **ounces cream cheese**
6 to 8 **ounces crab meat, fresh, frozen or canned (drained)**
1   **clove garlic, finely minced**
¼   **cup mayonnaise**

1   **teaspoon prepared mustard**
1   **teaspoon powdered sugar**
Salt to taste
3 to 4 **tablespoons dry white wine**

Put all ingredients in the top of a double boiler. Heat over hot water until cream cheese is melted, stirring frequently. Serve in a chafing dish with French bread cubes.

Mrs. Terry Arndt (Barbara)

Casey's Crab Dip

2 cans (6½ ounces each) crab meat
4 eggs, hard cooked, chopped
3 cups soft bread crumbs, divided
3 tablespoons chopped parsley
2 tablespoons minced green pepper
3 tablespoons minced green onion
3 tablespoons lemon juice
Salt and pepper to taste
Onion salt to taste
Garlic powder to taste
1 can cream of mushroom soup
1 cup mayonnaise
2 cups half and half cream
2 teaspoons prepared mustard
Parmesan cheese

Combine crab meat, eggs, 2½ cups bread crumbs, parsley, green pepper, onion, lemon juice and seasonings. Mix soup with mayonnaise and mustard. Blend both mixtures together. Top with remaining bread crumbs and a generous sprinkling of cheese. Bake uncovered at 400° for 15 to 20 minutes in a 2½ quart casserole. To enhance the flavors, prepare the day before baking. Keep warm while serving. Serve with Melba toast rounds. *This dish is so rich that it can double as a light meal.*

Mrs. Larry Hall (Jane)

Spicy Shrimp Dip

1 pound shrimp, peeled, deveined, cooked and chopped
8 ounces cream cheese, softened
Juice of 1 lemon
1 cup mayonnaise
¼ cup Durkee's famous sauce
2 ribs celery, finely chopped
1 large green pepper, finely chopped
1 medium onion, finely chopped
1 clove garlic, finely chopped
½ teaspoon seasoned salt
2 tablespoons picante sauce

Combine shrimp, cream cheese and lemon juice. Blend well. Add rest of ingredients. Cover and refrigerate at least one day ahead of serving. This dip keeps in the refrigerator at least five days. Serve with vegetables or crackers.

Mrs. Jim Schultz (Mary Kay)

Cold Shrimp Dip

1½ cups cooked shrimp, cut up
8 ounces cream cheese
½ cup mayonnaise
¼ cup diced green onion

½ cup diced celery
1 teaspoon lemon juice
Salt and pepper to taste

Soften the cream cheese and mix all ingredients together. Chill overnight. Serve with chips or crackers. For emergencies, substitute 1½ cans (4½ ounces each) shrimp, and for a different flavor use garlic salt in place of regular salt.

Mrs. Larry Morris (Diane)

Salsa Caliente (Hot Sauce)

6 ripe tomatoes
8 to 10 fresh jalapeño or serrano peppers
2 large cloves garlic, chopped or ½ tablespoon garlic powder
1 teaspoon salt

¼ teaspoon freshly ground pepper
¼ teaspoon honey, optional
½ cup chopped green onions
¼ cup fresh cilantro, chopped

Bring two quarts of water to a rapid boil. Add tomatoes and boil until their skins split. Remove promptly and allow to cool 5 minutes. Peel tomatoes and cut them into large chunks. Remove seeds and stems from jalapeños. Blend one half of the tomatoes, garlic, salt, pepper, honey and jalapeños until the mixture is very finely chopped. The remainder of the ingredients will add texture to the sauce, so lightly blend the remaining half of tomatoes, green onions, and cilantro. Store covered in the refrigerator until ready to serve. Yields 2 cups. *Use rubber gloves if possible while deseeding the jalapeños, and be sure to stand near your cook top vent for better ventilation.*

Mrs. Dan Steakley (Susan)

Shrimp Ceviche

1½ pounds raw shrimp, peeled
  and deveined
1 cup fresh lime juice
1 can (4 ounces) chopped
  green chilies
½ cup chopped green onions
  with tops
2 large tomatoes, chopped
1 teaspoon salt

4 tablespoons olive oil
4 serrano chilies or 1
  jalapeño, chopped
1 clove garlic, finely minced
1 jar (4 ounces) chopped
  pimientos, drained
Fresh cilantro or parsley,
  chopped

Marinate bite size shrimp in lime juice in a covered flat dish for 2 to 3 hours. Mix remaining ingredients except cilantro; add to shrimp and lime juice. Marinate at least 8 hours. Drain. Garnish with cilantro or parsley. Serve cold in a chilled bowl. *This appetizer is best if the Mexican limones are used for the fresh lime juice.*

Mrs. Dudley Baker (Kathy)

Ceviche, Acapulco Style

2 pounds boneless fresh fish
2 cups lime juice, divided
2 tablespoons olive oil
¼ teaspoon ground oregano
¼ teaspoon cumin
2 teaspoons salt
½ teaspoon white pepper
¼ teaspoon Tabasco
6 green onions, chopped
3 large tomatoes, peeled and
  chopped

⅓ cup sliced stuffed green
  olives
6 to 8 pickled serrano chilies,
  sliced
3 tablespoons cilantro,
  chopped or ½ teaspoon
  coriander leaf
1 cup parsley, chopped
2 avocados, cubed

Cut fish into cubes and put in a glass container. Cover with 1½ cups lime juice. Refrigerate, tightly covered, for 4 to 5 hours. Stir several times to make sure fish is coated. About 30 minutes before removing fish from refrigerator, mix oil, ½ cup lime juice, dry spices and Tabasco. Add onions, tomatoes, olives, chilies, and parsley. Remove fish; drain, and add to the tomato mixture. Refrigerate tightly covered overnight or at least 8 hours stirring occasionally. One hour before serving, add avocados, making sure cubes are completely covered.

Mrs. Dudley Baker (Kathy)

Ceviche

2	pounds ocean trout, cut into 1 inch squares	4	tablespoons white wine
2	cups fresh lime juice	4	tablespoons olive oil
1	teaspoon salt	10	green onions, chopped
2	cups tomato juice	¼	teaspoon soy sauce
3	tablespoons chopped jalapeños	½	teaspoon Worcestershire sauce
2	medium tomatoes, diced	1	teaspoon salt
1	medium onion, diced	1	teaspoon oregano

Marinate fish in lime juice and one teaspoon salt for 3 to 4 hours. Rinse in a colander. Mix remaining sauce ingredients and add fish. Refrigerate overnight to allow the flavors to blend. Serve with crackers or tostado chips.

Mrs. Jim Rado (Vicki)

Guacamole

3	ripe avocados		Tabasco to taste
	Salt and pepper to taste	1	tomato, chopped
1½	teaspoons lemon juice		Tomato wedges for garnish, optional
¼	teaspoon garlic powder		
2	tablespoons finely minced onion		

Peel and mash avocados. Add salt, pepper, lemon juice, garlic powder, onion and Tabasco; mix well. Stir in chopped tomato. Garnish with tomato wedges, if desired. May be used as a dip; as a salad, served on a bed of lettuce; or as an appetizer to stuff cherry tomatoes.

Mrs. Marvin Sentell (Julie)

Avocado Dip

8	ounces cream cheese, softened		Dash Tabasco
2	very ripe avocados, mashed		Cayenne pepper to taste
½	small onion, grated		Salt to taste
1	clove garlic, mashed	2	tablespoons lemon juice
1	teaspoon Worcestershire sauce	2	heaping tablespoons mayonnaise

Combine all ingredients and mix well. Chill. Serve with Fritos or tostados.
Mrs. Robert Henderson (Dale)

Prairie Fire

1   stick butter
1   large onion, chopped
2 to 4 tablespoons bacon
     drippings
1   quart cooked pinto beans

8   ounces Provolone cheese
5   jalapeños, chopped (reserve
     liquid)
2   cloves garlic, chopped
Salt to taste

Melt butter in large pan; add onions and sauté them until soft. Add bacon drippings. Add beans and mash, adding bean juice if needed. Cook over low heat mashing and stirring until desired consistency is reached. Add remaining ingredients. Stir over low heat until cheese is melted. Taste for seasonings, adding reserved 1 tablespoon jalapeño juice if needed. Serve in a chafing dish with tostados or corn chips. This dip can be frozen or stored in the refrigerator. Flavors are enhanced if made the day before serving. Warm over a low heat and stir often.

Mrs. Dudley Baker (Kathy)

Bleu Cheese Artichoke Appetizer

¼   pound bleu cheese
1   pound butter, no substitute

4   cans (14 ounces each)
     artichoke hearts, drained

Melt butter; do not boil. Crumble bleu cheese and add to melted butter. Cut artichokes in half and add to mixture. Keep warm in a chafing dish.

Mrs. Lee Provinse (Dottie)

Artichoke Dip

1   can (14 ounces) artichoke
     hearts

1   package (.6 ounces) Italian
     salad dressing mix
1   cup mayonnaise

Drain and chop artichoke hearts. Mix salad dressing and mayonnaise. Stir in chopped artichoke hearts. Place in a serving dish and refrigerate until chilled. Yields approximately 2 cups.

Marcy Batey

Artichokes will turn a grayish color if cooked in aluminum or iron. For extra flavor, cook them in broth instead of water.

Andalé Dip

2 cans (4 ounces each)
chopped green chilies
2 cans (4 ounces each)
chopped black olives
4 to 6 chopped green onions

1 can (16 ounces) tomatoes,
drained and chopped
(reserve liquid)
2 tablespoons wine vinegar
1 tablespoon oil
Salt and pepper to taste

Mix all ingredients together. If the mixture seems a little dry, add reserved tomato liquid. This dip needs to be a little soupy. Refrigerate for several hours or overnight to blend flavors. Serve with Doritos or tortilla chips. Yields a generous 2 cups.

Mrs. Ken Moyer (Bonnie)

Spinach Dip

1 package (10 ounces) frozen
chopped spinach or 2 cups
fresh cooked spinach,
chopped
1 cup sour cream
½ cup mayonnaise

½ cup minced parsley
½ cup minced onion
1 teaspoon salt
½ teaspoon celery salt
¼ teaspoon pepper
⅛ teaspoon nutmeg

Thaw spinach; place in a colander and press out excess water. Mix spinach with remaining ingredients. Cover and refrigerate at least 24 hours. May be prepared up to 3 days in advance. Serve as a dip for fresh vegetables. Yields about 3 cups.

Mrs. Jim Rado (Vicki)

Broccoli Dip

2 packages (10 ounces each)
frozen chopped broccoli
2 tablespoons butter
1 medium onion, chopped
3 ribs celery, chopped
1 can (4 ounces) chopped
mushrooms, drained

1 or 2 rolls garlic cheese
1 can cream of mushroom
soup
⅛ teaspoon Worcestershire
sauce

Cook and drain broccoli. Melt butter and sauté onion, celery, and mushrooms. Melt cheese in a double boiler; add soup and Worcestershire sauce. Blend all ingredients together. Serve warm with chips or vegetables. For a variation try substituting frozen spinach for the broccoli.

Mrs. Joe Bowles (Mary)

Green Chile Dip

8	ounces cream cheese, softened	1	tablespoon mayonnaise
1	can (4 ounces) chopped green chilies	½	tablespoon lemon juice

Mix all ingredients together thoroughly. Refrigerate. Remove from refrigerator about 30 minutes before serving. Serve with chips.

Mrs. Jim Lederer (Anne)

Chile Con Queso

3	tablespoons butter	1	pound Velveeta cheese, diced
½	cup finely chopped onion		
3	tablespoons finely chopped green pepper	½	pound sharp Cheddar cheese, diced
1	can (4 ounces) chopped green chilies	½	pound American cheese, diced
1½	cups milk	¼	teaspoon cayenne
1½	cups water		

Melt butter. Add next three ingredients and saute until tender. Add milk and water; cook until boiling. Over very low heat, add Velveeta cheese, stirring constantly until melted. Continue stirring, adding sharp cheese. When melted, add American cheese stirring until melted. Add cayenne and blend well. Let set overnight; reheat in a double boiler. The mixture will be thin when first made but will thicken overnight.

Larry Hall

Dill Dip with Rye Bread

1	round (6 to 8 inches) uncut rye bread, Russian or Swedish	2	teaspoons dill weed
		2	teaspoons seasoned salt
1⅓	cups mayonnaise	2	tablespoons minced onion
1⅓	cups sour cream	2	tablespoons minced parsley

Cut center out of bread; cut this extra bread into cubes for dipping. Combine remaining ingredients and serve in the cut out round loaf of rye bread. Serve on a platter with bread cubes placed around the loaf of bread. The dip can be made ahead of time and refrigerated. Pour dip into bread just before serving. When cubes are all eaten, break off chunks from the loaf of bread to use for dipping. Serves 15 to 20.

Mrs. Robert Henderson (Dale)

Bagna Cauda (Hot Anchovy Dip)

½ cup butter
6 tablespoons olive oil
4 cloves garlic, minced

2 cans (2 ounces each) flat
   anchovy fillets, chopped
2 tablespoons chopped
   parsley

Heat butter, oil and garlic. Keep warm over very low heat for 5 minutes. Add anchovies. Increase heat until mixture begins to simmer. Do not boil. Stir until anchovies have dissolved. Just before serving, transfer to a small flameproof bowl; stir in parsley. Keep warm. Great with pumpernickel, French bread chunks, or raw vegetables.

Mrs. Jim Rado (Vicki)

June's Dip

8 ounces cream cheese,
   softened
1 pint mayonnaise
1 medium onion, grated or 2
   tablespoons onion juice

1 tablespoon B V beef extract
Salt and pepper to taste
Paprika to taste
2 ounces bleu cheese

Combine softened cream cheese and mayonnaise. Blend well. Add onion, beef extract, salt, pepper and paprika. Mix thoroughly. Crumble bleu cheese into mixture and stir gently. This dip keeps in the refrigerator for a long time. Serve with fresh vegetables.

Mrs. Bob Edgecomb (Mary)

Vegetable Christmas Tree

1 recipe of a sour cream
   based dip (Hidden Valley)
1 bunch fresh broccoli

1 head cauliflower
15 cherry tomatoes

Spread bottom of a large oblong pyrex dish with dip. Cut broccoli flowerlets into short pieces; cut cauliflower into bite size chunks. Clean one broccoli stalk for tree trunk. Arrange broccoli into a tree shape on top of dip; stud with tomatoes, and surround by cauliflower. *This is a really pretty and festive way to serve a dip for a Christmas party.*

Mrs. Jim Schultz (Mary Kay)

Marinated Broccoli and Curry Dip

1 large bunch fresh broccoli	2 cloves garlic, split
¼ cup cider or wine vinegar	1 teaspoon dill weed
¾ cup oil	

Cut broccoli into bite size flowerettes. Split large stems if necessary. Combine vinegar, oil, garlic and dill weed; shake well. Pour over broccoli; seal and refrigerate overnight. Drain broccoli and serve with curry dip.

Curry Dip:

1 cup mayonnaise	
1½ teaspoons dry mustard	1 teaspoon tarragon vinegar
1 teaspoon curry powder	2 tablespoons finely chopped onion

Combine all ingredients and store in the refrigerator. Use as a dip for the marinated broccoli.

Mrs. John Griggs (Judy)

Gourmet Paté

2 pounds chicken livers	1 teaspoon paprika
1½ cups butter, divided, no substitute	1 teaspoon curry
2 medium onions, finely chopped	¼ teaspoon salt
	¼ teaspoon pepper
	¼ cup Cognac

Wash chicken livers; pat dry, and chop. In a saucepan melt ½ cup butter; add livers, onions, paprika, curry, salt and pepper. Cover and simmer over low heat until livers are cooked and onions are transparent. Puree mixture in a blender. It should be a nice thick paste. Add remaining 1 cup butter, softened; blend again. Add Cognac and blend. Pack firmly in crocks or glass containers. Freezes well.

Mrs. Bob Edgecomb (Mary)

Paté

1	pound Braunschweiger liver sausage, at room temperature
1	carton (8 ounces) sour cream
8	ounces cream cheese, softened

1	package (1½ ounces) dry green onion dip
¼	teaspoon dill weed, optional
	Pine nuts or slivered almonds, optional

Mix sausage, sour cream, cream cheese, onion dip, and dill weed. Mold in a container of your choice and place in refrigerator until firm. Unmold and place pine nuts on top.

Mrs. Larry Nau (Rose)

Chicken Paté

8	tablespoons butter, melted
1	medium onion, thinly sliced
1	celery stalk, julienned
1	carrot, julienned
1	tablespoon salt

2	large chicken breasts (4 halves)
1	pork chop (6 or 7 ounces)
¾	pound butter, softened
⅓	cup Cognac
	Salt and pepper to taste

Combine butter, onion, celery, carrot and salt in a heavy three quart saucepan. Add chicken and pork chop. Cook, covered over medium heat until tender, about 45 minutes to 1 hour. Remove chicken and pork from saucepan and cool. Trim away skin, fat and bone. Dice about ¼ cup chicken and set aside. Grind remaining chicken and pork. Beat in softened butter and Cognac. Add salt and pepper to taste. Mix in reserved diced chicken. Butter a 9 × 5 inch loaf pan and line with wax paper. Press paté into the prepared pan and cover with plastic wrap. Refrigerate 24 hours before serving. Garnish with parsley, pimientos, cherry tomatoes or hard cooked egg whites arranged to suit your fancy.

Mrs. Joe Bowles (Mary)

Black Caviar Paté

11 ounces cream cheese,
   softened
½ cup grated Cheddar cheese
1 tablespoon mayonnaise
½ teaspoon Worcestershire
   sauce
2 tablespoons grated onion

Lemon juice to taste
Tabasco or cayenne pepper to
   taste
1 jar (2 ounces) Whitefish
   type black caviar
1 purple onion, chopped

Combine cheeses, mayonnaise, Worcestershire, grated onion, lemon juice and Tabasco or cayenne. Shape as for the type of dish you plan to use (oval or round). Cover with plastic wrap, and refrigerate. When ready to serve, place on a dish and top with a coating of black caviar. Arrange chopped purple onion around base of cheese. Serve with crackers of your choice.

Mrs. Jim Lederer (Anne)

Red Caviar Mousse

3 jars (2 ounces each) red
   salmon caviar
¼ cup chopped parsley
1 tablespoon grated onion
1 teaspoon grated lemon peel
3 green onions, chopped

3 tablespoons peeled, seeded
   and diced cucumber
2 cups sour cream
1 envelope unflavored gelatin
¼ cup water
1 cup whipping cream

Place caviar, parsley, onion, lemon peel, green onions and cucumber in a large bowl. Gently fold in sour cream. Sprinkle gelatin over water; cook over low heat until dissolved. Cool. Beat cream until stiff. Fold dissolved gelatin and whipped cream into sour cream caviar mixture. Pour into a 6 cup mold; cover and refrigerate until set, about 2 hours. May be prepared up to 24 hours in advance. Unmold on plate, and serve with sliced pumpernickel or crackers.

Mrs. Jim Rado (Vicki)

Crab Meat Mold

1   can cream of shrimp soup
6   ounces cream cheese
¼   cup finely chopped onion
1   cup mayonnaise
1   package unflavored gelatin

1   cup cold water
1   can (6½ ounces) crab meat, drained, flaked
1   cup finely chopped celery

Combine soup, cream cheese and onion. Heat and stir until cheese is melted. Blend in mayonnaise. Remove from heat. In another pan sprinkle gelatin over water, and stir over low heat until dissolved. Combine with soup mixture; add crab meat and celery. Pour into a 6 cup mold. Refrigerate 6 hours or until firm. Garnish with salad greens and lemon wedges. Serve with crackers. About 48 servings.

Mrs. John Griggs (Judy)

Seafood Mold

1   can cream of tomato soup
2   tablespoons unflavored gelatin
6   ounces cream cheese, softened

1   cup chopped celery
½   cup diced green pepper
1   tablespoon chopped onion
1   cup tuna, flaked
1   cup mayonnaise

Heat tomato soup. Soften gelatin in ½ cup cold water, and add to heated soup. Whip cream cheese and add to mixture along with rest of ingredients. Pour into a mold and chill. Serve with crackers. For a variation, use 1 pound boiled shrimp, peeled and chopped, instead of tuna.

Mrs. John Griggs (Judy)

Special Shrimp Spread

2   cans (4½ ounces each) shrimp, drained, chopped
3   green onions, chopped
1   cup mayonnaise

4   ounces Cheddar cheese, grated
Garlic salt to taste

Mix above ingredients together. Refrigerate 24 hours. Serve with crackers.

Mrs. Ken Moyer (Bonnie)

Crab Meat Spread

½ cup mayonnaise
8 ounces cream cheese
1 can (6½ ounces) crab meat

Dill seed
Paprika

Cream mayonnaise with cream cheese. Fold in crab meat. Place in a 9 inch pie plate. Sprinkle with dill seed and paprika. Bake at 300° for 20 minutes. Serve with crackers.

Mrs. Charlie Smith (Jeannie)

Three Layer Crab Spread

1 carton (12 ounces) whipped
   cream cheese, softened
2 cans (6½ ounces each) crab
   meat, drained

⅓ cup red cocktail sauce

Spread cream cheese evenly into an 8 inch pie plate. Layer crab meat over cheese; pour cocktail sauce over crab. Serve with crackers.

Nancy Young Moritz

New England Crab Meat Spread

8 ounces cream cheese
1 cup crab meat
2 tablespoons lemon juice

¼ cup mayonnaise
½ teaspoon horseradish
2 to 3 teaspoons curry powder

Mix cream cheese with crab meat until well blended. Add remaining ingredients. Pour into a buttered baking dish and bake at 375° for 30 minutes. Serve with assorted crackers.

Mrs. Ed Cornet (Kathi)

Salmon Ball

1 can (16 ounces) red salmon,
   drained
11 ounces cream cheese,
   softened
1 tablespoon chopped onion
2 teaspoons lemon juice

1½ teaspoons horseradish
1 teaspoon Worcestershire
   sauce
¼ teaspoon liquid smoke,
   optional
Chopped parsley, optional

Mix all ingredients and shape into a ball. Sprinkle parsley on top if desired. Refrigerate. Serve with assorted crackers.

Mrs. Jack Dempsey (Estelle)

Super Nachos

2 cans (16 ounces each) refried beans
1½ pounds ground meat
1 onion, chopped
Salt and pepper to taste
1 can (4 ounces) chopped green chilies
3 cups grated Cheddar cheese

2 to 3 cans (4 ounces each) taco sauce
Chopped green onions
Sliced ripe olives
Sour cream
Guacamole, frozen or homemade
Tostado chips

Spread refried beans in a large oblong pan. Brown meat and onion. Drain; season with salt and pepper, and layer over beans. Sprinkle green chilies over meat; cover with grated cheese and taco sauce. Bake at 400° for 25 to 30 minutes. Remove from oven and spread with chopped green onions and sliced ripe olives. Before serving, garnish with sour cream and guacamole. Use tostado chips for dipping.

Mrs. Robert Henderson (Dale)

Jalapeño Cheese Balls

8 ounces cream cheese
½ pound mild Cheddar cheese
½ pound pimiento cheese
½ pound sharp Cheddar cheese
½ pound jalapeño cheese
½ cup chopped pecans

1 medium onion
2 to 3 cloves garlic
3 small dried hot peppers
Salt and pepper to taste
Paprika
Dried parsley flakes

Grind all ingredients except paprika and parsley in a meat grinder. Mix with hands and form into balls (any size you desire). Roll in paprika or dried parsley flakes or a combination of the two. Refrigerate until ready to serve. May be frozen.

Mrs. Robert Henderson (Dale)

Ham Cheese Ball

8 ounces cream cheese, softened
¼ cup mayonnaise
2 cups chopped ham
½ cup chopped fresh parsley

½ cup chopped green onions
¼ teaspoon Tabasco
¼ teaspoon dry mustard
Chopped pecans to garnish

Form ingredients into a ball. Chill; roll in chopped pecans. Refrigerate until serving.

Mrs. Larry Nau (Rose)

Texas Cheese Log

3 ounces cream cheese,
   softened
½ pound Velveeta cheese,
   softened
1 cup grated Cheddar cheese,
   softened

1 tablespoon Worcestershire
   sauce
1 teaspoon garlic salt
6 dashes Tabasco
1 cup chopped pecans,
   optional
Chili powder

Mix all ingredients together except chili powder, and form into a log or ball. Chill until firm. Roll in chili powder to cover. Serve with crackers. This cheese log can be frozen.

Mrs. Larry Hall (Jane)

Bacon Cheese Mold

32 ounces cream cheese
1   cup mayonnaise
2   tablespoons lemon juice
1   large onion, chopped
2   green peppers, chopped

2   cans (4 ounces each)
    chopped green chilies,
    drained
1   pound bacon, cooked and
    crumbled
½   teaspoon garlic salt
½   teaspoon savory salt

Line a bundt pan or 10 × 14 inch round mold with plastic wrap. Mix cheese, mayonnaise and lemon juice until smooth. Add remaining ingredients; pour into prepared pan. Chill overnight. Invert on platter lined with greens. Sprinkle with more bacon if desired. Serve with crackers. Serves approximately 50. This spread may be divided in half for smaller groups.

Mrs. Jimmy Cox (Mary)

Cheese Ball

6   ounces bleu cheese at room
    temperature
10 ounces Cheddar cheese at
    room temperature
12 ounces cream cheese,
    softened

2   tablespoons grated onion
1   teaspoon Worcestershire
    sauce
½   cup parsley
½   cup chopped pecans

Combine cheeses, onion, and Worcestershire sauce. Chill. Shape into a ball and roll in parsley and pecans. Serve with assorted crackers.

Mrs. Joe Bowles (Mary)

Chutney Cheese Spread

6   ounces cream cheese,
    softened
1   cup grated Cheddar cheese
2   tablespoons dry sherry
¼   teaspoon salt

¼   teaspoon curry powder
¼   cup chopped chutney
1   tablespoon finely chopped
    chives

Combine all ingredients except chives. Place in a serving dish, and top with chives. Serve with assorted crackers. This cheese spread freezes well and may be doubled or tripled. Try topping the spread with macadamia nuts, toasted coconut chips or crushed banana chips.

Mrs. Jack Dempsey (Estelle)

Chipped Beef Cheese Ball

8   ounces cream cheese,
    softened
3   green onions, finely
    chopped, tops and all

2   tablespoons Worcestershire
    sauce
1   jar (6 ounces) dried beef,
    finely chopped

Mix cheese with onion, Worcestershire sauce and one half of the dried beef. Shape mixture into a ball and roll into the remainder of the dried beef to cover.

Mrs. B. L. Turlington (Jill)

Stuffed Edam Cheese

1   Edam cheese, about 2
    pounds
½   cup sherry or port wine
1   tablespoon grated onion

2   teaspoons caraway seed
½   teaspoon dry mustard
¼   teaspoon garlic powder

Remove a two or three inch wide horizontal slice from top of cheese. Scoop out cheese leaving a ¼ inch shell. With a sharp knife, cut a sawtooth pattern around edge of shell. Chop or shred cheese. Blend cheese with remaining ingredients. Mixture will be lumpy. Spoon cheese back into shell. Cover and refrigerate until 2 hours before serving. The cheese may be prepared up to 3 days in advance.

Mrs. Jim Rado (Vicki)

Spinach Spread

1   package (10 ounces) frozen
    chopped spinach, thawed
1   cup mayonnaise
1   carton (8 ounces) sour
    cream
1   package (1⅝ ounces) dry
    vegetable soup mix
1   can (8½ ounces) water
    chestnuts, finely chopped
1   small onion, finely chopped

Squeeze all water from spinach. Combine with other ingredients, and refrigerate for at least two hours. Better if made a day ahead. Serve with rye bread. *This spread works well as a dip in a hollowed out bread round, or as a stuffing for raw mushroom caps.*

Mrs. Larry Nau (Rose)

Vegetable Spread

2   large eggplants
3   large green peppers
½   teaspoon minced garlic
2   tablespoons lemon juice
3   tablespoons oil
1   teaspoon salt
Freshly ground pepper
2   tablespoons finely chopped
    parsley to garnish

Place eggplant and green pepper in baking pan. Bake at 500° for 25 minutes. Remove peppers; bake eggplants 15 to 20 minutes more. Cool, peel, and seed peppers. Cool and peel eggplant. Drain. In a blender or food processor mix garlic, lemon juice, and oil. Add peppers and eggplant; blend. Season with salt and pepper. Chill. Garnish with chopped parsley. Serve with crackers. Serves 6 to 8.

Mrs. Clark Rector (Sue)

Hot Artichoke Spread

1   can (14 ounces) artichoke
    hearts, drained and
    chopped
1   cup mayonnaise
¾   cup grated Parmesan cheese
Garlic powder to taste

Mix all ingredients and put in a chafing dish. Heat until bubbly. Serve with crackers. Yields 6 servings.

Mrs. Robert West (Linda)

Deep Fried Squid

1 pound fresh squid
½ cup flour
¼ cup cornstarch
½ teaspoon baking powder
½ teaspoon salt

1 egg, beaten
⅓ cup cold water
1½ tablespoons oil
Oil for deep frying

Clean squid and cut each into four parts. Blend flour, cornstarch, baking powder and salt. Add egg, cold water and oil. Beat mixture with an egg beater until batter is smooth. Dip squid in this batter to coat. Meanwhile, heat oil for deep fat frying. Add squid, a few pieces at a time, and deep fry until golden brown. Do not overcook. Drain on paper towels and serve.

Nancy Young Moritz

Chili Flavored Shrimp

1 stick butter, melted
1 tablespoon chili powder
¼ teaspoon garlic powder

1 pound medium sized
   shrimp, peeled
Bacon slices

Mix together butter, chili powder and garlic powder. Dip shrimp into mixture and wrap each with ¼ slice of bacon. Cook on barbecue grill, 5 minutes on each side.

Mrs. Tony Hall (Jane)

Beer Boiled Shrimp

5 pounds raw, headless
   shrimp
2 lemons, thinly sliced
1 onion, thinly sliced
¼ cup olive oil

1 tablespoon salt
1 box "shrimp or crab" boil
2 cans beer
12 cups water (to cover)

Bring all ingredients except shrimp to a boil and simmer 5 minutes. Add shrimp and boil for approximately 10 minutes. Drain liquid only. Serve shrimp over a bed of ice. The spices, lemon, peppers and onion rings are an interesting garnish.

Mrs. Denman Smith (Sandra)

Oysters Ernie

24 oysters
Salt and pepper to taste
Flour
2 tablespoons butter
¼ cup lemon juice
½ cup A-1 steak sauce

2 tablespoons Worcestershire sauce
2 jiggers sherry or Madeira wine
2 tablespoons flour
3 tablespoons water

Salt and pepper oysters and dredge in flour. Grill in buttered skillet until crisp and brown on both sides. Sprinkle with butter or oil while cooking. This browns and crisps them. In another pan, melt the butter over low heat. Add lemon juice, steak sauce, Worcestershire and sherry. Heat, but do not boil. Blend flour and water. Add to sauce and stir until thickened. Combine sauce with oysters; serve in a chafing dish.

Mrs. Jim Schultz (Mary Kay)

Hot Crab Meat Appetizers

1 can (6½ ounces) crab meat, drained
1 tablespoon sliced green onion
4 ounces Swiss cheese, grated
½ cup mayonnaise

¼ teaspoon curry
2 packages (6 count each) butterflake refrigerator rolls
1 can (8 ounces) sliced water chestnuts

Combine crab, onion, cheese, mayonnaise and curry. Separate each roll into three layers and place on ungreased baking sheet. Spoon mixture over rolls and top with a water chestnut slice. Bake at 400° for 10 to 12 minutes or until brown on the bottom. Yields 36.

Mrs. Wayne Davison (Cindi)

The fruits of the sea—shrimp, clam, crab, and others—lend themselves to light, delicious appetizers to be enjoyed on a warm summer day, along with a cool drink.

Stuffed Mushrooms with Crab Meat

1 **pound very large mushrooms**	**Chopped chives**
½ **cup butter**	**Salt and pepper to taste**
1 **teaspoon soy sauce**	¼ **cup bread crumbs**
8 **ounces crab meat**	**Mayonnaise**
	Parmesan cheese

Remove mushroom stems and chop. Sauté caps in butter and soy sauce just until tender. Remove from pan and cool. In same pan, add crab meat, chopped chives, salt and pepper. Sauté for 3 minutes. Add bread crumbs and mushroom stems; mix together, and stuff into mushroom caps. Place mushrooms in a flat baking pan; spread mayonnaise on top of each one. Sprinkle with Parmesan cheese, and broil until lightly browned. Serve immediately. Serves 6.

Mrs. Don Bradford (Melinda)

Tempe's Stuffed Mushrooms

8 **ounces cream cheese**	¼ **teaspoon salt**
1 **can (6½ ounces) minced clams, reserve some liquid**	**Dash of pepper**
	1 **tablespoon milk**
2 **tablespoons finely chopped onion**	30 **large mushrooms**
	8 **tablespoons butter, divided**
½ **teaspoon horseradish**	½ **teaspoon garlic salt**

Combine cheese, clams, onion, horseradish, salt, pepper and milk. Add as much of the clam liquid as necessary to make the mixture soft. Cut stems from mushrooms and chop. Wash and dry mushroom caps. Sauté stem pieces in 4 tablespoons butter and garlic salt. Mix sautéed stems with cream cheese mixture. Melt remaining 4 tablespoons butter and dip caps. Stuff with cream cheese mixture; place on cookie sheet and bake at 375° for 20 minutes.

Mrs. Jimmy Williams (Tempe)

Bacon Stuffed Mushrooms

1 pound large mushrooms
5 slices bacon, finely chopped
½ to 1 green pepper, finely chopped

1 medium onion, finely chopped
8 ounces cream cheese
Bread crumbs to cover

Clean mushrooms; chop stems and save for stuffing. Cook bacon until nearly done; add peppers, onions, and stems. Continue cooking until vegetables are tender. Blend in cream cheese. Place mushrooms in a 9 × 13 inch pan. Fill each cap with stuffing and top with bread crumbs. Bake at 325° for 20 minutes. Serve hot. Yields approximately 24. These may also be heated in the microwave for 5 minutes on high.

Mrs. Bryan Healer (Georganne)

Ham Stuffed Mushrooms

24 large mushrooms, cleaned, stems removed
1 cup mushroom stems, finely minced
½ pound cooked ham, ground
1 clove garlic, finely minced

1 cup parsley, finely minced
½ cup fine white bread crumbs
½ cup grated Parmesan cheese
Salt and pepper to taste
½ cup melted butter.

Combine mushroom stems, ham, garlic, parsley, bread crumbs and cheese. Add salt and pepper to taste. Stuff prepared mushrooms. Place in a buttered casserole and pour melted butter over mushrooms. Bake at 375° for 25 minutes.

Mrs. Larry Hall (Jane)

Soy Sauce Mushrooms

3 tablespoons melted butter, no substitute
2 tablespoons Worcestershire sauce

2 tablespoons soy sauce
1 pound fresh mushrooms, cleaned with stems intact

Melt butter in a skillet and add both sauces. Add mushrooms and sauté about 5 minutes or until tender.

Mrs. Don Bradford (Melinda)

For a little different taste, try sautéing your mushrooms with a little sherry or your favorite spirit.

Cookbook Committee

Anticuchos

5	pounds tenderloin	1	achiote pepper or a long
3	aji, jalapeños, or other hot		green pepper
	peppers	1	teaspoon pepper
2	cloves garlic	1	teaspoon salt
½	teaspoon comino seed	1	cup red wine vinegar
		2	tablespoons melted butter

Cut meat into 1½ inch cubes. Crush all dry ingredients thoroughly; add vinegar. Marinate meat overnight in this mixture. When ready to cook, skewer two or three cubes of meat and broil over hot coals to desired doneness. While cooking baste meat with a mixture of reserved marinade and melted butter. An extra aji may be added to the marinade, but the dish will be really hot. For a variation try substituting pork, fish or shrimp for the meat. *This anticucho recipe was brought back from Peru and is now served regularly at the "Night In Old San Antonio" celebrations. These are a favorite at cocktail parties in the American Embassy in Peru, and now, they are a cocktail favorite in many Texas homes.*

Jack McKay

Five-Spice Chicken Wings

4	scallions or green onions, chopped	2	teaspoons Chinese five-spice powder
½	cup soy sauce	1	teaspoon sesame oil
½	cup medium dry sherry	4	pounds chicken wings, tips removed
¼	cup dark brown sugar, firmly packed		

In a heavy saucepan combine all ingredients except chicken and bring to a boil over moderate heat. Add chicken, and simmer, covered, turning several times, for 25 to 30 minutes, or until tender. Serves 12. *Five spice powder is a mixture of Chinese star anise, fennel, pepper, cloves and cinnamon, and is readily available in Oriental groceries.*

S. D. Jackman, Jr.

Peppered Beef

¼ cup coarsely ground black pepper
1 teaspoon ground cardamon
4 to 5 pounds boneless brisket, fat removed or sirloin strip

⅔ cup soy sauce
½ cup vinegar
1 tablespoon tomato paste
1 teaspoon paprika
1 clove garlic, chopped

Combine pepper and cardamon and spread evenly on a sheet of waxed paper. Place meat over mix; press down. Turn meat over; press pepper mix down into meat by hand. Cover both sides evenly and thoroughly, using all pepper mix. Place meat in a shallow dish. Combine soy sauce, vinegar, tomato paste, paprika and garlic. Pour over meat, being careful not to dislodge pepper. Cover and refrigerate overnight, turning meat occasionally. When ready to cook, carefully remove meat from marinade and wrap securely in heavy aluminum foil. Place in shallow pan and bake at 275° for about 4 to 5 hours or until meat is quite tender. Serve warm or cold. If serving cold, place meat in refrigerator until very cold. Before serving, remove from foil and slice very thin. Serve with a cold mustard sauce. Yields 8 main dish servings or 20 cocktail servings.

Mrs. Jim Shorey (Zann)

Drunken Meat Balls

3 pounds ground beef
1 large onion, finely chopped
Salt and pepper to taste
Garlic powder to taste

¼ cup water
1 bottle (14 ounces) catsup
1 can (12 ounces) beer

Combine meat, onions and seasonings. Form into bite size meat balls. Heat water, catsup and beer in saucepan; carefully drop meat balls into liquid. Boil slowly in sauce for 1 hour. Serve with sauce in chafing dish. May be prepared in advance. Yields 50 to 55 cocktail meat balls.

Mrs. Don Panter (Carolyn)

 Ground beef is a staple in many homes. Store it in the refrigerator for no more than 48 hours. In the freezer, it will keep up to three months.

Sauerkraut Balls

1	cup chopped onion	1	tablespoon horseradish
2	tablespoons butter	1	tablespoon prepared
1	pound cooked ham, ground		mustard
2	cups sauerkraut, drained,	1	teaspoon salt
	chopped	½	cup flour
2	tablespoons finely chopped	3	eggs, slightly beaten
	parsley	2½	cups cracker crumbs

Sauté the onion in butter until tender. Add ham, sauerkraut, parsley, horseradish, mustard and salt. Mix well and add flour. Roll into one inch balls. Dip each ball into the eggs; roll in cracker crumbs. Deep fry in hot fat until golden brown. Keep in a warm oven until ready to serve. *For a tasty diet snack, omit the egg and bread crumbs. Instead, serve balls well chilled and rolled in parsley.*

Nancy Young Moritz

Tamale Balls

1	pound ground beef	1	teaspoon salt
1	pound ground pork	½	teaspoon cayenne
1	cup V-8 juice	2	teaspoons paprika
4	eggs	2	teaspoons cumin
1½	teaspoons garlic powder	2	cans (16 ounces each)
2	tablespoons chili powder		stewed tomatoes
1	cup cornmeal	2	teaspoons salt
½	cup flour	1	tablespoon chili powder

Thoroughly mix meats, V-8 juice and eggs. Combine dry ingredients, and add to meat mixture. Be sure that all dry mix is evenly and thoroughly blended with meat. Pinch off a small amount and roll into marble size or bite size balls. Place on two large cookie sheets with sides. Bake at 350° for 30 minutes. Remove from oven and drain. While meatballs are cooking, place tomatoes in a pan. Stir in 2 teaspoons salt and 1 tablespoon chili powder. Bring to a boil; simmer for 30 minutes. The sauce should be slightly thick and the flavors well blended. Place sauce in a large chafing dish and add meatballs.

Mrs. D. D. Baker, Jr. (Agnes)

Sweet and Sour Party Meat Balls

1 pound lean ground beef
1 pound bulk sausage
Dash nutmeg
Salt and pepper to taste
1 cup cracker crumbs
½ cup crushed almonds
Oil for frying

1 can (16 ounces) pineapple chunks
2 cups vinegar
4 teaspoons cornstarch
1½ cups sugar
½ cup soy sauce

Combine meats, spices, crumbs and almonds. Form into bite size meat balls and brown in oil. Mix pineapple, vinegar, cornstarch, sugar and soy sauce; cook until thick. Serve meat balls with sauce in a chafing dish. The meat balls freeze nicely until you are ready to serve.

Mrs. Jette Campbell (Sally)

Spinach Balls

2 packages (10 ounces each) frozen chopped spinach
2 cups Pepperidge Farm stuffing mix

1 stick margarine
1 cup Parmesan cheese
6 eggs
Salt and pepper to taste

Cook spinach as directed; cool before handling. Lightly squeeze all water out of spinach. Mix all ingredients and form balls about the size of ping pong balls. Bake at 350° for 15 minutes. These appetizers freeze nicely.

Mrs. B. L. Turlington (Jill)

Fancy Franks

1 cup chili sauce
1 cup currant jelly
3 tablespoons lemon juice
3 teaspoons prepared mustard

4 packages (7 ounces each) cocktail franks
2 cans (13½ ounces each) pineapple chunks, drained

Combine all ingredients except franks and pineapple; blend well. Add remaining ingredients and simmer together 15 minutes. Serve with cocktail toothpicks. Two pounds of link sausage cut in bite size pieces may be substituted for the cocktail franks.

Mrs. Ken Moyer (Bonnie)

Sausage Caliente

1½ to 2 pounds link sausage
2 medium green peppers,
   sliced in strips
¼ cup chopped onion
3 tomatoes, cut into wedges

6 jalapeño peppers, seeded
   and chopped
1 can (12 ounces) beer
Salt and pepper to taste

Cut sausage into bite size pieces and brown. Drain grease. Add remaining ingredients and simmer until vegetables are soft. Serve warm in a chafing dish.

Mrs. Charles Tupa (Sidney)

Sausage is very popular in Texas. Each nationality has its own special method. English, Hungarian, Polish, Swiss, Yugoslav, German . . but the end result is always a spicy delicacy. It's a treat you shouldn't do without when touring the many community festivals.

Artichoke Nibbles

2 jars (6 ounces each)
   marinated artichoke hearts
1 small onion, finely chopped
1 clove garlic, minced
4 eggs, beaten
¼ cup fine bread crumbs
¼ teaspoon salt

⅛ teaspoon pepper
⅛ teaspoon oregano
⅛ teaspoon Tabasco
2 cups grated sharp Cheddar
   cheese
2 tablespoons minced parsley

Drain marinade from one jar of artichoke hearts into medium skillet. Drain second jar and discard marinade. Chop artichokes and set aside. Heat oil; add onion and garlic and sauté until limp, about five minutes. Combine eggs, bread crumbs, salt, pepper, oregano and Tabasco. Fold in cheese and parsley. Add artichokes and sautéed onions, blending well. Pour into a 9 inch square glass baking dish. Bake at 325° for 30 minutes. Allow to cool briefly before cutting into one inch squares. Can also be served cold. This dish may be prepared ahead of time and reheated 10 to 12 minutes.

Mrs. Don Panter (Carolyn)

Cold Spinach Squares

2   packages (10 ounces each) frozen chopped spinach
3   tablespoons butter
1   small onion, chopped
¼   pound mushrooms, sliced
4   eggs
¼   cup dry bread crumbs

1   can cream of mushroom soup
⅓   cup grated Parmesan cheese, divided
½   teaspoon pepper
½   teaspoon dry basil
½   teaspoon oregano
1½ teaspoons salt

Place spinach in a strainer and rinse under hot water to thaw; press out all excess water. Set aside. Over medium heat, melt butter; cook onion and mushrooms stirring constantly until onion is limp. Beat eggs; stir in bread crumbs, soup, two tablespoons Parmesan cheese and all the spices. Add spinach to mixture and blend well. Place in a well greased 9 inch square pan. Sprinkle with remaining cheese, and bake uncovered at 325° for 35 minutes or until lightly set. Cool slightly; then cover and refrigerate. Cut into 1 inch squares and serve cold. Yields 7 dozen squares. Freezes well.

Mrs. Marcus Bone (Beverly)

Spinach Hors D'Oeuvres

8   ounces Velveeta cheese
14 tablespoons margarine, divided

1   package (10 ounces) frozen chopped spinach, thawed
20 slices soft sandwich bread

In a double boiler, melt cheese with 6 tablespoons margarine. Drain spinach well, squeezing out all excess water. Add spinach to cheese and stir well. Remove from heat and let cool. Cut crusts off bread; flatten slices with a rolling pin. Spread filling on bread. Roll up each slice and cut in half. Place on a greased cookie sheet, seam side down. Melt remaining 8 tablespoons margarine and brush rolls. Bake at 350° for 15 to 20 minutes or until golden. Yields 40 rolls.

Mrs. Terry Arndt (Barbara)

Crystal City, a primary center for packing, processing and shipping vegetables, also has another claim to fame. Most famous for its spinach crop, the town boasts a statue of the cartoon character, Popeye, as a salute to this muscle builder.

Toasted Mushroom Rolls

1 pound mushrooms, chopped	¼ teaspoon thyme
¼ cup butter	¼ teaspoon marjoram
3 tablespoons flour	Salt to taste
1 carton (8 ounces) sour cream	1½ loaves sandwich type bread
	Chopped parsley

Sauté mushrooms 5 minutes in butter. Add flour; stir until mixture forms a thick paste. Add sour cream and seasonings. Remove crusts from bread and flatten with a rolling pin. Spread mushroom mixture on bread; sprinkle each with chopped parsley, and roll up as for jelly roll. Cut each roll into one-half inch slices. Bake at 350° for 15 minutes or until toasted. Yields 24 large and 48 small rolls. *To make bread roll easier, put a few slices at a time in a colander and place over boiling water for a few seconds.*

Mrs. Jerry Hunt (Gail)

Asparagus Roll Ups

1 cup mayonnaise	1 can (15 ounces) extra long asparagus, drained
½ cup chopped chives	
1 loaf white sandwich bread, crusts removed	Lemon-pepper marinade to taste

Mix mayonnaise and chives. Spread on prepared bread. Lay asparagus stalks diagonally across bread. Lightly sprinkle with lemon-pepper marinade. Roll up and secure with a toothpick. Heat in a 350° oven until lightly toasted. Remove toothpick before serving.

Mrs. John Perkins (Sandy)

Ham Rolls

Cream cheese	Sliced Danish ham
Pimiento cheese	

Combine two parts cream cheese to one part pimiento cheese. Blend until smooth. Spread a thin layer on a slice of Danish ham. Roll horizontally and place in the freezer for one hour. This hardens the cheese and makes it easier to slice. Slice rolls into bite size pieces. Usually yields four pieces per roll. For a variation omit the pimiento cheese and use cream cheese combined with chopped nuts, or thin cream cheese with milk and spread on ham topped with a sweet pickle.

Mrs. Charles Cantwell (Winn)

Bacon Squares

1 cup mayonnaise	8 slices bacon, cooked and
2 teaspoons Worcestershire	crumbled
sauce	⅓ cup chopped peanuts
½ teaspoon salad seasoning	4 green onions, sliced
¼ teaspoon paprika	14 slices white bread
2 cups grated Cheddar cheese	

Mix mayonnaise, Worcestershire sauce, salad seasonings and paprika. Stir in cheese, bacon, peanuts and onions. Spread about three tablespoons bacon mixture over each slice of bread. Bake at 400° on an ungreased cookie sheet for 10 minutes. Cut each slice into 4 pieces. Serve hot. Yields 56 appetizers.

Marian Carlson Hidell

Bacon Hors D'Oeuvres

1½ teaspoons dry mustard	3 eggs, beaten
1½ teaspoons cayenne	1 pound sliced bacon
3 teaspoons cider vinegar	Cracker or cornflake crumbs

Mix mustard, cayenne, and vinegar into a paste. Stir in beaten eggs. Cut bacon into fourths. Dip each individual bacon piece into egg mixture; then roll in crumbs. Bake at 350° for 15 to 18 minutes. Drain on paper towels. Store in the refrigerator in a covered dish. Reheat at 200° for 10 minutes. Serves 10 to 12. *The bacon can be cooked in the microwave, making this a super easy dish.*

Mrs. Jim Schultz (Mary Kay)

Cheese Crisps

2 sticks butter	2 cups grated Cheddar cheese
2 cups flour	2 drops Tabasco

Mix all ingredients together and knead until smooth. Roll out and cut with biscuit cutter, or pinch into balls and then flatten. Bake on a greased cookie sheet at 400° for 15 to 18 minutes.

Mrs. Jim Rado (Vicki)

Olive Cheese Puffs

½ pound Cheddar cheese,
    grated
1¼ cups flour

½ cup melted butter
1   jar (13 ounces) stuffed green
    olives

Mix cheese and flour until crumbly. Add melted butter. Take one tea-spoon of dough; flatten and put olive inside. Roll into a ball. Place on cookie sheet and bake at 400° for 15 to 20 minutes. Yields approximately 48 appetizers.

Mrs. Bill Butler (Stephanie)

Cheese Squares

1 jar (6 ounces) Old English
   cheese
1 can (4 ounces) chopped
   green chilies

1 stick margarine
1 loaf Pepperidge Farm very
   thin white bread

Melt cheese, green chilies and margarine together. Remove crusts from bread. Spread each slice with cheese mixture and place one slice on top of another to make sandwiches. Cut sandwiches in half and then cut each half into thirds. Bake at 350° for 20 to 30 minutes until toasted. Freezes well. If frozen, warm at 350° about 30 minutes. Yields approx-imately 60 squares.

Mrs. Ron Garrick (Bonnie)

Jalapeño Cheese Squares

1 pound Longhorn Cheddar
   cheese, grated
1 pound Monterey Jack
   cheese, grated
1 can (4 ounces) jalapenõs,
   chopped

2 eggs
1 can (13 ounces) evaporated
   milk
½ cup flour

Layer cheese and jalapeños in 9 inch square pan. Mix together eggs, milk and flour. Pour over top. Cook at 350° for 45 minutes. Cool slightly; cut into squares and serve.

Mrs. Jim Carney (Jean)

Green Chili Pie

1 to 2 cans (4 ounces each)
   whole green chilies
1   pound Monterey Jack
   cheese, grated

4   eggs, beaten

Cut chilies in half lengthwise; remove seeds, rinse with water and pat dry. Lightly butter a 9 or 10 inch glass pie pan, or a 9 × 13 inch pyrex dish. Line the prepared pan with green chilies; cover the bottom and half way up the sides. Spread grated cheese making sure that the chilies are completely covered. Pour eggs evenly over the cheese. Bake at 275° for 45 minutes until a knife inserted in the center comes out clean. Cool slightly and cut in squares or pie wedges. Serve warm.

Mrs. Bob Edgecomb (Mary)

Jalapeño Pie

1 to 2 cans (4 ounces each)
   jalapeño peppers
8   ounces sharp Cheddar
   cheese, grated

4 to 6 eggs, beaten

Butter bottom of a 9 inch square pyrex dish. Cut jalapeños into strips and place close together on the bottom of the dish. Press grated cheese on top of peppers, covering them completely. Pour the beaten eggs over cheese. Be sure you have used enough eggs to completely cover cheese. Mixture will seep through the layers to the bottom. Bake at 350° for 40 minutes. Cut into small pieces to serve. May be served warm or at room temperature. Yields 20 to 24 squares.

Mrs. Ken Moyer (Bonnie)

Jalapeños are a staple much like flour in the Texas kitchen. A few slices placed on top of a chip with melted cheese, or a couple chopped into an everyday casserole can make an ordinary snack or meal distinctive.

Sausage Egg Rolls

1	pound bulk sausage	1	tablespoon white wine or
3	tablespoons oil		sherry
3	cups finely chopped celery	½	teaspoon sugar
½	pound fresh beansprouts or	1	tablespoon cornstarch
	1 pound canned	2	tablespoons cold water
¼	cup fresh mushrooms	1	package egg roll skins
2	teaspoons salt	1	egg, beaten
1	tablespoon soy sauce	3	cups oil

Cook sausage until done; drain grease, and set aside. Pour 3 tablespoons oil in skillet or wok, and heat for 30 seconds. Add celery; stir fry for 5 minutes. Add beansprouts, mushrooms and salt; mix well. Add sausage, soy sauce, sugar and wine; stir well. Continue cooking until liquid begins to boil. Dissolve cornstarch in water and add to sausage mixture. Cook until liquids have thickened slightly and coated the ingredients with a light glaze. Cool. Shape ¼ cup of filling to form a cylinder. Place diagonally across center of egg roll skin. Lift lower triangular flap over filling, tucking point under. Bring sides over to center. Brush upper and exposed triangle with egg to seal; roll wrapper into a neat package. Fry in 3 cups oil at 375° until browned. These egg rolls will keep for an hour or so in a 250° oven. Yields 16 egg rolls.

Mrs. Sam White (Jane)

Crab Empanadas

Pastry:

4	cups sifted flour	2	teaspoons salt
4	teaspoons baking powder	1	cup ice water (approximate)
½	cup shortening		

Crab Filling:

1	tablespoon butter	1	tablespoon minced parsley
1	medium onion, minced	1	jar (3 ounces) pimiento
1	large tomato, peeled,		stuffed olives, chopped
	chopped	1	teaspoon lemon juice
8	ounces cooked crab		Salt and pepper to taste

Sift together flour, baking powder, and salt; add shortening and work into flour as for pastry, adding enough water to hold dough together. Divide into 24 even pieces. Roll out each piece into a 5 inch round. Sauté onion in butter until tender, but not brown. Add tomato and cook a few minutes. Add crab, parsley, olives, lemon juice, salt and pepper. Mix well and use as filling for dough. Place a spoonful of mixture on one half of each round; wet edges with water, and fold the other half over, pressing edges firmly to seal. Fry empanadas in hot oil until golden brown, or bake at 400° for 15 to 20 minutes. Yields 24. Freezes well.

S. D. Jackman, Jr.

Cream Cheese Pastry Dough

1 cup butter	1 egg yolk
8 ounces cream cheese	2 teaspoons half and half
½ teaspoon salt	cream
2 cups flour	

Beat butter, cream cheese and salt until smooth and blended. Work in flour to form a smooth dough. Flatten dough to form a rectangle and wrap in foil. Chill overnight or several days. Divide dough and roll on floured pastry cloth with floured rolling pin or between two sheets of waxed paper. Shape as directed; chill before baking. Brush all tops with egg yolk beaten with cream. Bake in 350° oven unless otherwise specified. Filled turnovers and rolls freeze well. Preheat oven before removing appetizers from the freezer; bake without defrosting and add 5 to 10 minutes to the baking time. Watch carefully. The color should be a rich, golden brown.

Cookbook Committee

Appetizer Quiches

½ cup bacon or bacon bits	½ teaspoon Worcestershire
½ cup grated Swiss cheese	sauce
1 tablespoon dried parsley	1 tablespoon grated Parmesan
2 eggs, well beaten	cheese
½ cup half and half cream	Paprika
½ teaspoon salt	½ recipe cream cheese pastry
¼ teaspoon dry mustard	

Shape dough into two dozen balls and press into tiny muffin pans. Layer bacon, cheese and parsley into unbaked dough. Beat eggs with cream, salt, dry mustard and Worcestershire sauce. Pour over bacon, cheese and parsley. Sprinkle with Parmesan cheese and paprika. Bake at 350° for 30 minutes or until brown on top. These may be frozen and then warmed in a 200° oven. Yields 2 dozen.

Mrs. Larry Hall (Jane)

Hot Mushroom Tartlets

4 tablespoons butter	¼ teaspoon thyme
8 ounces fresh mushrooms, chopped	3 tablespoons flour
	½ cup sour cream
1 large onion, chopped	1 recipe cream cheese pastry
1 teaspoon salt	1 egg, beaten

Melt butter and sauté mushrooms and onion until tender. Blend in salt, thyme and flour; add sour cream. Cook until slightly thick. Chill. Roll dough and cut into 3 inch circles. Place 1 teaspoon filling on one half of dough. Moisten edges with egg; fold over other half, and press edges with a fork. Prick center of tartlet; brush top with egg. Place on ungreased cookie sheet and chill covered. Bake at 450° for 12 minutes or until golden brown.

Mrs. Dudley Baker (Kathy)

Parmesan Twists

½ recipe cream cheese pastry	1 egg yolk
1 cup finely grated Parmesan cheese	2 teaspoons half and half cream

Divide pastry in half and roll in a rectangle ¼ inch thick. Sprinkle heavily with Parmesan cheese. Press cheese lightly into dough with rolling pin. Fold dough over itself into thirds; roll again. Sprinkle with more cheese; press with a pin and fold again. Roll into a 4 × 8 inch rectangle, ¼ inch thick. Brush tops with egg yolk beaten with cream. Sprinkle with more cheese. Cut into strips about 1 × 4 inches. Twist strips into spirals and place on ungreased cookie sheet. Repeat with remaining dough. Brush ends with egg yolk mixture. Chill 1 hour. Bake at 350° for 15 to 20 minutes or until crisp and golden. Carefully remove from the sheet at once. Yields about two dozen.

Mrs. Larry Hall (Jane)

Spicy Empanadas

1½ recipes cream cheese pastry
1 pound ground beef
1 package (1½ ounces)
   spaghetti sauce mix
¼ cup minced onion
1 teaspoon seasoned salt

2 medium tomatoes, peeled
   and chopped
½ cup water
¼ cup grated Parmesan cheese
½ cup grated Cheddar cheese

Make pastry and chill. Brown beef until crumbly. Stir in sauce mix, onion, salt, tomatoes and water. Simmer 15 minutes; remove from heat. Add cheeses; mix and cool. Divide pastry into fourths. Roll ⅛ inch thick and cut in 3 inch rounds. Stack leftover dough and reroll. Place 1 teaspoon filling in each round a little off center; moisten edges. Fold pastry over and press edges. Seal and crimp with floured fork. Bake at 350° for 20 minutes or until golden brown. Yields 7½ dozen.

Mrs. Larry Hall (Jane)

Beverages

Lake Austin Cooler

1 glass tea, unsweetened
1 jigger Peppermint Schnapps

Ice

Fill tall glass with ice. Add one jigger Peppermint Schnapps and fill with tea. Serves one. To make full use of our wonderful Texas sun, place 1 gallon of water, 3 family size tea bags into a gallon jar. Secure lid and place in sun for 3 to 4 hours. This tea with the Peppermint Schnapps is a real refreshing drink when spending the day on Lake Austin.

Nancy Young Moritz

Cadillac Bar's Ramos Gin Fizz

1 ounce dry gin
Juice of one lemon
1 teaspoon powdered sugar

1 egg white
3 ounces whipping cream
6 drops orange flower water

Mix all ingredients in blender. Serve over crushed ice in tall glass. Serves one.

Mrs. Denman Smith (Sandra)

Kahlua Kolada

1 ounce Kahlua	1 tablespoon cream of
½ ounce orange juce	coconut
½ ounce pineapple juice	Pineapple and cherry garnish
1½ ounces half and half cream	

Blend all liquid ingredients with ice and garnish with pineapple and cherry. Serves one.

Mrs. Jim Rado (Vicki)

Velvet Nightcap

3 parts champagne	Lemon slices
1 part Grand Marnier	Sugar

Mix champagne and Grand Marnier. Rub a lemon slice around rim of brandy snifter; then dip rim in sugar. Add ice and champagne mixture for an elegant after dinner drink.

Mrs. Jim Rado (Vicki)

Norman's Margaritas

1 can (6 ounces) frozen limeade concentrate, thawed	6 ounces tequila
	2 ounces Triple Sec

Combine all ingredients in blender. Add ice to fill. Blend until smooth. Store in freezer indefinitely. Rub a lemon slice around rim of glass and dip in salt. Serves 3.

Mrs. Larry Nau (Rose)

Piña Colada

¾ cup light rum	½ cup cream of coconut
1 cup unsweetened pineapple juice	¼ cup whipping cream
	2 cups crushed ice

Combine in blender container and whirl until smooth. Yields 6 servings. Pour over crushed ice; garnish with pineapple spears.

Roger Borgelt

Mai Tai

2¼ cups light rum
1½ cups dark rum
¾ cup orange curacao

¾ cup lime juice
¼ cup sugar
1½ teaspoons aromatic bitters

Combine all ingredients in a large pitcher and stir well. Can be prepared ahead and refrigerated. Yields 12 servings. Pour over crushed ice and garnish with mint.

Roger Borgelt

Yellow Bird

2 cups sugar
1 cup water
2 ounces orange juice
1 ounce lemon juice

1 ounce light rum
½ ounce apricot brandy
½ ounce banana liqueur

Make a simple syrup by boiling the first two ingredients for two minutes without stirring. Store in refrigerator. When ready to serve, combine ½ ounce simple syrup with other ingredients. Shake and serve in a tall glass. Serves one. *This drink is a specialty of the house at the Grand Bahama Hotel.*

Mrs. Denman Smith (Sandra)

Hot Buttered Rum

1 pound brown sugar
1 pound powdered sugar
1 pound butter
1 quart vanilla ice cream
1 teaspoon allspice

1 teaspoon cinnamon
1 teaspoon nutmeg
Rum
Brandy

Mix all ingredients except liquors. Heat very slowly, stirring until mixture is like thin cake batter. Remove from heat; cool. Cover and freeze. When ready to serve, put 2 teaspoons frozen mixture in a mug, and add 1½ ounces each of rum and brandy. Fill remainder of cup with hot water and stir to melt frozen mixture. Sprinkle with nutmeg. Serves 50. *This recipe is handy to have in the freezer on those cold nights when a Texas "norther" blows through.*

Mrs. Jim Smith (Diane)

Insomnia Special

6 ounces hot milk
1½ ounces Kahlua

1½ ounces vodka

Heat, mix, drink and sleep! Serves one.

Mrs. Denman Smith (Sandra)

Café Brulot

1 cinnamon stick, 4 inches
long
12 whole cloves
Peel of 2 oranges, cut in thin
slices
Peel of 2 lemons, cut in thin
slices

6 sugar cubes
8 ounces brandy
2 ounces Curacao
1 quart strong, black coffee

Over low heat mash cinnamon, cloves, peels, and sugar with a ladle in a skillet. Add brandy and Curacao and stir. Ignite brandy and mix until sugar is dissolved. Gradually add black coffee and continue mixing until flame flickers out. Serve hot. Serves 10 to 12.

Mrs. Larry Hall (Jane)

Mint Cappuccino

1 cup very strong coffee
1 package (1 ounce) instant
chocolate mix
2 teaspoons brandy

2 teaspoons Vandermint
2 teaspoons creme de cacao
Whipped cream

Mix the coffee, chocolate and liqueurs together. Top with whipped cream and serve while hot. Serves one.

Mrs. John Perkins (Sandy)

Flaming foods are special and they look spectacular. Do you know how easy it is? Just start with hot food and an 80-proof liquor such as rum, brandy or a fruit-flavored liqueur. Heat the liquor in a small long-handled pan, then ignite carefully—long matches are recommended—and pour the flaming liquid over the food and stir. The alcohol burns off but the flavor remains. Dim the lights and you're set for another hit!

Dudley's Famous Bloody Marys

⅛ teaspoon garlic powder
1 teaspoon onion powder
1¼ teaspoons salt
1 can (46 ounces) V-8 juice
2 ounces lime juice
2 ounces Herdez Salsa
Casera*

½ teaspoon Tabasco sauce
Dash Worcestershire sauce,
optional
15 ounces vodka
Celery stalks to garnish

*2 ounces any red chili salsa may be substituted

Mix dry ingredients and add a little V-8 juice to dissolve. Then add all the other ingredients except the vodka. Stir until mixed. Fill each glass with ice and add 1½ ounces of vodka. Fill with mix. Garnish with a stalk of celery. Serves 8 to 10. *This is a great Bloody Mary! It's a real eye-opener for a Sunday morning brunch. You can freeze all the ingredients, except the V-8 juice and the vodka, and keep it ready for any occasion.*

Dudley Baker

Skip and Go Barefoot

1 can (6 ounces) frozen
limeade concentrate,
thawed

6 ounces vodka
6 ounces beer

Empty can of limeade into blender and fill ¾ full of crushed ice. Add vodka and beer and blend until smooth. Serves 4. *Fantastic way to break the ice.*

Mrs. Randy Hagan (Robin)

Frozen Daiquiri

1 fifth light rum
2 cans (6 ounces each) frozen
pink lemonade concentrate
1 can (6 ounces) frozen
limeade concentrate

42 ounces water
½ cup grenadine syrup,
optional

Mix all ingredients in a gallon container with lid (a milk carton will do). Freeze over night. Leave in freezer until ready to serve. Spoon into punch bowl. Makes 12 to 14 (6 ounce) servings. *This is a good do ahead party punch.*

Mrs. Jack Dempsey (Estelle)

Quickie Apple Daiquiris

1 can (12 ounces) frozen apple juice concentrate	1 small apple, cored and unpeeled
½ to ¾ cup light rum	2 tablespoons lemon juice

Place all ingredients in blender. Add enough ice to fill container. Blend until slushy. Serves 6.

Nancy Young Moritz

Peach Daiquiri

4 ounces rum	4 peaches peeled, or 1 can (29 ounces) peaches, drained
2 ounces Rose's lime juice	
½ cup sugar	

Mix ingredients together in a blender. Add ice cubes and blend until smooth. If using canned peaches, reduce the sugar to ¼ cup. Serves 4.

Mrs. Ron Garrick (Bonnie)

Frozen Flamingo

1 can (6 ounces) frozen Hawaiian Punch concentrate, thawed	1 can (8½ ounces) cream of coconut
	1⅛ cups rum
1 can (6 ounces) frozen limeade concentrate, thawed	¾ cup water
	Crushed ice

Combine all the ingredients except ice. Place one-half mixture in blender; fill with crushed ice and blend. Repeat with the second half. Serves 10 to 12. This makes a beautiful sweet drink.

Mrs. Wayne Davison (Cindi)

Tarzan's Frozen Tonic

1 can (6 ounces) frozen limeade concentrate, thawed	2 ounces gin or vodka
	2 ounces rum
	2 ounces tequila

Place all the ingredients in a blender. Fill ¾ full with crushed ice and blend until thick and frozen. Serves 6 to 8. *Guaranteed to make you swing from trees.*

Mrs. John Carrell (Jane)

Vodka Slush

1   can (6 ounces) frozen
    orange juice concentrate,
    thawed
2   cans (6 ounces each) frozen
    lemonade concentrate,
    thawed
2   cans (6 ounces each) frozen
    limeade concentrate,
    thawed

1   cup sugar
3½ cups water
2   cups vodka
2   bottles (32 ounces each)
    lemon-lime carbonated
    drink, chilled

Combine the frozen concentrates, sugar, water and vodka. Mix well. Freeze this mixture for 48 hours, stirring occasionally. For each serving, spoon ¾ cup frozen mixture into a tall glass, then fill with the lemon-lime drink. Yields 16 (8 ounce) servings.

Mrs. Ron Garrick (Bonnie)

Mimosa

1   quart freshly squeezed
    orange juice, chilled

1   fifth champagne, chilled

Mix and pour into stemmed glasses. Serves 10 to 12. *As sweet and refreshing as the blossom it's named for.*

Cookbook Committee

Tropical Champagne Punch

1   can (46 ounces) Hawaiian
    Punch
¼   cup sugar, optional
½   cup brandy

1   fifth champagne, chilled
    Orange slices to garnish
    Strawberries to garnish

Combine Hawaiian Punch and sugar, stirring until sugar dissolves. Add brandy and chill. When ready to serve, stir in champagne. Add ice and serve. Garnish with orange slices and/or strawberries. Yields 20 (4 ounce) servings.

Mrs. Marcus Bone (Beverly)

Relaxed entertaining calls for good drinks and tasty appetizers. Texas' fresh seafood, bountiful fruits, and crisp vegetables are all fine choices as ice breakers.

Milk Punch

1 pint vanilla ice cream, softened	¼ cup light rum
1 cup milk	3 tablespoons brandy
½ cup bourbon	Nutmeg, to garnish

Mix ice cream, milk, bourbon, rum and brandy. Serve with a dash of nutmeg on top. Yields 1 quart.

Mrs. Don Panter (Carolyn)

Strawberry Wine Punch

1 cup sugar	1 cup fresh strawberries or 1 package frozen strawberries, thawed and drained
½ cup water	
2 cups rosé wine	
2 cups orange juice	1 quart club soda
½ cup lemon juice	Ice

Cook sugar and water together to the boiling point and then boil 5 minutes. Cool. Combine with the wine, juices and strawberries. Pour over ice in a punch bowl and add club soda. The berries will stay prettier if added just before the club soda. Serves 12 to 15.

Mrs. Chris Williston (Janice)

Banana Slush Punch

5 bananas	1 can (46 ounces) pineapple juice
1 can (12 ounces) frozen orange juice concentrate	
1 can (6 ounces) frozen lemonade concentrate	Water
	4 quarts club soda, ginger ale or lemon-lime drink, chilled
2 to 3 cups sugar	

Mash bananas thoroughly and add slightly thawed frozen juices. Sprinkle sugar over mixture. Add pineapple juice, stirring well to dissolve the sugar. Put into a gallon container and fill with water. Freeze to a slush. Put mixture into a two gallon punch bowl and add the mixers. If lemon-lime or ginger ale is used, use less sugar. This punch base can be frozen and kept indefinitely. Allow several hours for the mixture to reach the slush stage before serving. Yields 2 gallons. *This is a great punch. We've served it at all kinds of receptions and parties. It never fails to get compliments. In place of 2 quarts of the mixer, add champagne for a lovely morning punch. We have also used rum and vodka. This punch seems to go well with any liquor.*

Mrs. Dudley Baker (Kathy)

Iced Tea Cooler

1 cup sugar	4 cans (6 ounces each) cold
6 cups strong tea	water
2½ cups pineapple juice	Sprigs fresh mint, to garnish
1 can (6 ounces) frozen	
lemonade concentrate	

Dissolve sugar in hot tea and cool. Add other ingredients and mix well. Chill. Serve as a punch or over ice in tall glasses. Serves 15 to 20. *Great with hot gingerbread!*

Mrs. Don Panter (Carolyn)

Whiskey Sour Punch

1 can (12 ounces) frozen	12 ounces bourbon
orange juice concentrate,	42 ounces water
thawed	1 to 2 ounces lime juice,
1 can (6 ounces) frozen pink	optional
lemonade concentrate,	Orange slices
thawed	Cherries

Mix the frozen juice concentrates, bourbon, water, and lime juice. Store in the refrigerator or freezer. Garnish with the orange slices and cherries. Serves 12 to 16.

Mrs. Robert Henderson (Dale)

Sangria

1 gallon Zinfandel or	¼ cup Cointreau
burgundy wine	1 quart club soda
1 quart orange juice	2 oranges, thinly sliced
1 cup lemon juice	1 lemon, thinly sliced
½ cup sugar	Ice ring
½ cup brandy	

Mix and chill wine, orange juice, sugar, brandy and Cointreau. Add the soda. Pour into a punch bowl over an ice ring. Float the lemon and orange slices on top. Recipe can be doubled easily. Yields 50 (4 ounce) servings.

Mrs. Dudley Baker (Kathy)

Sangria Slush

1   can (8 ounces) crushed
    pineapple, undrained
2½ cups dry red wine
1½ cups orange juice
½   cup lemon juice

½   cup sugar
2   tablespoons grated lemon
    peel
Orange slices and mint sprigs
    to garnish

Place all ingredients in blender. Blend on high speed for 5 seconds. Pour mixture into a 9 inch square pan and freeze. Before serving, let stand a few minutes at room temperature. With spoon stir until semi-thawed. Spoon into 8 wine or sherbert glasses. Garnish with orange and mint. Serves 8.

Mrs. Jim Schultz (Mary Kay)

Passionate Fruit Punch

1   bottle (28 ounces) passion
    fruit juice
2   bottles (64 ounces each)
    orange juice
2   cans (46 ounces each)
    unsweetened pineapple
    juice

6   ounces grenadine
2   bottles (8 ounces each) lime
    juice
8   bottles (32 ounces each)
    ginger ale

Mix juices and chill. When ready to serve pour over frozen fruit ring. Add chilled ginger ale just before serving. For a more spirited punch add vodka, rum or gin. Serves 100.

Fruit Ring: In a ring mold arrange alternating slices of lemon, limes, and oranges with unhulled strawberries. Add just enough water to partially cover fruit. Too much water will float the fruit. Freeze until set, and add water to fill mold almost full. Freeze. Unmold and float ring, fruit side up in punch bowl. For a clear ice ring, boil water and cool before using.

Mrs. Marcus Bone (Beverly)

Molly Hogans

6 eggs	1 can (6 ounces) frozen
1 cup sugar	limeade concentrate
1 tablespoon vanilla	1 quart gin
1 can (12 ounces) frozen	7-Up
orange juice concentrate	

Put eggs in blender. Slowly add sugar, vanilla, and juices. Blend well. Pour into large container and add gin. Let stand at least one hour in refrigerator. In large glasses pour 2 ounces gin mixture; add ice; fill with 7-Up. Serves 50.

Mrs. Jerry Hunt (Gail)

Eggnog

1 dozen eggs, separated	½ teaspoon salt
1 cup sugar, divided	3¼ cups bourbon whiskey
1½ cups brandy, divided	2 quarts milk
1 quart whipping cream	Nutmeg

Beat egg whites until stiff; gradually add ½ cup sugar. Add ¼ cup brandy and beat until smooth and very stiff. Beat whipping cream until stiff; gradually add ½ cup sugar. Beat thoroughly. Fold egg whites and whipped cream together. Beat egg yolks and salt until thick and fluffy. Slowly add whiskey, beating well. Stir in milk and remaining brandy. Fold in egg white and whipped cream mixture. Carefully pour into punch bowl so that mixture remains thick. Top with nutmeg. *This is an old family favorite brought from Kentucky and was served often in our home. My father loved to sip a cup of eggnog and reminisce about his horse, Wintergreen, that won the Kentucky Derby in 1909.*

Mae Respess Ross

Christmas Eggnog

12 eggs, separated	1 quart whipping cream
¾ cup sugar	1 quart eggnog ice cream,
6 ounces bourbon	softened

Beat egg yolks. Slowly add sugar and bourbon; set aside. Beat egg whites until frothy but not stiff. In separate bowl, whip cream, but do not stiffen. Fold whipped cream into yolks. Next add egg white mixture, then ice cream. Mix until smooth. Serves 12 to 15. *This is the drink for sipping around an open fire.*

Mrs. Charles Cantwell (Winn)

Chocolate Eggnog

3 quarts eggnog, chilled	3 tablespoons sugar
1¼ cups chocolate syrup	1 tablespoon cocoa
¾ cup rum, optional	½ square (1 ounce) semisweet
1½ cups whipping cream	chocolate, grated to garnish

In large punch bowl combine eggnog, chocolate syrup, and rum. In small bowl with electric mixer at high speed, whip cream, sugar and cocoa until stiff. Spoon cream onto eggnog. Sprinkle with chocolate. Yields 24 (½ cup) servings.

Mrs. Joe Bowles (Mary)

Hot Cranberry Cider

3 quarts apple cider	6 sticks cinnamon
1 quart cranberry juice	1 teaspoon whole allspice
cocktail	2 cups rum, optional
¼ cup sugar	1 teaspoon bitters, optional
3 oranges, pierced with a fork	¼ cup sugar, optional
16 cloves	

Place cider, cranberry juice and sugar in a large (30 cup) percolator. Put pierced oranges, cloves, cinnamon and allspice in the top basket and perk as for coffee. After cider has perked add the rum, bitters and additional sugar, if desired. Yields 32 (4 ounce) servings.

Mrs. Jerry Hunt (Gail)

Wassail Rockford

2 cups sugar	4 allspice berries
1 quart water	3 cups orange juice
12 whole cloves	2 cups lemon juice
4 cinnamon sticks	2 quarts cider
2 tablespoons ginger, chopped	

Make syrup by boiling sugar and water for 10 minutes. Add cloves, cinnamon, allspice, and ginger. Let syrup stand covered in warm place for one hour. Add orange and lemon juice and cider. Bring quickly to boil and serve at once. Yields 36 (4 ounce) servings. *Served to the girls at Rockford College at a Christmas Party before going home for the holidays; very nice with donuts in cold weather.*

Mrs. Bob Edgecomb (Mary)

Yule Glögg

1 orange	2 teaspoons cinnamon
1 lemon	½ gallon red wine
1 quart water	½ quart brandy
¾ cup sugar	½ cup raisins
8 whole cloves	½ cup peeled almonds

Peel lemon and orange and then squeeze the juices into a large pan. Add water, sugar, fruit peels, cloves and cinnamon. Boil for 5 minutes. When ready to serve, add red wine, brandy, raisins and almonds. Simmer; do not boil. Then serve. Yields 24 servings. *This is a perfect hot punch for a winter party. It does warm you up!*

Mrs. Larry Keith (Virginia)

Mexico Wallop

1 quart tequila	2 quarts fresh fruits, cubes or
1 bottle champagne	balls
4 bottles sauterne	Sugar to taste

Sweeten to taste; chill thoroughly, and add ice cubes just before serving. Place in large punch bowl and serve in sherbet cups.

Marian Carlson Hidell

Screwdriver Punch

1 can (10 ounces) Mandarin oranges	1 bottle (28 ounces) orange carbonated beverage, chilled
1 cup vodka	
1 can (6 ounces) frozen orange juice, thawed	1 bottle (⅘ quart) Rhine wine, chilled
	Ice cubes or ice ring
	Lemon slices and fresh mint to garnish, optional

Drain orange syrup into punch bowl; reserve orange sections. Add vodka and orange juice to the bowl, stirring to blend. Just before serving, add carbonated beverage and wine. Carefully add ice cubes or slide in ice ring; then add orange sections. Garnish with thinly sliced lemon and sprigs of fresh mint. Yields 20 four-ounce servings.

Cookbook Committee

Both the oil well and mesquite trees are familiar sights throughout Texas. "Old Spindletop" came in as a gusher at Beaumont in 1901 and changed the scope of industry forever in East Texas. The mesquite tree is indispensable to Texans in quite another way. Often called the "miracle mesquite," every portion of the tree was used for survival in the early days. Pioneers soon learned that water could usually be found within five miles of one. Its beans were used for food and its roots for fuel during especially cruel winters. The mesquite is said to have medicinal powers, as well, and the sap has been used for balm, glue, black dye, tea and gum drops.

Soups, Salads and Sandwiches pictured: Portuguese Soup, Avocado Soup, No Name Soup, Seven Layer Salad, Potato Salad, Mary Koock's Bombay Shrimp, Lamb Burger and Healthy Hero.

Soups, Salads and Sandwiches

Chilled Avocado Soup

3   ripe avocados, peeled and
    coarsely chopped
1   cup chicken broth
1   cup half and half cream
1   teaspoon salt

¼   teaspoon onion salt
White pepper to taste
1   teaspoon lemon juice
Lemon slices to garnish
Purple onion slices to garnish

Combine avocado and chicken broth in blender container. Cover and blend until smooth. Remove from blender and stir in half and half, salt, onion salt, and white pepper. Cover and refrigerate overnight. Stir in lemon juice before serving; garnish with lemon and purple onion slices. Serves 4 to 6.

Mrs. John Carrell (Jane)

Cold Avocado Cucumber Soup

1   can cream of celery soup
1   can water
1   avocado, diced
½   green pepper, diced
1   medium tomato, diced

1   medium cucumber, diced
3   green onions, chopped
2   tablespoons oil
1   tablespoon wine vinegar
Salt, pepper, garlic salt, and dill
    weed to taste

Combine all ingredients and chill. *This is a great light soup that will still allow you to enjoy the entrée without being full.*

Mrs. Robert Henderson (Dale)

Chilled Cucumber Soup

3   medium cucumbers, peeled,
    chopped, and seeded
3   tablespoons chopped green
    pepper

2   cups chicken broth
1   cup sour cream
1   teaspoon salt
2   teaspoons dill weed

Combine all ingredients and purée in blender. Chill and serve. Serves 6 to 8.

Mrs. James Carney (Jean)

Cold Squash Soup

¼ cup butter
1½ cups finely chopped onion
4 cups chopped summer squash
2 cups chicken broth
¼ teaspoon sugar

2 cups whipping cream
Salt to taste
White pepper to taste
Nutmeg to taste
Parsley or chives to garnish

In saucepan melt butter, add onion and cook at low heat until soft but not brown. Add squash and chicken broth. Cook until squash is tender. Add sugar. Put the mixture through a sieve or purée in blender. Cool. Add cream and season with salt, pepper, and nutmeg. Serve well chilled and sprinkled with chopped parsley or chives. Yields 10 to 12 servings. *For a less rich soup, you may substitute light cream.*

Mrs. Don Panter (Carolyn)

Gazpacho

1 clove garlic, minced
3 tomatoes, chopped
1 cucumber, peeled and diced
½ onion, chopped fine
½ green pepper, chopped, optional
Freshly ground pepper

½ teaspoon salt
2 tablespoons olive oil
1 tablespoon white vinegar
1 can (46 ounces) Campbell's tomato juice
Croutons to garnish, optional

Combine all ingredients. Chill overnight. *I always double this recipe, as it is the best summer diet lunch available.*

Mrs. John Baker (Jo)

Quick Vichyssoise

1½ cups water
2 tablespoons snipped parsley
2 chicken bouillon cubes
2 cups half and half cream, divided

Instant mashed potato mix (4 servings)
1 package (4 ounces) whipped cream cheese with onion
Snipped chives

Combine water, parsley and bouillon in saucepan. Cover and bring to a boil, stirring to dissolve bouillon. Remove from heat, add 1 cup cream; stir in potatoes. Cool at room temperature 15 minutes. Transfer mixture to blender container. Add cream cheese; blend until smooth, chill well. Add remaining cup of cream. Chill well. Garnish with chives. Serves 4.

Mrs. Robert Henderson (Dale)

Gourmet Potato Soup

½ pound fresh mushrooms, sliced
1 onion, chopped
3 tablespoons butter or margarine
3 tablespoons flour
2 cups milk
3 cups chicken broth
2 cups potatoes, peeled and chopped

1 teaspoon Worcestershire sauce
2 tablespoons parsley
1 tablespoon lemon juice
Salt and pepper to taste
Sour cream and chives, to garnish, optional
Parmesan cheese, to garnish, optional

Slice mushrooms and sauté with onions in butter until soft, but not brown. Stir in flour. Add liquids, potatoes, and seasonings. Simmer 30 minutes or until potatoes are done. Serves 4 to 6.

Mrs. Jim Schultz (Mary Kay)

Leek and Potato Soup

1½ pounds (6 to 8) potatoes
1 pound leeks
6 tablespoons butter
Salt and pepper to taste

3 cups water or broth
½ pint half and half cream
Bacon bits as optional garnish

Peel and cube potatoes. Wash, trim, and remove most of the green tops of leeks and then chop the remaining portion. Mix potatoes, leeks, butter, salt, and pepper. Cover with water or broth and bring to a boil; reduce to simmer and cook until potatoes are tender, about 30 to 35 minutes. If a thicker soup is desired, drain some of the liquid at this time. Add cream and heat before serving. Serves 6 to 8.

Mrs. Bernie Vise (Marion)

No-Name Soup

1 package (10 ounces) frozen broccoli or 1½ cups fresh
4 to 5 new potatoes
1 bunch green onions

2 cans chicken broth
Salt and pepper to taste
Sour cream as garnish

Cook vegetables with salt and pepper in broth until tender. Purée in blender. Serve hot with a tablespoon of sour cream on top of each bowl. Serves 6 to 8. *This is an East Texas "country" dish. It has no name and no known origin but is quick and great for last minute company.*

Mrs. Tom Hollis (Doris)

Creamy Broccoli Soup

1½ pounds broccoli
1 teaspoon beef bouillon
3 tablespoons chopped onion
2 tablespoons butter
1 tablespoon lemon juice

Salt and pepper to taste
1½ cups milk
⅓ cup sour cream
Paprika to garnish

Heat 1 inch of salted water in a saucepan to boiling. Cut broccoli and add to water along with bouillon. Cover and heat to boiling. Reduce heat and simmer until broccoli is tender, about 10 to 12 minutes. Purée 1 cup broccoli and 2 tablespoons cooking liquid in blender. Repeat until all broccoli has been puréed. Cook onion in butter over medium heat until tender, about 5 minutes. Stir in broccoli purée, lemon juice, salt and pepper. Add milk and sour cream gradually. Heat over low heat, stirring constantly. Garnish each serving with paprika. Serves 4 to 6.

Mrs. Larry Wisian (Kay)

Broccoli-Ham Soup

1 cup finely chopped ham
2 cloves garlic, minced
2 tablespoons salad oil
1 cup canned tomatoes
1 package (10 ounces) frozen chopped broccoli or 2 cups chopped fresh broccoli

½ teaspoon ground nutmeg
5 cups bouillon
1½ cups uncooked elbow, shell, or spiral macaroni
Salt and pepper to taste
Grated Parmesan cheese

Sauté ham and garlic in salad oil in large saucepan until delicately browned. Add tomatoes, broccoli, nutmeg, and bouillon; simmer about 20 minutes. Add macaroni and continue cooking for 5 to 10 minutes or until macaroni is tender. Add salt and pepper. Top with cheese. Yields 6 servings.

S. D. Jackman, Jr.

To remove excess salt from soup, drop in a sliced, raw potato. Remove just before serving.

Carrot Cream Soup

4 tablespoons butter or
  margarine
1 cup chopped onion
1 clove garlic, chopped
10 carrots, peeled and chopped
5 potatoes, peeled and
  chopped

6 cups chicken broth
½ teaspoon salt
½ teaspoon sugar
½ teaspoon white pepper
1 cup half and half cream

Sauté onion and garlic in butter until tender. Add broth, carrots, potatoes, and seasonings and simmer until vegetables are cooked, about 1 hour. Put soup through blender until smooth. Reheat before serving and add cream.

Mrs. Denman Smith (Sandra)

 For a tastier soup or stew, rub the inside of the soup pot with a cut garlic clove.

Cream of Cauliflower Soup

4 cups water
2 teaspoons chicken bouillon
1 small head cauliflower
  broken into very small
  pieces
1 medium carrot, grated
3 tablespoons chopped celery

3 tablespoons butter
3 tablespoons flour
Salt and pepper to taste
1 egg yolk
½ to 1 pint of half and half
  cream
Parsley to garnish

Heat water and bouillon to boiling; add cauliflower, carrots, and celery. Bring to a boil, then simmer covered for 20 minutes. Melt butter in large saucepan. Stir in flour, salt, and pepper. Cook, stirring constantly, over medium heat 1 minute. Gradually stir in bouillon and vegetables. Cook and stir until thick, about 5 minutes. Remove from heat. Combine egg yolk and cream; gradually add to hot mixture. Garnish each serving with parsley. Serves 6.

Mrs. Larry Wisian (Kay)

Okra Gumbo

2 tablespoons oil	½ to 1 pound okra
1 tablespoon flour	2 ripe tomatoes
½ onion, chopped	Salt and pepper to taste
2 garlic cloves, chopped	2 cups boiling water
½ green pepper, chopped	Rice
2 celery stalks, chopped	

Heat oil and stir in flour. Sauté onion, garlic, green pepper, and celery. When onion is clear, add okra, tomatoes, salt and pepper. Stir and add 2 cups boiling water. Cook for 45 minutes and serve over rice.

Mrs. Bill Butler (Stephanie)

French Onion Soup

3 cups sliced onions	1 teaspoon Worcestershire
2 tablespoons butter	sauce
2 cans (15½ ounces each) beef broth	1 loaf French bread
	Grated Parmesan cheese
1½ cups water or dry white wine	

In a large covered saucepan, cook onions in butter over low heat about 30 minutes, stirring occasionally. Add beef broth, water, and Worcestershire sauce. Heat to boiling. Reduce heat; cover and simmer about 30 minutes. Cut French bread into thin slices and toast lightly. Place ½ slice bread in bottom of each soup bowl. Pour hot soup over bread and sprinkle with Parmesan cheese. Serve immediately. Serves 4 to 6.

Mrs. Ken Moyer (Bonnie)

Mrs. Dean's Corn Soup

2 strips bacon, cut into pieces	1 corn can of milk
1 small onion, finely chopped	¼ teaspoon paprika
1 can (16 ounces) cream style corn	Salt and pepper to taste
	Chopped chives to garnish

Sauté bacon pieces until done but not crisp. Remove bacon. Sauté onion in bacon drippings until onion is transparent. Return bacon to pan. Add creamed corn, milk, paprika, salt and pepper. Heat just to boiling, stirring frequently. Garnish each bowl with chopped chives. Serves 4.

Mrs. Daniel O'Donnell (Sharon)

Mexican Corn Soup

4 cups fresh corn kernels
¼ cup chopped onion
2 tablespoons butter
2 tablespoons flour
Salt and pepper to taste
2 cups chicken broth

2 cups milk or cream
1 cup grated Cheddar cheese
1 can (4 ounces) green chilies, chopped, optional
Tortilla chips
½ cup crisp bacon, crumbled

Sauté corn and onion in butter until tender. Add flour, salt and pepper; cook 1 minute. Gradually add broth, alternating with milk or cream, until thickened. Add Cheddar cheese and green chilies; do not over heat. Serve soup in individual bowls, stirring in 4 or 5 tortilla chips; garnish with crumbled bacon.

Mrs. George Dolezal (Sharon)

Posole Soup

1 pound dried or frozen posole, or 2 cans (1 pound each) hominy, undrained
2 pounds cooked, cubed pork
1 tablespoon salt
1 large onion, chopped

2 cloves garlic, minced
Pinch ground oregano
1 teaspoon cumin
2 cans (4 ounces each) diced green chilies

If dried posole is used, soak in water overnight. Simmer posole in 8 to 10 cups water for 3 hours. During the final hour, add remaining ingredients. If using hominy, add enough water to make it soupy and then add ingredients and simmer for an hour. Yields 2 quarts. *Can be frozen. For some reason, this soup seems to get hotter in flavor as time goes by!*

Mrs. Ken Moyer (Bonnie)

Cumin and comino are one and the same! The seeds originated in Egypt, but are a popular seasoning in many Mexican dishes.

Vegetable Soup

1   soup bone
1½ quarts cold water
1   large onion, quartered
3   teaspoons salt
¼   teaspoon black pepper
1   carrot, cubed
1   turnip, diced
1   can (20 ounces) tomatoes,
    undrained

12 pods okra, cut in one inch
    rounds
1   ear corn, scraped
1   celery rib, sliced
12 green beans, cut in ½ inch
    pieces
12 pea pods, shelled
1   potato, diced
10 to 12 pieces of spaghetti,
    broken into small pieces
12 ounces tomato juice

Place soup bone in cold water with onion, salt and pepper. Bring to a boil, then cover and lower heat. Simmer for 1½ hours. Add vegetables, spaghetti, and tomato juice. Simmer another 1½ hours. *May delete or substitute almost any vegetables.*

Mrs. Ron Garrick (Bonnie)

Vegetable and Cheese Soup

2½ cups water
1   cup diced, peeled potatoes
½   cup chopped onion
½   cup finely chopped celery
½   cup chopped green pepper
½   cup chopped carrots
Seasoned salt to taste
2   tablespoons butter

2   tablespoons flour
1   cup milk
¾   teaspoon seasoned salt
Scant teaspoon pepper
¼   teaspoon dry mustard
1   teaspoon Worcestershire
    sauce
1   cup grated American cheese

In large pot, cook vegetables slowly in water, adding a dash of seasoned salt. When tender, cool slightly. Melt butter in skillet and add flour, blending well. Cook slowly 2 to 3 minutes. Combine milk with ¾ teaspoon seasoned salt, pepper, dry mustard and Worcestershire. Blend well; then add gradually to butter-flour mixture. Cook until mixture thickens, stirring often. Add grated cheese, stirring until cheese melts. Add cheese mixture to vegetables. Heat well but do not boil. Serve while hot. Serves 4 to 6.

Mrs. Ken Moyer (Bonnie)

Cheddar Cheese Soup

6 tablespoons margarine	8 to 10 ounces Cheddar cheese,
3 chopped green onions	grated
3 stalks celery, chopped	Salt and pepper to taste
2 carrots, grated	3 drops Tabasco sauce
2 cans chicken broth	8 ounces sour cream
4 cans potato soup	

Sauté onions, celery, and carrots in margarine. Add chicken broth and simmer 30 minutes. Add potato soup, cheese, salt and pepper, Tabasco, and sour cream. Simmer 15 minutes. Do not boil. Makes 10 cups.

Mrs. Chris Williston (Janice)

To change a cream soup into a low-calorie soup; blend 1 cup ricotta or cottage cheese with 1 cup lowfat milk. This makes a satisfying replacement for the conventional flour, butter and cream version.

Calico Cheese Soup

½ cup finely chopped carrots	3 tablespoons flour
½ cup finely chopped green	2 cups milk, scalded
peppers	2 cups chicken broth
½ cup finely chopped celery	2 cups shredded Cheddar
Boiling water to cover	cheese
2 tablespoons minced onion	¼ cup salad oil
Garlic to taste, chopped	¼ cup grated Parmesan cheese
4 tablespoons butter	Box of croutons

Place carrots, green pepper and celery in boiling, salted water to cover; cover and cook until crisp-tender. Drain and set aside. Sauté onion and garlic in butter until tender. Stir in flour, milk and broth, blending well. Cook, stirring constantly, until slightly thickened. Add cheese, stir until melted. Add vegetable mixture, cook 10 minutes. Combine oil, Parmesan cheese and toss with croutons. Serve on top of hot soup. Serves 4 to 6. *Good with grilled sandwiches. Very filling soup.*

Mrs. H. C. Carter (Joan)

Crab Bisque

¼ pound butter or margarine
½ cup finely chopped onion
½ cup finely chopped green pepper
¼ cup finely chopped parsley
2 cups sliced fresh mushrooms

4 tablespoons flour
2 cups milk
1 teaspoon salt
1 teaspoon white pepper
2 cups half and half cream
3 cups chopped crab
3 tablespoons sherry, optional

Heat butter and sauté onion, green pepper, parsley, and mushrooms until soft. Add flour and stir to dissolve. Add milk, salt, and pepper and simmer until thickened and well blended. Add cream and crab and simmer for 15 minutes. Can be served immediately, but flavor is enhanced when refrigerated overnight and then reheated. Add sherry just before serving.

Mrs. Denman Smith (Sandra)

Crab Meat Soup

6 to 8 ounces crab meat
1 can tomato soup

1 can cream of asparagus soup
1 pint half and half cream

Drain crab meat. Mix all ingredients together and simmer in crockpot 2 or 3 hours. Soup may also simmer on stove at a very low temperature. Serves 4. *This rich soup should not be diluted with water.*

Mrs. Jack Dempsey (Estelle)

Seafood Gumbo

6 tablespoons flour
½ cup shortening
6 cloves garlic, chopped
½ cup chopped onions
½ cup chopped green peppers
½ cup chopped celery
2 pounds peeled raw shrimp
1 cup tomato sauce

3 quarts shrimp stock
1 pound crab meat
½ bunch parsley
½ teaspoon thyme
6 bay leaves
1 pound frozen okra
Salt and pepper

Prepare roux by slowly browning flour in shortening; add garlic and cook until golden brown. Add onions, green pepper and celery and cook until transparent. Add shrimp and tomato sauce; simmer 10 minutes and then add stock, blending for a few minutes. Add remaining ingredients and cook an additional 30 minutes. Remove bay leaves. Serve over steamed rice. Yields 1 gallon.

Mrs. Charles Cantwell (Winn)

Instant Shrimp Gumbo

¼	pound bacon	4	cups chicken stock
¼	cup chopped onion	2	cups shrimp
¼	cup diced celery	2	cups chopped okra
¼	cup diced green pepper	1	cup cooked rice
2	cups fresh or canned tomatoes		

Dice and sauté bacon; add onion, green pepper, and celery. Sauté until tender. Add tomatoes and stock. Cook until vegetables are soft. Add shrimp, okra and rice. Cook for 10 minutes. Serves 6.

Mrs. Charles Perry (Carolyn)

Tiffany's Bean Pot Soup

2	cups pinto beans, uncooked	4	tablespoons brown sugar
1	pound cooked ham, cubed	1	tablespoon chili powder
2	cans (12 ounces each) tomato juice	1	teaspoon monosodium glutamate
4	cups chicken stock	1	teaspoon salt
3	onions, chopped	1	teaspoon crushed bay leaf
3	gloves garlic, minced	1	teaspoon oregano
3	tablespoons chopped parsley	½	teaspoon ground cumin
¼	cup chopped green pepper	½	teaspoon crushed rosemary
½	teaspoon celery seed	½	teaspoon thyme
½	teaspoon marjoram	½	teaspoon basil
¼	teaspoon curry powder	1	cup sherry, optional
4	whole cloves		Green onions, chopped for garnish

Wash and soak beans overnight, drain. Cover with water and bring to a boil and let boil one hour. Add all ingredients except sherry. Bring to a boil; cook slowly until beans are tender. Add sherry and heat just before serving. Serve garnished with chopped green onions, if desired. Serves 8 to 10 generously.

Mrs. Larry Lerche (Gail)

Forget to soak the beans last night? Try this quickie version: measure your beans into a large pot. Cover with water and boil, covered, for two minutes. Remove from heat and soak them covered in the cooling water for one hour. Then proceed with your recipe.

Three Bean Soup

½ cup dry baby lima beans
½ cup dry garbanzo beans
½ cup dry green split peas
Water
1 teaspoon salt
1½ pounds ham hock with meat
1 tablespoon vegetable oil
½ pound white onions, chopped
½ tablespoon chopped garlic
2 cups diced celery
1 cup diced carrots
½ tablespoon thyme, crumbled
¼ teaspoon dried crushed red pepper
½ teaspoon salt
2 teaspoons pepper
⅛ teaspoon Tabasco
4 cups sliced fresh mushrooms
1 tablespoon flour

Soak beans and peas overnight in 1½ quarts salted water. Brown ham hock in oil in Dutch oven. Stir in onion and garlic; sauté until onion is soft. Add 1 quart water; cover and simmer 1 hour. Refrigerate overnight. Next day skim fat and discard. Remove meat from bone; cut in pieces and return to pot. Drain beans and peas. Add to meat with 1 quart water and remaining ingredients except mushrooms and flour. Cover, simmer 50 minutes. Add mushrooms. Blend flour with one cup of pan sauce. Add to pot; simmer 10 minutes longer to thicken. Yields 1 gallon.

S. D. Jackman, Jr.

Black Bean Soup

1 pound black beans
10 cups water
5 slices bacon, cut into small pieces
2 stalks celery, chopped
2 medium onions, chopped
2 tablespoons flour
2 smoked ham hocks, split (1½ pounds)
3 pounds beef bones
3 sprigs parsley
2 bay leaves
2 cloves garlic, halved
2 carrots, cut into pieces
2 parsnips, coarsely chopped
¼ teaspoon black pepper
2 teaspoons salt
¾ cup Madeira wine or sherry

Wash beans; cover with cold water and soak overnight. Drain and wash again. Place in casserole; add 10 cups of water, cover and simmer about 90 minutes. Cook bacon in a large pot; add celery and onions and cook until tender, but do not brown. Blend in flour and cook, for one minute, stirring often. Add ham and beef bones, parsley, bay leaves, garlic, carrots, parsnips, pepper, salt and the beans with the cooking liquid. Cover and simmer over low heat, stirring occasionally, for 4 hours. Add more water if necessary. Remove bones and hocks and put soup through a sieve, straining thoroughly. Chop the meat fine and return to the soup. Reheat soup. Add the wine and mix well. Serve hot. Serves 8.

Mrs. Larry Hall (Jane)

Frijole Bean Soup

1½ pounds pinto beans
1 tablespoon salt
1 cup salt pork, cut in pieces
½ cup bacon, cut in pieces
3 strips salt pork rind, if available
1 tablespoon bacon drippings
2 cups finely chopped yellow onion
½ tablespoon minced fresh garlic
3 bay leaves

½ teaspoon fresh ground black pepper
½ teaspoon whole thyme, pulverized
½ teaspoon oregano, pulverized
Pinch sweet basil
Pinch marjoram
¼ teaspoon cayenne pepper
⅛ teaspoon Tabasco
Fifth of sherry and/or 6 pack of beer, optional

Wash beans and place in 1 gallon pot. Cover with 6 cups water, add salt, stir and soak overnight. Cook in same water. Render and discard excess fat from salt pork, bacon and rind, and add to pot when water is bubbling. In same skillet add bacon drippings and sauté onions and garlic until soft. Add to beans. Add remaining seasoning; stir in and simmer until beans are tender, about 5 to 6 hours. Add hot water if liquid does not cover contents by 1 inch. Either mash about ⅓ of beans on side of pot with wooden spoon or in blender and return to pot; test for seasonings. Let sit for an hour; test for seasonings again. Serve hot with fresh hot flour tortillas. Yields 6 pints. *The optional items are for spouse and cook respectively during the 5 to 6 hours cooking time. Soup is better the next day.*

S. D. Jackman, Jr.

Split Pea Soup

1 ham hock (1 pound) or 2 to 3 cups diced ham
1 package (1 pound) dry split peas
8 carrots, sliced

1 onion, diced
1 teaspoon salt
Pepper to taste
10 cups water or broth

Put all ingredients into large pot. Bring to a boil and cook until carrots are tender and peas are mushy. Stir often when peas begin to soften to prevent scorching. Cook a total of about 1½ hours. Serves approximately 10.

Mrs. Larry Wisian (Kay)

Green Pea Soup with Turkey

2	tablespoons butter	½	teaspoon ground pepper
1	tablespoon oil	1	tablespoon curry powder
1	onion, finely chopped	3	tablespoons flour
½	cup chopped celery	2	cups chicken broth
1	package (10 ounces) frozen peas	1	cup half and half cream
1	teaspoon salt	¾	cup finely chopped, cooked turkey

Heat butter and oil; add onion and celery. Sauté until tender. Add peas, salt, and pepper. Cook until peas are very soft. Add curry powder and remove from heat; stir in flour. Gradually add chicken broth. Stir soup as it cooks over medium heat until it comes to a boil. Blend soup until smooth in blender. Pour soup back in pan and add cream and turkey. When ready to serve, reheat but do not boil. Yields 2 quarts. *This soup is good cold as well as hot and is a great way to use leftover turkey.*

Mrs. Charles Tupa (Sidney)

Mulligatawny Soup

¼	cup finely chopped onion	4	cups chicken broth
1½	teaspoons curry powder	1	can (16 ounces) tomatoes, undrained and chopped
2	tablespoons oil		
1	tart apple, peeled, cored, and chopped	1	tablespoon chopped parsley
¼	cup chopped carrot	2	teaspoons lemon juice
¼	cup chopped celery	1	teaspoon sugar
2	tablespoons chopped green pepper	2	whole cloves
		¼	teaspoon salt
3	tablespoons flour		Dash of pepper
		1	cup diced cooked chicken

In large saucepan, cook onion and curry powder in oil until onion is tender. Stir in apple, carrot, celery, and green pepper. Cook, stirring occasionally, until vegetables are crisp-tender, about 5 minutes. Sprinkle flour over vegetables. Stir to mix well. Add broth, tomatoes, parsley, lemon juice, sugar, cloves, salt and pepper. Bring to a boil, then add chicken. Simmer for 30 minutes, stirring occasionally. Serves 6.

Mrs. Clark Rector (Sue)

Inn at Brushy Creek's Portuguese Soup

2 cups chopped onion
6 cloves garlic, chopped
6 tablespoons oil
1 pound garlic flavored smoked pork sausage, sliced
10 cups beef stock
1 can (16 ounces) kidney beans with liquid

1 head green cabbage, cored and chopped
12 small new potatoes, scrubbed and quartered
¼ to ½ cup vinegar
2 cups catsup
Salt and pepper to taste

Sauté onions and garlic in the oil. When the vegetables are transparent, add sausage slices and brown lightly. Add remaining ingredients. Bring to a boil, stirring to prevent scorching. Reduce heat. Simmer 35 to 45 minutes, stirring occasionally. Correct seasonings to taste. Yields 1 gallon.

Mrs. Jim Rado (Vicki)

Sausage Chowder

2 links of smoked garlic flavored sausage
1 medium onion, chopped
2 cans (16 ounces each) peeled tomatoes, chopped with liquid
½ cup mild pepperoncini peppers, chopped

2 cans (15 ounces each) Ranch Style beans
Garlic powder, salt, pepper, oregano to taste
1½ cups water
6 medium potatoes, diced

Slice sausage into ½ inch thick pieces. Place sausage, onion, chopped tomatoes, peppers, beans, and seasonings in a large Dutch oven. Add 1½ cups water. Simmer for one hour; then add diced potatoes and continue to cook until potatoes are done. Mix a little flour and water and use to thicken the chowder. Serves 8. *This is our favorite substitute for chili. It can be made as hot in flavor as you like by adding more peppers. I always serve it with jalapeño cornbread, and it is really a good dish for cold weather.*

Mrs. Rush McGinty (Carol)

Old Country Borscht

1 pound beef brisket	2 bay leaves
12 cups water	Salt
2 large onions, chopped	2 beets, grated
4 stalks of celery, sliced	1 can (6 ounces) tomato paste
4 medium beets, diced	2 tablespoons vinegar
5 carrots, sliced	2 teaspoons salt
1 small head cabbage, cut into 6 wedges	1 cup sour cream

Cut brisket into at least 6 pieces and put in large pot with water, onions, celery, diced beets, carrots, cabbage, bay leaves, and bring to a boil. Reduce heat; cover and simmer about 3 hours. Add grated beets, tomato paste, and vinegar. Return to simmer for 20 minutes. Cool and refrigerate overnight. Skim fat from top and discard. Bring soup slowly to a boil and simmer covered 15 minutes. Adjust salt. Serve topped with sour cream. Serves 6 to 8.

Mrs. Dudley Baker (Kathy)

Plaza II Steak Soup

1 stick butter, melted	1 tablespoon Accent
1 cup flour	2 tablespoons B-V beef extract
½ gallon water	1 teaspoon pepper
1 pound ground chuck	Kitchen Bouquet for color
1 cup diced onion	1 teaspoon celery salt
1 cup diced celery	1 teaspoon onion salt
1 cup diced carrots	1 teaspoon garlic salt
1 package (10 ounces) frozen mixed vegetables	Salt to taste
1 can (16 ounces) tomatoes, strained	Dash basil

Melt butter and stir in flour and water until mixture is smooth. Add meat and bring to a boil. Add vegetables, Accent, B-V, and pepper. Bring to a boil and simmer 4 hours. Add Kitchen Bouquet to darken. Add remaining seasonings to taste. Yields about 1 gallon.

Mrs. Wayne Davison (Cindi)

Egg Drop Soup

2 eggs
2 teaspoons water
6 cups chicken stock
1 teaspoon dry sherry

1 tablespoon soy sauce
Salt to taste
2 scallions, chopped

Beat eggs and stir in water. Bring chicken stock to a boil. Reduce heat to medium and stir in sherry, soy sauce, and salt. Pour eggs in slowly, a little at a time, so that soup continues to boil at all times. Keep stirring constantly, until eggs separate into shreds. Garnish with scallions. This typical Chinese soup may be changed by adding any one or combination of these ingredients: soaked, dried black mushrooms, bamboo shoots, lean pork, sesame oil, black pepper or shredded chicken. Serves 8.

Mrs. Thomas Schwartz (Ellana)

The railroads brought the Chinese to Texas in 1870, but they came to help build them, not ride them. Since that time, the Chinese influence in cooking has gained in popularity.

Almond Soup

2 tablespoons butter, melted
2 tablespoons instant-
    dissolving flour
2 tablespoons grated onion
3 cups chicken broth
1½ cups finely ground almonds
¼ teaspoon basil
1 teaspoon sugar
¼ teaspoon ground mace

¼ teaspoon dry mustard
¼ teaspoon paprika
1 clove garlic, minced
Salt and pepper to taste
1 cup whipping cream
2 tablespoons sweet sherry
Slivered, toasted almonds to
    garnish

Combine butter and flour in a saucepan; blend until smooth. Cook 1 minute. Add onion; cook 2 minutes. Stir in chicken broth; cook, stirring constantly, until thickened. Combine almonds, basil, sugar, mace, mustard, and paprika; stir into soup. Cook 20 minutes over medium low heat. Add garlic, salt and pepper. Remove from heat; whisk in cream. Heat slowly, do not bring to a boil. Add sherry just before serving. Garnish with slivered, toasted almonds. Yields about 6 servings.

Nancy Young Moritz

Case Noodle

Dough:

3 to 4 cups flour

3 eggs

Water

Filling:

1½ pounds cottage cheese	½ teaspoon allspice
½ teaspoon salt	4 slices bread, cubed, divided
¼ teaspoon pepper	¼ cup butter
3 tablespoons minced onion	1 pint sour cream

Dough: Put flour in bowl and make a nest for liquid. Put three eggs into a 2 cup measure and fill to 1½ cups with water. Pour this into the nest and mix with the flour until all the flour is mixed with the liquid. Put dough onto floured brown paper or pastry cloth and knead to the right consistency for a noodle dough, about 5 minutes. Divide the dough into four pieces, roll out to ⅛ to ¼ inch thick and cut into 4x4 inch squares.

For filling, mix cottage cheese, salt, pepper, onion, allspice and 2 slices cubed bread. To assemble and cook, put a heaping tablespoon of cheese mixture on each noodle and seal by folding the corners into the center and crimping together into a flat little pouch. When all noodles are filled and crimped, drop into 12 cups boiling salted water and cook about 10 to 15 minutes. While noodles are boiling, brown remaining bread cubes in butter. When noodles are done, add the sour cream and croutons. Rinse crouton skillet with broth for extra richness. Serves 6 to 8. *This is a very special German soup that everyone asks for.*

Mildred May

Salads

Avocado Grapefruit Salad

1 head bibb or romaine lettuce	2 cans (11 ounces each) Mandarin oranges, drained
2 avocados, sliced	1 small red onion, sliced in rings
3 Ruby Red grapefruit, sectioned and membranes removed or 2 cans (16 ounces) grapefruit sections, drained	Prepared poppy seed dressing or celery seed dressing

Line salad bowl with salad greens. Tear some greens into bite size pieces. Add avocado, grapefruit and orange slices. Lightly toss with prepared dressing of your choice. Place onion rings on top of salad to add color and flavor. Serves 6 to 8.

Mrs. Dudley Baker (Kathy)

Strawberry Soufflé Salad

⅓ cup evaporated milk
2 teaspoons lemon juice
½ cup sliced bananas
1½ cups cold cooked rice
1 cup coconut
½ cup chopped pecans

1 cup fresh or frozen
strawberries, sliced and
drained
2 tablespoons lemon juice
6 tablespoons powdered sugar

Chill evaporated milk in refrigerator tray in freezer until soft crystals form around edges of tray, about 15 to 20 minutes. Sprinkle 2 teaspoons lemon juice over bananas. Mix bananas with rice, coconut, pecans, and strawberries. Whip chilled milk until stiff. Add 2 tablespoons lemon juice and whip very stiff, approximately 2 minutes. Beat in powdered sugar. Fold whipped milk mixture into strawberry mixture. Spoon onto lettuce leaves. Serves 6.

Mrs. Ron Garrick (Bonnie)

Orange Apricot Salad

2 packages (3 ounces) orange
gelatin
2 cups boiling water
Pinch of salt
2 cups miniature
marshmallows
1 can (12 ounces) apricot
nectar
1 can (15¼ ounces) crushed
pineapple, drained (save
juice)

3 heaping teaspoons flour
1 egg, beaten
½ cup sugar
Pinch of salt
2 tablespoons butter
1 cup whipped topping
5 ounces Cheddar cheese,
grated

Mix boiling water and salt with gelatin. Add marshmallows to gelatin mixture and stir until melted. Set aside ½ cup of apricot nectar and ½ cup pineapple juice for topping. Add remaining apricot nectar, pineapple juice and crushed pineapple to gelatin. Pour into 2 quart casserole and refrigerate until set.

Topping: Cook flour, egg, sugar, salt, reserved juice and butter over low heat until thick, stirring constantly. It scorches easily. When cooled, fold in whipped topping. Spread over gelatin just before serving. Cover with grated cheese.

Mrs. Chris Williston (Janice)

Mandarin Orange Salad

1   carton (8 ounces) sour
    cream
1   small package (3 ounces)
    orange gelatin
1   can (11 ounces) Mandarin
    slices, drained

1   can (20 ounces) crushed
    pineapple, drained
1   carton (8 ounces) whipped
    topping, thawed

Mix sour cream and powdered gelatin thoroughly. Add drained fruit to sour cream mixture. Stir in whipped topping. May be served immediately or can be refrigerated for later use. Serves 8. *Variation: Use strawberry jello, strawberries, and bananas.*

Mrs. Ron Garrick (Bonnie)

Bing Sherry Salad

1   can (16½ ounces) pitted
    bing cherries, drained
    (reserve juice)
2   cups orange juice
1½ cups sherry
1   cup sugar

3   tablespoons unflavored
    gelatin
¾   cup chopped pecans
Whipped topping or
    mayonnaise to garnish

Mix cherry juice with 1½ cups of the orange juice, sherry, and sugar; bring to a boil. Soak gelatin in remaining ½ cup orange juice. Dissolve in hot fruit syrup. Chill mixture until partially set; pour into a mold or a 9 inch square pan. Stir in cherries and nuts and distribute evenly. When congealed, top with whipped topping or mayonnaise. Serves 12.

Mrs. Robert West (Linda)

Cranberry Cherry Salad

1   can (20 ounces) white
    cherries, halved and pitted
1   scant cup reserved cherry
    juice
1   small package cherry
    gelatin

1   can (16 ounces) whole
    cranberry sauce
2   tablespoons lemon juice
3   ounces cream cheese, diced
    small
½   cup chopped pecans

Heat cherry juice to boiling; add gelatin and stir until dissolved. Blend in cranberry sauce and lemon juice. Chill until partly set. Fold in cherries, cream cheese, and pecans. Pour into ring or other mold. Serves 8.

Mrs. B. L. Turlington (Jill)

Cranberry Salad Mold

1 pound fresh cranberries	1 cup chopped pared apple
1 cup sugar	1 cup chopped pecans or
1 envelope unflavored gelatin	walnuts
½ cup orange juice	Mayonnaise or whipped cream
1 cup chopped celery	to garnish

Wash cranberries; drain and remove stems. Put through food processor or food chopper. Add sugar. Let stand 15 minutes, stirring occasionally. Sprinkle gelatin over orange juice and stir until dissolved over low heat. Add gelatin mixture, celery, apples, and nuts to cranberries, mixing well. Put in a 1 quart mold. Refrigerate 6 to 8 hours. Serve with mayonnaise or whipped cream. Serves 10 to 12.

Mrs. James Carney (Jean)

Frosted Lemon Salad

1 package (6 ounces) lemon gelatin	2 bananas, sliced
	½ cup sugar
2 cups boiling water	2 tablespoons flour
2 cups ginger ale	1 cup pineapple juice
1 can (20 ounces) crushed pineapple	1 egg, slightly beaten
	2 tablespoons butter
1 cup miniature marshmallows	1 cup whipping cream, whipped

Dissolve gelatin in boiling water; stir in ginger ale. Chill until partially set. Drain pineapple, save juice. Fold pineapple, marshmallows and bananas into partially set gelatin mixture. Pour into a 9 × 13 inch dish. Chill until firm. For whipped cream topping combine sugar and flour in a saucepan. Stir in the pineapple juice and beaten egg. Cook over low heat until thickened. Remove from heat and add butter; let cool and chill. Fold into whipped cream. Frost gelatin mixture and chill overnight. Serves 15.

Mrs. David Armour (Betsy)

Salad molds made from everyday kitchen utensils: muffin pans, custard cups, ice trays, and even empty tin cans—turn ordinary molded salads into something special. Cans can be filled, chilled, and the salad pushed out when ready.

Mango Salad

2   small packages orange
    gelatin
1   small package lemon
    gelatin
1   cup boiling water

1   can (29 ounces) mangos and
    juice
8   ounces cream cheese, cut
    into 8 pieces
Juice of 1 to 2 limes

Dissolve orange and lemon gelatins in boiling water, in large bowl. Mixture will be sticky. Blend mangos with juice; pour one-half into gelatin mixture, stirring to mix. In blender add cheese one at a time until well blended. Pour into gelatin mixture, stirring well. Add lime juice to taste. Pour into ring mold or 9 × 13 dish, and chill. Serves 10 to 12. *This is a cool, delicious tropical treat. If mangos are unavailable in your area, you can substitute one large can of peaches or apricots.*

Mrs. Bob Edgecomb (Mary)

Strawberry Nut Salad

2   small packages strawberry
    gelatin
1   cup boiling water
2   packages (10 ounces each)
    frozen sliced strawberries,
    thawed, reserve juice
1   can (1 pound 4 ounces)
    crushed pineapple, drained

3   medium bananas, mashed
1   cup coarsely chopped
    walnuts or pecans
1   pint sour cream
Lettuce for garnish

Combine gelatin with boiling water, stirring until dissolved. Fold in strawberries, pineapple, bananas and nuts. Pour one half of the strawberry mixture into an oblong baking dish. Refrigerate until firm. About 1½ hours later evenly spread top with sour cream. Gently spoon on remainder of strawberry mixture. Cut into squares and serve on a bed of lettuce. Serves 10 to 12.

Mrs. Larry Strickland (Linda)

Poteet, Texas, proudly boasts a monument of a strawberry, which is not surprising as this small community produces almost half of the state's crop.

Dill Salad

Salad:
4 to 6 heads romaine, bibb or
    other lettuce
½ cup fresh dill, chopped or ¼
    cup dried
5 green onions, chopped

3 avocados, chopped,
    optional
2 cups sliced mushrooms,
    optional

Dressing:
1½ cups salad oil
½ cup white distilled vinegar
1½ teaspoons powdered beef
    broth
1 onion, quartered

1 teaspoon salt
½ teaspoon dried basil
½ teaspoon sugar
¼ teaspoon dry mustard
¼ cup water

For salad, wash greens and drain well. Tear into bite size pieces and place in large salad bowl. Add dill and green onions and toss. Cover with a damp paper towel. Refrigerate at least one hour to let flavors penetrate. Pour on dressing just before serving; toss until well coated. Serves 24. For dressing, purée all ingredients in blender until smooth. Cover and refrigerate up to 1 week.

Mrs. Jim Rado (Vicki)

Artichoke Tossed Salad

½ cup oil
¼ cup lemon juice
3 tablespoons tarragon vinegar
2 tablespoons sugar
1 clove garlic, crushed
½ teaspoon dry mustard
1 teaspoon salt
Fresh ground pepper
2 tablespoons onions, minced
1 or 2 cans (14 ounces each)
    artichokes, drained

1 cup croutons
2 tablespoons butter
1 large head lettuce, torn into
    bite size pieces
1 large head romaine, torn
    into bite size pieces
6 to 8 radishes, sliced
1 avocado, cubed

Combine oil, lemon juice, vinegar, sugar, garlic, dry mustard, salt, pepper, and onions into a large jar. Cover and shake until well mixed. Add artichokes; refrigerate overnight. Brown croutons in butter stirring until toasted on all sides. Toss greens and radishes in a large serving bowl. Add artichokes and dressing; toss well. Add avocados and croutons. Serves 12. *Croutons are best served warm. Reheat just before serving if needed.*

Mrs. Ernest Butler (Sarah)

Romaine Salad

4 strips crisp fried bacon, reserve drippings	¼ teaspoon pepper
	½ teaspoon salt
¾ cup oil	1 tablespoon sugar
¼ cup vinegar	1 head romaine lettuce
¼ cup bacon drippings	3 slices bread, crusts removed
1 egg	¼ cup oil
¼ teaspoon dry mustard	1 clove minced garlic

Blend ¾ cup of oil, vinegar, bacon drippings, egg, and spices in a blender for 1 minute. Refrigerate for at least one hour. Serve over torn romaine lettuce pieces, and top with crumbled bacon and homemade croutons. Cut prepared bread in cubes for croutons. In ¼ cup oil, sauté one clove garlic; add bread and coat with oil. Remove from heat and let stand one hour. Toast in 350° oven until brown. Serves 8.

Mrs. Jette Campbell (Sally)

Layered Salad

Salad greens	1 to 2 tablespoons sugar, optional
Green pepper, chopped	
Celery, chopped	1 package (.04 ounces) dry Ranch dressing mix, optional
Green onions, chopped	
Fresh mushrooms, sliced	
Water chestnuts, sliced	2 cups grated cheese, Cheddar or Swiss
Olives, well drained and chopped	
1 to 2 packages (10 ounces each) frozen peas	Parmesan cheese, grated
	8 to 10 slices bacon, cooked and crumbled
1 cup mayonnaise	
1 carton (8 ounces) sour cream	

The first layer should be your favorite salad greens or a mixture of several, such as spinach, romaine, bibb, or red leaf lettuce. Tear into bite size pieces. Greens should equal about 1½ heads. Place in a large straight sided, clear bowl. Next, layer any combination of the following: green pepper, celery, onions, mushrooms, water chestnuts, and olives to equal 1½ to 2 cups. The third layer should be frozen peas. For the fourth layer, combine mayonnaise and sour cream. If you like it sweet add sugar. If not add the dry Ranch dressing mix to the mayonnaise-sour cream mixture. Spread dressing evenly on top, making sure edges are sealed. Next sprinkle cheese, Cheddar or Swiss. Cover generously with Parmesan and top with crumbled bacon. Do not mix. Cover tightly with plastic wrap. Refrigerate overnight. Serves 10 to 12.

Mrs. Ken Moyer (Bonnie)

Wilted Spinach Salad à la Villa Demos

1	pound spinach	¼	cup sugar
1	pound bacon, thick sliced	3	ounces Italian dressing
1	medium onion, sliced thin	3	ounces white vinegar
8	ounces fresh mushrooms, sliced thin		Seasoned croutons

Wash spinach and drain; then refrigerate at least 1 hour. Fry bacon until crisp; drain and crumble. In large skillet, sauté onion in ½ cup bacon drippings. Add sugar, dressing and vinegar. Pour over spinach which has been tossed with bacon and mushrooms. Top with croutons and serve immediately. Serves 6. *This is the famous salad served at the Villa Demos Restaurant in Acapulco.*

Mrs. Robert Kelly (Margaret)

Spinach Salad

6	slices bacon, cooked and crumbled	2	hard cooked eggs, sliced
1	tablespoon bacon drippings		Small onion, peeled and cut into rings
4	tablespoons olive oil	1	cup fresh mushrooms, sliced
3	tablespoons red wine vinegar		Salt and pepper
1	pound fresh spinach		

In a small jar or bowl combine bacon drippings, olive oil and vinegar. Mix well and set aside. Place spinach, eggs, onion, mushrooms, and bacon in a salad bowl. Season with salt and pepper. Sprinkle with dressing and toss well.

Mrs. Larry Hall (Jane)

Spinach and Mandarin Orange Salad

1½	pounds fresh spinach, torn in bite size pieces	10	bacon slices, cooked and crumbled
1	can (11 ounces) Mandarin oranges, drained	1	can (15 ounces) pineapple chunks, drained, optional

Combine all ingredients and toss with the honey dressing, see Index, or with any fruit salad dressing.

Mrs. Wayne Davison (Cindi)

Spinach Salad and Dressing

2 pounds fresh spinach
2 cups thinly sliced water
   chestnuts
4 hard cooked eggs, chopped
1 cup bean sprouts, drained
½ pound bacon, fried crisp
   and crumbled
1 cup salad oil

½ cup dark vinegar
1 teaspoon Worcestershire
   sauce
1 medium onion, finely
   chopped
2 teaspoons salt
½ cup catsup
½ cup sugar

Clean spinach and tear into bite size pieces for salad. Add chestnuts, eggs, sprouts, and bacon and toss. Combine the remaining ingredients for dressing. Pour over salad just before serving; toss to coat. Serves 12.

Mrs. Bob Edgecomb (Mary)

Calypso Slaw

1 cup mayonnaise
2 tablespoons sugar
2 tablespoons vinegar
4 tablespoons prepared
   mustard
½ teaspoon celery seed
Salt and pepper to taste

4 cups cabbage, shredded
1 can (12 ounces) Mexicorn,
   drained
½ cup chopped onion
½ cup diced Cheddar cheese
2 tablespoons ripe olives,
   sliced

Combine mayonnaise, sugar, vinegar, mustard, celery seed, salt and pepper. This is best if made a day ahead. Combine cabbage, corn, onions, cheese and olives, and toss with dressing. Serves 6. *This is a very different and colorful salad.*

Mrs. Nelson Poldrack (Elaine)

Creamy Cabbage Slaw

1 cup mayonnaise
2 tablespoons sugar
2 tablespoons vinegar
2 teaspoons celery seed
1 teaspoon salt

6 cups shredded cabbage
½ cup shredded carrots,
   optional
¼ cup sliced scallions

Mix mayonnaise, sugar, vinegar, celery seed and salt. Add to cabbage, carrots, and scallions. Toss well and serve immediately. Serves 6 to 8.

Mrs. Ernest Butler (Sarah)

Farmhouse Slaw

4	cups shredded cabbage	½	cup mayonnaise
¾	cup raisins	2	tablespoons salad oil
1	chopped apple	1	tablespoon sugar
½	cup chopped celery	½	teaspoon salt
¼	cup chopped onion	¼	teaspoon pepper

Combine all ingredients, toss and chill 30 minutes. Serves 8.

Mrs. Randy Hagan (Robin)

Chef's Cabbage Salad

Thousand Island Dressing:

3	cups mayonnaise	⅓	cup minced hot garlic dill pickles
½	cup catsup		
½	cup minced green onions	1	tomato, minced
2	hard cooked eggs, diced		

Chef's Salad:

1	large red cabbage, chopped	1	pound chicken, bologna or summer sausage, diced
1½	pounds cooked ham, sliced in thin strips		
		4	ribs celery, diced
1	large cucumber, thinly sliced		

Mix together all dressing ingredients. Cover and refrigerate. Place salad ingredients in a large bowl. Add salad dressing and toss gently. Serves 15.

Mrs. Tom Hollis (Doris)

Twenty-Four Hour Slaw

12	cups shredded cabbage	1	cup white vinegar
2	large red onions, thinly sliced and separated into rings	1	teaspoon salt
		1	teaspoon celery seed
		1	teaspoon dry mustard
2	large green peppers, thinly sliced, optional	1	teaspoon dill weed
		¼	teaspoon white pepper
1	cup sugar	½	cup salad oil

Alternate cabbage, onion and green pepper in glass bowl, ending with onion rings. Combine remaining ingredients, except oil, and bring to a boil. Remove from heat and add oil. Drip hot mixture over cabbage mixture. Do not stir. Cover and refrigerate 24 hours or longer before serving. Serves 12.

Mrs. Denman Smith (Sandra)

Marinated Fresh Asparagus

¼ cup lemon juice
⅓ cup olive oil
½ cup oil
½ teaspoon salt
Dash of pepper
½ teaspoon dry mustard
1 tablespoon chopped
   pimiento

1 tablespoon capers
1 tablespoon chopped parsley
1 pound fresh asparagus,
   cooked
Salad greens
Tomatoes to garnish

Combine lemon juice, oils, salt, pepper and mustard, stirring until well blended. Add pimiento, capers and parsley. Place cooked asparagus in a shallow 1½ quart casserole and pour marinade over all; cover and chill two hours. Drain asparagus and reserve marinade as needed for dressing for salad greens. Serve on a bed of lettuce, garnished with tomatoes.

Mrs. D. D. Baker, Jr. (Agnes)

Five Bean Salad

1 can (16 ounces) green beans
1 can (16 ounces) yellow
   beans
1 can (15 ounces) kidney
   beans
1 can (16 ounces) garbanzo
1 can (15 ounces) lima beans

1 red or white onion, thinly
   sliced
1 cup sugar
½ cup salad oil
½ cup tarragon or white
   vinegar
1 tablespoon salt
1 teaspoon pepper

Drain all beans. Make marinade of remaining ingredients. Combine with beans and onion. Mix well and refrigerate overnight. Serves 10.

Mrs. Denman Smith (Sandra)

Dilled Green Bean and Cucumber Salad

2 packages (10 ounces each)
   frozen green beans
2 cucumbers, pared, sliced
   and chilled
1 cup sour cream or yogurt

1½ teaspoons dill weed
1½ teaspoons salt
¼ teaspoon white pepper
1 tablespoon lemon juice

Cook green beans until crisp and tender, then chill. Mix sour cream, dill weed, salt, white pepper and lemon juice. Chill at least 2 hours. Toss with chilled cucumbers and green beans at serving time. Serves 6 to 8.

Mrs. Denman Smith (Sandra)

Ruth's Bean Salad

1 can (16 ounces) Italian cut green beans
1 can (16 ounces) wax beans
1 can (16 ounces) kidney beans
1 medium red onion, sliced
1 jar (4 ounces) sliced pimientos
1 can (8 ounces) water chestnuts, sliced

1 can (14½ ounces) artichoke hearts
¾ cup sugar
¾ cup vinegar
Salt to taste
Tabasco to taste
1 teaspoon dill seed
1 package Garlic-Cheese salad dressing mix

Drain all beans well. Add remaining vegetables and mix well. For dressing, boil sugar and vinegar until well blended. Add salt, Tabasco, garlic, dill seed, and dry salad mix. Put in a large jar or covered bowl and refrigerate. Stir occasionally. Keeps indefinitely. Serves 8 to 10.

Mrs. Jim Schultz (Mary Kay)

Marinated Green Bean Salad

2 cans (15½ ounces each) whole green beans, drained
1 large onion, thinly sliced
2 tablespoons oil

2 tablespoons white wine vinegar
Salt to taste
Cracked black pepper
Lettuce to garnish

Horseradish Sour Cream Dressing:
½ cup sour cream
¼ cup mayonnaise
½ teaspoon lemon juice
⅛ teaspoon dry mustard

1½ to 3 teaspoons prepared horseradish, depending on taste

Place beans and onion in dish. Make marinade of oil and vinegar, and pour over beans; add salt and cracked pepper. Refrigerate at least two hours or overnight, tossing several times to coat all beans. Meanwhile combine ingredients for horseradish sour cream dressing, and refrigerate while beans are marinating. When ready to serve, drain marinade from beans and mix with prepared salad dressing. Toss beans with enough dressing to coat generously. Serve on a bed of lettuce. Serves 6 to 8. *This horseradish dressing is also good on cold roast beef.*

Mrs. Dudley Baker (Kathy)

Marinated Carrots

5 cups cooked sliced carrots	1 teaspoon dry mustard
1 onion, thinly sliced	1 teaspoon salt
1 green pepper, thinly sliced	½ teaspoon pepper
½ cup oil	1 teaspoon celery seed
¾ cup sugar	1 teaspoon basil
¾ cup vinegar	1 teaspoon Worcestershire
1 can tomato soup	sauce

Combine first three ingredients in a large bowl. Mix remaining items for marinade. Pour over carrot mixture. Refrigerate at least 12 hours before serving cold. Serves 12. *This is a great dish for picnics! And the marinade keeps well for at least two weeks. Simply add more vegetables when necessary.*

Mrs. Charlie Cantwell (Winn)

Chilled Sweet and Sour Red Onions

1 pound red onions	2 tablespoons oil
1 tablespoon soy sauce	1 large clove garlic, mashed
2 tablespoons wine vinegar	¼ teaspoon salt
2 tablespoons sugar	

Peel and cut each onion into 1 inch wide wedges. Separate the layers. Combine soy sauce, wine vinegar, and sugar in a small bowl and stir until sugar dissolves. Heat wok until hot. Add the oil and swirl and heat for 30 seconds. Toss in garlic and press into the oil. Toss in the onions and stir rapidly in turning motion for about 40 seconds, until they glisten with oil. Sprinkle in the salt and stir briskly. Splash in the sauce and as it sizzles, stir a few times. Let cool and serve.

S. D. Jackman, Jr.

Gümber Salad

1 cucumber, peeled and sliced	1 hard cooked egg, chopped, optional
½ head lettuce, torn into bite size pieces	2 cups buttermilk
1 small onion, sliced	1 tablespoon salt
	Pepper to taste

Toss cucumber, lettuce, onion, and egg; cover with buttermilk. Add salt and pepper. Serve immediately. Serves 6. *This is an authentic German salad that is a family favorite.*

Mrs. Denman Smith (Sandra)

Yogurt Cucumber Salad

¼ cup wine vinegar
Juice of ½ lemon
1 clove garlic, minced
1 teaspoon Dijon mustard
1 teaspoon chopped herbs,
(basil, parsley, and thyme)

Salt and ground pepper to taste
1 cup plain yogurt
2 pounds cucumbers, peeled
and thinly sliced
1 small red onion, thinly
sliced

Mix together vinegar, lemon juice, garlic, mustard, herbs, salt and pepper. Stir in yogurt and toss with cucumbers and onions. Chill. Toss again before serving. Serves 8. *This is a good low calorie salad.*

Mrs. B. L. Turlington (Jill)

Cu-Cu Salad

1 small package (3 ounces)
lime gelatin
1 cup hot water
1 cup grated cucumbers

¼ cup chopped onion
1 cup cottage cheese
½ cup mayonnaise
½ teaspoon salt

Mix gelatin with water; stir until blended. Add remaining ingredients and mix well. Refrigerate overnight in a 9x13 inch glass dish. Serves 6. *This is nice because you don't have to wait for gelatin to firm up before adding the other ingredients. Quick and easy to do ahead.*

Mrs. Robert West (Linda)

Pickled Cucumbers

¼ cup water
¾ cup white vinegar
⅓ cup sugar
¼ cup finely chopped parsley

¾ teaspoon salt
⅛ teaspoon pepper
4 medium cucumbers, pared
and sliced

Early in day or day before, combine water with vinegar, sugar, parsley, salt and pepper. Add cucumbers and toss well. Refrigerate at least 3 hours covered. Serves 10.

Mrs. Jerry Hunt (Gail)

Marinated Pea Salad

1 can (12 ounces) shoe peg
corn, drained
1 can (16 ounces) French style
green beans, drained
1 can (8½ ounces) English
peas, drained
1 cup chopped celery
1 green pepper, chopped
1 small onion, chopped

1 jar (2 ounces) pimientos,
drained and chopped
½ cup oil
½ cup cider vinegar
1 cup sugar
Salt
Paprika
½ teaspoon garlic salt

Combine all ingredients. Refrigerate for one or two days. Serves 12.

Mrs. John C. Waller (Elsie)

Spicy Tomato Salad

5 medium tomatoes, sliced ¼
inch thick
½ cup olive oil
2 tablespoons wine vinegar or
lemon juice
1 tablespoon basil, crushed

¼ teaspoon salt
Freshly ground pepper
2 tablespoons sliced green
onions or shallots
1 to 2 tablespoons parsley,
chopped

Arrange tomato slices in a glass serving dish. Combine remaining ingredients and pour over tomatoes. Chill until cold. Serves 6.

Mrs. Jack Dempsey (Estelle)

Marinated Vegetable Salad

1 jar (7 ounces) artichoke
hearts, undrained
1⅓ cups Italian dressing
¼ cup parsley, snipped
2 carrots, sliced diagonally
1 green pepper, chopped
1 cup cauliflower pieces

1 cup broccoli pieces
8 ounces fresh mushrooms,
sliced
1 medium cucumber, sliced
1 package (10 ounces) frozen
brussel sprouts, thawed and
drained

Mix undrained artichokes, Italian dressing, and parsley. Pour over carrots, green pepper, cauliflower, broccoli, mushrooms, cucumber and brussel sprouts. Refrigerate covered at least 2 hours. Drain vegetables reserving marinade for future use. Salad stays fresh in dressing for days. Serves 4 to 6.

Burlie Randall

Artichoke Salad

1 envelope (1 ounce)
unflavored gelatin
1 can (17 ounces) tiny peas,
well drained, reserve liquid
1 cup mayonnaise
1 tablespoon lemon juice
1 jar (2 ounces) pimientos,
drained

2 green onions, finely
chopped
Salt and pepper to taste
1 can (14 ounces) artichokes,
drained and quartered

Soften gelatin in ¼ cup heated pea liquid and stir until dissolved. Add mayonnaise and stir until smooth. Carefully add peas and remaining ingredients until well blended. Pour into ring mold and refrigerate until firm. Unmold on bed of greens. Serves 10 to 12.

Mrs. Dudley Baker (Kathy)

Patchwork Cauliflower Salad

1 cup mayonnaise
1 package (7 ounces) dry
garlic cheese dressing mix
1 cup sour cream
1 head cauliflower, chopped
and broken into pieces

1 cup thinly sliced radishes
1 or 2 sliced cucumbers
¼ cup chopped green onions
1 cup thinly sliced carrots

Mix the first three ingredients and pour over the vegetables. Refrigerate. Flavor is enhanced when made a day ahead. Serves 8.

Mrs. Charlie Smith (Jeannie)

Broccoli Cauliflower Salad

1 bunch broccoli, finely
chopped
1 head cauliflower, finely
chopped

1½ cups grated carrots
1 large tomato, finely
chopped
1 onion, finely chopped

Dressing:
1 cup mayonnaise
2 teaspoons prepared mustard
2 teaspoons sugar

2 teaspoons vinegar
Dash of Worcestershire sauce
Salt and pepper to taste

Make dressing and pour over finely chopped vegetables. Mix well and chill thoroughly. Serves 10 to 12. *It is a great salad for a picnic or a covered dish affair.*

Mrs. Jette Campbell (Sally)

Broccoli Salad

1   package (10 ounces) frozen
    broccoli
2   teaspoons unflavored
    gelatin
¼   cup water
½   cup consommé, heated
2   tablespoons Worcestershire
    sauce

1   tablespoon lemon juice
Salt to taste
Dash of Tabasco
½   cup mayonnaise
2   hard cooked eggs, sliced

Cook broccoli according to package directions; drain, and chop coarsely. Dissolve gelatin in cold water and add to consommé. Stir in Worcestershire sauce, lemon juice, salt, Tabasco sauce. Blend in mayonnaise until well mixed. Carefully fold in broccoli and eggs. Put in mold and chill until set. Serves 6 to 8.

Mrs. Dudley Baker (Kathy)

Guacamole Mousse

2   tablespoons unflavored
    gelatin
½   cup cold water
3   cups mashed ripe avocado
2¼ teaspoons lemon juice
2½ teaspoons finely chopped
    green onion, tops and
    bottoms
3   teaspoons picanté sauce

1   teaspoon Worcestershire
    sauce
Salt to taste
½   cup whipping cream,
    whipped
½   cup mayonnaise
Leaf lettuce, optional
Cherry tomatoes, optional

Sprinkle gelatin over water and place over low heat, stirring constantly until dissolved. Cool. Combine avocado, lemon juice, green onion, picanté sauce, Worcestershire sauce and salt in mixer and blend. Combine whipped cream and mayonnaise; add gelatin. Combine avocado and cream mixtures. Pour into an oiled 1½ quart ring mold. Chill until firm. Unmold on a platter covered with leaf lettuce; fill center and surround mold with cherry tomatoes for garnish. Serves 12. *A versatile dish, this could be served as an appetizer with Melba rounds.*

Mrs. Marcus Bone (Beverly)

Tomato Aspic

2 envelopes (1 ounce each) unflavored gelatin	½ cup shredded carrots
1½ cups cold water	½ cup finely chopped celery
1 can beef consommé	¼ cup chopped green pepper, optional
1 can tomato soup	Salad greens
2 tablespoons vinegar	Mayonnaise or sour cream for garnish
4 drops Tabasco sauce	
¼ cup minced onion	

In a saucepan, sprinkle gelatin on cold water to soften. Place over low heat and stir until gelatin dissolves. Remove from heat and stir in soups, vinegar, Tabasco, and onion. Chill until slightly thickened. Fold in carrots, celery, and green pepper. Spoon into 1½ quart mold; chill until firm. Unmold onto salad greens, serve with mayonnaise or sour cream. Serves 12.

Mrs. Joe Bowles (Mary)

Potato Salad

10 medium large California potatoes	1 bunch green onions, sliced thin, with tops
2 cups mayonnaise	5 hard cooked eggs, diced
2 tablespoons prepared mustard	Salt and pepper to taste
1 jar (10 ounces) sweet pickle relish	

Cut potatoes in half and boil in jackets. Mix mayonnaise, undrained pickle relish and onions together in large flat pan. Add diced eggs and mix thoroughly. Skin and cube potatoes a few at a time, tossing in dressing mixture while potatoes are still warm. Salt and pepper to taste. Cover and chill overnight before serving. Serves 8 to 10.

Mrs. Bob Bluntzer (Jo)

Salad Cocktail

Gouda cheese	Apple
Green and red peppers	Celery

Cut all ingredients into small bite size pieces and combine in a bowl. Proportions can vary to taste. Add lemon and oil dressing spiked with a little salt and toss until coated lightly. Serve on bed of Boston lettuce. *This is a favorite salad served in the Cumberland Hotel in London.*

Mrs. Randy Hagan (Robin)

Cracked Wheat Salad

1 cup cracked wheat	1 large firm tomato, diced
2 cups boiling water	Salt and coarse ground pepper
2 cups parsley, finely chopped	to taste
1 cup mint, finely chopped	Juice of one lemon
4 green onions, finely chopped	Olive oil

Pour boiling water over cracked wheat and let sit ½ hour. Mix parsley, mint, and green onions. Add tomatoes. Squeeze excess water from cracked wheat. Wring out in clean cloth. Add cracked wheat to parsley mixture. Salt and pepper to taste. Add lemon juice and toss. Then coat lightly with smallest amount of olive oil until salad is coated. Refrigerate and serve cold. Serves 8.

Mrs. James Stockton (Judy)

Spaghetti Salad

¾ cup mayonnaise	½ cup green olives, chopped
2 cloves garlic, crushed	1 can (10 ounces) Ro-Tel
¼ cup chopped onion	tomatoes and green chilies,
½ teaspoon cumin seeds, crushed	drained and chopped
Salt to taste	1 package (10 ounces) spaghetti, cooked and
¼ cup diced celery	rinsed

Mix mayonnaise, garlic, onion, cumin seeds, salt, and tomatoes. Add a little juice if too thick. Toss with spaghetti, celery, and olives until well coated. Serves 8 to 10.

Mrs. Don Panter (Carolyn)

Rice Salad

2 cups cooked rice	¼ cup chopped onion
2 tablespoons oil	1 cup chopped celery
1 tablespoon vinegar	¾ teaspoon curry powder
1 package (10 ounces) frozen English peas, cooked	¾ cup mayonnaise

Marinate rice, oil, and vinegar overnight. Combine peas, onion, and celery, and add to marinated rice. Stir curry powder into mayonnaise. Mix with rice mixture being careful not to crush the peas. Serves 4 to 6.

Mrs. Don Panter (Carolyn)

Artichoke Rice Salad

1 package (8 ounces) chicken flavored rice mix	2 jars (6 ounces each) artichoke hearts, reserve liquid
4 green onions, thinly sliced	
½ green pepper, chopped	¾ teaspoon curry powder
12 to 24 pimiento stuffed olives, sliced	⅓ cup mayonnaise

Cook rice mix as directed (no butter). Cool and add onions, pepper and olives. Drain artichoke hearts, reserving liquid. Cut artichokes in half or less. Combine liquid, a little at a time, with curry powder and mayonnaise. Use only enough liquid to moisten. Add to rice mixture and marinate for several hours. *For a one-dish meal, 1 cup of chopped chicken, ham, or turkey can be added.*

Mrs. Dudley Baker (Kathy)

Mexican Chef Salad

1 pound ground beef	4 ounces Cheddar cheese, grated
1 can (15 ounces) kidney beans, drained	
	8 ounces Italian dressing
1 package (1¼ ounces) taco seasoning mix	Hot sauce to taste
	1 large avocado
¼ teaspoon salt	1 bag (12 ounces) tortilla chips
1 onion	
4 tomatoes	Tomato and avocado slices for garnish
1 head lettuce	

Brown ground beef; drain drippings. Add kidney beans, taco mix and salt; simmer 10 minutes. Chop onions, tomatoes and lettuce. Toss with cheese, Italian dressing and hot sauce. Slice and add avocado. Add hot ground beef mixture to salad. Break tortilla chips and add to salad. Decorate with extra tortilla chips, avocado and tomato slices. Serve pronto!

Mrs. Charles Strong (Ginny)

Cottage Cheese Salad

¾ cup sour cream
1 carton (12 ounces) cottage cheese, well drained
¼ cup green pepper, diced
¼ cup green onion, chopped

2 tablespoons pimiento, chopped
¼ teaspoon salt
Pepper to taste
Dill weed to garnish

Blend by hand sour cream and cottage cheese. Stir in green pepper, onion, pimiento, salt and pepper. Serve as a salad on a bed of lettuce. Sprinkle with dill. *This is especially pretty when used to stuff tomatoes. It also makes a delicious low calorie dip.*

Mrs. A. J. Saegert (Pat)

Zucchini Toss

6 small zucchini
2 cups ripe cherry tomatoes
1 small red onion, thinly sliced
1 can (4 ounces) diced pimiento
8 ounces Mozzarella cheese, grated

1 can (7 ounces) tuna
¼ cup sliced black olives
1 teaspoon salt
¼ teaspoon freshly ground pepper
½ tablespoon red wine vinegar
1 tablespoon lemon juice
5 tablespoons olive oil

Cook zucchini in boiling salted water about 8 minutes. Drain and run under cold water. Cut zucchini in half lengthwise, then slice crosswise into large bowl. Add tomatoes, onion, pimiento, cheese, tuna and olives. Combine salt, pepper, vinegar, lemon juice and olive oil in small jar. Shake, then pour over salad. Toss. Serves 4.

Kay Doughty

Marinated Tuna Salad

2 cans (7 ounces each) all white tuna
1 large red onion, thinly sliced
2 green peppers, sliced
2 oranges, halved and sliced
¼ cup olive oil

½ cup fresh lemon juice
1 cup fresh orange juice
2 bay leaves
½ teaspoon crumbled oregano
¼ teaspoon salt
Salad greens

Break tuna into large pieces. Cover with slices of onion, green pepper and orange. Combine olive oil, lemon juice, orange juice, bay leaves, oregano, and salt. Pour over fish. Refrigerate for several hours. Garnish with greens. Serves 4 to 6 as a main dish, or 8 to 10 as a side dish.

Mrs. Marcus Bone (Beverly)

Cold Tuna Stuffed Zucchini

8 small whole zucchini	⅓ cup mayonnaise
1 can (7 ounces) tuna, drained	1 teaspoon salt
2 tablespoons oil	¼ teaspoon freshly ground
2 tablespoons minced green	pepper
onion	1 tablespoon lemon juice
2 tablespoons minced dill	Sliced tomato for garnish,
pickle	optional

In large saucepan, precook zucchini in salted boiling water 8 to 10 minutes, or until tender. Drain. Cut a ¼ inch slice lengthwise off top of each zucchini. Scoop pulp out; chop coarsely. Meanwhile, drain zucchini on a paper towel. Flake tuna into bowl. Add zucchini pulp and all remaining ingredients. Mix well and fill zucchini shells. Chill before serving for several hours. Garnish with fresh sliced tomato. Serves 4. *This is a light, filling luncheon dish or great on a hot summer day. Just serve on bed of lettuce and pass the crackers!*

Kay Doughty

Marcia's Fish Salad

2 pounds firm white fish fillets	Dash Tabasco
	Salt and pepper to taste
½ cup white wine	1 can (7¾ ounces) salmon,
4 ribs celery, coarsely chopped	drained
	3 ribs celery, diced
1 medium onion, sliced	½ cup finely chopped onion
Water	Cherry tomatoes, to garnish,
½ cup mayonnaise	optional
2 tablespoons lemon juice	1 avocado, sliced, optional
2 teaspoons horseradish	

Poach fish with wine, celery, sliced onion, and water to barely cover. Cook until fish flakes easily with fork. Carefully remove fish and refrigerate. Mix mayonnaise, lemon juice, horseradish, Tabasco, salt and pepper. In bowl coarsely flake cold fish fillets and salmon. Add 3 ribs celery and ½ cup onions; toss with mayonnaise mixture. Serve on bed of lettuce and garnish with cherry tomatoes and avocado slices. Serves 8 to 10.

Mrs. Thomas Schwartz (Ellana)

Shrimp Bombay

1 small fresh pineapple	½ pound shrimp, cooked and
3 tablespoons butter	peeled
3 tablespoons flour	Leaves to garnish
1 teaspoon grated onion	2 tablespoons toasted
¼ teaspoon salt	coconut
3 cups half and half cream	2 tablespoons toasted
1 tablespoon curry powder	slivered almonds
2 tablespoons milk	4 tablespoons chutney

Split pineapple in half, leaving top leaves intact. Cut around each pineapple half with sharp knife, within ½ inch of outer shell. Remove and discard core; cut pineapple meat into small cubes and let drain in colander. Wrap pineapple shells securely in foil, leaving leaves exposed and place in deep, hot water. Do not let boil.

Make a white sauce by melting butter in top of double boiler. Add flour and cook until bubbly, about 5 minutes; add onion and salt. Slowly add half and half cream, stirring briskly with wire whip. Mix curry powder with milk until smooth and add to mixture. Taste for desired seasoning. Remove from heat, add shrimp and ¾ cup of pineapple cubes. Unwrap pineapple halves. Place on plate of grape, fig or mint leaves. Fill cavity with shrimp mixture, sprinkle coconut and almonds over top and add generous servings of chutney at each end. Serves 2. *This is a lovely summer treat, served with a rice salad and fresh mangos for dessert.*

Mary Faulk Koock

South Seas Salad

6 large fresh tomatoes	2 tablespoons red wine
2 cups cooked diced shrimp	vinegar
1½ cups chilled cooked rice	½ teaspoon salt
½ cup chopped celery	¼ teaspoon dry mustard
¼ cup diced ripe olives	¼ teaspoon paprika
1 tablespoon fresh snipped	1 small clove garlic, minced
parsley	Fresh lettuce
¼ cup salad oil	

With tomato stem end down, cut each into six wedges, cutting to but not through base. Spread wedges slightly apart and carefully scoop out pulp. Dice and drain this pulp. Combine tomato pulp, shrimp, rice, celery, olives and parsley. Blend oil and vinegar with spices. Pour over shrimp mixture and toss slightly. Fill tomato wedges with this mixture and serve on a bed of lettuce. Serves 6. *This is a really nice dish for a luncheon . . . very showy.*

Mrs. Ken Moyer (Bonnie)

Stuffed Tomatoes

16 ounces tuna or crab meat
1 cup finely diced celery
½ cup grated onion
Salt and pepper to taste
Mayonnaise

8 regular tomatoes or 100
  cocktail tomatoes
Parsley to garnish

Mix thoroughly tuna or crab meat, celery, onion, salt and pepper. Add enough mayonnaise to make a thick paste. Cut out inside of tomatoes and fill with the mixture. Top with parsley.

Mrs. Marcus Bone (Beverly)

Fancy Chicken Salad

3 cups cold cooked chicken,
  diced
1 cup finely chopped celery
½ cup sliced almonds
2½ tablespoons parsley, minced

Seedless grapes, sliced,
  optional
1 teaspoon salt
1 cup mayonnaise
½ cup whipping cream,
  whipped

Combine chicken, celery, almonds, parsley, grapes, salt and mayonnaise. Fold in whipping cream. Chill until ready to serve. Serves 8.

Mrs. John Perkins (Sandy)

Imperial Chicken Salad

2 chickens, cooked and cubed
1½ cups chopped celery
2 tablespoons chopped
  onions
4 tablespoons sweet relish
1 cup chopped pecans
1 cup sliced mushrooms
2 tablespoons mayonnaise

1 apple, chopped fine
2 envelopes (1 ounce each)
  gelatin
¾ cup hot chicken broth
1 cup hot water
Mayonnaise to garnish
Lettuce to garnish

Mix chicken, celery, onions, relish, pecans, mushrooms, mayonnaise and apple, and spread evenly in 9 × 13 inch dish. Dissolve gelatin in hot water and mix with heated broth. Carefully pour over chicken mixture. Chill until firm. Cut into squares and place on lettuce. Garnish with mayonnaise. Serves 20.

Mrs. Leon Melton (Vera)

Party Chicken Salad

3 cups diced chicken
1 cup cooked rice
1 tablespoon salt
2 tablespoons lemon juice
1 cup chopped celery
1 can (11 ounces) Mandarin oranges, drained

1 cup pineapple chunks, drained
½ cup toasted almonds
½ cup mayonnaise

Combine first five ingredients. Fold in fruits and almonds. Chill. Add mayonnaise when ready to serve. Serves 8.

Mrs. Don Harris (Nancy)

Festive Frozen Cranberry Salad

1 can (16 ounces) cranberry sauce
1 carton (8 ounces) sour cream
1 cup miniature marshmallows

1 can (8 ounces) crushed pineapple, drained
1 banana, sliced into small pieces
½ cup nuts
½ cup sugar

Place cupcake papers in muffin tins. Mix all ingredients together and fill liners ⅔ full. Cover with foil or plastic wrap before freezing. Serves 12.

Mrs. Chris Williston (Janice)

Frozen Fruit Confetti

3 ounces cream cheese, softened
⅓ cup mayonnaise
1 teaspoon lemon juice
2 egg whites
⅓ cup sugar
1 cup whipping cream, whipped

5 to 6 large marshmallows, diced
¼ cup Mandarin orange slices
1 can (17 ounces) fruit cocktail, drained
2 tablespoons chopped Maraschino cherries

Blend cheese, mayonnaise and lemon juice. Beat egg whites until foamy. Add sugar, a tablespoon at a time, until stiff peaks form. Fold whipped cream into egg whites. Fold into cheese mixture. Add marshmallows and fruits. Pour into an 8 inch square pan. Freeze. Serves 6 to 8.

Mrs. Wayne Davison (Cindi)

Frozen Butter Mint Salad

1 can (20 ounces) pineapple, drained	1 box (12 ounces) Kraft butter mints
1 small box lime gelatin	1 carton (12 ounces) whipped topping

Mix pineapple and dry gelatin mixture and refrigerate overnight. Crush mints. Add mints and whipped topping to gelatin mixture and freeze. Serves 10.

Mrs. Denman Smith (Sandra)

Frozen Fruit Medley

1 can (10½ ounces) Royal Anne cherries, drained	2 bananas, sliced
1 can (15 ounces) pineapple chunks, drained	½ cup mayonnaise
1 jar (6 ounces) Maraschino cherries, drained and halved	½ cup whipping cream, whipped
	Lettuce to garnish

Mix Royal Anne cherries, pineapple, Maraschino cherries and bananas with mayonnaise. Carefully fold in whipped cream. Freeze until firm. Slice into squares and serve on lettuce leaves. Serves 12.

Mrs. Jim Smith (Jare)

Individual Frozen Pineapple Salads

8 ounces cream cheese, softened	1 can (15½ ounces) crushed pineapple, well drained
¼ cup sugar	2 cups pineapple yogurt
¼ cup brown sugar	½ cup finely chopped pecans

Blend cream cheese and sugars, beating well; add pineapple and yogurt. Spoon into cupcake liners in muffin tins. Sprinkle with pecans. Cover and freeze until firm. Remove from freezer 10 minutes before serving. Serves 8.

Mrs. Jim Schultz (Mary Kay)

Salad Dressings

Poppy Seed Dressing

¾ cup sugar
1 teaspoon dry mustard
1 teaspoon salt
⅓ cup vinegar

1 tablespoon onion juice
1 cup oil
1½ tablespoons poppy seed

Mix thoroughly sugar, dry mustard, salt, vinegar, and onion juice. Slowly add oil, beating continuously, until thick. Add poppy seeds. Yields approximately 2 cups. *This dressing keeps indefinitely in the refrigerator and is especially good on fruit salads.*

Mrs. Bill Hayes (Ginger)

Whipped Fruit Salad Dressing

1 egg yolk
½ cup sugar
1 tablespoon flour
½ cup pineapple juice

¼ cup lemon juice
1 cup whipping cream, whipped

Beat egg yolk until thick. Combine sugar and flour. Blend into beaten egg yolk. Gradually add fruit juices. Cook in top of double boiler until thick, stirring constantly. Cool thoroughly. Fold in whipped cream. Store in covered container in refrigerator. Yields 2 cups.

Mrs. Ron Garrick (Bonnie)

Honey Lime Dressing

1 cup sugar
½ cup honey
2 tablespoons dry mustard
1 tablespoon ground ginger

⅓ cup lime juice
⅓ cup water
2 cups corn oil

Blend all ingredients, except oil, in blender. Slowly add corn oil and blend. Yields 1 quart. *This is great on fresh fruit.*

Mrs. Jim Rado (Vicki)

Celery Seed Dressing

½ cup sugar
1 teaspoon salt
1 teaspoon paprika
1 teaspoon dry mustard

¼ cup vinegar
1 cup oil
3 tablespoons onion juice
1 teaspoon celery seed

Combine sugar and dry spices; add vinegar and set aside for 5 minutes. Slowly add oil, beating continuously. Carefully stir in onion juice and celery seed. Yields 1½ cups. *Excellent on grapefruit and avocado salads.*

Mrs. George Wade (June)

Red Barn Salad Dressing

2 cups mayonnaise
1 avocado, mashed
6 green onions, finely chopped
1 can (2 ounces) anchovies, mashed with oil
4 tablespoons buttermilk
1½ teaspoons Tabasco
1½ tablespoons Worcestershire sauce

1½ tablespoons soy sauce
Juice of ½ lemon
½ teaspoon celery seed
½ teaspoon dry mustard
½ teaspoon white pepper
½ teaspoon leaf oregano
½ teaspoon salt
½ teaspoon garlic powder

Mix all ingredients together until well blended. Yields one quart of salad dressing. *This would also be great as a sauce to accompany beef fondue.*

Florence Batey

Creamy Celery Seed Dressing

2 egg yolks
1 to 1½ tablespoons Dijon mustard
1 cup olive oil
1 cup sour cream
2 tablespoons diced green onions

1 tablespoon celery seed
1½ teaspoons Worcestershire sauce
1 teaspoon white wine vinegar

Use food processor or blender. Whisk egg yolks and mustard until pale yellow. Drizzle in oil to consistency of mayonnaise. Mix in remaining ingredients and blend well. Refrigerate. Yields 2½ cups. *This is especially good on a fresh spinach salad.*

Mrs. Jim Rado (Vicki)

Caesar Dressing

1 cup salad oil
2 cloves garlic, finely chopped
½ teaspoon ground pepper
½ teaspoon salt
1 egg

4 tablespoons lemon juice
½ cup Parmesan cheese
2 tablespoons Worcestershire sauce

Soak garlic in oil for 30 minutes. Blend all ingredients in blender for a few seconds.

Mrs. Marcus Bone (Beverly)

Sandwiches

Curried Lamb Sandwiches

1 pound lean ground lamb
1 small onion, finely chopped
½ cup cottage cheese
⅓ cup raisins
½ cup sunflower seeds
2 teaspoons curry powder
2 tablespoons milk

1 egg
1 teaspoon salt
2 tablespoons salad oil
4 or 5 pieces pocket bread, cut in halves
Condiments

Combine lamb, onion, cottage cheese, raisins, sunflower seeds, curry powder, milk, egg, and salt; mix well until well blended. Form meat mixture into 8 to 10 oval shaped patties, about ½ inch thick. Pour oil in a wide frying pan; when hot, add patties to pan and cook until browned on both sides, about 3 to 4 minutes per side. Place the lamb patties inside pocket bread and serve with condiments. Choose 3 or 4 of the following for condiments: unflavored yogurt, chutney, diced cucumber or green pepper, shredded lettuce, thinly sliced tomato or green onion. Serves 8 to 10.

Mrs. Denman Smith (Sandra)

Pimiento Cheese

1 package (8 ounces) Cheddar
cheese, grated
1 teaspoon grated onion
1 teaspoon finely chopped
parsley

3 pimientos, chopped fine
Dash black pepper
1 tablespoon salad dressing

Combine all ingredients with enough salad dressing to attain spreading consistency desired.

Mrs. Daniel O'Donnell (Sharon)

Monte Cristo Sandwich

2 slices white bread
Butter
1 thin slice baked or boiled
ham
1 thin slice Swiss cheese
1 thin slice baked or boiled
chicken

1 thin slice American cheese
1 egg
Dash of salt and pepper
1 tablespoon cold water
1 tablespoon salad oil
Butter and oil for frying

Spread both bread slices with butter. Place ham on one slice, top with Swiss cheese, add chicken, then American cheese. Cover with second slice of bread. Press sandwich firmly together. Wrap prepared sandwich in damp cold towel. Refrigerate until well chilled or until ready to cook. Combine egg, salt, pepper, cold water and salad oil. Blend well with wire whisk. Holding sandwich firmly together, dip it in the egg mixture on both sides. Fry sandwich in a heavy skillet in ⅔ part oil and ⅓ part butter, having enough mixture to cover bottom of skillet to ⅛ inch. When brown on both sides, transfer to a shallow baking dish. Place in preheated 350° oven for 8 to 10 minutes. Allow sandwich to cool, then drain briefly on paper towels.

Mrs. Larry Hall (Jane)

Corny Dogs

1 package wieners
⅔ cup corn meal
1 cup flour
1½ teaspoons baking powder
1 tablespoon sugar

1 teaspoon salt
¾ cup milk
1 egg
Oil

Boil wieners; drain on paper towels. Combine other ingredients and mix well. Dip wieners into batter and drop into hot oil. Fry until golden brown. Sticks can be inserted if you like after frying.

Mrs. Tim Bauerkemper (Pam)

Tuna on French Bread

2   cans (7 ounces each) grated
    tuna
1   can (5 ounces) water
    chestnuts, sliced thin
½   cup mayonnaise
1   tablespoon onion, minced
1   small garlic clove, crushed

1   teaspoon lemon juice
1   teaspoon soy sauce
½   teaspoon curry powder
6 to 8 slices French bread, ½
    inch thick
Cheddar cheese, grated

Mix tuna, water chestnuts, mayonnaise, onion, garlic, lemon juice, soy sauce, and curry powder together. Spread on French bread and sprinkle heavily with Cheddar cheese. Place under broiler until cheese is melted.

Mrs. James Carney (Jean)

Crab Meat Muffinwiches

1   pound Velveeta cheese,
    softened
1   stick margarine, softened
Dash Worcestershire sauce

6 to 8 ounces fresh, frozen or
    canned crab meat, drained
12 English muffins, split

Mix together first four ingredients. Spread on English muffins. Cut each muffin in quarters. Broil until bubbly and golden, or bake at 400° for 10 minutes. These freeze beautifully before cooking.

Mrs. Terry Arndt (Barbara)

Sloppy Joes

1   pound hamburger meat
1   medium onion, chopped
2   tablespoons butter or
    margarine
2   tablespoons vinegar
2   heaping tablespoons brown
    sugar

1   tablespoon lemon juice
1   cup catsup
1   cup water
½   teaspoon celery salt
½   teaspoon salt
1½ to 2 teaspoons
    Worcestershire sauce

Brown hamburger meat with onion. Drain. Add remaining ingredients and simmer until thick, about 15 to 20 minutes. Spoon mixture over toasted buns. Serves 6 to 8. *Also great for left over roast.*

Mrs. Chris Williston (Janice)

Barbecue Beef

3 to 4 pounds chuck roast
2 beef bouillon cubes
½ teaspoon rosemary
1 teaspoon oregano
1 teaspoon garlic powder
1 teaspoon savory salt
1 teaspoon salt
1 teaspoon pepper
1 can (6 ounces) tomato paste
Water to cover
2 cups barbeque sauce
Toasted buns

Place roast, bouillon cubes, spices and tomato paste in Dutch oven. Cover with water. Bring to boil; simmer covered for four hours. Uncover and simmer four more hours. Add barbecue sauce and cook uncovered until tender and falling apart. Remove bones and fat and serve beef on toasted buns. Serves 6 to 8.

Mrs. Daniel O'Donnell (Sharon)

Healthy Hero

1 pound ground beef
1 teaspoon salt
½ teaspoon pepper
¼ teaspoon dry mustard
½ medium onion, chopped
½ cup chopped green pepper
½ cup tomato sauce
½ teaspoon oregano
½ cup olives
4 loaves (6 inches each) French-type bread
1 pint sprouts
2 cups chopped olives
Onions, pickles, cheese, etc.

Sauté ground meat until done. Drain grease and return to skillet. Add salt, pepper, mustard, onion and green pepper and cook 10 minutes. Add tomato sauce, oregano and olives. Simmer for 15 minutes. Taste for seasonings and adjust to your taste. Warm French loaves in oven, split, and remove some of the dough from lower half. Fill with meat mixture and garnish with onions, pickles, cheese or whatever sounds exciting. Top with sprouts.

Mrs. Denman Smith (Sandra)

Sandwiches have come a long way from the brown bag. In fact, these versions feature a masterful blending of satisfying fillings and different breads.

Olive Nut Sandwiches

8　ounces cream cheese, room
　　temperature
½　cup mayonnaise
½　cup chopped green olives
½　cup chopped pecans

½　teaspoon onion powder
White pepper to taste
24　bread slices, buttered
　　lightly

Blend cream cheese and mayonnaise. Add olives, pecans, onion powder, pepper, and mix well. Trim crusts off bread. Spread with sandwich spread mixture. Cut into halves or thirds. Cover tightly in refrigerator until ready to serve. Serves 12.

Louise Holt

Leftover cooked vegetables are a wonderful treat in sandwiches. Add enough mayonnaise to bind them together and flavor with curry powder or your favorite seasoning.

Pocket Sprout Sandwiches

3　pita bread rounds
1　container (4 ounces)
　　whipped cream cheese with
　　chives
2　medium avocados
2　teaspoons lemon juice

1½ cups alfalfa sprouts
1　cup shredded lettuce
½　cup diced tomato
2　tablespoons Green Goddess
　　dressing
2　tablespoons sour cream

Cut pita bread in half to make six pockets. Spread the inside of each pita with whipped cream cheese. Dice avocados and toss with lemon juice. Mix sprouts, lettuce and tomatoes; toss with salad dressing and sour cream. Fill pita halves. *Substitute any salad dressing you like!* Serves 4 to 6.

Mrs. Denman Smith (Sandra)

Deluxe Pizza

Pizza Dough:

1 package dry yeast	¾ teaspoon salt
½ cup warm water	1 egg
2 to 2¼ cups flour	1½ teaspoons oil
1 teaspoon sugar	

Sauce and Topping:
Oil

1 can (8 ounces) tomato sauce
1 can (6 ounces) tomato paste
1 large clove garlic, crushed
2 teaspoons sugar
1 teaspoon oregano
¾ teaspoon basil
¼ teaspoon crushed red pepper
¼ pound sweet Italian sausage, casings removed or pork sausage, browned and drained

⅛ pound pepperoni, thinly sliced
½ cup mushrooms, thinly sliced
⅓ cup onion, chopped
⅓ cup green pepper, chopped
1 can (2 ounces) anchovies, drained, optional
10 ounces Mozzarella cheese, shredded
¼ cup Parmesan cheese, grated

Combine yeast and warm water for dough. Stir until dissolved. Add 1 cup flour, sugar and salt, mix well. Add egg and oil, stirring until smooth and glossy. Stir in 1 cup, or enough flour to keep dough from sticking. On lightly floured surface, knead dough until smooth and elastic, about ten minutes. Place in a greased bowl, turning to grease top. Cover with plastic wrap and clean dish towel. Let rise in warm place until more than double, one hour. Punch down, chill for ten minutes. Let dough reach room temperature before shaping.

To assemble, gently stretch or roll out dough to fit a greased 16 inch pizza pan or two 12 inch circles; place on greased cookie sheet. Crimp edge to form a rim. Brush dough with oil. Bake without toppings on lowest rack in pre-heated 450° oven for 3 to 4 minutes or until bottom of crust is slightly golden. For sauce, mix tomato sauce and paste, garlic, sugar, oregano, basil and red pepper. Spread evenly over crust. Top with sausage, pepperoni, mushrooms, onions, green pepper and anchovies. Bake 15 minutes at 450°, then sprinkle with Mozzarella and Parmesan cheese. Bake 5 to 10 minutes or until cheese is melted and crust is golden. Serves 4. *The dough can be made hours ahead of time or the night before for faster preparation.*

Mrs. Larry Hall (Jane)

Thick Crust Pizza

1 package yeast	1 teaspoon salt
1⅓ cups warm water	1 cup whole wheat flour
2 tablespoons cooking oil	3 cups flour

Dissolve yeast in warm water. Stir in oil. Sift flours and salt together and stir into oil and water mixture. Knead until all flour is worked in, approximately 10 minutes. Form into a ball and place in a well greased bowl to rise, from 1 to 3 hours. Divide into two parts and roll out on a floured board to fit a 14 inch round pan or a cookie sheet which has been greased and floured. Let rise 45 minutes and then bake at 350° for 15 minutes. Build the rest of the pizza to your own taste. First, spread with a pizza sauce, then toppings of hamburger, pepperoni, olives, mushrooms, and ½ pound of grated Mozzarella cheese can be added. Bake at 350° for 25 minutes or until brown and cheese is melted. *The dough mixture is not hard but is time consuming and needs to be started 3 to 5 hours before you plan to serve the pizza.*

Mrs. Mike Leathers (Nancy)

Mini Pizzas

1 pound hamburger meat	1 jar (10¾ ounces) pizza
2 cans (10 count each)	sauce
biscuits	1 cup Cheddar cheese, grated

Brown hamburger meat and drain. Add pizza sauce to meat and stir in Cheddar cheese. Roll each biscuit very thin. Place 2 tablespoons of meat mixture on each biscuit, and bake at 350° for 10 minutes, or until brown and bubbly. Serves 20. *These make cute little appetizers, if the biscuits are cut in half.*

Mrs. Charles Cantwell (Winn)

English Sausage Sandwich

1 pound bulk pork sausage	¼ teaspoon red pepper
1 jar (4 ounces) Old English	¼ teaspoon garlic powder
cheese, room temperature	5 English muffins
1 stick margarine, room	
temperature	

Cook sausage and drain. Mix sausage, cheese, margarine, pepper and garlic powder together. Spread mixture on English muffin halves. Broil or bake in hot oven until brown or bubbly. *Can be frozen.*

Mrs. B. L. Turlington (Jill)

Nature has blessed Texas with a profusion of native wildflowers. The most famous is the state flower, the bluebonnet. As a delightful announcement of spring, the bluebonnet, Indian paint brush, and buttercup appear in March, and for a few weeks, the Bluebonnet Trails of Texas are abloom with a breathtaking array of beautiful wildflowers. There are many interesting legends surrounding the bluebonnet; perhaps this is one of the most endearing. One night a little Indian girl overheard her parents talking about the severe drought. Everything had been done to appease the gods and still there was no rain. The parents worried that the sacrifice of their son might be expected. The little girl, who loved her brother dearly, was frightened by this. Thinking of the one other thing she loved almost as much, her simple corn husk dolly with a coat of blue, she slipped out into the night. Placing her doll on the nearest hilltop, she prayed that this sacrifice would be enough. The rain began to fall, and the next morning, in the spot she had left her treasure, stood a beautiful wildflower, the bluebonnet. Every year after that, bluebonnets covered the fields as a reminder of the girl's love for her brother.

Vegetables pictured: Dilled Carrots, Spinach Stuffed Tomatoes, Peas and Water Chestnuts, Elegant Asparagus and Calabazo Mexicano.

Vegetables

Elegant Asparagus

4 cups fresh asparagus, cut up, or 2 packages (8 ounces each) frozen cut asparagus
1 can cream of shrimp soup
½ cup sour cream
2 tablespoons shredded carrots
1 tablespoon grated onion
⅛ teaspoon pepper
½ cup stuffing mix
1 tablespoon butter, melted

Cook asparagus and drain. Combine soup, sour cream, carrots, onion and pepper. Fold in asparagus. Turn into 1 quart baking dish. Combine stuffing mix and melted butter; sprinkle around edge of asparagus mixture. Bake at 350° for 30 to 35 minutes. Serves 6.

Mrs. Jim Rado (Vicki)

Asparagus in Wine

1 pound fresh asparagus
1 tablespoon olive oil
¼ cup dry white wine
¼ teaspoon salt
Garlic powder to taste
Juice of ½ lemon

Break off tough ends of asparagus and wash. Slice large stalks in half. Slowly heat olive oil over low-medium heat; add asparagus. Add wine immediately. Sprinkle with salt and garlic powder. Simmer until tender, approximately 10 minutes. Squeeze the juice of half a lemon over asparagus just before serving. Serves 4.

Mrs. Art DeFelice (Connie)

Chili Beans

1 pound dry pinto beans
2½ cups cold water
½ pound salt pork
Crushed red peppers to taste
1 clove garlic
1 medium onion, chopped
1 can (6 ounces) tomato paste
1½ teaspoons chili powder
1 teaspoon salt
1 teaspoon cumin
½ teaspoon marjoram

Soak beans overnight. When ready to cook, drain and put beans and water into a large pot. Bring to a boil; cover and simmer one hour. Stir in remaining ingredients. Cover and simmer 3 hours, or until tender, adding extra water if necessary. Serves 8 generously. *Great with any kind of barbecue! Can also be cooked in a crock pot.*

Mrs. Tom Palmer (Jan)

Frijoles Borrachos (Drunk Beans)

4 cups pinto beans, two pounds	½ teaspoon sugar
1 tablespoon baking soda	2 tablespoons chili powder, optional
2 chopped onions	1 tablespoon cumin, optional
2 garlic cloves, chopped	1 teaspoon oregano, optional
4 slices bacon	1 can beer
1 tablespoon salt	

Cover beans with water and soak overnight. Drain and discard any bad beans. In a large pot about four times as deep as beans, cover beans with an inch of water and bring to a boil. Boil for about 15 minutes; reduce heat and slowly add baking soda. Stir until mixture foams to the top of pot, about 1 minute, and then quickly drain and rinse in a colander. Return to pot; add onion, garlic, bacon and water to cover by about two inches; cover pot and cook slowly for 2 to 4 hours. Add salt and other optional spices during the last ½ hour of cooking time along with your favorite Texas beer. Serves 8 to 10. *These beans are better the second day if there are any left.*

Denman Smith

Frijoles Refritos (Refried Beans)

2 cups black, pinto or kidney beans	2 onions, finely chopped or grated
3 quarts water	2 cloves garlic, minced
¼ to ½ cup bacon drippings	Salt to taste

Using a colander, wash the dried beans in cold running tap water for one minute. In a 4 quart pot, bring three quarts water to a rolling boil. Drop beans slowly into the pot so that boiling does not stop. Cook, covered, at a low boil for 3 hours, checking the water level each hour. When a bean mashes easily between two fingers; only then, are they suitable for refrying. Drain beans. In a medium sized pan, using as little drippings as possible, sauté the onions and garlic. Then add some beans, mashing them well with a wooden spoon or potato masher. Continue adding beans, mashing and cooking. Salt to taste. If too dry, add a little of the bean liquid while mashing them. Serves 12.

Mrs. Dan Steakley (Susan)

Baked Beans

1 **pound dried Navy beans**	½ **cup molasses**
14 **ounces 7-Up**	¼ **cup brown sugar**
1 **can (14½ ounces) tomatoes**	½ **cup catsup**
6 **slices bacon, diced**	1 **tablespoon prepared**
2 **teaspoons salt**	**mustard**
½ **teaspoon pepper**	1 **tablespoon Worcestershire**
1 **medium onion, diced**	**sauce**
½ **green pepper, diced**	2 **teaspoons vinegar**
2 **stalks celery, diced**	1 **can (2 ounces) mushroom**
1 **can (8 ounces) tomato**	**pieces**
sauce	

Wash and soak beans overnight. In large pan or Dutch oven combine beans, 7-Up, tomatoes, bacon, salt, and pepper. Cover and simmer for 1 hour. Add onion, green pepper, celery, tomato sauce, molasses, brown sugar, catsup, mustard, Worcestershire, and vinegar. Cover and simmer another hour. Add mushroom pieces. Put in covered casserole and bake at 250° for 3 or 4 hours. Remove cover and bake one more hour. Serves 8 to 10.

Mrs. Daniel O'Donnell (Sharon)

BBQ Beans

2 **cans (16 ounces each) pork**	1 **tablespoon Worcestershire**
and beans	**sauce**
1 **cup canned tomatoes,**	1 **teaspoon seasoned salt**
drained	1 **teaspoon dry mustard**
1 **cup apple cider**	½ **teaspoon pepper**
½ **cup catsup**	¼ **teaspoon monosodium**
½ **cup brown sugar**	**glutamate**
½ **onion, chopped**	
2 **tablespoons horseradish,**	
optional	

Mix all ingredients in shallow 3 quart baking pan. Bake uncovered at 350° for 1½ to 2 hours. Serves 10 to 12. *A favorite from Stephenson's Restaurant in Kansas City.*

Mrs. Wayne Davison (Cindi)

Mixed Bean Casserole

1 clove garlic, minced
1 medium onion, chopped
3 tablespoons bacon
  drippings
1 can (15 ounces) baked
  beans
1 can (15 ounces) kidney
  beans

1 can (15 ounces) lima beans
½ cup catsup
3 tablespoons vinegar
1 tablespoon brown sugar
1 teaspoon dry mustard
1 teaspoon salt
¼ teaspoon pepper

Cook garlic and onions in bacon drippings until onion is limp. Pour all ingredients into a 2 quart casserole and mix. Bake at 350° for 45 minutes. Serves 6. *A great dish to serve with barbecue.*

Mrs. Porter Young (Chris)

 There's no denying that vegetables brighten and enliven a menu. Whether fresh, frozen or canned, vegetables can be dressed up in numerous exciting ways.

Chinese Pickled Beets

1 cup sugar
2 tablespoons cornstarch
1 cup vinegar
24 whole cloves
3 tablespoons catsup
3 tablespoons oil

Dash of salt
1 teaspoon vanilla
1½ cups beet juice
3 cans (16 ounces each)
  beets, reserving juice

In a large skillet, mix sugar and cornstarch. Add vinegar, cloves, catsup, oil, salt and vanilla. Stir well. Add the beet juice. Cut the beets into bite size pieces and place in the pan. Cook over medium heat for three minutes, stirring constantly, until thickened. Serves 12.

Mrs. Larry Hall (Jane)

Broccoli Supreme

2   packages (10 ounces each) chopped broccoli
3   cups creamed cottage cheese
3   eggs
6   tablespoons butter, softened, divided
⅓   cup flour
¼   cup finely minced onion

1   can (8 ounces) whole kernel corn, drained
½   pound Cheddar or Swiss cheese, diced
½   teaspoon salt
¼   teaspoon pepper
Dash hot pepper sauce
2   slices soft bread
½   cup crumbled, cooked bacon

Cook broccoli according to directions and drain. Combine cottage cheese, eggs, 4 tablespoons butter and flour in blender or mixer bowl. Blend or mix until cottage cheese mixture is smooth and creamy. Fold in broccoli, onion, corn, cheese, salt, pepper, and hot pepper sauce. Pour cottage cheese mixture into a greased deep 2½ quart casserole. Make soft bread crumbs by tearing one bread slice and placing in a blender. Blend until soft crumbs have formed. Repeat with other slice. Melt remaining 2 tablespoons butter in skillet. Add crumbs and sauté until brown. Sprinkle crumbs and bacon over broccoli mixture. Bake at 350° for 1 hour or until mixture is set. Serves 8 to 12.

Mrs. B. L. Turlington (Jill)

Broccoli-Rice Casserole

½   cup chopped celery
1   cup chopped onion
1   can (8½ ounces) water chestnuts, drained and chopped
3   tablespoons butter
2   packages (10 ounces each) frozen chopped broccoli

1   cup cooked rice
1   can cream of mushroom soup
1   can cream of chicken soup
1   jar (8 ounces) Cheez Whiz

Sauté celery, onion and water chestnuts in butter. Prepare broccoli according to package directions; drain. Combine all ingredients in large bowl. Pour into large buttered casserole dish and bake at 350° for 30 minutes. May be frozen before baking. To cook, place in 300° oven for 1 hour. Serves 6 to 8.

Mrs. Robert Kelly (Nell)

Dill Carrots

6 to 8 carrots, peeled
1   cup sliced onion
1   clove garlic, finely minced
¼   cup oil
1   tablespoon flour
1   can cream of celery soup

1   cup milk
½   teaspoon dill seed
1   teaspoon sugar
Salt, pepper and garlic powder
    to taste

Cut carrots into julienne strips; a food processor may be used. Sauté carrots, onion and garlic in oil for 5 minutes. Sprinkle with flour. Stir in soup and milk. Add dill and sugar. Simmer covered until carrots are tender. Season to taste with salt, pepper and garlic powder. Serves 6.

Mrs. Jim Rado (Vicki)

Stuffed Carrots Anaccacho

8 to 10 medium carrots,
    approximately one pound
2   tablespoons butter
½   cup finely chopped onion
¼   cup finely chopped green
    pepper
½   cup finely chopped celery
1   tomato, chopped
3   tablespoons chicken stock
¼   teaspoon Beau Monde
    seasoning

½   cup cooked, chopped
    chicken
1   egg, slightly beaten
Salt
Cracked black pepper
¾   cup grated Old English
    cheese
4   tablespoons buttered bread
    crumbs

Peel carrots; cook whole. Carefully remove carrots from water. Do not prick with fork. Halve carrots lengthwise. Scoop out centers and reserve. Melt butter in skillet and sauté onion, green pepper and celery. Add chopped tomato and chicken stock; cook until liquid is reduced. Remove skillet from heat; add chopped carrot centers, Beau Monde and chicken. Stir in egg and season with salt and cracked pepper. Arrange carrot shells on ovenproof plate in a semi-circle. Fill each carrot with the vegetable mixture. Sprinkle with grated cheese. Top with bread crumbs. Bake at 350° for 15 minutes, until cheese is melted and bubbly. Serves 6. *These carrots are a lot of work; however, they are a beautiful way to perk up an ordinary vegetable for a really special party.*

Mrs. Dudley D. Baker (Kathy)

Jean's Curried Carrots and Pineapple

2 tablespoons margarine	3 tablespoons water
1 teaspoon curry powder	1 tablespoon cornstarch
1 can (8 ounces) pineapple chunks, reserving liquid	6 medium carrots, sliced and cooked
½ cup pineapple syrup	

Melt margarine in large skillet. Stir in curry powder. Combine ½ cup pineapple liquid, water and cornstarch until smooth. Add to skillet mixture; cook until sauce is smooth and thick. Stir in pineapple chunks and carrots before serving. Serves 4.

Mrs. Larry Morris (Diane)

Braised Celery

6 ribs celery	1½ teaspoons salt
6 tablespoons butter, divided	Freshly ground pepper
1 onion, sliced	2 cups chicken broth
2 carrots, pared and sliced	1 bay leaf

Trim celery stalks into 7 inch lengths. Scrape off tough outer fibers. Cut each stalk in half lengthwise and rinse well. Parboil celery for 10 minutes in 3 quarts of water. Drain. In large skillet melt 3 tablespoons butter; add onion and carrots and sauté for 5 minutes. Spoon into 9x13 inch pan. Melt remaining butter in same skillet and sauté celery for 5 minutes until lightly browned. Place celery in baking dish in a single layer, cut side up. Sprinkle with salt and pepper. Heat broth and bay leaf in skillet; pour over celery. Bake in a preheated 350° oven for 30 minutes or until tender. Remove bay leaf. Serve 8.

Mrs. Larry Hall (Jane)

Corn Pudding

4 ears fresh corn	1 teaspoon sugar
2 beaten eggs	Dash salt
1 cup milk	2 tablespoons butter

Cut corn from cobs and scrape ears. Combine all ingredients in buttered 1½ quart casserole. Bake at 350° for 45 minutes, or until set. Serves 6. *This is an old family recipe.*

Mrs. K. L. McConchie (Katherine)

Squaw Corn

2 packages (10 ounces each)   1 medium onion, diced
  frozen whole kernel corn   1 teaspoon salt
6 bacon slices   Dash of pepper
1 medium green pepper, diced   ½ cup whipping cream

About 40 minutes before serving, prepare corn as directed; drain well and set aside. Fry bacon slices until crisp; drain off drippings, reserving 2 tablespoons. In same skillet, sauté green pepper and onion. Add corn, salt, pepper, cooking until corn is hot. Crumble bacon and stir into corn mixture along with cream. Serves 6 to 8.

Mrs. Don Panter (Carolyn)

Mexican Corn

8 ounces cream cheese   2 cans (16 ounces each)
¼ cup milk   whole kernel corn, drained
2 tablespoons butter   2 cans (4 ounces each)
¼ teaspoon garlic salt   chopped green chilies

Melt cream cheese, milk, butter, and garlic salt over low heat. Add corn and chilies. Put in casserole and bake uncovered at 350° for 20 to 25 minutes. Serves 6.

Florence Batey

Corn-Cheese Casserole

36 saltine crackers, crushed   1½ cups grated Cheddar cheese
1 teaspoon dry mustard   1 tablespoon butter, melted
1 teaspoon salt   1 can (17 ounces) cream style
3 eggs, separated   corn
1 cup milk, scalded   Paprika for garnish
¼ teaspoon Tabasco sauce

Combine cracker crumbs, mustard and salt. Beat egg yolks well; gradually stir milk and Tabasco into eggs. Add crumb mixture, cheese, butter and corn. Beat egg whites until stiff but not dry; fold into mixture. Pour into 1½ quart greased casserole. Bake uncovered at 325° for 40 minutes, or until golden brown and slightly firm to touch. Sprinkle with paprika. Serves 8.

Mrs. Clark Rector (Sue)

Stuffed Eggplant

1 large eggplant	1 clove garlic, minced
2 slices bacon	½ cup half and half cream or
1 tablespoon butter	evaporated milk
1 can (4 ounces) mushroom	Salt and pepper to taste
pieces, drained	Buttered bread crumbs for
1 small onion, chopped	garnish

Cut lengthwise slice off top of eggplant. Remove pulp and cube, leaving shell ½ inch thick. Cook cubes in boiling water 10 minutes; drain. Cook bacon, reserving drippings; drain on paper towel. Melt butter in bacon grease; add mushrooms, onion and garlic and brown. Place mushroom mixture and bacon in blender and chop coarsely. Add eggplant cubes and blend. Add cream and blend. Season with salt and pepper. Fill eggplant shell and top with crumbs. Bake uncovered at 350° for 45 to 55 minutes. Serves 4 to 6. *Filling may also be baked in buttered 8 inch square Pyrex dish.*

Mrs. Larry Nau (Rose)

Eggplant Dressing

4 tablespoons butter	1 teaspoon salt
1 large onion, chopped	Pepper to taste
1 cup chopped celery	½ teaspoon thyme
1 cup chopped mushrooms,	1 cup beef bouillon
fresh or canned	1 package (8 ounces) herb
1 medium eggplant, peeled	seasoned stuffing mix
and cut in 1 inch pieces	2 cups grated Swiss cheese
1 can (16 ounces) tomatoes	

Sauté onion and celery in butter until soft. Add mushrooms and eggplant; cook over medium heat stirring for about 5 minutes. Add remaining ingredients, except cheese, and stir until well mixed. Put into a 9x13 inch baking dish and bake covered at 350° for 30 minutes. Uncover during last 10 minutes and sprinkle with cheese. Cook until cheese is melted. Serves 8 to 10. *More beef bouillon should be added if mixture seems too dry before baking. This should be about the consistency of turkey dressing.*

Mrs. Denman Smith (Sandra)

Ratatouille

1 tablespoon olive oil	1 large eggplant, peeled and
6 scallions or 1 onion,	chopped
chopped	1 green pepper, chopped
6 small zucchini, sliced	3 tomatoes, chopped and
4 cloves garlic, minced	seeded
1 teaspoon salt	2 teaspoons basil
¼ teaspoon pepper	2 tablespoons parsley

Sauté scallions, zucchini, and garlic in olive oil for 2 minutes. Add salt and pepper. Add rest of ingredients and sauté 2 minutes. Cover and simmer 10 minutes. Uncover and simmer until thick, about 1½ hours. Serves 6.

Mrs. Tom Schwartz (Ellana)

Island Nut Bananas

4 to 6 bananas, peeled and	¼ cup lime juice
sliced	1 can (5 ounces) macadamia
¼ cup honey	nuts, coarsely chopped

Dip banana slices in mixture of honey and lime juice; roll in nuts to cover. Refrigerate until serving time. *I use this as an accompaniment with pork, but it would be nice as an appetizer, too.*

Nancy Young Moritz

Hot Spiced Fruit

1 can (29 ounces) fruit for	2 large bananas, cut in large
salad	chunks
½ jar (8 ounces) maraschino	⅓ cup brown sugar
cherries	2 tablespoons cornstarch
1 can (16 ounces) dark pitted	1½ teaspoons curry power
cherries	¼ cup butter, melted

Drain fruit well, mixing all the juices together. Combine dry ingredients and melted butter. Place fruit in 9x13 inch casserole; add dry ingredients with melted butter. Cover with reserved juices. Bake at 350° for 40 minutes. Serves 4 to 6. *Be sure to get fruit for salad and not fruit cocktail.*

Mrs. Larry Morris (Diane)

Scalloped Pineapple

1 cup margarine
2 cups sugar
4 eggs, beaten
¼ cup milk

4 cups white bread cubes
1 can (20 ounces) crushed
  pineapple

Cream together margarine, sugar and eggs. Mix all ingredients together. Place in buttered oblong casserole. Bake at 375° for 15 minutes, then at 350° for 1 hour. Serves 6 to 8. *This is a great dish with ham or turkey dinners. It is served as a vegetable rather than a dessert.*

Mrs. B. L. Turlington (Jill)

Caliente Green Beans

1 green pepper, chopped
1 large onion, chopped
1 can (4 ounces) green chilies,
  minced
2 tablespoons bacon
  drippings
1 can (16 ounces) cut green
  beans, drained

1 can (16 ounces) whole
  tomatoes
1 can (4¾ ounces) tomato
  purée
Salt and cayenne to taste
1 cup grated Cheddar cheese

Sauté green pepper, onion and green chilies in bacon drippings until tender. Add green beans, tomatoes, tomato purée, salt and cayenne. Cook slowly for 1 hour until almost dry. Pour into a buttered 1½ quart casserole and top with cheese. Bake, uncovered, at 350° for 15 minutes, or until cheese melts. Serves 8.

Mrs. Bill Hayes (Ginger)

Green Beans with Horseradish Sauce

1 pound fresh green beans
1 cup mayonnaise
2 hard boiled eggs, chopped
2 tablespoons horseradish
1 teaspoon Worcestershire
  sauce
Salt

Pepper
Garlic powder
Celery salt
Onion salt
1½ teaspoons parsley flakes
Juice of 1 lemon

Steam green beans 12 minutes. Blend remaining ingredients, the spices to taste. Set aside at room temperature. When ready to serve pour over hot beans. Serves 4. *Beans are also good cold.*

Mrs. Jim Lederer (Anne)

Company Green Bean Casserole

1½ sticks of butter, divided
½ cup chopped onions
1 can (8½ ounces) sliced button mushrooms, drained, reserving juice
1 can (8 ounces) water chestnuts, drained, thinly sliced
½ cup flour
1 teaspoon salt
½ teaspoon pepper

1 cup milk
½ cup mushroom juice
2 cups grated sharp cheese
2 teaspoons Tabasco sauce
3 boxes (10 ounces each) frozen French cut green beans, thawed and patted dry
1 can (3 ounces) French fried onions

In one-half stick of butter sauté onions, mushrooms, and water chestnuts until tender. Set aside. Melt a stick of butter; blend in flour, salt and pepper. Gradually add milk and mushroom juice. Next, add cheese and Tabasco and stir until melted. In the bottom of a buttered 9x13 baking dish, layer half the vegetable mixture and half the green beans. Cover with half the cheese sauce. Repeat for second layer and top with remaining cheese sauce. Bake uncovered at 350° for 15 minutes. Sprinkle crumbled French fried onions on top and return to oven; bake for 10 more minutes. Serves 8 to 10. *This dish can be made ahead and kept in the refrigerator, but the cooking time must be increased a little.*

Mrs. Jim Williams (Tempe)

Cheese Grits

1 quart milk
1 cup quick grits
2 sticks butter
Salt and pepper to taste

8 or 9 triangles Gruyere cheese, grated
1 cup Parmesan cheese

Bring milk to boil and slowly add grits and 1 stick of butter. Stir constantly over medium heat and cook until consistency of cereal. Remove from heat and beat for 3 minutes. Add other stick of butter and grated Gruyere cheese, salt and pepper. Pour into a 9x13 inch greased baking dish. Sprinkle top with Parmesan cheese and bake at 350° for 30 minutes until brown on top. Serves 8 to 10. *This casserole is good at any meal. For spice add jalapeño peppers.*

Mrs. Charlie Carpenter (Judy)

Grits Soufflé

1½ cups grits
6   cups water
3   eggs, separated
1   roll (6 ounces) garlic cheese
    spread

1½ sticks butter
2   teaspoons salt
½   teaspoon paprika

Cook grits in water for 10 minutes. Add egg yolks, garlic cheese, butter, salt and paprika. Beat egg whites until stiff peaks form. Fold whites into grits mixture. Bake at 250° for 1 hour. Serves 8. *We serve with ham. Keeps well for the next day.*

Mrs. Larry Hall (Jane)

Sausage Cheese Grits

1   package (1 pound) bulk hot
    saugage
1   cup instant grits
1   teaspoon salt
4   cups boiling water

1   stick margarine
1   roll (6 ounces) garlic cheese
2   eggs, slightly beaten
½   cup milk, approximately

Cook hot sausage in skillet until brown; drain and set aside. Add salt to boiling water and stir in grits. Cook according to package directions. Add 1 stick margarine and the roll of garlic cheese to hot grits. Put beaten eggs into a measuring cup and fill with enough milk to make one cup. Add to grits mixture. Crumble cooked sausage into grits mixture and place in a buttered 2 quart casserole. Bake at 350° for one hour. Serves 6 to 8.

Mrs. Ken Moyer (Bonnie)

Creamy Hominy Casserole

2   cans (29 ounces each)
    hominy, drained
2   cans (4 ounces each)
    chopped green chilies,
    drained
1   carton (8 ounces) sour
    cream

½   pint whipping cream
Salt and pepper to taste
¼   cup margarine
1   cup grated Jack or Gruyere
    cheese

In a bowl, mix hominy, green chilies, sour cream, whipping cream, salt and pepper. Pour into deep casserole dish. Dot with margarine and sprinkle with cheese. Cover and bake at 350° for 30 minutes. Serves 8.

Mrs. Larry Wisian (Kay)

Texas Hominy

4 slices bacon
2 large onions, chopped
1 green pepper, chopped
1 can (4 ounces) mushrooms, drained
1 can (29 ounces) hominy, drained

1 teaspoon Worcestershire sauce
1 can (10 ounces) Ro-Tel tomatoes and green chilies
1 teaspoon salt
¼ teaspoon pepper
1 cup grated cheese

Fry bacon until crisp; drain and crumble. Add onion and green pepper to drippings; sauté until tender. Stir in mushrooms, hominy, Worcestershire, tomatoes, and seasonings. Cook 20 to 30 minutes. Stir in bacon. Alternate layers of hominy mixture and cheese in greased 2 quart casserole, ending with cheese. Bake, uncovered, at 350° for 20 minutes. Serves 6 to 8.

Mrs. Don Panter (Carolyn)

Mushrooms in Sour Cream

2 pounds mushrooms, cleaned
¼ pound butter
1 whole onion, peeled
1 tablespoon minced parsley or 1 teaspoon dried parsley flakes

½ teaspoon granulated beef bouillon
1 teaspoon salt
½ teaspoon pepper
1 tablespoon flour
1 carton (8 ounces) sour cream

Cut very large mushrooms in half. Sauté in butter about 2 minutes. Add onion and parsley; cover and simmer gently for 15 minutes. Remove onion. Add bouillon, salt and pepper; stir gently. Sprinkle flour over mushrooms and stir. Add sour cream; heat, but do not boil. Serves 4 to 6.

Mrs. Terry Arndt (Barbara)

 Never soak or wash mushrooms before storing them. Simply clean by wiping with a damp cloth or paper towel right before using.

✓

Noodle Casserole

8 ounces one-quarter inch noodles, cooked	**1** teaspoon Worcestershire sauce
2 cups cottage cheese	**Dash of Tabasco**
1¼ cups sour cream	**3** tablespoons fresh parsley, chopped
¼ cup margarine, melted	**Salt and pepper to taste**
¼ cup finely chopped onions	**Paprika to garnish**
1 clove garlic, finely minced	
1 can (4 ounces) chopped green chilies, drained	

Combine cottage cheese, sour cream, margarine, onions, garlic, green chilies, and all seasonings except paprika. Add noodles and turn into buttered 2 quart casserole. Sprinkle with paprika. Cover and bake at 350° for 45 minutes. Serves 8 to 10. *This side dish is also delicious served under beef tips or beef stroganoff.*

Mrs. Ron Garrick (Bonnie)

Our ancestors brought many vegetable and flower seeds with them on their treks to the West. Since space was scarce in their covered wagons, they sewed the seeds into the hems of their dresses or made small pockets in their clothing to insure their arrival in the "new land."

✓ # Okra Casserole

½ cup chopped onion	**1¼** cups sliced okra
½ cup chopped green pepper	**2** cups chopped tomatoes
⅓ cup margarine, melted	**½** teaspoon basil
2 tablespoons flour	**4** slices American cheese, cut in triangles
1 teaspoon salt	
½ teaspoon pepper	

Sauté onion and green pepper in margarine. Stir in flour, salt, and pepper. Add okra, tomatoes and basil. Spoon into lightly greased 1½ quart casserole. Top with cheese. Bake uncovered at 350° for 25 to 30 minutes. Serves 4. *May be assembled early in the day.*

Mrs. William Bush (Carolyn)

Fried Onion Rings

1½ cups flour
1½ cups beer, active or flat,
  cold or at room temperature

3 very large yellow onions
3 to 4 cups shortening

Make a batter by combining flour and beer in a large bowl; blend thoroughly. Cover the bowl and allow the batter to sit at room temperature for no less than 3 hours. Preheat oven to 200°. Carefully peel the onions and cut into ¼ inch thick slices. Separate the slices into rings and set aside. Melt enough shortening in a 10 inch skillet to come to a two inch depth. Heat the shortening to 375°. Dip onion rings into the batter and place in hot fat. Fry rings, turning once or twice, until they are a golden color. Drain on paper towels. To keep warm, place on middle shelf of preheated oven. To freeze, arrange on a cookie sheet. When frozen, pack in plastic bags. To reheat, arrange on cookie sheets and place in a preheated 400° oven for 4 to 6 minutes. Serves 6.

Mrs. Larry Hall (Jane)

Chinese Green Peas

¼ cup olive oil
¼ cup salad oil
3 packages (10 ounces each)
  frozen peas
3 small onions, chopped
1½ cups chopped celery

1 can (8 ounces) water
  chestnuts, drained and
  sliced
4 teaspoons cornstarch
1 cup beef broth
1 teaspoon soy sauce
Salt to taste

Heat oils in a large skillet. Add all vegetables and, when peas start sputtering, cover and turn heat to low. Cook 10 to 15 minutes, stirring occasionally. Do *not* overcook vegetables; they should be crisp. Dissolve cornstarch in ¼ cup of the broth; then combine with remaining broth. Pour over vegetables and cook, stirring constantly, until slightly thickened. Add seasonings and cook 1 minute longer. Serves 10.

Mrs. Ron Garrick (Bonnie)

Peas Oriental

3   packages (10 ounces each) frozen peas
2   cans (8 ounces each) sliced water chestnuts, drained
1   can (15 ounces) bean sprouts, drained
1   can (4 ounces) sliced mushrooms
2   cans cream of mushroom soup
2   cans (3 ounces each) French fried onion rings

Pre-cook peas briefly. Mix all ingredients except onion rings in a 2 quart casserole and bake at 350° for 30 minutes. Crumble onion rings over top and bake 5 or 10 minutes longer. Serves 10.

Mrs. Wayne Davison (Cindi)

Potato-Cheese Puff

3   eggs, separated
¼   cup milk
3   cups mashed potatoes
1½ teaspoons grated onion
2   cups grated Cheddar cheese
Salt and pepper to taste

Combine egg yolks and milk. Add remaining ingredients, except egg whites. Beat egg whites until stiff; then fold into potato mixture. Bake in greased 2 quart dish at 375° for 40 minutes, until knife inserted in center comes out clean and top is brown. Serves 6.

Mrs. Robert West (Linda)

Oven Potato Fans

2   large potatoes, peeled
¼   cup butter, melted
⅛   teaspoon seasoned salt

Cut potatoes in half lengthwise. Place outside down in baking dish. Score diagonally about ½ through with knife. Pour melted butter and salt over. Bake at 325° for 1 hour, until golden brown. Spoon butter over occasionally. Serves 4 (or 2 if you're skinny).

Mrs. Jim Schultz (Mary Kay)

New Potatoes with Mushrooms

8   new potatoes, washed and
    scrubbed
¼   cup butter
2   cans (4 ounces each) sliced
    mushrooms, drained or 1
    cup fresh

3   green onions, chopped,
    stems and all
Salt and pepper to taste

Boil new potatoes in jackets until just tender. Drain and cut into bite size pieces in pan. Stir in butter, mushrooms and onions, adding enough butter so mixture is moist. Serves 4. *These potatoes are great reheated, too.*

Mrs. Robert Henderson (Dale)

Gourmet Scalloped Potatoes

4 to 5 potatoes
¼   teaspoon salt
¼   teaspoon pepper
1   clove garlic
¼   pound margarine, divided

3   cans (4 ounces each)
    mushrooms, chopped, or
    one pound fresh
1   cup grated Cheddar cheese
½   cup chopped parsley
1   small onion, chopped
1   pint whipping cream

Peel and thinly slice potatoes; season with salt and pepper. Rub a 2½ quart baking dish with sliced garlic, then with two tablespoons of the margarine. Alternate layers of potatoes and drained mushrooms, sprinkling each layer with cheese, parsley, and onion. Repeat layers until all ingredients are used, ending with potatoes and reserving some cheese. Pour cream over potatoes; sprinkle remaining cheese over cream. Dot with remaining butter. Bake at 375° for 1 hour 15 minutes. Serves 6 to 8.

Mrs. Don Panter (Carolyn)

A general rule for cooking vegetables covered or uncovered: vegetables that grow underground should be cooked covered, those that grow above ground should be cooked uncovered.

Cheese Potatoes

1   can Cheddar cheese soup
½   cup milk
Pepper
4   cups potatoes, peeled and
    sliced

1   small onion, sliced
2   tablespoons butter
Paprika to garnish

Mix soup, milk, and pepper. Butter casserole dish and place a layer of potatoes, a layer of onion, and a layer of cheese sauce. Repeat layers once more. Dot top with butter and sprinkle with paprika. Bake covered at 375° for 1 hour. Uncover and bake 15 minutes more. Serves 6.

Mrs. Ron Garrick (Bonnie)

Potatoes Romanoff

5   green onions, chopped
1   carton (12 ounces) cottage
    cheese
1   carton (8 ounces) sour
    cream

5   large potatoes, cooked and
    cubed
Salt and pepper to taste
1   cup grated Cheddar cheese

Combine onions, cottage cheese, sour cream, potatoes, salt, and pepper in a 1½ quart casserole. Top with grated cheese. Bake at 350° for 40 minutes. Serves 6.

Mrs. Larry Strickland (Linda)

Arroz Con Salsa Verde

1   carton (8 ounces) sour
    cream
1   can (4 ounces) Herdez Salsa
    Verde or green chilies,
    chopped

2   cups cooked rice
6   ounces Monterey Jack
    cheese, grated
2   ounces American cheese,
    grated

Combine sour cream and salsa (or green chilies). Place thin layer of rice in bottom of buttered 1½ quart casserole. Add a layer of Monterey Jack cheese, topped by the sour cream mixture. Repeat layers, ending with rice. Bake at 350° for 10 to 15 minutes. Put reserved American cheese on top. Return to oven until cheese melts, approximately 5 minutes. Mixture should be heated through and cheese melted. Serves 6.

Mrs. Dudley D. Baker (Kathy)

Curried Orange Rice

¼ cup butter
1 medium onion, thinly sliced
2 teaspoons curry powder
1 cup uncooked rice
1 cup orange juice

1 cup chicken broth
1 teaspoon salt
½ cup seedless raisins
1 bay leaf

Melt butter in heavy saucepan. Sauté onion until soft and golden but not brown. Stir in curry and rice. Cook two minutes longer, stirring constantly. Add remaining ingredients; stir with fork. Bring to boiling; lower heat; cover and simmer 15 to 20 minutes, or until rice is tender and liquid has been absorbed. Remove bay leaf before serving. Serves 6.

Mrs. B. L. Turlington (Jill)

Mexican Rice

2 cups uncooked rice
⅓ to ½ cup oil
2 green onions with tops, chopped
½ green pepper, chopped
1 tomato, thinly sliced
½ cup tomato sauce

½ teaspoon pepper
½ teaspoon garlic powder
Salt to taste
¼ teaspoon cumin
3½ cups chicken broth
1 package (10 ounces) frozen peas

Heat rice in oil until golden. Add remaining ingredients and stir. Cover and cook over low heat about 20 minutes or until rice is tender and most of the liquid is absorbed. Serves 8.

Mrs. Jim Rado (Vicki)

Rice Pilaf

2 cups uncooked rice
1 stick margarine
2 cans onion soup

2 cans (3 ounces each) whole mushrooms

In saucepan brown rice in 1 stick margarine. When browned thoroughly, add soup and mushrooms, juice and all. Simmer, covered until done, about 45 minutes. Serves 6 to 8.

Mrs. Robert Henderson (Dale)

Dirty Rice

2 medium onions, finely chopped	½ cup bacon drippings or oil
1 green pepper, finely chopped	⅓ cup flour
2 ribs celery, finely chopped	2 cups water
3 cloves garlic, crushed	Salt and pepper to taste
½ pound chicken giblets, finely chopped	Tabasco to taste
1 pound bulk sausage, crumbled	4 green onion tops, chopped
	6 sprigs parsley, chopped
	8 to 10 cups hot cooked rice

Prepare vegetables as directed in food processor or food chopper. Add crushed garlic. Chop chicken giblets in same manner; set aside. Brown sausage in large pot. Remove and set aside. To sausage drippings, add enough bacon drippings or oil to make ½ cup. Add flour and brown, stirring constantly, over medium heat until the roux is very dark brown, about the color of an old penny. Be very careful not to scorch this roux. Immediately add chopped vegetables and stir and cook a few minutes; then add chopped chicken giblets and cook until the pink color is gone. Add water, the sausage and seasonings and simmer two hours or more. Thirty minutes before serving, add onion tops and parsley. Before serving add hot cooked rice and mix well. Serves 16 to 20. *A favorite Cajun accompaniment to barbecue also good with roast beef or turkey. It's even better on the second day. I often divide the base of the dressing into two parts before adding rice and freeze half for later use.*

Mrs. John Baker (Jo)

Wild Rice Casserole

2 boxes (6 ounces each) wild rice, cooked	1 jar (4½ ounces) sliced mushrooms or
2 to 3 stalks celery, chopped	8 to 10 fresh mushrooms, sliced
2 to 3 green onions, chopped	¼ pint whipping cream
½ green pepper, chopped	½ cup Parmesan cheese

Blend cooked rice with celery, onions, mushrooms and green pepper. Put entire mixture in 2 quart casserole. Cover with cream. Sprinkle with Parmesan cheese. Bake at 350° for 15 minutes or until heated. Serves 6 to 8. *This is a good accompaniment to fowl or game.*

Mrs. B. L. Turlington (Jill)

Gourmet Spinach

¼ pound bacon
1 large onion, chopped
3 packages (10 ounces each) frozen spinach

8 ounces cream cheese
Salt and pepper to taste
2 tomatoes, sliced
Bread crumbs to garnish

Cook bacon and crumble. Sauté onions in bacon drippings; drain. Cook spinach according to directions and drain well. Mix spinach, onions, cream cheese, salt and pepper. Pour into a 9 inch square glass dish. Place tomatoes on spinach mixture. Sprinkle bacon and bread crumbs on top. Bake at 350° for 25 to 30 minutes or until hot throughout. Serves 8.

Mrs. Leo Mueller (Nancy)

Spinach Madeleine

2 packages (10 ounces each) frozen chopped spinach
4 tablespoons butter
1 medium onion, chopped
2 tablespoons flour
½ cup evaporated milk
½ cup vegetable liquid
½ teaspoon pepper
¾ teaspoon Beau Monde powder

½ teaspoon garlic powder
½ teaspoon salt
1 teaspoon Worcestershire sauce
Red pepper to taste
1 roll (6 ounces) Jalapeño cheese, cubed
½ to ¾ cup buttered bread crumbs

Cook spinach according to directions. Drain and reserve liquid. Melt butter in saucepan over low heat. Sauté onions until soft, then remove from pan. Stir in flour and mix until blended and smooth, but not brown. Slowly add liquid, stirring constantly; cook until smooth and thick over low heat. Blend in seasonings and onions, stirring well. Add cheese to flour mixture, stirring until melted. Add spinach; pour into casserole. Top with crumbs. Bake at 350° until bubbly around the edges, 15 to 20 minutes. Serves 5 to 6. *This dish is better prepared the day before.*

Mrs. D. D. Baker, Jr. (Agnes)

Cheese and Spinach Pie

½ cup chopped onion	1 pound ricotta, drained
¼ pound mushrooms, sliced	1 cup grated Mozzarella
1 small zucchini, sliced	cheese
1 green pepper, diced	3 eggs, beaten
3 tablespoons oil	2 tablespoons olive oil
1 cup diced cooked ham	Nutmeg
1 package (10 ounces) frozen	Salt and pepper to taste
chopped spinach	1 tablespoon dill

Sauté onion, mushrooms, zucchini and green pepper in oil until vegetables are tender. Add diced ham and sauté for 2 minutes. Thaw and squeeze dry spinach. Combine spinach, ricotta, Mozzarella, eggs, olive oil, and spices. Add vegetables to cheese mixture. Pour into two 8 inch buttered pie plates and bake at 350° for 45 minutes. Serves 8.

Mrs. Thomas Schwartz (Ellana)

Quick Spinach and Artichoke Casserole

1 can (14 ounces) artichokes, drained and cut in half	1 stick butter, softened
2 packages (10 ounces each) frozen chopped spinach, cooked and drained	1 can (8½ ounces) water chestnuts, chopped
	Salt and pepper to taste
8 ounces cream cheese, softened	½ cup seasoned Italian bread crumbs
	2 tablespoons butter

Arrange artichoke halves in 9 inch square baking dish. Mix remaining ingredients, except bread crumbs and butter. Pour over artichokes. Cover with crumbs, dot with butter. Bake uncovered at 350° about 20 minutes. Serves 6. *This is a great freeze ahead, too.*

Mrs. Jim Schultz (Mary Kay)

Carol's Spinach Casserole

3 boxes (10 ounces each) chopped spinach	1 envelope onion soup mix
1 carton (8 ounces) sour cream	2 cups dry stuffing mix
	1 stick butter

Cook and drain spinach according to package directions. Mix sour cream and soup; add spinach and stir well. Pour into 2 quart casserole and cover with stuffing mix. Dot with butter. Bake at 350° for 30 minutes. Serves 6 to 8. *This is an easy do ahead dish and can be refrigerated before adding stuffing and butter. Complete recipe when ready to serve.*

Mrs. Jim Rado (Vicki)

Spinach Casserole

2 packages (10 ounces each) frozen chopped spinach	3 tablespoons flour
1⅓ cups cottage cheese	4 tablespoons margarine
⅓ pound Cheddar cheese, grated	3 eggs, beaten
	Salt and pepper to taste

Cook and drain spinach. Add all other ingredients. Pour into a greased 5 x 9 inch pan. Bake at 350° for 1 hour. Let stand 5 to 10 minutes. Serves 6.

Mrs. Chris Williston (Janice)

Calabazo Mexicano

3 to 4 medium yellow squash	1 can (4 ounces) chopped green chilies, drained
1 small onion, chopped	2 medium tomatoes, diced
½ teaspoon salt	

Slice squash into ½ inch pieces. Cook squash and onion in saucepan with salted water to cover, until soft, approximately 10 minutes. Drain off liquid and add chilies and tomatoes. Serves 4.

Mrs. Ken Moyer (Bonnie)

Squash Casserole

2   pounds yellow squash
1   carton (8 ounces) sour
    cream
4   medium carrots, grated
1   medium onion, chopped
1   can cream of mushroom
    soup
1   package (8 ounces) herb
    stuffing mix, divided

1   jar (4 ounces) chopped
    pimientos
1   can (4 ounces) mushrooms,
    optional
Salt and pepper to taste
1   stick margarine

Cook squash, drain and mash. Add other ingredients except half the stuffing and margarine. Mix well and pour into a 2 quart casserole. Melt margarine and mix with remaining stuffing. Sprinkle on top of casserole. Bake at 350° for 40 minutes or until brown and bubbly around edges. Serves 6 to 8.

Mrs. George Barton (Mindy)

Green and Gold Squash Pie

1   unbaked 10 inch pastry
    shell
2   medium zucchini, thinly
    sliced
2   medium yellow squash,
    thinly sliced
½   medium onion, sliced
1   medium tomato, peeled and
    chopped
1   medium green pepper, finely
    chopped

1   large clove garlic, minced
¾   teaspoon salt
¼   teaspoon pepper
½   teaspoon basil
2   tablespoons butter, melted
3   eggs, beaten
½   cup whipping cream
¼   cup Parmesan cheese

Prick bottom and sides of pastry shell. Bake at 450° for 8 minutes until lightly browned. Set aside to cool. Combine vegetables, garlic, salt, pepper, basil and butter in large skillet. Sauté until vegetables are tender. Spoon into pastry shell, spreading evenly. Combine eggs and cream, mixing well. Pour over vegetables. Sprinkle with cheese and bake at 350° for 30 minutes, or until set. Serves 6 to 8.

Mrs. Wayne Davison (Cindi)

Zucchini Tomato Bake

1 onion, chopped	3 tablespoons chopped
4 tablespoons margarine	parsley
4 zucchini, sliced in rings	Garlic salt and pepper to taste
3 tomatoes, chopped	¼ cup Parmesan cheese
¼ pound fresh or 1 can (4 ounces) mushrooms, sliced	¼ pound Cheddar cheese, grated
½ teaspoon basil	

Sauté onion in margarine until soft. Add zucchini and sauté until tender. Add tomatoes and mushrooms. Sauté briefly, then add seasonings. Put in 1½ quart buttered casserole. Toss with Parmesan; top with Cheddar cheese. Cook at 350° for 20 to 30 minutes. Can be frozen. Serves 4 to 6. *Try this shortcut: Sauté everything longer, approximately 10 minutes. Right before serving, add cheeses and stir to melt. Forget the oven!*

Mrs. Jim Schultz (Mary Kay)

Zesty Zucchini

2 pounds zucchini	Salt and pepper to taste
1 bunch green onions, chopped	¼ teaspoon sugar
4 tablespoons butter	¼ teaspoon basil, optional

Grate squash; sprinkle with salt and place in colander for 2 hours to remove moisture. Drain and sauté squash and green onions in butter for about 6 minutes. Add salt, pepper, sugar and basil during last 2 minutes. Serves 6.

Mrs. Jerry Dow (Annette)

Zucchini Soufflé

6 medium zucchini, cooked and mashed	¼ cup minced onion
2 eggs, beaten	Salt and pepper to taste
½ cup bread crumbs	1 cup Parmesan cheese
	2 tablespoons butter

Combine all ingredients except cheese and butter and blend well. Put in 1½ quart casserole. Cover with cheese and dot with thin slices of butter. Bake uncovered at 350° for approximately 30 minutes. Before serving, place under broiler for a few minutes. Serves 6.

Mrs. Larry Morris (Diane)

Grilled Tomatoes

10 large firm ripe tomatoes
4 cups finely grated dry
   French bread crumbs
4 to 6 tablespoons butter,
   melted

2 cloves garlic, minced
4 green onions, minced
2 teaspoons dried oregano,
   crushed
Salt and pepper

Cut tops off tomatoes and scoop out the pulp; save for another recipe. Combine remaining ingredients. Fill the tomato shells and bake at 350° for about 20 minutes. Then, place under broiler just until golden on top. Serves 10. *Baked tomatoes add a colorful note to almost any meal. These can be changed by adding your favorite herbs or a bit of Parmesan cheese.*

Mrs. Lee Provinse (Dottie)

Spinach-Stuffed Tomatoes

12 tomatoes
2 packages (10 ounces each)
   frozen chopped spinach
2 large onions, chopped
¼ cup parsley, chopped
1½ cups celery, chopped
1 large green pepper, chopped
4 carrots, chopped
6 tablespoons butter, melted

1½ cups seasoned bread
   crumbs
⅔ cup milk
2 eggs, beaten
Dash of Creole seasoning,
   optional
Salt and pepper to taste
Parmesan cheese to garnish

Scoop centers from tomatoes, salt inside, and turn upside down to drain. Cook spinach according to package directions; drain. Sauté onions, parsley, celery, green pepper and carrots in butter until onion is soft. Add crumbs, milk, eggs, Creole seasoning, salt and pepper. Fill tomatoes and top with Parmesan cheese. Place in buttered 9x13 inch dish. Bake at 400° for 20 minutes. Serves 12.

Gayle Lewis

Yams Flambé

2 yams, boiled and sliced	Sugar
4 slices pineapple	¼ cup rum
½ cup flour	¼ cup sherry
½ cup milk	
4 maraschino cherries to garnish	

Roll pineapple and sliced yams in flour, milk, and then in flour again. Fry pineapple and yams in oil until golden brown. Put cherry in center of each pineapple. Place pineapple and yams in oven dish and sprinkle with sugar. Bake in 325° oven for 5 minutes. When ready to serve, pour rum over mixture, light with match, and then pour sherry over all. Serves 4.

Mrs. Ben DuBilier (Lillian)

Bourbon Yam Casserole

5 large sweet potatoes or yams	1 teaspoon cinnamon
2 tablespoons oil	¼ teaspoon grated nutmeg
6 tablespoons butter, divided	⅛ teaspoon cloves
⅓ cup Curaçao	½ teaspoon salt
¼ cup bourbon	⅛ teaspoon freshly ground pepper
½ cup sugar	

Scrub sweet potatoes or yams. Rub skins with oil; place in shallow dish, and bake at 450° for 30 minutes. Cool slightly; then peel and cut in ¾ inch slices. In saucepan, melt 4 tablespoons of butter; add remaining ingredients and mix thoroughly. Remove from heat. Butter 3 to 4 quart casserole dish and add yam slices in three layers, pouring ⅓ of seasoned butter sauce over each layer. Bake covered, at 350° for 20 minutes. Remove from oven and stir, cutting the yam slices in half. When mixed, smooth and flatten top. Dot surface evenly with remaining two tablespoons butter. Bake uncovered for 20 minutes. Serves 8. *A large can (40 ounces) of yams may be substituted for fresh in this dish.*

Mrs. Larry Hall (Jane)

Sub Gum Vegetables

4   tablespoons oil, divided
½   teaspoon salt, divided
1   onion, sliced in strips
1   green pepper, sliced
2   stalks celery, sliced
½   cup fresh mushrooms,
    sliced
2   dried mushrooms, cut in
    strips, optional
¾   cup bean sprouts

2   carrots, diagonally sliced
½   cup bamboo shoots
½   cup water chestnuts, sliced
4   tablespoons water
2   tablespoons soy sauce
1   tablespoon sherry
1   tablespoon cornstarch
2   tablespoons water
½   teaspoon sesame seed oil

Heat 2 tablespoons oil and ¼ teaspoon salt in wok or skillet; stir fry onion and pepper for one minute; remove. Add one tablespoon oil; stir fry celery and mushrooms 1 minute; remove. Add bean sprouts; stir fry for ½ minute; remove. Add one tablespoon oil, stir fry carrots and bamboo shoots for 1½ minutes; add water chestnuts. Combine 4 tablespoons water, soy sauce, sherry, and remaining salt; bring to a boil. Add vegetables; cover and cook 2 minutes. Add cornstarch, 2 tablespoons water and sesame seed oil. Stir briefly to heat. Serves 6.

Mrs. Thomas Schwartz (Ellana)

Creole Vegetables

½   cup chopped onion
½   cup chopped green pepper
2   tablespoons butter
1   can (16 ounces) tomatoes or
    2 cups fresh tomatoes,
    peeled
2   cups diced celery
2   cups fresh or frozen okra,
    sliced

1½ teaspoons salt
¼   teaspoon pepper
½   teaspoon basil or oregano,
    optional
¼   teaspoon Tabasco sauce,
    optional

In a large skillet, sauté onion and green pepper in butter until tender. Add diced tomatoes, including liquid to skillet. Stir in remaining ingredients. Cook until celery is soft, 20 to 25 minutes. Serves 8 to 10.

Mrs. Ken Moyer (Bonnie)

Vegetable Pudding

4   eggs, beaten
3   cups canned cream style
    corn
2½ cups half and half or milk
1   can (16 ounces) green
    beans, drained
3   cups chopped tomatoes
1   cup chopped onion
2   medium green peppers,
    chopped
2   cans (4 ounces each)
    pimientos
2   cups sliced or chopped ripe
    olives
1   cup sliced mushrooms
½   teaspoon Tabasco
1½ teaspoons salt
½   teaspoon chili powder
½   teaspoon paprika
1½ cups yellow corn meal
1   pound bacon, fried crisp
    and crumbled

Combine all ingredients as listed, except crumbled bacon and mix thoroughly. Pour into 5 quart casserole or pan. Bake at 325° for 1½ hours or until firm. Garnish with crumbled bacon. Serves 30. *Can be refrigerated before or after baking; also freezes well.*

Mrs. Jim Smith (Jare)

Almond Sausage Dressing

1   pound bulk sausage
8   cups dry bread crumbs
2   cups blanched, shredded
    almonds
1   cup strong beef bouillon,
    made with two cubes
2   cups finely chopped green
    celery leaves
1   cup chopped onion
1   cup sliced fresh mushrooms
¼   cup chopped parsley
¼   cup chopped chives
¼   cup chopped green pepper
¼   teaspoon pepper
Dash cayenne
¼   teaspoon mace
¼   teaspoon marjoram
¼   teaspoon sage
¼   teaspoon thyme
¼   teaspoon nutmeg
4   eggs, well beaten
¼   cup evaporated milk

Sauté sausage until well browned. Remove from skillet to bowl; combine with bread crumbs. Toast almonds in fat; pour over bread crumbs; mix well. Rinse pan with beef bouillon; pour into bowl. Add celery leaves, onion, mushrooms, parsley, chives, green pepper, and spices to bowl. Mix thoroughly. Mix eggs with milk and add to bowl. Toss lightly to loosen and coat all ingredients. Stuff turkey or bake in casserole at 350° for 45 minutes to 1 hour.

Mrs. Daniel O'Donnell (Sharon)

Lyndon Baines Johnson, the 35th President of the United States and a native Texan, often escaped the pressures of his office at the LBJ Ranch. It is easy for us to imagine, as we gaze at his rocker and famous Stetson hat, how he must have enjoyed the lazy afternoons of summer from the front porch of his home. Nestled along the banks of the Pedernales River, the stately ranch house was often the setting for casual, yet elegant entertaining by the President and his gracious wife, Lady Bird. Old friends and international dignitaries alike yielded to the charm and romance of the old West, when invited to the "Texas White House."

Main Dishes pictured: LBJ Pedernales River Chili, Beef Wine Stew, Braised Red Cabbage, Apples and German Sausage, Spiedi Marinade Shish Kabobs, Lone Star Ribs and Tacos.

Main Dishes

Artichoke Quiche

2   jars (6 ounces) marinated artichoke hearts
12 green onions, sliced with tops
1   clove garlic, minced
4   eggs
6   crackers, crushed
½   pound sharp Cheddar cheese, grated
Salt and pepper
1   unbaked (9 inch) pie shell

Drain artichokes, reserving some marinade; chop. Sauté onions, tops and garlic in reserved marinade. Beat eggs; slowly add crackers and onion mixture. Blend in artichokes, cheese, salt and pepper. Pour into pie shell and bake at 325° for 30 to 40 minutes. Cool slightly before cutting. Serves 6 to 8.

Mrs. Larry Strickland (Linda)

Chilies and Sausage Quiche

2   uncooked (8 inch) pie shells
1   can (7 ounces) whole green chilies
1   pound hot bulk sausage, cooked and crumbled
4   eggs, lightly beaten
2   cups half and half cream
½   cup grated Parmesan cheese
½   cup grated Swiss cheese
Salt and pepper to taste

Line bottom of pie shells with split and seeded whole green chilies. Sprinkle sausage over chilies. Combine eggs, cream, cheeses and seasonings. Pour over sausage. Bake at 350° for 30 to 40 minutes or until top is golden brown. Remove from oven and allow to set 5 minutes before serving. Serves 8. This quiche can be made in a 9 × 13 inch casserole without the crust. Cut into squares and serve as an appetizer.

Mrs. Chris Williston (Janice)

French Onion Pie

1 unbaked (9 inch) pie shell
2 cans (3 ounces) French fried onions
3 eggs
1½ cups milk

1¼ teaspoons salt
Dash cayenne pepper
1 cup grated sharp Cheddar cheese

Spread onions over pastry. In small bowl beat eggs; add milk, salt and pepper. Pour egg mixture over onions. Spinkle with grated cheese. Bake at 425° for 15 minutes. Reduce heat to 350° and bake an additional 15 to 20 minutes or until custard is set. Cool slightly before cutting. Serves 6.

Mrs. Clark Rector (Sue)

Quiche Lorraine

8 ounces Swiss cheese, cut into thin strips
2 tablespoons flour
1½ cups half and half cream
4 eggs, slightly beaten

8 slices bacon, cooked and crumbled
½ teaspoon salt
Dash of pepper
1 unbaked (9 inch) pie shell

Toss cheese with flour. Add cream, eggs, bacon and seasonings; mix well. Pour into pastry shell and bake at 350° for 40 to 45 minutes or until set. Serves 8. Try substituting ¾ cup chopped ham for the bacon. It is just as good.

Mrs. Larry Morris (Diane)

Shrimp Quiche

1 unbaked (9 inch) pie shell
1 pound fresh or frozen shrimp, peeled and deveined
3 eggs
1 cup half and half cream

1 cup grated Swiss cheese
½ teaspoon salt
1 teaspoon pepper
¾ cup chopped onion
4 tablespoons butter

Cook shrimp; drain. Mix eggs, cream, cheese, salt and pepper. Sauté onion in butter until soft; add to egg mixture along with shrimp. Reserve some shrimp for garnish. Pour into pie shell and bake at 350° for 40 to 45 minutes. Serves 6.

Mrs. Robert West (Linda)

Spinach Quiche

3   ounces cream cheese,
    softened
1   cup half and half cream
½   cup soft bread cubes
¼   cup grated Parmesan cheese
2   eggs, slightly beaten
1   package (10 ounces) frozen
    chopped spinach, thawed
    and drained

¼   cup margarine
1   large onion, chopped
½   pound fresh mushrooms,
    sliced
¾   teaspoon salt
1   unbaked (9 inch) pie shell

Mash cream cheese; add cream, bread cubes, Parmesan cheese, and eggs; beat to break up bread cubes. Stir in spinach. Melt margarine, and sauté onions and mushrooms; add to spinach mixture. Add salt, and pour into pie shell. Bake at 400° for 25 minutes. Let stand about 10 minutes before cutting. Serves 6 to 8. *The filling can be made ahead of time, but do not put into pie shell until ready to bake.*

Mrs. Bob Courts (Belva)

Eggs Sonora

Salsa:
1   can (28 ounces) tomatoes
1   can (4 ounces) chopped
    green chilies, drained
1   large onion, finely chopped
2   tablespoons oil

1   teaspoon salt
¼   teaspoon dried oregano,
    optional
1   clove garlic, minced
¼   teaspoon sugar

Drain tomatoes; reserving liquid. Chop tomatoes and combine with reserved liquid and remaining ingredients. Mix well. Cover and chill for at least 2 hours before using.

Filling:
6   flour tortillas
8   eggs, scrambled
3   cups shredded Cheddar
    cheese
1   pound bacon, cooked,
    drained and crumbled

1   medium onion, finely
    chopped
1   cup guacamole
¼   cup sliced ripe olives
Sour cream
Salsa

Warm tortillas. Layer eggs, cheese, bacon, onion, guacamole and olives evenly on each tortilla. Top with sour cream and salsa. Serves 6.

Nancy Young Moritz

Mom's Sunday Morning Sausage Ring

2 pounds bulk sausage
2 eggs, beaten
2 tablespoons grated onion

1½ cups fine dry toast or bread
crumbs
¼ cup chopped parsley,
optional

Lightly butter a 9 inch ring mold. Mix ingredients well and pack into mold. Bake at 350° for 20 minutes. Remove from oven, and pour off excess fat. Bake an additional 20 minutes. Turn onto heated platter and fill with 8 to 12 scrambled eggs or other egg mixture. Serves 4 to 6.

Mrs. Stephen Scheffe (Betsy)

Chile Rellenos

6 canned whole green chilies
Monterey Jack cheese, cut in
strips
2 eggs, separated
2 tablespoons flour
Oil for frying
1 clove garlic, minced
1 small onion, minced

1 tablespoon oil
1 cup canned tomatoes
1 cup chicken broth
1 teaspoon salt
1 teaspoon pepper
1 teaspoon powdered
marjoram

Remove seeds from chilies and wrap around cheese strips. Beat egg whites until stiff. Beat egg yolks and flour together; fold into egg whites. Drop chilies into egg mixture, remove with a spoon and place in hot skillet with a small amount of oil. Fry until golden; drain. Sauté garlic and onion in 1 tablespoon oil; add remaining ingredients. Season to taste. Add chilies and heat before serving. Serves 4 to 6.

Mrs. Jerry Dow (Annette)

To remove skins from fresh green chilies, parch whole peppers by placing 4 to 6 inches under broiler. Roast, turning often, until uniformly blistered. Place hot chilies in a plastic bag for 15 minutes. Remove; start at stem end and peel skin downward.

Green Enchiladas

1   package (10 ounces) frozen
    chopped spinach, thawed
    and drained
1   can (14 ounces) chicken
    broth
1   can cream of mushroom
    soup
1   can cream of chicken soup

2   cans (4 ounces each)
    chopped green chilies
1   pint sour cream
12 to 16 ounces Monterey Jack
    cheese, grated
2   medium onions, chopped
2   tablespoons oil
24 corn tortillas, softly fried

Combine spinach, broth, soups and chilies in a blender until smooth. Add sour cream and set aside. Sauté onion in oil and combine with cheese, reserving some cheese for topping. Place 1 heaping tablespoon of onion mixture on each tortilla and roll up. Place in a large casserole dish; cover with reserved sauce and top with cheese. Bake at 325° for 30 minutes or until cheese melts. Serves 10 to 12.

Mrs. Denman Smith (Sandra)

Chile Rellenos Casserole

6   eggs, beaten
3   cups cream style cottage
    cheese
¾   cup crushed rich round
    crackers
1   can (4 ounces) chopped
    green chilies, drained

2 to 3 jalapeños, optional
¾   cup shredded Cheddar
    cheese
¾   cup shredded Monterey
    Jack cheese

Combine eggs, cottage cheese, cracker crumbs, chilies, optional jalapeños and half the shredded cheeses. Turn into a buttered oblong baking dish. Bake at 350° for 45 minutes or until set. Sprinkle with remaining cheeses; bake an additional 2 to 3 minutes or until cheese melts. Let stand 5 minutes before serving. Serves 10 to 12.

Mrs. Jim Rado (Vicki)

Audrey's Golden Egg Bake

8 to 10 hard cooked eggs,
    halved lengthwise
2   tablespoons mayonnaise
1   teaspoon vinegar
1   teaspoon mustard
Dash salt

1   can cream of chicken soup,
    undiluted
⅓   cup milk
¾   teaspoon curry powder
1   cup grated Cheddar cheese
1   tablespoon chopped onion

Devil the eggs with a mixture of mayonnaise, vinegar, mustard, and salt. Refill egg whites. Place in a 9 inch square baking dish. Combine soup, milk, curry, cheese and onion; spread over eggs. Bake at 350° for 12 to 15 minutes. These can be served on toast. Serves 8.

Mrs. Johnny Johnson (Marcy)

Linguine Giuseppe

1   stick butter
1   pound linguine
1   tablespoon salt
½   cup freshly grated Parmesan
    cheese

2   tablespoons Tellicherry
    pepper or coarse ground
    black pepper
2   egg yolks
½   cup whipping cream
Salt to taste

Melt butter in chafing dish. Cook linguine al dente in at least 8 quarts of boiling water. Add 1 tablespoon salt to water just before adding pasta. Fork linguine carefully from water to drain. Do not use a colander. Place into melted butter; toss and turn until all strands are coated with butter. Continue tossing pasta; alternate adding cheese and pepper until each strand is evenly coated. Add unbeaten egg yolks and toss until yolks are well mixed. Pour in cream and toss again. Adjust salt and serve immediately. Serves 4 to 6.

Joe Pascucci

Manicotti

Meat or Tomato Sauce (your
favorite)

Batter:
2½ cups flour
2½ cups water
8 eggs

2 tablespoons grated Romano
or Parmesan cheese
Salt and pepper

Filling:
2 pounds Ricotta cheese
8 ounces Mozzarella cheese,
diced

¼ cup grated Parmesan cheese
2 eggs
1 tablespoon chopped parsley
Salt and pepper

Combine batter ingredients and beat until smooth. Heat a lightly greased 8 inch skillet to approximately 300°. Spoon about 4 tablespoons of batter into pan to cover bottom. Cook until top is dry. If bottom browns, the heat is too high. Do not flip. Stack between wax paper. Mix well all filling ingredients. Spoon 2 tablespoons filling into center of each manicotti and fold. Ladle some of your favorite meat or tomato sauce into a large baking dish. Place manicotti, seam side down into pan in a single layer. Spoon additional sauce over manicotti. Cover pan and bake at 325° for 30 minutes. Serves 10 to 12.

Mrs. Art DeFelice (Connie)

Frittata

1 cup finely chopped onions
2 tablespoons butter
Thyme to taste
Dash salt
1 cup chopped tomatoes
3 eggs, beaten

1 cup milk
½ teaspoon salt
½ cup grated Parmesan cheese
1 cup grated Swiss cheese
2 large tomatoes, sliced ¾
inch thick

Sauté onions in butter until transparent. Add thyme, salt and tomatoes; cover and simmer 5 minutes. Uncover pan; mash tomatoes and cook until mixture is dry and thick. Set aside to cool. Beat eggs with milk and salt. Stir in grated cheeses and cooled tomato mixture. Put sliced tomatoes on bottom of a 9 inch square pan, and pour mixture on top. Bake at 350° for 30 to 35 minutes. Cut into squares and serve. Serves 4 to 6.

Mrs. Jim Carney (Jean)

Eggs and Cheese Casserole

8	slices white bread, crusts removed	6	eggs
1	pound sharp cheese, grated	3	cups milk
		½	teaspoon salt

Butter bread thickly and cut into ½ inch cubes. Lay side by side in a buttered 9 × 13 inch dish. Cover heavily with cheese. Beat eggs well; add milk and salt. Beat again, and pour over cheese and bread. Cover with plastic wrap and refrigerate at least one night, preferably two. Remove from refrigerator and let warm to room temperature. Bake at 375° for 35 minutes. Serves 8. *For a spicy variation, add cayenne pepper to taste and top with shrimp, chicken, ham or whatever.*

Mrs. Jim Lederer (Anne)

Brunch Puff

16	slices bacon, cooked and crumbled, reserve drippings	8	eggs, beaten
2	onions, sliced	4	cups milk
12	slices white bread, quartered	1½	teaspoons salt
		¼	teaspoon pepper
½	pound Cheddar cheese, grated	½	teaspoon dry mustard

Sauté onion in bacon drippings until soft. Place ½ of the bread in the bottom of a greased 9 × 13 inch pan. Sprinkle ½ of bacon, onions and cheese on bread; repeat these layers. Combine eggs, milk and spices; pour over top layer. Refrigerate for at least 24 hours before cooking. Remove from refrigerator one hour before serving. Bake at 350° for 45 to 50 minutes. Serves 10 to 12. *Instead of bacon, add any one of the following: 1 pound cooked bulk sausage, 1 pound crab meat, 1 pound shrimp, cooked Italian sausage, chopped spinach or chopped broccoli.*

Mrs. Bob Kelly (Margaret)

The brunch is not as modern as we think. Called a "company breakfast" in the late 1880's, it was a popular type of entertainment in literary and artistic circles.

Rolled Chicken Washington

½ cup chopped fresh
   mushrooms
2 tablespoons butter
2 tablespoons flour
½ cup half and half cream
¼ teaspoon salt
Dash of cayenne pepper
1¼ cup grated sharp Cheddar
   cheese

6 to 7 boned whole chicken
   breasts, skinned
¾ cup fine dry bread crumbs
Flour
Salt
2 eggs, beaten
Bread crumbs
Oil for deep frying

Cook mushrooms in butter about 5 minutes. Blend in flour; stir in cream. Add salt and cayenne; cook and stir until mixture becomes very thick. Stir in cheese; cook over low heat, stirring until cheese is melted. Turn mixture into pie pan. Cover; chill thoroughly. Cut into 6 or 7 equal portions; shape into short sticks. Set aside. Place each piece of chicken, boned side up between two pieces of plastic wrap. Working from center out, pound to form cutlets not quite ¼ inch thick. Peel off plastic wrap. Place a cheese stick on each chicken breast. Tucking in sides, roll as for jelly roll. Press to seal well. Dust chicken rolls with flour; dip in slightly beaten egg, then roll in bread crumbs. Cover and chill. Fry rolls in a deep fat fryer at 375° for 5 minutes. Drain and bake at 325° for 30 to 45 minutes. Serves 6.

Mrs. Dudley Baker (Kathy)

Chicken Saltimbocca

6 halved chicken breasts,
   skinned, boned
6 thin slices boiled ham
3 slices Mozzarella cheese,
   halved
½ cup chopped tomato
½ teaspoon dried sage,
   crushed

⅓ cup fine dry bread crumbs
2 tablespoons grated
   Parmesan cheese
2 tablespoons minced parsley
4 tablespoons butter, melted

Wrap chicken in plastic wrap and pound lightly into 5 inch squares. Remove plastic. Place a ham slice and a half slice of cheese on each piece of chicken. Top with tomato and sage to taste. Tuck in sides and roll up, jelly roll style. Hold together with a toothpick. Combine bread crumbs, Parmesan cheese and parsley. Dip chicken in butter then in bread crumbs. Place in shallow baking pan. Bake at 350° for 40 to 45 minutes. Serves 6.

Wendy Tarpley

Easy Chicken Divan

2 packages (10 ounces each)
frozen broccoli stalks
2 cups sliced cooked chicken
1 cup mayonnaise
2 cans cream of chicken soup
1 teaspoon lemon juice

½ teaspoon curry powder
½ cup shredded sharp cheese
or ⅓ cup grated Parmesan
cheese
½ cup bread crumbs
1 tablespoon butter, melted

Cook broccoli as directed until tender; drain. Arrange stalks in a greased oblong baking dish. Place chicken over broccoli. Combine mayonnaise, soup, lemon juice and curry powder. Pour over chicken. Sprinkle with cheese. Combine crumbs and butter and sprinkle over all. Bake at 350° for 25 to 30 minutes. Serves 6.

Mrs. Ed Cornet (Kathi)

Festive Chicken Asparagus

1 package (10 ounces) frozen
asparagus
2 chicken breasts, halved
2 tablespoons flour
3 tablespoons oil

¼ cup dry white wine
¼ cup bleu cheese
1 can cream of chicken soup
½ teaspoon salt
¼ teaspoon pepper

Thaw asparagus. Coat chicken with flour and brown lightly on all sides in oil. Meanwhile, in shallow casserole, combine wine, bleu cheese, soup, salt and pepper. Place chicken in soup mixture and spoon sauce over chicken. Bake at 375° for 30 minutes. Separate asparagus into individual stalks. Remove casserole from oven and arrange asparagus between chicken pieces. Spoon some sauce over the chicken and asparagus. Cover tightly and bake an additional 30 minutes. Serves 4.

Mrs. Jerry Hunt (Gail)

Continental Chicken

1 package dried beef
6 to 8 chicken breasts, boned
6 to 8 slices bacon
1 can cream of mushroom
soup

¼ cup sour cream
¼ cup flour
Hot buttered noodles

Arrange dried beef on bottom of greased crock pot. Wrap each piece of chicken with bacon and lay on top of the dried beef. Mix soup, sour cream and flour together; pour over chicken. Cover and cook on low 8 to 10 hours or high for 3 to 4 hours. Serve over hot buttered noodles. Serves 6 to 8.

Mrs. Larry Lerche (Gail)

Chicken and Wild Rice Casserole

2 fryer chickens	2 packages long grain wild
1 cup dry sherry	rice with seasonings
1½ teaspoons salt	1 pound mushrooms
½ teaspoon curry powder	¼ cup margarine
Onion	1 cup sour cream
½ cup sliced celery	1 can cream of mushroom
	soup

Cook chicken in water, sherry, salt, curry, onion, and celery. Simmer until done. Strain broth and reserve; debone chicken. Using broth, cook rice according to directions for firm rice. Slice mushrooms and sauté in margarine. Reserve a few mushrooms for topping and combine the rest with the chicken and rice. Blend sour cream and soup. Combine with chicken mixture. Arrange mushrooms on top. Bake covered at 350° for 1 hour. Serves 10 to 12.

Mrs. Thomas Schwartz (Ellana)

Savory Chicken Casserole

6 chicken breasts	1 can (6 ounces) mushrooms,
1 cup chopped green pepper	sliced
1 cup chopped onion	1 jar (7½ ounces) stuffed
1 cup chopped celery	olives, sliced
½ cup butter	1 package (12 ounces) green
½ pound Velveeta cheese	noodles
1 can cream of mushroom	
soup	

Boil chicken in salted water; drain and reserve chicken stock. Bone and dice chicken. Sauté green pepper, onion, and celery in butter. Add Velveeta and melt. Blend in soup, mushrooms and olives. Add chicken and 1 cup of reserved stock. Boil noodles in remaining stock until done; add to chicken mixture. Bake at 350° for 30 minutes in a large casserole dish. Serves 8 to 10.

Mrs. Wayne Davison (Cindi)

Chicken Sauterne

1 small onion, finely chopped	1 cup chicken stock
6 ounces fresh mushrooms, sliced	½ teaspoon Worcestershire sauce
6 tablespoons butter	¼ teaspoon Tabasco
2 tablespoons flour	1 cup half and half cream
1 teaspoon salt	1 package (10 ounces) frozen peas and onions, thawed
½ teaspoon Beau Monde spice	
½ teaspoon paprika	2 cups cooked chicken, diced
½ teaspoon oregano	2 cups cooked rice
½ cup sauterne wine	

Sauté onions and mushrooms in butter. Add flour, salt, Beau Monde, paprika, and oregano; cook for about 2 minutes. Slowly add wine, chicken stock, Worcestershire sauce, and Tabasco, stirring over heat until thickened. Cool slightly; stir in cream, peas and onions, and chicken. Reheat, but do not boil. Serve over hot fluffy rice. Serves 6 to 8.

Mrs. Dudley Baker (Kathy)

Jalapeño Chicken

2 cups chopped onions	4 green onions, tops only
2 tablespoons butter	½ teaspoon salt
1 package (10 ounces) frozen chopped spinach, cooked and drained	1 large package (12 ounces) Doritos
6 jalapeño peppers	4 to 6 cups chopped, cooked chicken
1 pint sour cream	2 cups grated Monterey Jack cheese
2 cans cream of chicken soup	

Sauté onions in butter; blend in spinach, jalapeños, sour cream, soup, onion tops and salt. In a large pyrex pan alternate layers of Doritos, chicken, spinach mixture and cheese. Layer again ending with cheese. Bake at 350° for 30 to 40 minutes. Serves 10 to 12.

Mrs. Jim Schultz (Mary Kay)

Creamy Chicken Tacos

1   can (4 ounces) chopped
    green chilies
1   large onion, chopped
3   tablespoons butter
2   tablespoons flour
2   cups tomato juice

2   cups grated Cheddar cheese
2   cups half and half cream
1   chicken, cooked and boned
12 tortillas
Oil

Sauté green chilies and onion in butter. Add flour and tomato juice; simmer a few minutes. Cool. Melt cheese with cream in double boiler. Dice chicken and add to tomato mixture; gradually add cream mixture. Slightly fry tortillas in hot oil. Place alternate layers of tortillas and chicken mixture in an oblong casserole. Bake at 350° for 30 to 40 minutes or until thoroughly heated. Serves 4 to 6.

Mrs. Jimmy Hall (Sue)

Chicken Enchiladas

12 corn tortillas
½   cup oil
2   packages (8 ounces each)
    Monterey Jack cheese
1   chicken, cooked and diced
¾   cup chopped onion

¼   cup butter
¼   cup flour
2   cups chicken broth
1   cup sour cream
1   can (4 ounces) jalapeños or
    green chilies, sliced

Spicy Sauce:
1   finely chopped tomato
½   cup chopped onion
2   jalapeños, chopped

¼   cup tomato juice
½   teaspoon salt

Dip tortillas in hot oil until soft. Place 2 tablespoons cheese, 1½ tablespoons chicken, and 1 tablespoon onion in each tortilla; roll up. Place seam side down in a 9x13 inch casserole. Melt butter in saucepan; blend flour. Add broth; cook, stirring constantly until mixture thickens and bubbles. Stir in sour cream and peppers. Cook until heated through, but do not boil. Pour over tortillas. Bake at 350° for 30 minutes. Sprinkle remaining cheese on top and cook 5 more minutes or until cheese melts. Mix spicy sauce ingredients and serve on top of the enchiladas. Serves 6.

Mrs. Don Panter (Carolyn)

Brunswick Stew

1 fryer (2 to 3 pounds), cut into serving pieces
1 teaspoon salt
1 teaspoon paprika
¼ cup butter
2 medium onions, sliced
2 green peppers, diced
1 pound ham or bacon, cut in bite size pieces, optional
2 to 3 cups water
2 cups canned tomatoes, undrained
2 tablespoons chopped parsley
½ teaspoon Tabasco
½ teaspoon salt
1 teaspoon Worcestershire sauce
2 cups canned or frozen corn
1 package (10 ounces) frozen lima beans
2 cups okra, fresh or frozen, optional
1 cup chopped mushrooms, optional
3 tablespoons flour
¼ cup cold water

Sprinkle chicken with 1 teaspoon salt and paprika. Brown in butter in a Dutch oven; remove and set aside. Brown onion, green pepper, and ham in drippings. Return chicken to pan along with water, tomatoes, parsley, Tabasco, salt and Worcestershire sauce. Bring to boil; cover. Reduce heat and simmer for 30 minutes. Add corn, lima beans, okra and mushrooms; cook 20 minutes more. Blend flour and water, and gradually stir into stew. Cook 10 minutes more. Serves 10 to 12.

Mrs. Denman Smith (Sandra)

Chicken Cacciatore

2 frying chickens, about 2½ pounds each
1 tablespoon salt
1 teaspoon pepper
2 green peppers, cut into ¼ inch strips
½ pound fresh mushrooms, sliced ¼ inch thick
2 cloves garlic
2 bay leaves
½ cup olive oil
1 can (20 ounces) Italian style tomatoes
2 tablespoons sugar
¼ cup Italian red wine

Quarter chicken. Wash and dry; season with salt and pepper. Place skin side down one layer deep in a shallow baking pan which has been coated with olive oil. Top with peppers, mushrooms, garlic and bay leaves. Sprinkle with olive oil. Bake at 450° for 45 minutes or until browned, turning chicken once. Combine tomatoes and sugar. Pour over chicken. Reduce heat to 400°; bake 30 minutes. Add wine and bake 10 minutes more. Serves 8.

Mrs. Larry Hall (Jane)

Paella

1 chicken, cut in serving pieces	1 large green pepper, diced
1 large onion, diced	1 jar (4 ounces) diced pimientos
2 cloves garlic, diced	2 packages (10 ounces each) frozen green peas and onions
¾ cup olive oil	
1 can (28 ounces) tomatoes	
1½ quarts chicken broth	2 cans (14 ounces each) artichokes
1 to 2 bay leaves	
1 tablespoon salt	1 pound cooked Italian or German sausage
2½ to 3 cups uncooked white rice	
½ teaspoon saffron	1 pound shrimp in shells
	1 dozen clams in shells

Fry chicken with onion and garlic in olive oil for about 30 minutes. Add tomatoes and broth; boil for 5 to 10 minutes, mashing large tomatoes. Add bay leaf, salt, rice, saffron and green pepper. Cook, stirring for 2 minutes. Place in a large baking dish and bake at 375° for 15 to 20 minutes; add remaining ingredients. Return to oven and bake another 15 minutes or until rice is tender and has absorbed the moisture. Serves 12 to 15.

Mrs. Dudley Baker (Kathy)

Chicken Caliente

3 pounds chicken breasts, cooked, reserving 1 cup broth	1 can cream of mushroom soup
1 large onion, chopped	1 can (10 ounces) Ro-Tel tomatoes and green chilies, drained and crushed
1 large green pepper, chopped	
2 tablespoons margarine	12 corn tortillas, cut into strips
1 teaspoon chili powder	½ pound Cheddar cheese, grated
Dash garlic salt	
1 can cream of chicken soup	

Bone chicken and cut into bite-size pieces. Sauté onion and green pepper in margarine. Combine chili powder, garlic salt, soups, broth and Ro-Tel. Place ½ of chicken in a large casserole; top with ½ soup mixture, tortilla strips, onion and green pepper, then cheese. Repeat layers. Cook covered at 350° for 30 minutes; then uncover and bake an additional 15 minutes. Serves 8.

Mrs. Jim Schultz (Mary Kay)

Chicken Paprikash

1   roasting chicken, cut up
Salt and pepper
¼   cup butter
Paprika
1   can (14½ ounces) chicken
    broth, undiluted
1   tablespoon paprika
1   jar (1 pound) small white
    onions, or 8 small peeled
    onions

¼   cup flour
¼   cup water
¾   teaspoon salt
1   cup sour cream
1   tablespoon chopped parsley
1   package (10 ounces) egg
    noodles, cooked

Rinse chicken; pat dry. Sprinkle both sides with salt and pepper. Brown chicken in butter in a 4 quart Dutch oven. Remove pieces as they brown. Sprinkle each piece with paprika. Return chicken to pan. Add chicken broth, 1 tablespoon paprika, and onions. Cook covered over low heat until chicken is done; about 30 to 40 minutes turning chicken twice. Remove chicken and onions. Blend flour with water to make a smooth paste. Stir into hot liquid until smooth. Add ¾ teaspoon salt; bring to a boil. Remove from heat. Slowly stir in sour cream. Stir until well blended. Add chicken and onions. Heat through. Serve over hot noodles. Serves 4 to 6.

Mrs. Jim Rado (Vicki)

Oven Baked Chicken with Spicy Sauce

1   cup flour
2   teaspoons salt
¼   teaspoon pepper

2   teaspoons paprika
½   cup butter
1   chicken, cut in pieces

Spicy Sauce:
½   cup sliced onion
1   teaspoon salt
1   tablespoon vinegar
1   tablespoon Worcestershire
    sauce

1   tablespoon sugar
¼   teaspoon chili powder
¼   teaspoon pepper
½   cup catsup
¼   cup water

Mix flour, salt, pepper and paprika in a paper bag. Melt butter in a shallow baking pan. Shake chicken pieces in the bag to coat with flour; place in baking pan and coat with butter. Bake skin side down in a single layer at 400° for 30 minutes. While chicken is baking, simmer all ingredients for spicy sauce 15 minutes. Turn chicken and pour spicy sauce over the pieces; return to oven and continue to bake an additional 30 minutes or until tender. Serves 6.

Mrs. Jerry Hunt (Gail)

Mrs. Lyndon B. Johnson's Recipe for Barbecued Chicken

1   chicken, quartered
Salt and pepper to taste
¼   cup butter
Garlic, to taste
Chopped onion, to taste

¼   cup lemon juice
¼   cup vinegar
¼   cup catsup
¼   cup Worcestershire sauce

Wash and drain chicken. Season with salt and pepper and place in pan large enough that pieces do not overlap. Melt butter in saucepan, add garlic and onion, if desired, and sauté until transparent. Add remaining ingredients and bring to a boil. Broil chicken until golden brown on both sides. Add sauce and cook uncovered in oven for about 1 hour or until nice and tender. Baste often.

LBJ Ranch

Old Fashioned Chicken and Dumplings

4   chicken breasts or 1 whole
    chicken
6   cups water
1   teaspoon salt
1   tablespoon minced onion
1   tablespoon instant chicken
    bouillon

1   tablespoon dried parsley
2   tablespoons margarine
¼   teaspoon celery seed
1   teaspoon pepper
1   cup milk

Dumplings:
2   cups flour
1   teaspoon salt

2   eggs
½   cup milk

In a large pot combine chicken, water, salt and onion, and boil until done. Remove chicken, cool and debone. Cut into bite size pieces. Save broth for cooking.
Mix dumpling ingredients to form a very stiff dough and drop by teaspoons into boiling chicken broth. Add deboned chicken, and remaining ingredients; boil 20 minutes, stirring occasionally. Keep warm until serving. If broth is not thick enough, add flour and water. If broth is too thick, add more milk. Serves 6.

Mrs. Larry Wisian (Kay)

Chicken Crepes

Crepe Batter:

4 eggs
2¼ cups milk
¼ cup melted margarine

¼ teaspoon salt
2 cups flour
Butter

Filling:

1 chicken, cooked, skinned,
  boned and chopped
3 to 4 green chilies, chopped

2 cups grated Swiss cheese
1 cup grated Cheddar cheese

Cream Sauce

2 tablespoons butter
2 tablespoons flour
2 cups chicken stock or broth
1 cup half and half cream

Salt and pepper
Grated onion to taste
Cheddar cheese

To make crepes, combine eggs, milk, margarine, salt and flour in a blender container; blend. Let batter stand overnight in the refrigerator. Lightly grease crepe pan or 6 inch skillet with butter. Put large tablespoon of batter in skillet and roll it evenly around the bottom, pouring any excess back into the batter. Cook over medium heat until set, turning one time. Yields 34 to 36 crepes.

For filling, mix chicken, chopped chilies and cheeses. Place a large tablespoon of mixture on center of each crepe. Fold in sides and roll up to keep filling from leaking. Place seam side down in a lightly greased large casserole.

Make a cream sauce by melting butter and adding flour. Cook until bubbly. Remove from heat and add chicken stock and cream, stirring until smooth. Return to heat and cook until thickened. Season with salt, pepper and onion. Pour sauce over crepes and then sprinkle with cheese. Heat at 325° for 20 minutes or until warm. Serves 12 to 14.

Mrs. Chris Williston (Janice)

For perfect crepes, discard the first crepe. It is used only to absorb excess oil from pan. The crepe filling goes on top of the last side cooked. It is unattractive and should be hidden! Stack crepes between waxed paper. If the crepe batter gets too thick, thin with a small amount of milk.

Grilled Stuffed Bantams

8   chicken breasts or thighs,
    boned

Salt
Monosodium glutamate

Filling:
1   egg, beaten
1   cup packaged herb
    seasoned stuffing
½   can cream of mushroom
    soup
1   can (6½ ounces) crab meat,
    drained, flaked

¼   cup chopped green pepper
1   tablespoon lemon juice
2   teaspoons Worcestershire
    sauce
1   teaspoon prepared mustard
¼   teaspoon salt

Basting Sauce:
½   can cream of mushroom
    soup
¼   cup oil

1   teaspoon Kitchen Bouquet
¼   teaspoon onion juice
Dash of pepper

Sprinkle inside of chicken breasts with salt and monosodium glutamate. Mix filling ingredients together. Top each breast with ⅛ of filling mixture. Skewer each breast closed. Combine basting sauce ingredients. Broil chicken over hot coals 30 minutes or until tender, turning frequently. During last 15 minutes brush with basting sauce. Serves 8.

Mrs. Clark Rector (Sue)

Lemon Honey Chicken

1   fryer (3 pounds), cut in
    pieces
Salt and pepper
¼   cup oil
¼   cup honey

1   egg yolk, slightly beaten
2   tablespoons lemon juice
2   tablespoons soy sauce
¼   teaspoon nutmeg
1   teaspoon paprika

Season chicken with salt and pepper; place in a baking dish. Combine remaining ingredients and mix until well blended. Pour over chicken and bake uncovered at 350° for 1 hour or until tender. Turn and baste chicken while baking. Serves 4 to 6.

Mrs. David Armour (Betsy)

Deviled Chicken

12 chicken legs and thighs
12 chicken wings
3   cups catsup
¾   cup prepared mustard

⅓   cup horseradish
1   tablespoon Worcestershire
    sauce
4   cloves garlic, crushed

Arrange chicken on 2 shallow foil lined pans. Combine remaining ingredients; brush generously over chicken. Bake at 350° for 30 minutes. Turn chicken and brush with sauce; bake 15 minutes more. Turn chicken again; brush once more with sauce and bake a final 15 minutes. Serves 20.

Mrs. Clark Rector (Sue)

Parmesan Chicken

1   fryer, skinned and cut in
    pieces
1   stick melted butter
2   cups cracker crumbs
⅓   cup grated Romano cheese

½   cup grated Parmesan cheese
¼   cup chopped parsley
1   teaspoon garlic salt
Salt and pepper to taste

Dip chicken pieces in butter, then in a mixture of remaining ingredients. Place chicken in a large baking pan and bake uncovered at 350° for 1 hour. Serves 4 to 6.

Mrs. Norman Snider (Natalie)

Chicken Breasts Supreme

2   tablespoons butter, divided
Salt and pepper
4   chicken breasts, skinned
½   pint whipping cream

1   tablespoon cornstarch
⅓ to ½ cup white wine or
sherry
1   cup grated Swiss cheese

Melt 1 tablespoon butter in a large skillet with salt and pepper. Add chicken breasts and brown lightly. Remove to a casserole. In same skillet add another tablespoon of butter, whipping cream, and cornstarch. Cook slowly and stir; add white wine. When sauce thickens, pour over the chicken. Cover generously with grated cheese. Bake covered at 350° for 1 hour. Remove top the last few minutes so the cheese will brown. Serves 4.

Mrs. Joe Bowles (Mary)

Sweet and Sour Barbecued Chicken

1 jar (8 ounces) apricot preserves	1 bottle (8 ounces) Russian dressing
1 envelope dry onion soup mix	2 broiler chickens, quartered

Mix together sauce ingredients. Place chicken in large baking pan. Spoon sauce over chicken and bake at 350° for 1½ hours. Serves 8.

Mrs. Jerry Hunt (Gail)

Baked Cornish Hens

8 Cornish hens	¼ cup Kitchen Bouquet
Salt and pepper	1 jar (8 ounces) orange marmalade
8 whole medium onions	
¾ cup butter	

Clean and dry hens. Season inside and out with salt and pepper; refrigerate overnight. When ready to bake, insert a whole onion in cavity of each hen and place in open roasting pan. Melt butter; add Kitchen Bouquet and orange marmalade until blended. Spoon over hens and bake at 350° until hens are tender, about 1½ hours, basting often. If sauce cooks down before hens are done, add a little hot water to the pan to assure having some sauce. If hens appear to be drying out during the baking, cover loosely with foil. Yields 8 servings.

S. D. Jackman, Jr.

Picnic Cornish Hens

Cornish hens	Minced shallots
Salt and pepper	Butter
Dijon mustard	White wine
White bread crumbs	

Rub each bird with salt and pepper and one tablespoon mustard. Sprinkle with bread crumbs. Place in a square of foil and fold up sides. Add 1 teaspoon minced shallots, 1 tablespoon butter and 3 tablespoons wine to each package. Seal foil over tightly. Bake at 400° for 45 minutes. Open foil; baste hen, and bake 15 minutes more until browned. Reseal foil and carry to picnic. Good served cold. If serving at home, stuff cavity with fresh parsley and serve juices separately. Servings equal number of hens prepared.

Mrs. Leo Mueller (Nancy)

Elegant Campfire Chicken

3   large chicken breasts, split,
    skinned and boned
Salt to taste
Lemon pepper to taste
2   tomatoes, cut in wedges
½   cup sliced ripe olives
½   cup chopped onion
⅓   cup sherry

1½ tablespoons lemon juice
1   teaspoon Beau Monde
¼   teaspoon dried basil
½   teaspoon dried marjoram
2   avocados, sliced
6 to 8 ounces sliced Monterey
Jack cheese

Sprinkle chicken breasts with salt and pepper. Place each breast half on an 18x12 inch sheet of heavy duty foil. Arrange tomato wedges on top each breast. Sprinkle with olives and onions. Combine sherry, lemon juice, and spices, and drizzle over top of chicken. Seal completely. Cook over medium coals until chicken is tender, about 45 minutes. Do not turn. Open packages and add avocado and cheese. Reseal until cheese melts. Serves 6.

Mrs. Dudley Baker (Kathy)

Chicken Macadamia

6   whole chicken breasts,
    boned
Peanut oil for deep frying

Macadamia nuts for garnish
Fried Rice

Batter:
2   eggs
½   cup flour
¼   cup cornstarch
½   cup cold water
1   inch minced ginger
1   whole onion, grated

½   teaspoon black pepper
2   tablespoons peanut oil
2   tablespoons brandy
2   tablespoons soy sauce
Salt to taste

Sweet Sour Sauce:
4   tablespoons brown sugar
2   tablespoons soy sauce
2   tablespoons cornstarch

¼   cup vinegar
¼   cup cold water

Cut each chicken breast into six pieces. Mix batter ingredients thoroughly in a blender. Marinate chicken in batter for at least 20 minutes. Fry in peanut oil in a deep fat fryer at 350° for 8 to 10 minutes or until done. Simmer sweet and sour sauce over low heat for 15 minutes. Serve cooked chicken on a bed of fried rice, with plenty of sauce and a garnish of shaved and whole macadamia nuts. Serves 8 to 10. *This recipe comes from the Cannon Club in Honolulu.*

Mrs. Dudley Baker (Kathy)

Chicken Beverly

1   fryer, about 3 pounds
¾ cup soy sauce
4   tablespoons honey
1   large clove garlic, minced

1   can (8 ounces) crushed
    pineapple
Wild rice or rice pilaf for serving

Cut chicken into serving pieces. Mix remaining ingredients and marinate chicken overnight in a covered dish. Remove from refrigerator 2 hours before cooking. Grill chicken 30 to 45 minutes or until done. Serve with wild rice or rice pilaf. Serves 4.

Mrs. Marcus Bone (Beverly)

Chinese Chicken

8   boned chicken breasts
¾ cup white wine or dry sherry
2   tablespoons soy sauce
½ cup flour
¼ cup oil
1   teaspoon ginger
½ teaspoon salt
1   large green pepper, chopped

¼ cup chopped green onion
¼ pound fresh mushrooms,
    sliced
¼ cup sliced almonds
1   can (8 ounces) sliced water
    chestnuts
Hot rice or fried rice

Cut breasts into bite size pieces. Marinate in wine and soy sauce for 1½ hours. Lightly coat chicken in flour and brown. Set aside. Place oil, ginger and salt in skillet or wok; stir fry green pepper, onions and mushrooms. When just tender, add chicken, almonds and water chestnuts. Stir fry until well mixed. Serve with rice or fried rice. Serves 6 to 8.

Mrs. Sam White (Jane)

Lemon Chicken Supreme

3   whole chicken breasts, split
    and boned
¼ cup flour
½ teaspoon salt
⅛ teaspoon pepper

3   tablespoons margarine
1   cup hot water
1   chicken bouillon cube
Juice of ½ lemon

Pound breasts until about ¼ inch thick. Combine flour, salt and pepper; coat chicken. Save remaining flour. Heat margarine in a skillet and brown breasts on both sides, adding more margarine if necessary. Remove chicken from skillet. Reduce heat to low; add remaining flour, scraping the skillet. Add water, bouillon cube and lemon juice. Return chicken to pan; cover and simmer 5 minutes. Serves 4 to 6. *It is easier to bone chicken if the meat is partially frozen.*

Mrs. Jim Schultz (Mary Kay)

Lemon and Mushroom Turkey Breast

½ turkey breast, 2 to 3 pounds
2 tablespoons flour
Salt and pepper
2 tablespoons butter
1 tablespoon oil

8 ounces fresh mushrooms, chopped
1 bunch green onions, chopped
Juice of 1 lemon

Cut turkey breast across grain into ½ inch slices. Put between sheets of wax paper and pound smooth and flat (¼ inch or less). Dust each slice with flour, salt and pepper. Melt butter and oil in heavy skillet until golden. Add turkey, mushrooms, onions, and ½ of the lemon juice. Cook turkey 3 minutes on one side; push vegetables aside and turn turkey. Add remaining lemon juice; cover and cook 2 to 3 more minutes until just done. Remove meat to serving platter, stir fry vegetables 1 or 2 minutes longer and spoon over turkey. Serve immediately. Serves 4 to 6. *This is an elegant but simple dish for dinner parties. This recipe is also good with boned chicken breasts or veal.*

Mrs. Don Bradford (Melinda)

Moussaka

1 large eggplant, peeled and sliced in ¼ inch slices
Salt
½ cup onion
1 pound lean ground beef
½ cup dry white wine
¼ cup tomato sauce
2 tablespoons water
1 tablespoon dried parsley flakes
½ teaspoon paprika
¼ teaspoon pepper

1 teaspoon salt
1½ to 2 cups dried bread crumbs, divided
1 can (16 ounces) tomatoes, diced, undrained
2 fresh tomatoes, peeled and sliced
1 cup plain yogurt
2 egg yolks
¼ cup flour
1 cup grated Cheddar cheese

Salt eggplant and set aside for 1 hour. In heavy frying pan, sauté onion and ground beef. Mix wine, tomato sauce, water, parsley flakes, paprika, pepper and salt. Pour over meat in pan and simmer for 30 minutes. Dredge eggplant slices in flour and brown in hot oil. Butter a long deep casserole and coat dish with dried bread crumbs, reserving ¾ cup for topping. Alternate eggplant slices and meat in dish. (Stop here if you want to freeze this dish.) Put tomatoes over top of casserole. By hand, beat together yogurt, egg yolks and ¼ cup flour. Pour over casserole. Sprinkle with grated cheese and reserved bread crumbs. Bake at 350° for 45 minutes. Serves 6 to 8.

Mrs. Rush McGinty (Carol)

Round Steak Parmesan

1 pound round steak or veal	1 onion, minced
Salt and pepper	1 cup tomato paste
1/3 cup Parmesan cheese	2 cups hot water
1/3 cup dry bread crumbs	1/2 teaspoon marjoram
1 egg, beaten	Sliced Mozzarella cheese,
1/4 cup oil	(10 ounces)
2 tablespoons butter	

Cut meat into serving pieces; salt and pepper. Combine Parmesan cheese and bread crumbs. Dip meat into egg, and then coat with cheese mixture. Heat oil in a skillet and fry meat pieces until brown. In another pan, fry onion in butter until soft; add remaining ingredients, except Mozzarella cheese. Boil a few minutes. In a casserole layer one half of sauce with meat; then add all the Mozzarella cheese. Top with rest of sauce and bake uncovered at 350° for 30 minutes. Serves 6.

Mrs. Larry Hall (Jane)

Lazy Lasagne

8 to 10 lasagne noodles	1 tablespoon oregano
2 pounds ground meat	1 tablespoon basil or tarragon
1 onion, diced	2 teaspoons salt
1 clove garlic, diced	1/2 pound American cheese,
3 tablespoons olive oil	grated
1/2 cup chopped green pepper	1/2 pound Mozzarella cheese,
1 can (4 ounces) mushrooms	grated
1 can (20 ounces) tomatoes	2 cartons (8 ounces each)
1 can (8 ounces) tomato	sour cream
sauce	Parmesan cheese
1 tablespoon sugar	

Rinse lasagne noodles under warm water until completely soft. Do not cook. Sauté meat, onion, garlic and green pepper until done. Combine mushrooms, tomatoes, sauce, sugar and spices; add to meat mixture. Simmer 30 minutes or until sauce is thickened. In a large casserole or lasagne pan, make 2 layers, starting with noodles, meat sauce, cheeses and sour cream. Top with Parmesan cheese. Bake at 375° for 30 minutes. Let stand 10 minutes. Serves 8 to 10.

Mrs. Jette Campbell (Sally)

Lasagne

Marinara Sauce:

½   cup olive oil
4   cups chopped onion
1   cup sliced carrots
3   cloves garlic, finely minced
8   cups canned Italian
    tomatoes

Salt and pepper
1   tablespoon parsley, minced
½   cup butter
1½ teaspoons oregano
2   tablespoons fresh basil or 2
    teaspoons dried

Heat oil; add onions, carrots and garlic. Cook until golden brown. Strain tomatoes and add to the vegetables. Season with salt and pepper. Partially cover skillet and simmer 15 minutes. Purée entire mixture in a blender; return to skillet and simmer 30 minutes more. Stir occasionally.

Meat Sauce:

1   pound sweet Italian sausage
1   pound ground chuck
Salt and pepper

1½ pounds mushrooms, sliced
1   teaspoon garlic, chopped
6   cups Marinara sauce

Cook sausage in a skillet over medium heat until brown. Remove and set aside. Pour off fat; add ground chuck with salt and pepper. Cook, breaking up lumps. Add mushrooms and garlic. Stir until brown. Skin sausages and slice thin. Add to ground meat along with 6 cups Marinara sauce. Partially cover and simmer 45 minutes, stirring occasionally.

White Sauce:

3   tablespoons butter
3   tablespoons flour
1   cup milk

1¼ cups whipping cream
Salt and pepper
¼   teaspoon nutmeg

In a saucepan over low heat, melt butter; stir in flour until blended. Gradually stir in milk until thickened. Add cream and seasonings. Set aside.

1   package (1 pound) lasagne
    noodles
½   pound Mozzarella cheese,
    cubed

½   pound Parmesan cheese,
    grated
6   tablespoons butter, melted,
    divided

Cook lasagne al dente. Drain half of the water from pot and fill with cool water until pasta is cool enough to handle; dry on paper towels. Spoon a layer of meat sauce to cover the bottom of a large lasagne pan. Arrange remaining layers as follows: 3 to 4 tablespoons white sauce, layer of pasta, layer of meat sauce, layer of white sauce, layer of Mozzarella cubes, layer of Parmesan, and 2 tablespoons butter. Repeat these layers. Bake at 375° for 45 minutes. Let stand 10 minutes before cutting. Serves 12. To prepare lasagne with ricotta, combine 1 pound ricotta cheese, 3 eggs, 1 cup freshly grated Parmesan cheese, 2 tablespoons chopped parsley, salt and pepper. Spread this mixture between the layers of meat sauce and white sauce.

Mrs. Larry Hall (Jane)

Zucchini Italian Style

6	tablespoons butter	2	cans (20 ounces each) tomatoes
4	tablespoons flour	1	green pepper, chopped in small squares
1	teaspoon basil		
2	bay leaves	4	green onions, minced with tops
1	clove garlic, finely chopped		
Salt and coarse ground pepper to taste		12	small zucchini
3	pounds ground round		

Melt butter in skillet; blend in flour, seasonings, ground round, tomatoes, green pepper and green onions. Cook slowly for 10 to 20 minutes. Slice the zucchini thin, but do not peel or parboil. Arrange zucchini in buttered casserole or baking dish, and top with meat sauce. Bake at 350° for 2 hours. Serves 8.

Mrs. Jim Kimbell (Ellen)

Cheese Stuffed Meatloaf

2	pounds ground beef	¼	teaspoon pepper
2	eggs	1	large onion, minced
½	cup bread crumbs	Butter	
1	cup tomato juice	6	slices cooked ham
½	teaspoon salt	Mozzarella cheese, grated	
1	teaspoon oregano		

Combine beef, eggs, bread crumbs, tomato juice, salt, oregano, and pepper. Sauté onion in a little butter until golden brown. Add onion to meat mixture and mix well. Turn meat out on a sheet of foil or wax paper. Flatten meat into oblong shape about 1 inch thick. Place ham on meat, keeping it about 1 inch from edge. Sprinkle Mozzarella cheese on ham. Use the foil to roll meat as for jelly roll. Press meat on sides and top to seal all openings. Turn loaf from foil into a greased loaf pan. Bake at 325° for 60 to 75 minutes. Serves 6 to 8.

Mrs. Art DeFelice (Connie)

Beef Tips Burgundy

3 tablespoons butter, divided
1½ pounds fresh mushrooms, sliced
1 tablespoon oil
3 pounds sirloin steak, cut into 1 inch cubes
¾ cup beef bouillon
¾ cup burgundy wine
2 tablespoons soy sauce
1 clove garlic, minced
½ onion, grated
2 tablespoons cornstarch
⅓ cup beef bouillon
½ can cream of mushroom soup
Salt, optional
Cooked noodles or rice

Heat 1½ tablespoons butter in skillet. Add mushrooms and cook until brown. Put into a deep casserole. Add remaining butter and oil to skillet and heat. Brown meat cubes; add to the mushrooms. Stir into skillet the ¾ cup bouillon, wine, soy sauce, garlic and onion. Heat thoroughly. Blend cornstarch with ⅓ cup bouillon. Add to skillet, stirring constantly, and cook until mixture thickens. Pour into casserole; cover and cook at 275° for 1 hour. Stir in the mushroom soup until smooth. Taste for salt as needed. Serve over noodles or rice. Serves 8.

Mrs. Ron Garrick (Bonnie)

Beef Stroganoff

4 tablespoons flour, divided
½ teaspoon salt
1 pound sirloin steak, cut into strips
4 tablespoons butter, divided
1 cup mushrooms, thinly sliced
½ cup chopped onion
1 clove garlic, chopped
1 tablespoon tomato paste
1¼ cups beef bouillon
1 cup sour cream
2 tablespoons sherry
Hot cooked rice or noodles

Dust meat with 1 tablespoon flour and salt. Brown quickly in 2 tablespoons butter. Add mushrooms, onion and garlic, and cook until onions are barely tender. Remove meat; add 3 tablespoons flour, 2 tablespoons butter, and tomato paste. Slowly stir in beef bouillon. Cook until thickened; add meat, sour cream, and sherry. Heat but do not boil. Serve over rice or noodles. Serves 4 to 6.

Mrs. Jack Dempsey (Estelle)

Veal and Sour Cream

½ to 1 pound veal, cut in
serving pieces
6 green onions, chopped
1 clove garlic, chopped

2 tablespoons oil
1 can beef consommé
½ cup sour cream
Hot cooked brown rice

Sauté lightly floured veal, onion and garlic in hot oil. Add consommé and simmer covered for 20 minutes. Add sour cream and simmer another 10 minutes. Serve with brown rice. Serves 4. *For a little variation try substituting dry white wine for half of the consommé.*

Mrs. Jerry Dow (Annette)

Liver Louisianne

6 slices bacon, cut in 1 inch
pieces
2 pounds liver, sliced ½ inch
thick
¼ cup flour
1½ teaspoons salt

¼ teaspoon chili powder
⅛ teaspoon cayenne pepper
⅛ teaspoon garlic salt
1 can (16 ounces) tomatoes
½ pound onion, sliced
⅓ cup diced green pepper

Cook bacon until crisp. Combine flour and salt. Dredge liver and brown lightly on each side in bacon drippings. Pour off drippings. Sprinkle spices over liver; add tomatoes, onion, and green pepper. Cover tightly and cook slowly for 20 minutes. Remove liver to warm platter and sprinkle bacon on top. Thicken vegetable mixture with flour if desired. Serves 6 to 8.

S. D. Jackman, Jr.

Hungarian Liver

1 pound calves liver
1 medium onion, chopped
Oil to cover bottom of skillet
Salt and pepper to taste

Paprika to taste
½ cup water
1 tablespoon flour
1 tablespoon water

Slice liver into strips ½ inch wide. Sauté onion in oil until transparent. Add liver, season with salt and pepper and sprinkle generously with paprika. Cook 5 minutes. Add water and bring to a boil. Add flour mixed with remaining water and simmer until liver is done and gravy is thickened, about 20 minutes. Serves 3 to 4. *This traditional dish is served with cubed potatoes that have been boiled and seasoned with salt, pepper, butter, and parsley.*

Jim Rado

Peppered Rib Eye Steak

1	rib eye (6 to 8 pounds), fat removed	1	onion, chopped
2	tablespoons oil	1	carrot, sliced
Salt		1	rib celery, chopped
¼ to ½ can cracked or fresh ground pepper		½	cup red burgundy wine
		1	can beef consommé

Rub meat with oil, salt, and pepper. The amount depends on taste. Spread onion, carrot and celery in a shallow pan. Place meat on top and roast uncovered at 350° for 15 minutes for each pound. Baste frequently with a mixture of wine and consommé. Serves 12 to 14.

Mrs. Randy Hagan (Robin)

Beef Bordelaise

5 to 6 pound rolled rib, rib eye, or rump roast		4 to 5	sprigs parsley
2	cups sliced onion	1	teaspoon salt
½	cup sliced shallots	2	cups dry red wine
2	cloves garlic, crushed	5	tablespoons melted butter, divided
1	bay leaf		
½	teaspoon thyme, crumbled	2	cans (14½ ounces each) beef broth
1	teaspoon whole peppercorns	1	tablespoon flour

Combine meat and vegetables in large casserole. Mix herbs, salt and wine together. Pour over meat and vegetables; cover and refrigerate 8 to 12 hours, turning meat occasionally. Heat oven to 475°. Remove meat from marinade and dry. Strain marinade; reserve liquid and vegetables. Place meat on rack in shallow pan. Roast at 475° for 30 minutes, basting occasionally with 4 tablespoons butter. Reduce heat to 400°; add reserved vegetables to pan and roast 40 to 45 minutes, basting occasionally. (Cook about 12 minutes per pound for a rare roast.) Let meat stand 15 minutes before carving. Heat pan drippings to boiling; cook 1 minute, skimming off fat. Add reserved marinade, and boil until only a few tablespoons are left. Add beef broth. Blend 1 tablespoon butter and flour; add to pan. Cook, stirring constantly until sauce is thick and smooth. Taste for seasoning. Serves 8 to 10.

Mrs. Larry Hall (Jane)

LBJ's Pedernales River Chili

4 pounds chili meat*
1 large onion, chopped
2 cloves garlic
1 teaspoon oregano, ground
1 teaspoon comino seed
6 teaspoons chili powder (or more if needed)

1½ cups canned whole tomatoes
2 to 6 generous dashes liquid hot sauce
Salt to taste
2 cups hot water

Place meat, onion, and garlic in large heavy fry pan or Dutch oven. Cook until light-colored. Add oregano, comino seed, chili powder, tomatoes, hot pepper sauce, salt and hot water. Bring to boil, lower heat and simmer about 1 hour. Skim off fat during cooking. *Chili meat is coarsely ground round steak or well-trimmed chuck. If specially ground, ask butcher to use ¾ inch plate for coarse grind.

Mrs. Lyndon B. Johnson

Fireside Chili

2 pounds chili meat
1 pound ground beef
2 tablespoons bacon drippings
1 pint hot water
1 can (10½ ounces) tomato purée
1 teaspoon Tabasco
1 chili pepper pod or more to taste

2 large onions, finely chopped
2 cloves garlic, finely chopped
3 heaping tablespoons chili powder
1 tablespoon oregano
1 tablespoon cumin
1 teaspoon paprika
1 teaspoon ground mustard
¼ teaspoon cayenne pepper
1 teaspoon salt

Brown meats; add bacon drippings and cook 5 minutes. Add hot water, tomato purée, Tabasco, pepper, onion and garlic; simmer 30 minutes. Add rest of the ingredients and simmer slowly for 1 to 2 hours. *Serve with crackers, raw onion, grated sharp Cheddar cheese and plenty of ice cold Texas beer.* Serves 6 to 8.

Mrs. Lawrence Christian (Joyce)

Chili—a word that makes your eyes water and your tastebuds tingle! It's the survival kit of the West, wherever beef, Mexican chilies and sometimes a few dried beans could be found. It's been said that villains would plan their escapades for towns that claimed a good "jailhouse chili." Will Rogers titled it a "bowl of blessedness."

San Antonio Chili

3 pounds coarsely ground meat	½ tablespoon cayenne pepper
6 tablespoons chili powder	2 large cloves garlic, minced
1 tablespoon oregano	1 teaspoon Tabasco
1 tablespoon cumin	1½ quarts water
1 tablespoon salt	¼ cup white corn meal

In Dutch oven, brown ground meat; drain. Add seasonings and water; heat to boil. Reduce heat, cover and simmer for 1 hour and 30 minutes. Skim off fat. Stir in corn meal and simmer uncovered for 30 minutes. Stir occasionally. Serves 8. *I usually use part ground beef, pork and venison, but all beef is almost as good.*

Mrs. Jim Rado (Vicki)

From Mexico, Texas gained independence and chili con carne! A favorite with most Texans, this spicy, tantalizing dish was served first in the border towns and brought home to the ranch house by satisfied cowboys.

Gourmet Chili Con Carne

Oil	3 teaspoons oregano
2 medium onions, finely chopped	2 pounds ground beef
1 cup finely chopped green and red peppers	1 tablespoon salt
6 cloves garlic, pressed	½ teaspoon black pepper
4 tablespoons chili powder	3½ to 4 cups tomatoes or 1 can (2 pounds), undrained
2 teaspoons ground cumin	2 cans (1 pound each) red kidney beans, undrained

Heat oil in a 4 or 5 quart pot. Sauté onion until clear; add peppers and garlic, and sauté until limp. Add chili powder, cumin, oregano, ground beef, salt and pepper. Cook slowly, stirring often until meat is brown and broken apart. Add tomatoes and kidney beans including liquid. Stir well to combine ingredients. Cover; simmer slowly at least 1 hour, preferably 2 to 3 hours. Taste and adjust seasoning, if necessary. Stir often so as not to burn. Serves 6 to 8.

Mrs. Daniel O'Donnell (Sharon)

Enchilada Casserole

2	pounds ground meat	1	can golden mushroom soup
1	large onion, chopped	1	carton (8 ounces) sour
1	package (10 ounces) frozen		cream
	chopped spinach, optional	¼	cup milk
1	can (16 ounces) tomatoes	¼	teaspoon garlic powder
1	can (10 ounces) Ro-Tel	16 to 20 corn tortillas	
	tomatoes and green chilies	1	can (4 ounces) chopped
1	teaspoon salt		green chilies
½	teaspoon pepper	½	pound Cheddar cheese,
1	can cream of mushroom		grated
	soup		

Cook and drain meat. In separate skillet, cook onion until transparent and add to meat. Cook and drain spinach. Mix with tomatoes, Ro-Tel, salt and pepper. Combine with meat and simmer until thickened. Mix soups, sour cream, milk and garlic powder. Place tortillas on the bottom and sides of a 3 quart casserole. Spoon the meat mixture into the casserole. Scatter green chilies on top. Next, layer some grated cheese. Place a layer of tortillas on the cheese and cover with soup mixture. Sprinkle with more cheese. Bake at 350° for about 35 to 40 minutes. Serves 8 to 10. This is best if made ahead of time and refrigerated or frozen.

Mrs. Jimmy Hall (Sue)

Beef and Chilies Enchiladas

1	small onion, chopped	½	pound Velveeta cheese
1	pound lean ground beef	1	can (4 ounces) chopped
½	pound Cheddar cheese,		green chilies
	grated	1	jar (2 ounces) diced
1	can cream of chicken soup		pimientos
1	can (5.33 ounces)	1	dozen corn tortillas
	evaporated milk		

Brown onion and meat in a large skillet; drain fat. Add grated Cheddar cheese. Heat soup, milk and Velveeta cheese until cheese melts. Add chilies and pimientos. Set aside. Steam tortillas a few at a time in a colander over boiling water. Fill tortillas with meat mixture; roll and place in an oblong casserole. Pour cheese mixture on top. Cover and bake at 350° for 30 minutes. Serves 4 to 6.

Jean Rogers Carney

Enchilada Squares

1 pound ground beef	1 envelope enchilada sauce
¼ cup chopped onion	mix
4 eggs	⅓ cup pitted ripe olives
1 can (5.33 ounces)	2 cups corn chips
evaporated milk	1 cup shredded Cheddar
1 can (8 ounces) tomato	cheese
sauce	

Cook beef and onion in skillet until beef is brown and onion is tender. Drain off excess fat. Spread beef in bottom of an oblong baking dish. Beat together eggs, milk, tomato sauce, and enchilada sauce mix. Pour over meat layer. Sprinkle with olives; top with corn chips. Bake uncovered at 350° for 20 to 25 minutes or until firm in center. Sprinkle with cheese and return to oven until cheese has melted. Serves 4 to 6.

Mrs. Larry Strickland (Linda)

Dorito Delight

1 pound ground meat	1 can (4 ounces) chopped
1 medium onion, chopped	green chilies
Salt and pepper to taste	1 package (8 ounces) Doritos
1 can cream of mushroom	½ pound American cheese,
soup	grated
1 can cream of chicken soup	
1 can (5.33 ounces)	
evaporated milk	

Brown ground meat, onion, salt and pepper. Add and heat the soups, milk and chilies. Spread Doritos in the bottom of a 9x13 inch pan. Put meat mixture over Doritos and top with grated cheese. Bake at 350° for 20 minutes. Serves 8.

Mrs. Leo Mueller (Nancy)

 Beer and Mexican food naturally go together. The Mexican way to drink beer is to squeeze lime juice on top of the open can and sprinkle with salt. Sip and enjoy!

Tostada Granadas

1 recipe Taco Filling, recipe
   follows
1 can (15 ounces) refried
   beans
¼ teaspoon garlic powder
½ teaspoon cumin seed
1 tablespoon bacon drippings
8 large, flat chalupa or
   tostada shells

1½ cups shredded lettuce
1   cup diced tomatoes
1½ cups grated Cheddar cheese
¾ cup sour cream
Sliced avocados for topping,
   optional
Picante sauce

Season refried beans with garlic powder, salt, cumin, and bacon drippings. Heat slowly. Heat taco shells at 250° for 10 minutes. Spread each with beans and taco filling, about ½ cup each. Cover with lettuce, tomatoes, grated cheese and a dollop of sour cream. Serve with picante sauce. Serves 6 to 8.

Taco Filling:
2 pounds ground beef
1 teaspoon garlic powder
2 teaspoons cumin seed
2 teaspoons seasoned
   chicken base

1 teaspoon pepper
1 can (8 ounces) tomato
   sauce
⅓ cup chopped onion
⅓ cup chopped green pepper

Combine all ingredients and simmer slowly for 1 hour.

Mrs. Jim Schultz (Mary Kay)

Tacos

1 pound lean ground beef
1 medium onion, chopped
1 can (8 ounces) tomato
   sauce
1½ teaspoons chili powder
Salt and pepper to taste

Garlic powder to taste
8 crispy taco shells
2 tomatoes, diced
½ head lettuce, shredded
2 cups grated Cheddar cheese
Picante sauce

Brown ground beef and onion in skillet. Drain and add tomato sauce, chili powder, salt, pepper and garlic powder. Simmer 10 minutes. Warm taco shells. To prepare tacos, put meat in shell and top with tomatoes, lettuce, and cheese. Add picante sauce for extra zing. Serves 4 to 6. *For soft tacos, substitute warm flour tortillas and wrap around filling.*

Mrs. Jim Schultz (Mary Kay)

Carne Guisada

1 pound sirloin in strips or chunks	1 cup water
¼ cup oil	1 hot pepper, jalapeño or serrano, chopped
1 onion, chopped	2 tablespoons cumin
2 tomatoes, chopped	8 flour tortillas
2 tablespoons flour	

Brown meat in oil. Add onions and sauté; add tomatoes. Mix flour with water and add to tomatoes. Add chopped pepper and cumin. Simmer until meat is tender and sauce begins to thicken. Heat tortillas; put meat mixture in tortilla. Roll and serve. Serves 4.

Mrs. Bill Butler (Stephanie)

Fajitas

1½ pounds round or skirt steak	Pepper
Worcestershire sauce	Flour tortillas
Garlic salt	

Trim excess fat and gristle from meat. Tenderize with a mallet. Cut into long strips 1½ inches wide by 6 inches long. Marinate with the Worcestershire sauce, garlic salt and pepper for 6 hours or overnight in the refrigerator. Grill over charcoal, 5 minutes on each side. Place in an attractive covered dish, along with any juices from cooking. In separate bowls, provide an array of garnishes such as chopped tomatoes, chopped green onions, sliced avocado and refried beans. To serve place meat and garnishes in flour tortilla and roll.

Mrs. Dan Steakley (Susan)

Marinated Flank Steak

1½ pounds flank steak	¼ cup honey
¾ cup oil	¼ cup soy sauce
2 tablespoons wine vinegar	1½ teaspoons ginger
2 tablespoons minced green onions	1 clove garlic, crushed

Marinate steak overnight. Barbecue on a grill and baste often while turning. Cook according to taste. Cut meat on the diagonal. Serves 4.

Mrs. Linden Welch (Phyllis)

Spiedi Marinade

¾ cup olive oil
¼ cup vinegar
¼ cup wine
1 tablespoon oregano
¼ teaspoon garlic powder
½ teaspoon onion powder
1 teaspoon chives
1 teaspoon Italian seasoning

¼ teaspoon mint sauce
½ teaspoon salt
½ teaspoon pepper
1½ ounces Worcestershire
   sauce
2 slices lemon, squeezed with
   rind

Mix all ingredients well. Let stand at least overnight. Spiedis are chunks of lamb, pork, beef, or a combination of all three that have been marinated in this special sauce. The meat should marinate at least overnight. Two or three days is even better. Place the meat on skewers and cook over a charcoal grill. When done, serve on a piece of Italian bread with no other accompaniment.

Mrs. Jim Smith (Diane)

Bierocks

2 pounds ground meat
Salt and pepper to taste
12 cups chopped cabbage
1 onion, chopped
2 or 3 packages dry yeast

4 cups warm water, divided
1½ tablespoons salt
3 tablespoons sugar
½ cup butter
9 cups flour

Brown meat with salt and pepper. Drain fat from meat, return to skillet; add cabbage and onion and cook until tender. Add more salt and pepper to taste and set aside to cool. Sprinkle 2 or 3 packages of dry yeast on one cup warm water (3 packages of yeast will make dough rise faster). To the other three cups warm water, add salt, sugar and butter. Dissolve well and add to yeast mixture. To this yeast mixture, gradually add the nine cups of flour and mix until well blended. Set the dough aside to rise until double. Beat down and divide into four pieces. Roll each piece out on floured surface to ¼ inch thick and cut into 3x3 inch squares. Fill each square with one heaping tablespoon of the filling; fold the corners into the center and crimp the seams to make pouches. Heavily grease a cookie sheet; lay Bierocks seam side down on sheet and then turn over and arrange ½ inch apart. Let rise about 30 minutes and bake at 400° for 15 to 20 minutes until brown. Yields 3 to 4 dozen. *This is an old German favorite that is served in the back yard with big slices of watermelon.*

Mildred May

Spiced Round

10 pound piece round of beef, bone removed	2 pounds kidney suet, finely cut
1 tablespoon saltpeter	2 tablespoons ground cloves
1 cup salt	2 tablespoons ground allspice
½ cup sugar	1 tablespoon sugar

Mix saltpeter, salt and ½ cup sugar; rub this well onto the top, bottom, and sides of the round. Place it in a crock to cure for a week or 10 days, turning over daily. If the weather is cold all the time, this may be left out; if not, it should be kept in the refrigerator. When meat is ready to be cooked, mix the rest of the ingredients. The suet and spice mixture should be stuffed into deep slits that have been cut into meat with the point of a sharp butcher knife. Slits should be cut both top and bottom at 1½ inch intervals. Pack suet and spice mixture tightly into each slit. Any mixture left should be put on top of round during baking. Take clean white strips of cloth about 3 inches wide and bind the roast all over, very securely—sides, top and bottom. Tie these as tightly as possible to prevent the roast from falling apart during cooking.

Place meat in roaster, adding a little water and cook at 350° for 5 to 6 hours or until tender. When done, remove from liquid. While still hot, put round in a clean crock, and place a heavy weight on top. This may be done by placing about 10 pounds on an inverted dinner plate which has been placed on top of the round. This keeps the meat compressed. After the round is thoroughly cooled, 12 hours or more, it is ready to serve. It is very important that this round be cut properly. Cut the slices as thin as possible, across the grain of the meat on the cut side of the round.

Dudley D. Baker Jr.

The Easter Fires Pageant is a unique celebration held annually in the German town of Fredericksburg. It is a tradition born, not in the homeland, but on the frontier. During negotiations for a treaty with the Indians in the area, small fires were lit at night on the surrounding hilltops. To allay the children's fears about the fires, a loving mother explained that the Easter rabbit was boiling and dyeing eggs for the coming day. Now, each Easter Eve, the fires are lit in remembrance of that long-ago night, and traditional German foods are served for the Easter meal.

Oven Bar B Q Brisket

Brisket, 4 pounds or larger
1 tablespoon salt
1 tablespoon black pepper
1 tablespoon onion salt
1 tablespoon garlic salt

2 tablespoons celery seed
2 tablespoons Worcestershire
sauce
1 tablespoon Liquid Smoke

Sauce:
1 cup Woody's barbecue sauce
1 cup catsup

¼ to ½ cup brown sugar

Place meat fat side up in a pan lined with heavy foil. Mix marinade ingredients and put on top of meat. Wrap tightly with foil; refrigerate for 24 hours. Bake brisket at 300°, 1 hour per pound. Mix sauce ingredients together and bring to a boil. Open foil and drain off juice. One hour before serving, put sauce over meat; rewrap with foil and cook for 1 more hour at 300°. Serves 8 to 10.

Mrs. Chris Williston (Janice)

Barbecue holds a special place in the heart of Texans; almost any meat is enhanced by the slow, deliberate cooking and every cook has some "secret ingredient" for the basting sauce.

Best Ever Brisket

Beef brisket, about 10 to 11
pounds
Salt and pepper

2 large onions, sliced
¼ to ½ cup flour
1 cup water

Place meat fat side up in a large deep pan. Add water to ½ inch depth in pan bottom. Salt and pepper meat freely. Arrange onion slices on top; cover with foil and bake at 300° for 8 to 9 hours. When done, remove brisket to warm platter. Skim off fat from pan drippings and add a mixture of flour and water. Boil, stirring constantly for 3 to 5 minutes. Remove from heat and serve on top of meat.

Mrs. Larry Wisian (Kay)

Beef Brisket

1   beef brisket (10 to 15 pounds)
½   cup wine
¼   cup vinegar
⅛   cup Worcestershire sauce

⅛   cup soy sauce
Garlic salt to taste
Onion salt to taste
Celery salt to taste

Marinate brisket for 12 hours in a mixture of all the ingredients. Turn twice. Liberally apply coarse black pepper to meat and place on a roaster rack, meat side down. Add marinade and ¾ cup water. Cover and roast at 275° for 5 to 6 hours. If not brown, remove cover during last hour.

S. D. Jackman, Jr.

Chuck wagon cooks were among the first to perfect the art of cooking barbecue. While the cowboys rounded up the cattle, "Cooky" dug the pit and started the mesquite or oak wood burning.

Tagraline

1   medium onion, chopped
1   cup chopped green pepper
1   clove garlic, chopped, optional
2   pounds ground meat
Salt and pepper to taste
1   can (20 ounces) tomatoes
1   can (12 ounces) whole kernel corn

1   can (6 ounces) ripe olives
1   can (8 ounces) tomato sauce
1   package (16 ounces) wide noodles, cooked and drained
1½ cups grated Cheddar cheese

Sauté onions, green pepper and garlic with meat until meat is brown; drain. Salt and pepper to taste. Add tomatoes, corn, olives and tomato sauce. In a large rectangular casserole, alternate layers of noodles, meat and cheese, ending with cheese. Bake at 325° for 25 minutes. Serves 8 to 10.

Mrs. Jim Rado (Vicki)

Green Onion Casserole

2	pounds ground chuck	1	package (10 ounces) thin egg noodles
3	teaspoons salt		
4	teaspoons sugar	8	ounces cream cheese
½	teaspoon pepper	2	cups sour cream
2	cans (16 ounces each) tomatoes	12	green onions, chopped with tops
2	cans (8 ounces each) tomato sauce	2	cups grated sharp Cheddar cheese
4	cloves garlic, chopped		

Combine meat, salt, sugar, pepper, tomatoes, sauce, and garlic; simmer 10 minutes. Cook egg noodles; drain. Combine hot noodles with cream cheese. Add sour cream and green onions. In a 4 quart casserole, layer noodles, meat mixture and top with grated cheese. Bake at 325° for 30 minutes. Serves 8 to 10. This casserole can be made ahead of time and frozen. Great for drop-in company.

Mrs. B. L. Turlington (Jill)

Beef Wine Stew

2	pounds chuck, cut in bite-size chunks	1 to 2	cloves garlic, crushed
½	cup sliced onions	8	slices bacon
½	cup sliced carrots	1½	cups tomatoes, peeled, quartered and seeded
1¼	cups robust red wine	¼	cup sliced mushrooms
2	tablespoons olive oil	8 or more	black olives, pitted
Ground black pepper			
Bouquet of thyme, bay leaf and parsley, tied in cheesecloth			

Place chuck, onion, carrots, wine, oil and seasonings in glass bowl. Stir well; cover and refrigerate 4 hours or overnight. Next day, place ½ of the bacon in the bottom of a 1½ quart casserole. Put meat, vegetables and marinade on top. Add tomatoes and cover with remaining bacon. Cover tightly and cook at 300° for 4 hours or longer. Add mushrooms and olives for the last 30 minutes. Skim off fat if necessary. Serves 6.

Mrs. Clark E. Rector (Sue)

No Peep Stew

2 pounds good lean beef	Salt and pepper
2 large potatoes	Seasoned salt
1 cup chopped celery	2 tablespoons tapioca
1 large onion, chopped	2 cans (10 ounces each) Snap-
1 cup sliced carrots	E-Tom juice

Cube and mix together the meat and vegetables. Season to taste with salt, pepper and seasoned salt. Place in a Dutch oven. Dissolve tapioca in the tomato juice and pour over the mixture. Bake at 250° for 5 hours. Do not peep. Serves 6 to 8.

Mrs. Ron Garrick (Bonnie)

Since the arrival of the first German settlers in Galveston in 1844, their influence has been felt in Texas cooking. Never willing to waste a scrap of food, their use of potatoes, cabbage, bits of fruit and meat in a dish has given us some of our most cherished recipes.

Fiske's Beer Stew

3 pounds boneless beef chuck	1 bay leaf
½ cup flour	12 small white onions
½ teaspoon salt	6 carrots, peeled and
½ teaspoon pepper	quartered
4 tablespoons butter	6 medium potatoes, quartered
½ cup diced onions	½ pound mushrooms, sliced
1 cup beef bouillon	2 tablespoons flour, optional
2 cups beer	

Dredge meat in ½ cup flour, salt and pepper. In a heavy saucepan melt butter and sauté onions lightly. Add the meat and brown on all sides. Add bouillon, beer and bay leaf. Cover and simmer over low heat 1½ hours. Add white onions, carrots, potatoes and mushrooms. Cover and cook over low heat 40 minutes or until vegetables are tender. Taste for seasoning. If desired, thicken stew with 2 tablespoons flour mixed with ½ cup of gravy. Serves 8.

Mrs. Bob Edgecomb (Mary)

Braised Red Cabbage, Apples and German Sausage

4 tablespoons bacon drippings	2 tablespoons mild vinegar
2 tablespoons sugar	½ teaspoon caraway seeds
1 small onion, chopped	Salt and pepper to taste
4 cups red cabbage, shredded	6 links German sausage
2 tart apples, sliced	Water, stock, or red wine, optional

Heat drippings in a large skillet; add sugar and stir until brown. Add onion and cook slowly until golden. Add remaining ingredients laying sausage on cabbage. Cook slowly 45 minutes to one hour. Add a little water, stock, or red wine as necessary to keep from sticking. Serves 6.

Variation: For white cabbage, use ¼ cup sugar and only one table-spoon vinegar.

Mrs. Jerry Hunt (Gail)

Double Fruit Glazed Pork Chops

6 rib pork chops, 6 to 8 ounces each	6 whole coriander seeds, crushed
Salt and pepper to taste	6 slices each orange, lemon and lime
1 cup brown sugar	6 Maraschino cherries
¼ cup pineapple juice	1½ tablespoons cornstarch
¼ cup honey	2 tablespoons water
1 teaspoon dry mustard	¼ teaspoon salt
3 whole cloves	1 lemon slice

Brown chops in skillet; season with salt and pepper and place in a shallow baking pan. Combine brown sugar, pineapple juice, honey, dry mustard, cloves and coriander. Spoon about one tablespoon of the sauce over each chop. Bake uncovered at 350° about 1 hour and 15 minutes, basting with half of the sauce. With wooden pick, skewer one slice of orange, lemon and lime on each chop; top with a cherry. Baste fruit with the remaining sauce and bake an additional 10 minutes. Measure pan juices; skim off fat and add enough water to make 1⅓ cups. Blend cornstarch with 2 tablespoons water. Stir into juices. Add ¼ teaspoon salt and lemon slice. Cook, stirring constantly, until sauce is thickened and bubbly. Simmer 2 or 3 minutes, stirring occasionally. Remove lemon slice and serve sauce with chops. Serves 6. *A nice accompaniment are Island Nut Bananas* (see Index).

Nancy Young Moritz

Fabulous Ham Loaf

1 **pound lean smoked ham, ground**	¼ **cup chopped onion**
¾ **cup cracker crumbs**	¾ **teaspoon salt**
2 **well beaten eggs**	1 **teaspoon chopped parsley**
1 **cup milk**	¼ **cup brown sugar**
1 **pound lean pork, ground**	¼ **cup cider vinegar**
	¾ **teaspoon dry mustard**

Horseradish Sauce:

¼ **cup mayonnaise**	1 **tablespoon prepared horseradish**
¼ **cup sour cream**	
2 **tablespoons prepared mustard**	1 **teaspoon fresh lemon juice**
1 **tablespoon minced chives**	**Salt to taste**

Blend ham, crumbs, eggs, milk, pork, onion, salt and parsley thoroughly, and form into one loaf. Bake at 350° for 30 to 40 minutes. For glaze, combine sugar, vinegar and dry mustard; boil for 2 minutes. Pour off fat from ham; glaze and continue cooking 1 hour longer. Baste with glaze twice more during cooking time and continue to pour off fat as needed. Mix horseradish sauce ingredients and refrigerate until ready to use. Serve ham loaf either hot or cold with the horseradish sauce on the side. Yields about 6 to 8 servings. After this ham loaf is fully baked, it can be cooled; wrapped in foil and frozen until time to serve. Defrost ham and heat in foil for 30 to 40 minutes. This recipe doubles easily.

Mrs. Rush McGinty (Carol)

Glazed Ham Slice with Cranberry Raisin Sauce

1 **thick slice cooked ham**	**Dash salt**
Whole cloves	½ **cup orange juice**
½ **cup brown sugar**	1½ **cups cranberry juice**
2 **tablespoons cornstarch**	½ **cup seedless raisins**
Dash ground cloves	

Slash fat of ham and insert whole cloves in fat. Place in a shallow baking pan and bake at 325° for 30 minutes. Mix sugar, cornstarch, cloves, and salt. Add the remaining ingredients; cook and stir until mixture thickens and comes to a boil. Remove ham from oven; spoon some sauce over ham and bake 20 minutes or until glazed. Pass the remaining sauce with the ham. Serves 6.

Mrs. Jack A. Bone (Joyce)

Madeira Ham

10 pounds fully cooked ham	½ teaspoon pepper
1 cup Madeira wine	½ teaspoon ground allspice
½ cup brown sauce, recipe follows	½ teaspoon mace
	½ cup beef bouillon
1 cup brown sugar	Flour
1 tablespoon dry mustard	

Brown Sauce:

½ cup beef bouillon	2 teaspoons Worcestershire sauce
1 teaspoon brown gravy sauce mix	1 teaspoon catsup

Slice ham into ⅜ inch thick slices; reshape ham and tie securely. Place in a baking pan; pour wine over ham, basting to coat thoroughly. Bake at 350° for 15 minutes. Combine all sauce ingredients in a saucepan; boil rapidly for 5 minutes. Pour brown sauce over ham; bake 15 minutes. Combine brown sugar, mustard, pepper, spices and enough wine to make a smooth paste. Baste ham with pan drippings, then coat with brown sugar paste. Bake an additional 15 minutes. Remove and let stand. Drain pan drippings; stir in bouillon. Add flour, 1 teaspoon at a time, stirring constantly, until thickened. Keep warm. Run an 18 inch skewer lengthwise down each side of ham. Untie and remove strings; cut ham down the middle lengthwise. Garnish center with parsley and serve with pan sauce. If using plain skewers, top with a canned crab apple on each end.

Nancy Young Moritz

Herbed Pork Roast

1 teaspoon rosemary	1 pork loin roast
1 teaspoon thyme	1 cup water
½ clove garlic	½ cup dry white wine
Salt and freshly ground pepper	

Combine spices and rub over roast. Place in a baking dish with water and wine; bake at 350° for 2½ hours or until 185° on a meat thermometer. *Serve with rice seasoned with green pepper, onion, and tomatoes.*

Mrs. Ernest Butler (Sarah)

Canadian Christmas Pie

1 recipe double pie crust	1½ teaspoons seasoned salt
¾ cup chopped onion	⅛ teaspoon pepper
2 cloves garlic, minced	⅛ teaspoon allspice
2 tablespoons shortening	½ cup milk
½ pound ground veal	½ cup water
½ pound ground lean pork	2 cups diced cooked chicken
1 jar (4 ounces) pimientos,	or turkey
sliced and drained	1 egg, beaten
1 package (2 ounces) white	Parsley to garnish
sauce mix	

Make pie crust; put in pan and prick bottom. Sauté onion and garlic in shortening until golden. Add meats and brown; add pimientos, sauce mix, seasonings and liquids, blending well. Boil, stirring constantly. Turn into pie crust. Top with chicken or turkey; put top crust on. Brush with egg and bake at 375° for 40 to 45 minutes. Serves 6.

Mrs. Daniel O'Donnell (Sharon)

Sausage Lasagne

1 pound hot bulk sausage	¾ cup water
3 cloves garlic	8 ounces lasagne noodles
1 teaspoon basil	1 pound Ricotta cheese
½ teaspoon oregano	½ cup Parmesan cheese
1½ teaspoons salt	1 tablespoon parsley
2 cans (6 ounces each)	8 ounces Mozzarella cheese
tomato paste	

Brown and crumble sausage; drain off fat and add seasonings, tomato paste, and water. Simmer for about 1 hour. Add more water if needed. Cook noodles in salted water until tender. Drain; blanch and blot on paper towels. Place overlapping layers of noodles in the bottom of a large baking dish. Layer ½ of the Ricotta, the sauce, the Parmesan cheese and the parsley; top with half of the Mozzarella cheese. Repeat layering as established; bake at 375° for 45 minutes. Serves 8 to 10.

Mrs. John Baker (Jo)

Lone Star Ribs and Barbecue Sauce

3   pounds small pork ribs
1   part black pepper

1   part paprika
3   parts salt

Sauce:
1   pint catsup
1½ pints water
⅓   cup flour
1   tablespoon salt
4   teaspoons sugar
2½ teaspoons paprika

1½ teaspoons black pepper
1½ teaspoons chili powder
1   tablespoon prepared
    mustard
1½ teaspoons Liquid Smoke
1   cup Worcestershire sauce

Season the slab of pork ribs lightly on both sides with the above mixture. Place ribs on the grill in any type of covered smoker or barbecue pit, keeping away from direct heat so that the smoke does the cooking. Cook very slowly for 1½ to 2 hours, or until meat comes away from the bone easily. During the final 15 minutes of cooking, baste both sides of the meat with barbecue sauce. Cut ribs to serve.

To make sauce, combine catsup and water in large pot. Bring to a boil. Mix dry ingredients together. Add mustard, Liquid Smoke, and half of the Worcestershire sauce. Stir into a paste; then add remainder of Worcestershire. Pour this into heated mixture and boil slowly for 20 minutes. Refrigerate any unused portion. Keeps for several weeks. Sauce makes approximately one quart. Ribs serve 4.

Mrs. Ken Moyer (Bonnie)

Company Casserole

1   package (6 ounces) wild rice
1   package (10 ounces) frozen
    chopped broccoli
2   cups chopped cooked ham
1   can (4 ounces) mushrooms,
    drained

1   cup diced Cheddar cheese
1   can cream of celery soup
1   cup mayonnaise
2   teaspoons prepared mustard
1   teaspoon curry powder
¼   cup grated Parmesan cheese

Cook rice acording to package directions. Spread on bottom of a buttered 9x13 inch pan. Top with broccoli, ham, mushrooms and cheese. Blend soup with mayonnaise, mustard and curry. Pour soup mixture over all. Sprinkle with Parmesan cheese; bake at 350° for 45 minutes. Serves 6 to 8.   **Mrs. Larry Strickland (Linda)**

Shrimp and Pork Egg Rolls

½ pound fresh bean sprouts or 1 can (1 pound) bean sprouts
½ pound raw shrimp, shelled and deveined
3 tablespoons oil, divided
½ pound lean boneless pork, finely ground
1 tablespoon dry sherry
1 tablespoon soy sauce
½ teaspoon sugar
2 to 3 medium fresh mushrooms, sliced
4 cups finely chopped celery
2 teaspoons salt
1 tablespoon cornstarch
2 tablespoons cold chicken stock
1 package (1 pound) egg roll wrappers
1 egg, lightly beaten
3 cups peanut oil or salad oil

Rinse bean sprouts; drain and pat dry. Dice shrimp. Heat 1 tablespoon oil in a wok or skillet; add pork and stir fry for 2 minutes. Add wine, soy sauce, sugar, shrimp and mushrooms, and stir fry for 1 minute, or until shrimp turn pink. Transfer to a bowl and set aside. Pour remaining 2 tablespoons oil into wok; add celery and stir fry for 5 minutes. Then add the salt and bean sprouts; mix thoroughly. Return pork and shrimp mixture to pan, and stir until all ingredients are well combined. Cook over moderate heat, stirring constantly, until liquid starts to boil. Combine cornstarch and cold chicken stock, and add to mixture. Stir until cooking liquids have thickened slightly and coated the mixture with a light glaze. Cool to room temperature.

To assemble egg roll mixture, shape ¼ cup of filling into a 4 inch long cylinder and place diagonally across each egg roll wrapper. Lift the lower triangular flap over the filling, tucking the point under it. Bring each of the two small end flaps up to the top of the enclosed filling and press the points firmly down. Brush the upper and exposed triangle of dough with egg and continue rolling the wrapper. Cook immediately or store covered in the refrigerator. Deep fry 5 or 6 rolls at a time in oil heated to 375° for 3 to 4 minutes. Drain and serve as soon as possible. The egg rolls can be kept warm for an hour or so at 250°, or they can be reheated at 450° for about 10 minutes. Yields 16 egg rolls.

S. D. Jackman, Jr.

Pork was the mainstay of frontier cooking. Because of the value of other animals for milk, wool, feathers, etc., these animals were slaughtered for the family only as a last resort. Thus, many tasty dishes had pork as their main ingredient.

Calabaza with Pork

2½ pounds country pork ribs, cut in bite size pieces
Bacon drippings
1½ onions, chopped
4 cloves garlic, pressed
3 large calabaza or squash, peeled, seeded, and cut into bite size pieces
3 ears of corn, cut off kernels and scrape for milk
1 can (1 pound) whole tomatoes, cut in small pieces with juice

2 fresh tomatoes, peeled and cut in small pieces
Salt and ground pepper
1 teaspoon comino seeds, rubbed in your palms
5 squirts Tabasco
5 squirts Worcestershire sauce
3 squirts Angostura bitters
1 teaspoon Fines Herbes

Brown meat in bacon drippings. Sauté onion and garlic in drippings; add calabaza, simmering until soft. Add corn, tomatoes, and spices. Simmer until done. Serves 8 to 10. *Any pork cuts may be used as meat will be tender after cooking so slow and long. Also, zucchini may be substituted for calabaza.*

S. D. Jackman, Jr.

Apricot Pheasant

Two pheasants
Salt and pepper
1 cup celery leaves
2 lemon slices
2 thick onion slices
2 small apples, halved
2 cloves garlic

6 bacon strips
2 cups chicken broth
1½ cups apricot jam
1 teaspoon grated lemon rind
Chopped pheasant livers or chicken livers
Salt and pepper

Season birds inside and out with salt and pepper. Fill cavities with celery, lemon slices, onion slices, apple and garlic. Truss both birds. Place bacon slices over birds and roast uncovered at 350° for 20 minutes or until tender. Remove bacon slices before birds are done to brown evenly. Transfer pheasants to heated platter and keep warm. Pour off fat from roaster; add chicken broth and stir over medium heat, scraping up browned bits. Cook liquid down by half and add apricot jam, lemon rind, chopped liver, salt and pepper. Simmer 5 minutes; serve with birds.

Mrs. John Carrell (Jane)

Doves or Quail in Wine Sauce

15 doves or quail
Salt and pepper to taste
1 cup flour
½ cup oil
2 large onions, finely chopped
2 large ribs celery, finely chopped

2 cups sauterne wine
2 cups water
3 bay leaves
4 tablespoons butter

Salt and pepper doves or quail; dust with flour and brown in oil. Place onions and celery in bottom of a large Dutch oven; put bay leaves inside of each bird and dot with butter. Pour wine and water over birds. Cover casserole and bake at 375° about 2 hours or until birds are cooked. Baste often.

Mrs. Larry Morris (Diane)

"Jolly-Cholly-Holly" Peña Doves

12 canned jalapeños, halved
1 pound Monterey Jack cheese

24 doves or quail, breast only
24 slices thick bacon

Remove seeds from jalapeños. (If you like it hot, leave the seeds in. If you really like it hot, leave the seeds in and use a whole jalapeño for each bird.) Cut the cheese into 24 rectangles approximately 1½ by ¾ inches. Place a cheese rectangle on a pepper slice. If using the whole pepper, put the cheese between the two slices. Bone out the breast section of the birds. Each bird will have two sections of breast. On half the breast put the pepper and cheese. Press the other half of the breast on the other side so that the cheese and pepper are in the center. Then wrap one bacon slice, very tightly around the breast. Make sure the bacon covers the entire breast. Secure with toothpicks. It is important that the breast is tightly wrapped and secured at each end. Cook over a hot bed of coals for 30 to 45 minutes, turning often. For the best flavor use pecan or mesquite wood.

Charley Batey

Braised Quail with Bacon

6 quail	½ cup hot water
Salted water	4 tablespoons flour
18 strips bacon	6 slices toast, optional
2 tablespoons butter	

Before cooking, cover quail with salted water, using 1 tablespoon salt for each quart of water. Let stand 15 minutes; drain and pat dry. Place 1 strip bacon in cavity of each bird and place in shallow roasting pan. Layer a strip of bacon over the breast and over the legs of each bird. Bake at 450° for 5 minutes; reduce heat to 350° and continue cooking for 40 minutes, basting frequently with a mixture of butter and hot water. At the end of the baking time, sprinkle with flour and increase heat to 450° and brown for 7 to 10 minutes. Serve on toast if desired. Serves 6.

Mrs. Marcus Bone (Beverly)

Bradford's Country Fried Venison with Pan Gravy

2 pounds venison steak, thinly sliced	4 tablespoons pan drippings
½ cup flour	3 tablespoons flour
1 teaspoon salt	2¼ cups milk
¼ teaspoon pepper	1 teaspoon salt
½ cup oil	½ teaspoon pepper

Pound steak until ¼ inch thick. Cut into small pieces. Combine flour, salt and pepper, and coat steaks on both sides. In a heavy skillet, heat oil and sauté steaks on medium to high heat 5 minutes on each side. Remove from skillet and keep warm. Pour off all but 4 tablespoons pan drippings. Blend in 3 tablespoons flour, stirring constantly, scraping cooked juices on bottom of pan until bubbly. Stir in milk, salt and pepper. Continue cooking over medium heat, stirring and scraping bottom and sides until gravy thickens and bubbles for 1 minute. Serves 6 to 8. *For a hearty breakfast serve these steaks with eggs, biscuits and Bloody Mary's. People who think they don't like venison should try this version of the traditional chicken fried steak before deciding on the matter. This recipe is equally good with turkey breasts or beef round steak.*

Bill Butler

Venison Stew

3 to 4 pounds venison
¼ cup flour
3 tablespoons bacon
  drippings
1½ to 2 cups hot water
1½ cups red wine
2 cloves garlic, chopped
Tabasco to taste
Cayenne pepper to taste
1 teaspoon mixed herbs
  (thyme, marjoram, basil)

1 teaspoon dried parsley
1 large onion, sliced
1½ teaspoons salt
½ teaspoon pepper
4 carrots, peeled and
  quartered
4 potatoes, pared and
  quartered
1 cup mushroom pieces

Cut sinews and bones from venison. Cut meat into bite-size pieces; dredge in flour. Brown venison in hot bacon drippings. Add hot water, wine, garlic, Tabasco, cayenne, herbs, parsley, onion, salt and pepper. Cover and bring to a boil. Reduce heat and simmer about 2 hours. Add carrots and potatoes; cover and simmer for 1 hour. Add a little water if needed. Add mushrooms during the last 15 minutes. Serves 8.

S. D. Jackman, Jr.

 Sausage, steaks, chili and a whole lot more can be prepared from venison. And, with more than four million deer in Texas, the cooking of game presents a real challenge.

Roasted Wild Game

Venison roast or ham, wild
  turkey or goose
Meat tenderizer

1 tablespoon flour
1 envelope dry onion soup
  mix

Thoroughly moisten roast or ham; apply meat tenderizer, per directions on container. Skin turkey or goose, omitting tenderizer. Place flour in oven browning bag; shake to coat inside. Rub meat with dry onion soup. Place meat in bag, and cook following directions on box. Do not use drippings for gravy. However, these drippings may be used for reheating leftover meat to prevent dryness. Bone turkey or goose before serving. *Soup mix removes the "wild taste" of the game.*

Mrs. Bob Bluntzer (Jo)

Herbed Lamb

1 leg of lamb, about 6 pounds
4 to 5 cloves garlic
2 teaspoons salt
2½ teaspoons oregano
½ teaspoon pepper
1 cup claret wine or dry red
wine

¼ cup chopped green onions
with tops
2½ tablespoons lemon juice
2 tablespoons butter
2 tablespoons flour

Cut deep slits in lamb, about 2 inches apart, over entire surface. Crush garlic; mix with salt, oregano, and pepper. Press mixture evenly into all slits in meat. Place meat on rack in pan with fat side up. Do not cover. Roast at 325° 30 to 35 minutes per pound for medium. If using a meat thermometer, roast meat to 175° for medium or 180° for well done. Combine wine, green onions, and lemon juice; reserve ½ of this basting mixture for the gravy. Baste lamb often with remaining half of mixture. When meat is done, put on warm platter; skim fat off juices, reserving 1 cup. Melt butter and blend in flour. Stir in reserved wine mixture and meat juices. Cook and stir until thickened. Serve sauce separately.

Mrs. Dudley D. Baker (Kathy)

Irish Lamb Stew

2 pounds boneless cubed
lamb, reserve bones for
broth
5 cups water
2 teaspoons salt, divided
1 tablespoon shortening
3½ pounds red potatoes, peeled

1½ pounds onions, sliced
½ teaspoon coarsely ground
black pepper
1 bay leaf, optional
1 tablespoon chopped
parsley, optional

Put bones from lamb in a heavy pot with water and 1 teaspoon salt. Bring to a boil; skim off fat and simmer. Grease bottom of stew pot with shortening. Slice potatoes ¼ inch thick leaving 8 whole. Line bottom of pot with potatoes; spread half the onions evenly over the potatoes. Season lamb cubes with 1 teaspoon salt and pepper, and spread over onions. Top with remaining onions and 8 whole potatoes. Add bay leaf. Pour in 2½ to 3 cups lamb broth; cover and bake at 350° for 2 hours. After 2 hours, strain remaining broth and pour into pot. Cover and bake another 30 to 45 minutes. Remove from oven, sprinkle with parsley and serve at once. Serves 8. *If you do not have bones for your lamb broth, substitute 1 can chicken broth, diluted, mixed with 2½ cups water and omit the teaspoon of salt.*

S. D. Jackman, Jr.

Bengal Curry of Lamb

2½ pounds lamb shoulder or leg
    of lamb
4 tablespoons butter, divided
⅔ cup finely chopped onion
3 tablespoons chopped
    crystallized ginger
½ teaspoons sugar
⅛ teaspoon freshly ground
    pepper
2 teaspoons salt

2 to 3 tablespoons curry powder
¼ teaspoon crushed dried
    mint
3 cups milk, divided
1 cup coconut
½ cup freshly squeezed lime
    juice
½ cup whipping cream
Hot fluffy rice

Cut lamb into 1 inch cubes, removing bone and fat. Melt 2 tablespoons butter in a large heavy pan. Add onion and cook until tender, about 5 minutes. Remove from skillet and set aside. Add remaining butter and brown the lamb cubes. Return the onion to the pan; add ginger, sugar, pepper, salt, curry powder, mint and 2 cups milk. Mix well; cover and simmer over low heat 1 hour or more. Meanwhile, prepare fresh coconut milk by scalding 1 cup milk and adding 1 cup coconut. Blanch, and let stand 20 minutes. Strain; reserving coconut and milk. Add ½ cup coconut milk, and ½ cup coconut. Cover and cook 5 minutes. Gradually stir in lime juice and cream, adding them separately and in the order given. Simmer without boiling for 10 to 15 minutes. Serves 4 to 5. *Serve over hot fluffy rice with mango salad and a variety of condiments: chutney, preserved ginger, raisins, currants, chopped peanuts, chopped onions (raw or cooked), grated hard cooked egg yolks, chopped hard cooked egg whites, and/or coconut chips.*

Mrs. Bob Edgecomb (Mary)

Baked Fish Parmesan

1 box (12 ounces) Ritz
    crackers
¾ to 1 cup grated Parmesan
    cheese

Salt
¼ pound melted butter
1 pound fresh fish filets

Combine crackers and Parmesan cheese in blender. Add a little salt to the melted butter. Dip fish filets in butter and then in the cracker mixture. Bake at 400° for 15 minutes. Broil for 1 to 2 minutes. Serves 3 to 4. Fish can be prepared ahead of time and then popped into the oven 20 minutes before serving. Store leftover cracker mixture in a jar in the refrigerator.

Mrs. B. L. Turlington (Jill)

Pescado Veracruzana—Baked Fish

3   small onions, minced
1   green pepper, minced
3   tablespoons butter
1   clove garlic
1   can (16 ounces) tomatoes
1   can (8 ounces) tomato
    sauce

½   teaspoon oregano
Salt
1   tablespoon chili powder
Stuffed olives to taste
3 to 4 jalapeño peppers
1   redfish, 3 to 4 pounds, or
    any firm fish

Sauté onions and green pepper in butter until clear. Add garlic, tomatoes, tomato sauce, and seasonings. Simmer for 3 hours. Add olives and jalapeño peppers. Bake seasoned red fish until done. When ready to serve, pour sauce over fish and let stand a few minutes to absorb the flavor. Serves 6 to 8.

Mrs. Ellis Burges (Myrtle)

Stuffed Flounder

¼   cup chopped onions
¼   cup butter
1   can (3 ounces) mushrooms,
    drained, reserve liquid
1   can (6½ ounces) crab meat,
    drained
½   cup cracker crumbs
2   tablespoons chopped
    parsley

¾   teaspoon salt, divided
Pepper to taste
8   flounder filets
3   tablespoons butter
3   tablespoons flour
Milk
⅓   cup dry white wine
1   cup grated Swiss cheese
½   teaspoon paprika

Cook onion in ¼ cup butter until tender not brown. Stir in mushrooms, crab, cracker crumbs, parsley, ½ teaspoon salt, and pepper. Mix well; spread over filets. Roll filets and place seam side down in baking dish. In a saucepan, melt 3 tablespoons butter. Blend in flour and ¼ teaspoon salt. Add enough milk to mushroom liquid to equal 1½ cups. Combine with wine and gradually pour into saucepan. Cook and stir until mixture thickens and bubbles. Pour over filets. Bake at 400° for 25 minutes. Sprinkle with cheese and paprika. Return to oven and bake 10 minutes longer or until fish flakes easily with a fork. Serves 8.

Mrs. Jim Rado (Vicki)

Trout with Cream and Almonds

4   small trout, fresh or frozen
    or 1 pound fish filets
Flour
½   cup butter
½   cup slivered blanched
    almonds

½   cup heavy cream
Salt and pepper
Dash of parsley

Wash trout and dry well. Coat lightly with flour. Heat butter in skillet. Sauté trout in butter until browned on both sides. Remove fish to hot platter and keep warm. Sauté almonds in skillet until golden brown. Add cream; stir thoroughly to loosen all particles (sauce will be brown). Season to taste with salt and pepper; add parsley. Simmer gently for 2 minutes. Pour sauce over fish. Serves 2 to 3.

Mrs. Marcus Bone (Beverly)

Oysters Bienville

Sauce:
1   bunch shallots, chopped
1   tablespoon butter
1   tablespoon flour
½   cup chicken broth

½   cup shrimp, chopped
⅓   cup mushrooms, chopped
1   egg yolk
2   ounces white wine

Oysters:
Ice cream salt or coarse salt
1   dozen oysters on the half
    shell
Bread crumbs

Paprika
Grated cheese
Salt to taste

To prepare sauce, fry shallots in butter until brown; add flour and heat until brown. Add chicken broth, shrimp and mushrooms. Beat egg yolk and wine; slowly add to sauce, beating rapidly. Season to taste. Simmer 10 to 15 minutes, stirring constantly. Put ice cream salt in pie plate or cake pan. Place oysters on salt. Bake at 350° about 6 to 8 minutes or until partially done. Pour sauce over each oyster; cover with a mixture of bread crumbs, paprika and grated cheese. Place in broiler about 2 minutes to brown. Serves 2.

Mrs. Ben DuBilier (Lillian)

Baked Bass

1	pound sea bass filets	1	teaspoon instant minced
2	teaspoons salt		onions
½	teaspoon pepper	¼	cup olive oil
1	teaspoon basil	½	cup dry bread crumbs

Place cleaned bass in dish. Combine salt, pepper, basil, onion, and oil. Mix well and pour over bass. Marinate at least 2 hours. Place in 8 inch square baking dish. Pour marinade over fish. Sprinkle with bread crumbs and bake at 400° for about 20 minutes. Serves 3 to 4.

S. D. Jackman, Jr.

Fettuccine Al Frutti De Mare (With Seafood Sauce)

½	pound medium shrimp, peeled and deveined	⅔	cup dry white wine
½	pound scallops	1	pound fettuccine
1	cup mushrooms, quartered	2½	cups freshly grated Parmesan cheese
8	tablespoons butter, divided	1	cup whipping cream

In a heavy saucepan, sauté shrimp, scallops and mushrooms in 4 tablespoons butter just until seafood is cooked. Add wine and cook until liquids have reduced to a sauce consistency. Set aside. Cook fettuccine in boiling, salted water until al dente. Drain, and return to cooking pan. Add remaining 4 tablespoons butter, in pieces; then add cheese and cream. Toss together until cream sauce coats pasta. Serve immediately on a platter with seafood sauce on top. Serves 4 to 6.

Mrs. Bryan Healer (Georganne)

Barbecued Shrimp

1	teaspoon salt	¼	cup wine vinegar
1	teaspoon oregano	¼	cup catsup
½	teaspoon pepper	4	dashes Tabasco
2	cloves garlic, minced	3	pounds large shrimp, unpeeled
¼	cup white wine		

Mix marinade ingredients and pour over shrimp. Refrigerate at least 12 hours, stirring occasionally. Bake at 375° for 20 to 30 minutes, stirring occasionally. Broil for the last 5 minutes to brown. Serves 4 to 6.

Mrs. Don Panter (Carolyn)

Shrimp Etouffé

½ cup oil
½ cup flour
1½ pounds raw shrimp, peeled
1 onion, finely chopped
½ cup chopped green onions
½ green pepper, finely chopped
2 ribs celery, finely chopped

4 to 5 sprigs parsley, chopped
1 large tomato, peeled and finely chopped
1 can (8 ounces) tomato sauce
Salt and cayenne pepper to taste
Hot cooked rice

Make a roux with the oil and flour. Cook over very low heat until a light brown (tan) color. Add remaining ingredients. Cover pot and cook over very low heat 30 to 40 minutes or until there is sufficient gravy and shrimp are done. Stir occasionally. Since no water is added, this dish must be cooked slowly to avoid sticking. Serve over hot rice. Serves 6. *For a flavor variation try substituting scallops for half of the shrimp.*

Mrs. Jim Rado (Vicki)

Do not neglect the well-named "fruits of the Texas Coast." Protein-rich and with little waste, shellfish can be used for any course except dessert.

Spicy Hot Buttered Shrimp

4 pounds medium to large shrimp
1 pound butter

Garlic barbecue salt
Lemon pepper salt
Black pepper

Place unpeeled shrimp in a 9x13 inch pan. Dot butter over shrimp. Sprinkle heavily with garlic salt and lemon pepper salt. Completely cover the shrimp with black pepper. Bake uncovered at 300° for about 30 minutes. Stir twice during the baking to be sure all the shrimp are cooking. Serve in large bowls. Scoop up about ¼ cup of the black pepper mixture from the bottom and place in the bowl with the shrimp. Serves 4 to 5. Serve with hot French bread, a green salad and plenty of large napkins. *The secret of this recipe is to not skimp on the black pepper; you can't use enough.*

Mrs. Larry Morris (Diane)

Shrimp Scampi

7 tablespoons butter
2 teaspoons crushed garlic
3 tablespoons chopped
  parsley
2 tablespoons lemon juice

¼ teaspoon salt
½ cup dry white wine
½ teaspoon dry mustard
2 pounds large shrimp,
  shelled and deveined

Melt butter in a 9x13 inch baking pan. Add remaining ingredients except shrimp and mix well. Add shrimp and toss in mixture until coated. Broil shrimp approximately 5 minutes on each side or until done and lightly browned. Serves 6 to 8.

Mrs. Art DeFelice (Connie)

Glazed Shrimp Kabobs

2 pounds raw jumbo shrimp
18 lemon wedges
½ cup orange marmalade
¼ cup honey

½ cup orange juice
½ cup lemon juice
1 teaspoon pepper
Cornstarch

Peel all but last shell section of shrimp. Skewer 3 shrimp on a stick alternating with lemon wedges; repeat with remaining shrimp. Cover and refrigerate until ready to cook. Mix marmalade, honey, juices and pepper in a small saucepan with a little cornstarch. Stir over low heat to dissolve cornstarch and cook until thick. Grill and baste shrimp until done.

Mrs. Robert West (Linda)

Shrimp Kabobs

½ cup soy sauce
¼ cup oil
¼ cup Saki (Japanese wine)
1 teaspoon ground ginger
1½ pounds large shrimp,
  shelled

Mushrooms
Small onions
Cherry tomatoes
Rice pilaf

Combine soy sauce, oil, Saki and ginger; marinate shrimp about 2 hours. Skewer shrimp with a combination of mushrooms, onions, and tomatoes to taste. Broil 10 to 12 minutes, turning frequently. Serve with rice pilaf.

Mrs. Larry Keith (Virginia)

Butterflied Coconut Shrimp

1 pound large shrimp, shelled and deveined	1 egg
Oil	2 tablespoons cream of coconut or whipping cream
¼ cup flour	¾ cup flaked coconut
½ teaspoon salt	⅓ cup bread crumbs
½ teaspoon dry mustard	

Slit shrimp along curved side, cutting almost through. Place on paper towel. Heat 2 inches of oil in a saucepan to 350°. Combine flour, salt and dry mustard in a small bowl. Beat egg and cream of coconut in small bowl. In third bowl combine coconut and bread crumbs. Dip shrimp in flour mixture, then in egg mixture, then in coconut mixture. Refrigerate until ready to cook. When oil is hot, fry shrimp a few at a time for 2 minutes or until golden, turning once. Remove with slotted spoon and drain on paper towel. Keep warm in oven. Yields about 24 shrimp.

Mrs. Roger Borgelt (Cindy)

Shrimp Creole

½ cup oil	1 teaspoon salt
2 cups chopped onion	3 cups water
1 cup chopped green pepper	1 bay leaf
1 cup chopped celery	3 pounds raw shrimp, peeled and deveined
2 teaspoons minced garlic	
2 cups whole tomatoes	2 tablespoons cornstarch, optional
1 tablespoon paprika	Hot cooked rice
¼ teaspoon cayenne pepper	

Sauté in hot oil, onion, green pepper, celery and garlic until tender. Stir in tomatoes and brown. Add paprika, cayenne, salt, water and bay leaf. Simmer for 15 minutes. Add shrimp and continue simmering for 10 to 12 minutes more. If desired, thicken sauce with 2 tablespoons cornstarch. Serve with hot rice. Serves 4 to 6.

Mrs. Larry Hall (Jane)

Wild Rice and Shrimp Casserole

1 can cream of mushroom soup	1 tablespoon lemon juice
2 tablespoons chopped green pepper	2 cups cooked wild rice
2 tablespoons chopped onions	½ teaspoon Worcestershire sauce
½ cup sliced fresh mushrooms, optional	½ teaspoon dry mustard
2 tablespoons melted butter	¼ teaspoon pepper
	½ cup cubed cheese
	1 pound raw shrimp, deveined

Mix all ingredients together thoroughly. Pour into greased 1½ quart casserole and bake at 375° for 30 to 35 minutes. Serves 4.

Mrs. Bob Kelly (Margaret)

The Danish establishment of Danevang was established in 1894. The immigrants had many hardships to endure at first, until they started growing rice. Now, it is one of the major crops of the area and has become so important to the community's economy that one local restaurant serves it daily for lunch, as a reminder to all.

Seafood Divan

2 packages (10 ounces each) frozen broccoli	1½ cups milk, divided
1 can (5 ounces) lobster, drained and flaked	2 tablespoons flour
1 can (4½ ounces) shrimp, drained	¼ teaspoon salt
	1 tablespoon butter
	½ cup grated Swiss cheese
	Paprika

Cook broccoli as directed; drain and arrange in a greased oblong baking dish. Combine lobster and shrimp; spoon over broccoli. Beat together ¼ cup milk, flour, and salt; add 1¼ cups milk and butter blending well. Cook and stir milk mixture until thick and bubbly. Reduce heat and add Swiss cheese, stirring until melted. Pour over seafood; sprinkle with paprika and bake at 400° for 20 to 25 minutes. Serves 6 to 8.

Nancy Young Moritz

Shrimp and Artichoke Casserole

2 packages (10 ounces each)
 frozen artichoke hearts
1½ pounds cooked shrimp
¼ pound fresh mushrooms,
 sliced
2 tablespoons butter
2 tablespoons Worcestershire
 sauce

¼ cup dry white wine
1½ cups basic white sauce
½ cup grated Parmesan cheese
Lemon juice to taste
Onion flakes to taste
Salt and pepper to taste
Paprika to taste
Hot cooked rice to serve

Arrange artichokes in a buttered 9x13 inch baking dish; spread shrimp over artichokes. Sauté mushrooms in butter for 6 minutes; add to baking dish. Mix Worcestershire sauce with wine and cream sauce, and pour into the dish. Sprinkle with cheese and the remaining ingredients to taste. Bake at 375° for 30 to 40 minutes. Serve over rice. Serves 4 to 6.

Mrs. Robert Henderson (Dale)

Seafood Casserole

1 pound shrimp, peeled and
 deveined
1 pound crab meat
1 cup mayonnaise
1½ cups chopped celery
½ cup chopped green pepper

½ cup chopped onion
White pepper and salt to taste
1 to 2 teaspoons lemon juice
2 cups crushed potato chips
 or buttered bread crumbs

Cook shrimp in boiling water for 5 minutes; cool. Mix all ingredients except chips and put into a 9x13 inch pan. Top with chips or bread crumbs. Bake at 375° for about 30 minutes or until heated and bubbly around the edges. Serves 8.

Mrs. D. D. Baker, Jr. (Agnes)

 Texas is blessed with not only a beautiful coastline and seashore, but also an abundance of seafood. Our blue crabs are smaller and don't have as much meat as others, but are delicious.

Curried Crab over Rice

½ cup minced onion
1 cup sliced mushrooms,
    optional
½ cup chopped green pepper,
    optional
2 tablespoons butter

2 to 3 teaspoons curry powder
2 to 3 cans cream of shrimp
    soup
⅔ cup milk
1 pound claw crab meat
Hot cooked rice

Sauté onion, mushrooms and green pepper in butter until clear. Add curry powder, soup and milk. Cook until soup melts. Add crab meat and heat; do not boil. Serve over rice. Serves 4.

Mrs. Jim Carney (Jean)

Sister Barbara's Famous Tuna Jambalaya

1 large onion, chopped
1 large green pepper, chopped
1 rib celery, chopped
1 stick margarine
1 can (16 ounces) tomatoes
1 can (14 ounces) beef
    bouillon

½ can water
¾ to 1 cup raw rice
1 to 2 cans (6½ ounces each)
    tuna
½ teaspoon pepper
¼ teaspoon salt

Sauté onion, green pepper and celery in margarine. Combine tomatoes, bouillon and water; add to vegetables and bring to a boil. Add rice, tuna, pepper and salt to boiling water. Simmer tightly covered until rice is done. Serves 4.

Mrs. Randy Hagan (Robin)

Tuna Crunch Casserole

½ bag (1 ounce) sliced
    almonds
1 small onion, chopped
1 rib celery, chopped
2 tablespoons butter
1 can (6½ ounces) tuna

1 can (3 ounces) chow mein
    noodles
1 can cream of mushroom
    soup
2 cups chopped cabbage

Brown almonds, onions, and celery in butter. Mix all ingredients together in casserole, reserving ½ of the noodles. Sprinkle remaining noodles on top. Bake at 350° for 20 minutes. Serves 4 to 6.

Mrs. Ron Garrick (Bonnie)

Company Creamed Tuna

2   tablespoons finely chopped
    onion
3   tablespoons margarine
3   tablespoons flour
¼   teaspoon salt
Dash pepper
1¼ cups milk

½   cup sour cream
1   can (7 ounces) tuna, drained
3   tablespoons dry white wine
2   tablespoons snipped parsley
Toasted slivered almonds,
    optional
Toast points

Sauté onion in margarine until tender, but not browned. Blend in flour, salt, and pepper. Add milk and cook, stirring constantly until the mixture thickens and bubbles. Stir in sour cream; add tuna, wine and parsley. Heat through. Sprinkle with almonds if desired. Spoon over buttered toast points. Serves 4.

Mrs. Larry Hall (Jane)

Salmon Steaks Teriyaki

4   salmon steaks,
    approximately ½ inch thick
½   teaspoon sesame oil
4   teaspoons soy sauce

2   teaspoons lemon juice
1   garlic clove, minced
1   tablespoon butter, melted

Place steaks in a shallow pan. Mix remaining ingredients, except butter. Pour over salmon. Let stand twenty minutes at room temperature, turning occasionally. Remove steaks from marinade. Brush both sides with melted butter and broil 5 to 7 minutes on each side, until browned and easily flaked. Serves 4.

Cookbook Committee

Scallops Newburg

1½ tablespoons butter
1   pint scallops, cut small
½   cup sliced mushrooms
½   teaspoon salt
Dash paprika

⅛   teaspoon nutmeg
2   tablespoons cooking sherry
2   egg yolks, beaten
½   cup half and half cream
Pastry shells or toast

Melt butter in double boiler. Add scallops and mushrooms. Cook 3 to 5 minutes, stirring constantly. Add seasonings and sherry and let cook for one minute. Mix yolks and cream. Remove from fire, add egg mixture and beat until smooth. Return to fire and cook until mixture just begins to thicken, about one minute. Serve at once in pastry shells or on toast. Serves 6.

Mrs. Don Bradford (Melinda)

The present-day longhorn originated in Texas, although its ancestors wandered north from Mexico into the vast, open spaces of the state and were found roaming wild by the first Anglo settlers in 1821. This impressive animal was the salvation of Texas following the Civil War, when defeated soldiers returned to empty coffers and unplowed fields. Before the arrival of the railroad, great herds, often numbering from 10,000–15,000, were driven all the way to Kansas to market along the famous Chisholm and Western Trails. They were sold for as much as $11.00 a head to beef-hungry Easterners. In the late 1800's, Herefords were brought to the state in an effort to fatten the rangy longhorn breed. The trend at that time was toward marbled beef with heavy fat on each steak. However, in recent years, a greater awareness of good health has demanded a diet low in cholesterol and high in protein. These same genetic characteristics have brought the lean longhorn back into prominence. Now, Texas ranchers are once again breeding these magnificent, gentle longhorns to roam the range, much as the ones pictured here at the H. C. Carter Ranch outside Austin.

Breads pictured: French Bread, Croissants, Cookbook Coffee Cake, Sourdough Biscuits, Honey Wheat Bread, and Kolaches.

Honey Whole Wheat Bread

4 cups whole wheat flour, divided	3 cups water
½ cup instant nonfat dry milk	½ cup honey
2 packages dry yeast	2 tablespoons oil
1 tablespoon salt	4 to 4½ cups unbleached flour

Combine 3 cups whole wheat flour, dry yeast, dry milk and salt. Heat water, honey and oil in a saucepan over low heat until warm. Pour warm (not hot) liquid over flour mixture. Blend on low speed of electric mixer for 1 minute and then at medium speed for 2 minutes. By hand, stir in remaining whole wheat flour and regular flour. Turn dough onto a floured surface and knead about 5 minutes. Put dough in a greased bowl; cover and let rise until doubled in bulk, 45 to 60 minutes. Punch dough down; divide in half. Shape each half into a loaf by rolling dough out to a 7x14 rectangle. Starting with the 7 inch side, roll up jelly roll fashion. Place in 2 greased 5x9 inch or 4x8 inch loaf pans. Cover loaves; let rise until doubled in bulk, 30 to 40 minutes. Bake at 375° for 40 to 45 minutes or until loaf sounds hollow when lightly tapped. Remove from pan, cool on a wire rack before slicing. Yields 2 loaves.

Mrs. Larry Hall (Jane)

Monkey Bread

1 cup milk, scalded	1 teaspoon salt
1 cup butter, divided	1 package dry yeast
4 tablespoons sugar	3½ cups flour

Combine milk, ½ cup butter, sugar, and salt and stir until butter melts. Let cool to 105° to 115°. Add yeast and stir until dissolved. Place flour in large bowl; make well in center, and add liquid ingredients. Stir until blended. Cover; let rise until doubled. Turn onto floured surface and roll to ¼ inch thickness. Cut in 3 inch squares. Dip each in ½ cup melted butter. Layer in 10 inch tube or bundt pan. Let rise until double. Bake at 375° for 30 to 40 minutes. Yields 1 ring.

Mrs. Jerry Dow (Annette)

Cheese Herb Bread

5½−6 cups flour, divided
2 tablespoons sugar
2 teaspoons salt
¾ teaspoon oregano
¾ teaspoon basil
1 package dry yeast
1 cup milk

¼ cup butter
1 cup (2 servings) prepared instant mashed potatoes
2 eggs
2 cups (8 ounces) grated Cheddar cheese
Melted butter

Combine 2 cups flour, sugar, salt, oregano, basil and yeast. Heat milk and butter until very warm (120° to 130°). Gradually add to dry ingredients and beat 2 minutes at medium speed of mixer, scraping bowl occasionally. Add 1 cup flour, potatoes, eggs and cheese. Beat 2 minutes at low speed, scraping bowl occasionally. Stir in enough additional flour to make a soft dough. Knead on a lightly floured surface until smooth and elastic, 8 to 10 minutes. Place in buttered bowl, turning to butter top. Cover and let rise in warm place until doubled in bulk, about 1 hour. Divide dough into 6 equal parts. Shape each to form a 10½ inch rope. Braid together 3 ropes; repeat with remaining 3 ropes. Place 3 inches apart on large cookie sheet. Brush lightly with melted butter. Let rise in warm place until nearly doubled in bulk, about 45 minutes. Bake in 375° oven 25 to 30 minutes. Remove to wire rack to cool. Yields 2 loaves. *Delicious with spaghetti!*

Mrs. Don Panter (Carolyn)

White Braided Bread

1½ cups milk
3 tablespoons sugar
1 tablespoon salt
¼ cup butter
2 packages yeast

½ cup hot water
2 eggs, slightly beaten
7 cups flour, divided
Melted margarine

Heat milk, sugar, salt and butter until butter is melted. Then cool mixture some. Sprinkle yeast over hot water and dissolve. Add eggs and 4 cups of flour to the butter mixture along with the yeast mixture. Beat about 2 minutes. Gradually add 3 cups of flour, turn out and knead about 10 minutes. Place in a greased bowl. Cover and let rise about 1 hour or until double. Divide dough in half. Divide each into 3 parts. Roll into 15 inch strips and braid together; tuck ends underneath. Place on greased cookie sheets. Brush with melted margarine. Cover and let rise about 1 hour. Bake in a 400° oven about 40 minutes. If the crust browns too quickly, cover with foil. Yields 2 loaves.

Mrs. Larry Hall (Jane)

Zann's Wheat Germ Bread

2 cups milk
2 tablespoons sugar
3 teaspoons salt
⅓ cup oil
½ cup sorghum molasses
1 cup warm water (105° to 115°)

2 packages dry yeast
3 cups unsifted whole wheat flour
1 cup toasted wheat germ
2 cups unsifted white flour

Scald milk; stir in sugar, salt, oil and molasses. Cool to lukewarm. Measure warm water into large warm bowl. Sprinkle in yeast; stir until dissolved. Stir in lukewarm milk mixture, wheat germ, and whole wheat flour. Beat until smooth. Add remaining flour, ½ cup at a time to make a soft dough. Turn out on lightly floured board and knead until smooth and elastic, about 8–10 minutes. Place in greased bowl, turning to grease top. Cover; let rise in warm place, free from draft, until doubled in bulk, about 1½ to 2 hours, depending on room temperature. Knead until elastic, about 8 to 10 minutes. Let rise until doubled, about 1 hour. Punch down. Divide in half. Shape into loaves. Place in two greased bread pans. Cover; let rise in warm place until doubled in bulk, about 1 hour. Bake at 400° about 25 to 30 minutes. Remove from pans to cool.

Mrs. Jim Shorey (Zann)

Anne's Onion Bread

2 packages dry yeast
¾ cup warm water
3 tablespoons sugar
1 large onion, minced
⅓ cup oil

3 cups cottage cheese
1 teaspoon salt
¾ teaspoon baking soda
2 teaspoons beef bouillon
5½ to 6 cups flour

Combine yeast, warm water and sugar. Sauté onion in oil until soft; add cottage cheese, salt, soda and bouillon. Place yeast and cottage cheese mixtures in large bowl. Add 3 cups flour, and mix well. Stir in enough additional flour to make stiff dough, about 3 cups. Knead until elastic, about 8 to 10 minutes. Let rise until doubled, about 1 hour. Punch down; divide in half. Shape into loaves, and place in two greased bread pans. Cover; let rise in warm place until doubled in bulk, about 1 hour. Bake at 400° about 25 to 30 minutes. Remove from pans to cool. Yields two loaves.

Mrs. Jim Shorey (Zann)

Onion Lovers' Twist Bread

1 package dry yeast	**Filling:**
¼ cup warm water	¼ cup butter
4 cups flour	1 cup onion, chopped
¼ cup sugar	1 tablespoon Parmesan
1¼ teaspoons salt	cheese
½ cup hot water	½ cup Cheddar cheese
½ cup milk	1 teaspoon garlic salt
¼ cup butter, softened	1 teaspoon paprika
1 egg	1 teaspoon sesame seeds

Dissolve yeast in warm water in a large bowl. Add 2 cups flour and sugar, salt, water, milk, butter, and egg. Blend with electric mixer on low until moistened. Beat 2 minutes more on medium speed. By hand, stir in remaining 2 cups flour, forming a soft dough. Cover and let rise until light and doubled in size, about 1 hour. For filling, melt butter in a saucepan, and add onion. Parmesan cheese, Cheddar cheese, salt, paprika, and sesame seeds. Stir until cheese is melted and mixture is well blended. Grease a cookie sheet. Punch down dough and toss on a floured surface until it is no longer sticky. Roll to a 12x18 inch rectangle, and cut lengthwise into three 4x18 inch strips. Spread filling on each strip, then fold each one sealing the 18 inch side and ends. On the greased cookie sheet, braid the three strips together. Cover and let rise for 1 hour. Bake at 350° for 30 to 35 minutes, or until golden brown. Yields 1 large loaf.

Mrs. Edward Cornet (Kathi)

No Knead Dilly Bread

1 package dry yeast	1 egg, beaten
¼ cup hot water	¼ teaspoon baking soda
1 cup warmed cottage	1 teaspoon salt
cheese	2½ cups sifted flour,
1 tablespoon butter	approximately
2 tablespoons sugar	Melted butter
1 tablespoon minced onion	Salt
2 teaspoons dill seed	

Mix all ingredients and beat well. Let rise 1 hour or until double. Stir down and place in well greased loaf pan. Let double, 1 hour. Bake at 350° for 1 hour. Brush with butter and salt after removing from pan. Yields 1 loaf.

Mrs. Marcus Bone (Beverly)

Texas Beer Bread

3 cups self rising flour	1 egg, beaten
¼ cup sugar	1 tablespoon water
1 can Lite beer	Melted butter

Mix flour and sugar in bowl. Add beer; watch it foam, and mix just until blended. Pour into buttered loaf pan, preferably glass. Combine egg with water and brush top of loaf. Let rise 10 minutes. Bake at 350° for 40 to 45 minutes. Brush top with butter while hot. *Great for last minute.*

Don Bradford

Sour Cream Muffins

1 egg	2 teaspoons baking powder
1 cup sour cream	½ teaspoon baking soda
2 tablespoons butter, melted	½ teaspoon salt
2 cups sifted flour	¼ cup milk
¼ cup sugar	

Beat egg and sour cream until light and fluffy. Add melted butter. Sift flour, sugar, baking powder, baking soda, and salt together. Add to egg mixture with milk. Stir only until dry ingredients are dampened. Fill 12 greased muffin tins one half full. Bake at 400° for 20 minutes or until muffins are golden brown.

Ellie Winetroub

Quick and Easy Beer Muffins

2 cups buttermilk baking mix	12 tablespoons beer, at room
2 teaspoons sugar	temperature
Dash of salt	

Combine all ingredients, mixing well. Batter will be slightly stiff. Spoon into greased muffin tins. Bake at 450° about 10 minutes. Yields 8 muffins.

Mrs. James Hurlbut (Marsha)

 Has your bread dough risen enough? Press two fingers into the dough about ½ inch deep; if the impression remains, the dough is ready.

Six Week Muffins

5 teaspoons baking soda	4 cups flour
2 cups boiling water	1 teaspoon salt
1 cup shortening	4 cups All Bran
2 cups sugar	2 cups 40% Bran
4 eggs	2 cups chopped dates, raisins
1 quart buttermilk	or both

Add soda to boiling water; cool. Cream shortening and sugar; add eggs
and soda mixture. Add remaining ingredients; mix well. Store covered in
the refrigerator. Do not stir again. Spoon into muffin tins. Bake at 375°
for 25 minutes. Keeps up to six weeks.

Mrs. Elof Soderburg (Mary)

Angel Biscuits

6 cups biscuit mix	½ cup shortening
¼ cup sugar	1½ to 2 cups warm water
1 package dry yeast	¼ cup margarine, melted

Combine biscuit mix, sugar and dry yeast. Blend in shortening with a
fork or pastry blender. Add warm water slowly and stir until dough leaves
the sides of the bowl. Place dough on lightly floured board or pastry cloth.
Knead until smooth and elastic. Roll or pat dough into ½ inch thickness.
Cut with biscuit cutter and place on greased baking sheet. Brush with
melted margarine. At this point, biscuits can be frozen on the cookie sheet
and then transferred to plastic bags for freezer storage. Before cooking, let
thaw 40 minutes before putting in oven. Bake at 400° for 10 to 12 minutes or until golden brown. Yields 4 dozen.

Mrs. Larry Wisian (Kay)

Buttermilk Biscuits

2 cups flour	½ teaspoon baking soda
1 tablespoon baking powder	½ cup shortening
½ teaspoon salt	1 cup buttermilk

Preheat oven to 450°. Combine dry ingredients in bowl. Cut in the shortening. Blend in buttermilk. Put dough on floured board, but do not over
handle. Roll out to ½ inch thickness. Cut out with 2 inch biscuit cutter.
Bake at 450° for 12 to 15 minutes. Yields 16. *This is the best biscuit recipe I've ever made. I freeze these after baking and then reheat them in
the microwave for 20 seconds on high for breakfast.*

Mrs. John Perkins (Sandy)

Sour Dough Biscuits

1 package yeast	1 tablespoon salt
2 tablespoons warm water	3 tablespoons sugar
4½ cups flour	½ cup shortening or ⅓ cup oil
2 tablespoons baking powder	2 cups buttermilk
½ teaspoon baking soda	

Dissolve yeast in water. Combine dry ingredients; mix in oil, milk, and yeast mixture. Place in loose plastic bag; let rise until double in size. Do not punch down. Store in refrigerator for one or two days. Pinch off enough dough for a biscuit and put on a floured cookie sheet. Let rise at least four hours or overnight for breakfast. Bake at 400° for 12 to 15 minutes or until golden. Yields 4 to 5 dozen, depending on size of biscuit.

Ross Ayers

Spiral Herb Bread

1 loaf (1 pound) frozen white bread dough	
1 tablespoon oil	

Herb Filling:

1 tablespoon butter or margarine	1 tablespoon oregano
1 garlic clove, crushed	1 teaspoon salt
1½ cups chopped parsley	Pepper to taste
⅓ cup chopped green onions	¼ cup grated Parmesan cheese
	1 egg, lightly beaten

Brush all sides of frozen dough with oil. Thaw; let rise as directed on package.

Herb Filling: In skillet, melt butter; add garlic and sauté for one minute. Add parsley, green onions, oregano, salt and pepper. Cook for about 3 minutes or until tender. Stir in cheese and all but 1 tablespoon of egg (use the remaining egg for the bread). Grease a 9x5 inch loaf pan. Punch dough down and turn onto a lightly floured surface; let rest 5 minutes. Roll into a 14x9 inch rectangle. Brush dough with the reserved egg and spread with herb filling to within 1 inch of the edges. Roll up dough from 9 inch side; pinch edges to seal. Place in pan; brush top with remaining egg. Bake in 375° oven for 40 minutes. Remove from pan and cool on wire rack. Yields 1 loaf. *This gives you the fun of homemade without the hassle.*

Mrs. Jim Rado (Vicki)

Bran Refrigerator Rolls

2 packages dry or 2 cakes
   compressed yeast
1 cup warm water
1 cup shortening
¾ cup sugar
1 cup whole bran

2 teaspoons salt
1 cup boiling water
6½ cups sifted all purpose flour,
   divided
2 eggs, beaten

Soften active dry yeast in warm water (110°) or compressed yeast in luke-warm water (85°). Combine shortening, sugar, bran, and salt. Add boiling water and stir until shortening melts. Cool to lukewarm. Stir in 1 cup of flour; add eggs and yeast mixture. Beat in half the remaining flour. Add remaining flour and mix well. Place in bowl, greasing surface. Cover; chill in refrigerator until ready to use. Punch dough down and form into rolls. Using one ball of dough for each roll. Let rise until double, 1½ to 2 hours. Bake at 425° for 15 minutes. Yields 4 to 5 dozen.

Mrs. Ron Garrick (Bonnie)

Old Fashioned Rolls

½ cup lukewarm water
1 teaspoon sugar
1 package dry yeast
2 cups milk
½ cup sugar

1 teaspoon salt
½ cup shortening
1 egg
6 to 6½ cups flour, sifted
½ cup shortening, melted

Put yeast and 1 teaspoon sugar in water and let dissolve (this will also serve to proof the yeast—if it does not foam in the water, pour it out and start over). Scald the milk and allow it to cool to room temperature. Cream ½ cup sugar, salt, and ½ cup shortening. Beat in egg; then add milk and yeast. Add flour, ½ cup at a time and mix. The mixture should be sticky and if too much flour is added the rolls will not be light. Let dough rise in bowl until double in size. Punch down; cover with a thin layer of salad oil and place in refrigerator. Refrigerate at least overnight, but not more than 2 days. On floured surface, knead dough slightly; roll out and cut with biscuit cutter. Dip in butter; fold in half. To make folding easy, pull out slightly. Place on ungreased pan. Let rise until doubled. Bake at 400° for 10 minutes, or until golden brown. These may be baked until slightly brown and then frozen. *This recipe is at least 60 years old, and was written down as I watched my mother do it as her mother had done.*

Mrs. Jerry Hunt (Gail)

Garlic Bread Sticks

1 loaf very thin sliced bread, frozen
½ pound butter, melted

1 can (3 ounces) Parmesan cheese
Garlic powder

Remove crust from frozen bread; then cut into thirds. Dip each piece of bread into melted butter. Roll in a mixture of Parmesan cheese and garlic. Bake on greased cookie sheet at 350° about 10 minutes on each side until golden brown. Serve hot or at room temperature. Yields 60 bread sticks.

Mrs. Charles Strong (Ginny)

Sopaipillas

1¾ cups flour
2 teaspoons baking powder
1 tablespoon sugar
1 teaspoon salt
2 tablespoons shortening

⅔ cup milk
2 cups hot oil
Honey, if desired
Cinnamon sugar, if desired

Combine flour, baking powder, sugar, and salt in a large bowl. Cut in shortening with pastry blender until like corn meal. Add milk, mixing just until dough holds together in a ball. Turn out onto a lightly floured surface and knead about 1 minute. Cover dough and let rest 1 hour. Roll into a 12x15 inch rectangle, about ⅛ inch thick. Cut into 3 inch squares. Heat oil in deep fryer to 370° or 380°. Drop squares a few pieces at a time into oil, turning at once so they will puff evenly. Brown on both sides. Drain on paper towels. Serve hot with butter to accompany a meal, or with honey and cinnamon as a sweet treat. Serves 15 to 20.

Mrs. Jim Schultz (Mary Kay)

Blender Potato Pancakes

2 eggs
2 small onions, sliced
1½ teaspoons salt
½ of one carrot

2 cups raw potatoes, cubed
1 tablespoon to ¼ cup matzo meal or cracker meal
2 tablespoons flour

Put eggs in blender; add onion, salt, carrot and ½ of the potatoes. Blend on high for 5 seconds. Add meal, and remaining potatoes, stir to blend; blend 3 more seconds. Fry 8 minutes on each side until brown.

Mrs. Thomas Schwartz (Ellana)

Pancakes

1½ cups flour
2½ tablespoons sugar
3½ heaping teaspoons baking
    powder

1   teaspoon salt
1   egg, beaten
1½ cups milk
⅓   cup margarine, melted

Mix dry ingredients thoroughly. Add egg and milk, using only enough milk to make a thick or heavy pourable batter. Then add margarine. Yields 20 three inch pancakes.

Mrs. Jack Bone (Joyce)

Hush Puppies

⅔   cup yellow corn meal
⅓   cup flour
1   teaspoon sugar
1   teaspoon baking powder

Pinch soda
1   small onion, minced
Pinch salt
¼   cup milk

Mix dry ingredients. Add milk until mixture is pasty. Drop by spoonfuls into hot fat. Cook until golden brown; drain. Serve hot. Yields 12.

Mrs. Larry Keith (Virginia)

Mama's Corn Bread

1   cup yellow corn meal
¼   cup unbleached flour
1   teaspoon salt
1   tablespoon baking powder
½   teaspoon baking soda

1   cup plain yogurt
½   cup milk
½   cup safflower oil
1   egg
1   tablespoon honey

Grease an 8 inch cast iron skillet or pan and place in a 450° oven to pre-heat. Combine cornmeal, flour, salt, baking powder and soda in a bowl. Add yogurt, milk, oil, egg, and honey, stirring well. Pour batter into the hot skillet and bake at 450° for 20 minutes, or until golden brown. *Look for a coarse ground corn meal for a much chewier texture and a rich corn flavor.*

Mrs. Dan S. Steakley (Susan)

 Corn was grown in Texas even before Anglo settlers arrived in 1821. A favorite of the Indian tribes, they often made corn meal mush or "platter" bread, which was cooked on a flat rock, since they had no ovens.

Corn-Light Bread

3   cups white corn meal
1   cup flour
½   cup sugar
1   teaspoon salt

1   teaspoon soda
3   tablespoons oil
3   cups buttermilk

Mix all ingredients well. Grease and heat a square 9 inch pan. Pour mixture into hot pan. Bake 375° for 45 minutes. Remove; wrap in foil and chill. Slice, butter and toast. *Great with vegetables. Will keep in the refrigerator up to 3 weeks.*

Mrs. Jerry Dow (Annette)

Jalapeño Cornbread

3   cups cornbread mix
2   cups milk
½   cup oil
3   eggs, beaten
1   large onion, chopped
½   teaspoon garlic powder
4   slices crisp bacon,
    crumbled

3   tablespoons sugar
1   cup canned cream style
    corn
½   cup chopped jalapeños
1½ cups grated Cheddar cheese
1   jar (2 ounces) pimiento

Mix all ingredients together; pour into a 9x13 inch pan. Bake at 350° for about 30 to 40 minutes or until brown. *Freezes well.*

Mrs. Ken Moyer (Bonnie)

Mexican Spoon Bread

½   cup corn meal
1   tablespoon baking powder
1   teaspoon salt
2   eggs, slightly beaten
2   jalapeño peppers, chopped,
    or 3 tablespoons jalapeño
    relish

2   tablespoons green pepper,
    chopped
1   cup cream style corn
2   tablespoons chopped onion
1   cup sour cream
½   cup oil
1   cup sharp Cheddar cheese,
    grated

Combine dry ingredients. Add eggs, peppers, corn, onion and sour cream. Heat oil in 1½ quart casserole; pour into batter and mix. Pour ½ batter back into casserole and top with ½ cheese. Pour remaining batter and top with rest of cheese. Bake at 350° for 40 minutes. Serves 10 to 12.

Mrs. B. Lynn Turlington (Jill)

Patio Skillet Bread

1½ cups sifted flour
4 teaspoons baking powder
2 tablespoons sugar
2½ teaspoons salt
2 teaspoons sage
1 teaspoon thyme
1½ cups yellow corn meal

1½ cups chopped onion
1½ cups chopped celery
¼ cup chopped pimiento
3 eggs, beaten
1½ cups milk
⅓ cup shortening, melted

Sift flour, baking powder, sugar and salt. Add sage, thyme, corn meal, onion, celery, and pimiento. Stir to blend. Combine eggs, milk, and shortening and add to flour mixture; pour into a greased 10 or 11 inch skillet and bake at 400° for 35 to 40 minutes.

Mrs. Jerry Hunt (Gail)

Cinnamon Swirl Bread

2 packages dry yeast
½ cup warm water
2 cups scalded milk
⅓ cup honey
1 tablespoon salt
⅓ cup shortening

5½ to 6 cups sifted flour, divided
2 cups quick oats
Melted butter
⅔ cup brown sugar
1 teaspoon cinnamon

Soften yeast in warm water. Pour scalded milk over honey, salt, and shortening. Cool to lukewarm. Stir in 1 cup flour. Add yeast and oats. Stir in enough flour to make a soft dough. Turn out on floured board and knead until soft and satiny, about 10 minutes. Round dough into ball and place in greased bowl. Brush lightly with shortening. Cover and let rise about 1 hour. Punch down dough; divide in half. Roll one half into 7x14 inch rectangle. Brush with melted butter. Combine brown sugar and cinnamon for filling. Sprinkle rectangle with ½ of the filling. Starting with short side of dough; roll as for jelly roll. Place seam side down in greased loaf pan. Brush lightly with melted butter. Repeat with other dough. Cover and let rise 45 minutes. Bake at 375° about 20 minutes. Reduce heat to 350° and bake at least another 20 to 25 minutes or until golden.

Mrs. Don Panter (Carolyn)

Cinnamon Pinwheel Rolls

1 package dry yeast	¼ cup shortening
¼ cup water, warmed	1 teaspoon salt
1 cup milk	3 to 3½ cups flour
¼ cup sugar	1 egg

Filling:
¼ cup softened butter
½ cup sugar
2 teaspoons cinnamon

Soften the dry yeast in the ¼ cup warm water. Combine the milk, sugar, shortening and salt and heat to lukewarm (enough to melt the shortening). Add about half the flour and mix well. Add the softened yeast and the egg; beat well. Stir in remaining flour, or enough to make a moderately soft dough. Turn out on a lightly floured surface; knead until smooth and elastic (about 10 minutes). Place in a lightly greased bowl. Cover and let rise in a warm place until double (1½ to 2 hours). Punch down and shape in a ball; cover and let rest 10 minutes. Roll dough into a 18x10 inch rectangle, ½ inch thick. Spread with ¼ cup softened butter. Combine ½ cup sugar and 2 teaspoons cinnamon; sprinkle over dough. Beginning at wide side, roll up, jellyroll fashion. Seal edge well; cut in 1 inch slices. Place slices, cut side down, in greased 2¼ inch muffin cups. As you put each roll in pan, push center up from bottom so that it will rise more in the center than around the edges. Cover; let rise in a warm place until double (30 to 45 minutes). Bake in 375° oven 15 to 20 minutes or until done. Yields 1½ dozen rolls. *When these rolls are all gaily wrapped and placed in a basket, you have a perfect gift for all your friends.*

Mrs. Larry Hall (Jane)

Grapenut Bread

2 cups buttermilk	4 rounded teaspoons baking
1 cup Grapenuts	powder
1 cup sugar	1 teaspoon soda
3½ cups flour	Pinch of salt
	1 egg

Soak buttermilk, grapenuts and sugar for 10 minutes. Sift flour, baking powder, soda and salt together. Add egg to buttermilk mixture, then combine with dry mixture and mix well. Put in greased baking pans and let rest 1 hour. Bake at 350° for 35 to 40 minutes. Yields two loaves. *This bread is especially good toasted.*

Mrs. Clark Rector (Sue)

Danish Puff

Pastry Layer:

1 cup flour

1 stick butter

2 tablespoons water

Cream Puff Layer:

1 cup water

1 stick butter

1 cup flour

3 eggs

1 teaspoon vanilla or almond extract

Glaze:

Powdered sugar

Hot coffee

Nuts, pecans or almonds

For pastry layer combine flour and butter. Add water, blending as for a pie crust. Divide dough in half and pat into 2 inch rectangular strips, 3x12 inches, on an ungreased cookie sheet.

Bring butter and water to a rolling boil; remove from heat. Add flour, beating well until mixture forms a smooth ball. Add eggs one at a time, beating vigorously after each. Mix in flavoring. Spread this mixture evenly over the first layer. Bake at 350° for 1 hour.

Combine powdered sugar and coffee to form glaze. While pastry is still warm, frost. Sprinkle with nuts. Serves 10 to 12.

Mrs. Leo Mueller (Nancy)

Apricot Strudel

2 sticks margarine

2 cups flour

½ teaspoon salt

1 cup sour cream

1 jar (18 ounces) apricot preserves

1 can (3½ ounces) coconut, optional

½ cup slivered almonds, optional

Powdered sugar to decorate

Cut margarine into flour and salt until crumbly. Mix in sour cream. Chill dough. Roll out into two thin pieces. Spread preserves over each; sprinkle with coconut. Add a few almonds, if desired. Roll as for jelly roll. Place on well greased cookie sheet and bake at 350° for one hour. Remove and sprinkle with powdered sugar. Slice and serve. Yields 2 strudels; each serves 6 to 8. *May be prepared ahead of time and frozen.*

Mrs. Don Panter (Carolyn)

Cinnamon Crisps

3½ cups sifted flour, divided
1 package dry yeast
1¼ cups milk
1¾ cups sugar, divided
¼ cup shortening
1 teaspoon salt
1 egg

8 tablespoons butter, melted, divided
½ cup pecans, chopped
½ cup brown sugar
1½ teaspoons cinnamon, divided

In a large bowl, combine 2 cups flour and yeast. Heat milk, ¼ cup sugar, shortening and salt just until shortening melts. Add to dry ingredients; add egg and beat at low speed until mixed. Beat 3 minutes on high, then by hand stir in enough of the remaining flour to make a moderately soft dough. Place in a greased bowl; turning once to grease surface. Cover and let rise in a warm place until double, about 1½ to 2 hours. Turn out onto a lightly floured surface and divide in half. Roll out one portion of dough at a time into a 12 inch square. Combine 4 tablespoons of butter, brown sugar, ½ cup sugar and ½ teaspoon cinnamon. Spread half of this over the dough. Roll up jelly roll fashion; pinch the edges to seal. Cut into 12 pieces and place on a greased baking sheet. Flatten each to about 3 inch diameter. Repeat with other half of dough. Let rise about 30 minutes. Cover with waxed paper and flatten again. Remove paper and brush with 4 tablespoons butter. Combine 1 cup sugar, ½ cup pecans, and 1 teaspoon cinnamon; sprinkle over rolls. Cover with paper and flatten. Bake at 400° for 10 to 12 minutes. Remove immediately from baking sheets.

Mrs. Larry Hall (Jane)

Deep South Ginger Muffins

¾ cup butter
½ cup sugar
2 eggs
⅛ teaspoon cinnamon
1 teaspoon ginger
⅛ teaspoon allspice

½ cup buttermilk
1 teaspoon soda
½ cup dark molasses
½ cup chopped nuts
½ cup raisins
2 cups flour

Mix ingredients in order given. Put into well greased muffin tins or cup cake liners. Bake at 400° about 10 minutes. Yields 24. *Batter may be stored in refrigerator.*

Mrs. Wayne Davison (Cindi)

Blender Banana Bread

1   egg
¼   cup margarine
1   cup mashed bananas
1   cup sugar

1   cup raisins
2   cups flour
1   teaspoon baking soda
1   teaspoon salt

Put first five ingredients into the blender. Whirl on low until smooth. Combine the dry ingredients in a large bowl. Add blender mixture, and stir until moistened. Turn into a greased loaf pan. Bake at 325° for 60 minutes. Yields 1 loaf.

Mrs. Ken Moyer (Bonnie)

Pumpkin Bread

3   cups sugar
1   cup oil
4   eggs
2   cups canned pumpkin
¾   cup water

3½ cups flour
2   teaspoons baking soda
1½ teaspoons salt
2½ teaspoons cinnamon
2½ teaspoons nutmeg

In large mixing bowl combine sugar, oil, eggs, and pumpkin. Sift dry ingredients together and add to sugar mixture, alternating with water. Pour batter into a lightly greased bundt pan or into four ungreased one pound coffee cans, filling half full. Bake at 350° for 1 hour. *For a heartier cake, add 1 cup pecans and/or 1 cup raisins just before pouring into bundt pan. Slice bread rounds and serve with orange cream cheese for a sweet sandwich.*

Mrs. Bob Edgecomb (Mary)

Zucchini Bread

1   cup oil
3   eggs, slightly beaten
2   cups sugar
2   cups grated raw zucchini, peeled
2   teaspoons vanilla
3   cups all purpose flour

1   teaspoon baking soda
¼   teaspoon baking powder
1   teaspoon salt
3   teaspoons cinnamon
1   cup chopped pecans or walnuts

Combine oil, eggs, sugar, zucchini, and vanilla. Blend well. Stir in flour, baking soda, baking powder, salt, and cinnamon. Do not beat! Stir in nuts. Bake at 325° in greased and floured loaf pan for 1 hour or until done.

Mrs. Jim Rado (Vicki)

Kolache

2 packages dry yeast	½ teaspoon salt
1 tablespoon sugar	½ teaspoon mace
1 cup warm water	1 egg yolk
6 tablespoons butter	1 cup milk
¼ cup sugar	4 cups flour

Filling:

8 ounces dry cottage cheese	1 teaspoon flour
2 tablespoons pineapple preserves	1 teaspoon butter, melted
	Other fillings follow

Dissolve 2 packages yeast and sugar in warm water, and set aside. Cream butter and sugar; add salt, mace and egg yolk. Scald milk and let cool to luke warm. Add milk and yeast mixture to creamed mixture and begin adding flour ½ cup at a time until you have added the four cups. Continue to beat dough until it looks smooth and shiny. Put dough into a greased mixing bowl and let rise until double in bulk, about 20 to 30 minutes. Do not punch down but take out about half of the mixture and pat or roll on a floured surface to about ½ inch thick. Cut with a 3 inch cookie cutter and place on an oiled cookie sheet. Press holes immediately in the center of each, and fill with 1 teaspoon of any fruit or cheese filling. For filling, combine well drained cottage cheese, pineapple, and flour. Let buns rise 15 to 20 minutes after you add the fillings; then bake at 375° for 15 minutes or until brown. Yields 2 to 3 dozen. *Kolaches are a traditional Czech, Polish or German sweet bread made with leftover bread dough and whatever fruits might be on hand. Other fillings that can be cooked are seeded prunes, dried apricots, and dried or fresh apples (cooked and seasoned with cinnamon and sugar to taste). Canned pie filling may also be used.*

Mildred May

Cinnamon Pull Aparts

½ cup chopped nuts	½ cup sugar
3 cans (10 count) biscuits	1 stick margarine
1 teaspoon cinnamon	1 cup brown sugar

Grease bundt pan. Place nuts in bottom. Cut biscuits into quarters. Roll in cinnamon sugar mixture. Arrange in pan. Melt margarine and brown sugar. Pour over sugared biscuits. Bake at 350° for 30 to 40 minutes. Remove from pan. Serves 8 to 10.

Mrs. Jim Schultz (Mary Kay)

Strawberry Bread with Cream Cheese Spread

3 cups flour
2 cups sugar
1 teaspoon baking soda
1 teaspoon cinnamon
1 teaspoon salt
1 cup strawberry juice, divided

2 packages (10 ounces each) frozen strawberries, thawed
1 cup oil
4 eggs, well beaten
8 ounces cream cheese, softened

Combine and mix well flour, sugar, baking soda, cinnamon, and salt. Make a well in center and add ½ cup strawberry juice, strawberries, oil and eggs. Mix by hand. Grease and flour two 4x8 inch loaf pans. Bake at 350° for 1 hour or until toothpick inserted in center comes out clean. To prepare cream cheese spread, combine cream cheese with enough strawberry juice to make a spreadable mixture. Spread on bread and refrigerate until served. Yields 2 loaves. *Loaves can be frozen; slice thinly before completely thawed.*

Jan Palmer

Grandma's Banana Nut Bread

½ cup butter, no substitute
¾ cup honey
¼ cup molasses
2 eggs
1 cup mashed bananas
2¼ cups whole wheat flour
½ teaspoon soda

1 teaspoon baking powder
½ teaspoon salt
⅔ cup milk
1 teaspoon vanilla
1 cup coarsely chopped pecans

Cream butter, honey and molasses; add eggs and mix well. Stir in bananas. Sift dry ingredients together, and add to creamed mixture alternating with milk. Beat only until smooth. Add vanilla and nuts. Pour into well buttered loaf pan, bake at 350° for 60 to 80 minutes or until done. Yields 1 loaf.

Mrs. Dan Steakley (Susan)

Banana Pineapple Loaf

1	cup butter	¾	teaspoon salt
2	cups sugar	1	can (15½ ounce) crushed
4	eggs		pineapple, undrained
1	cup mashed ripe banana	1	cup shredded coconut,
4	cups sifted flour		optional
2	teaspoons baking powder	1	cup chopped pecans,
1	teaspoon baking soda		optional

Cream butter and sugar until light and fluffy. Add eggs and mix well. Stir in bananas. Sift together flour, baking powder, soda, and salt, and add to butter mixture. Fold in pineapple, and optional ingredients. Pour into greased and floured loaf pans to just over half full. Small or large pans may be used. Bake at 350° for 1 hour and 10 minutes or until done.

Mrs. Denman Smith (Sandra)

Cookbook Coffee Cake

Dough:

1	package dry yeast	1	teaspoon salt
¼	cup warm water	¾	cup milk
½	cup margarine	4¼	cups flour, divided
½	cup shortening	3	eggs, separated
3	tablespoons sugar	½	teaspoon vanilla

Filling:

1	cup sugar	1	teaspoon cinnamon
1	cup chopped pecans	1	cup chopped apples
1	cup raisins	1	cup chopped, dried
⅔	cup brown sugar		apricots, optional

Soften yeast in warm water (115° to 120°). Cream margarine, shortening, 3 tablespoons sugar and salt. Add milk, 1 cup flour, yeast mixture, egg yolks, and vanilla; beat well. Add 1¼ cups more flour; beat again. Gradually stir in remaining flour, using hands if necessary. Place in greased bowl, turning once to grease surface. Cover; let rise 2 hours. Punch down; divide into two parts. Let rest 10 minutes.

For filling beat egg whites to soft peaks. Gradually add 1 cup of sugar, beating until stiff peaks form. Set aside. Combine remaining filling ingredients. On a floured surface roll one part of dough to a 9 × 15 inch rectangle. Spread with ½ of meringue mixture to within one inch of edges. Sprinkle with ½ of filling. Fold in half lengthwise, pinching under edges to seal. Form dough into circle and pinch ends together. With scissors make slits on top of ring. Repeat with remaining dough. Bake at 350° for 25 minutes. Serves 24.

Cookbook Committee

Perfect Gingerbread

2 cups flour	¼ teaspoon salt
½ cup sugar	¾ cup molasses
1½ teaspoons ginger	1 cup buttermilk
½ teaspoon cinnamon	1 egg
2 teaspoons baking powder	¼ cup melted shortening
Scant teaspoon soda	1 to 2 teaspoons vanilla

Put all dry ingredients in sifter. Put wet ingredients in mixing bowl. Sift dry ingredients in the mixing bowl. Beat until smooth. Pour into greased 9x5 loaf pan. Bake at 350° for about 1 hour. *Delicious served plain. I also like a topping of whipped cream with bananas. Pecans may be added if desired.*

Mrs. Don Panter (Carolyn)

Sunday Morning Coffee Cake

2½ cups flour	**Topping:**
¾ cup sugar	¾ cup flour mixture
1 cup brown sugar	2 teaspoons cinnamon
1 teaspoon nutmeg	½ cup pecans, chopped
1 teaspoon salt	
¾ cup oil	**Icing:**
1 cup buttermilk	1 cup powdered sugar
1 teaspoon baking soda	¼ teaspoon vanilla
1 egg	1 tablespoon water

Mix flour, sugars, nutmeg, salt and oil. Remove ¾ cup of mixture and save for topping. Add buttermilk, soda and egg to the mixture remaining in bowl. Mix with hand mixer until smooth. Pour into greased and floured cookie sheet with sides. Combine topping ingredients and sprinkle over batter. Bake at 350° for 30 to 35 minutes. While hot, drizzle with icing.

Mrs. Robert West (Linda)

On Swedish Hill in Austin years ago, it was a custom for the ladies in the neighborhood to gather every afternoon at four for pastries and coffee. The hostess for the day hung a dish towel on her clothes line as an invitation. Many delectable pastries were consumed on these delightful afternoons.

Cinnamon Coffee Cake

1 box (18½ ounces) yellow cake mix	4 eggs
1 small box vanilla instant pudding	1 teaspoon vanilla
⅔ cup oil	1 teaspoon butter flavoring
¾ cup water	½ cup brown sugar
	¼ cup nuts, chopped

Filling:

¼ cup sugar	2 teaspoons cinnamon

Glaze:

1 cup powdered sugar	½ teaspoon butter flavoring
½ teaspoon vanilla	Milk

Mix cake mix, pudding, oil, water, eggs, vanilla, and butter flavoring and beat for 5 minutes. Grease and flour a bundt pan. Cover bottom of pan with brown sugar and sprinkle with chopped nuts. Mix sugar and cinnamon for filling. Alternate cake batter and filling in three layers of bundt pan. Bake at 350° for 40 to 50 minutes. Mix ingredients for glaze; pour ½ glaze over while it is still in pan. Cool cake for a few minutes, then remove from pan and top the cake with remaining glaze.

Mrs. Ron Garrick (Bonnie)

Pumpkin Spice Muffins

3 cups sugar	2 teaspoons baking powder
1 cup shortening	1 teaspoon ground cloves
3 eggs	1 teaspoon nutmeg
1 can (16 ounces) pumpkin	1 teaspoon cinnamon
3 cups flour	1 teaspoon allspice
1 teaspoon baking soda	1 teaspoon vanilla

Brown Sugar Glaze:

½ cup brown sugar	1 tablespoon milk, for spreading consistency
2 tablespoons melted butter, cooled	Pecan halves
1 cup powdered sugar	

Cream sugar and shortening; add eggs and pumpkin. Stir in dry ingredients. Add vanilla. Bake in greased and floured muffin pans for 15 to 20 minutes at 350°.

Cream sugar and butter. Add sugar, then milk. Spread over top of each muffin, placing 1 pecan half on each. Yields 24 muffins.

Mrs. Marcus Bone (Beverly)

Carrot Ring

3   sticks butter
1   cup brown sugar
4   eggs separated
3   cups grated carrots
2   tablespoons water
2   tablespoons lemon juice

2   cups flour
1   teaspoon baking soda
2   teaspoons baking powder
1   teaspoon salt
¼   cup bread crumbs

Cream butter, sugar, and egg yolks. Add other ingredients except egg whites and mix well. Beat egg whites until stiff and fold into batter. Pour into large ring mold that has been greased and dusted with bread crumbs. Bake at 350° for 1 hour. Let cool for 15 minutes before removing from pan. *This is a sweet bread that can be served with peas in a light cream sauce in the middle of the ring.*

Mrs. Jerry Dow (Annette)

Chocolate Tea Bread

¼   cup butter or margarine
⅔   cup sugar
1   egg
2   cups flour, sifted
1   teaspoon baking soda
¾   teaspoon salt

½   cup Hershey's Cocoa
1   teaspoon cinnamon
1   cup buttermilk
1   cup raisins, optional
1   cup chopped nuts

Cream butter; add sugar, a small amount at a time, mixing well after each addition. Add egg and beat well. Mix the dry ingredients and add to creamed mixture alternately with the buttermilk, beating well after each addition. Stir in raisins and nuts. Put in greased 9x5 inch pan. Bake at 350° for 1 hour. Yields one loaf.

Mrs. Robert West (Linda)

For over 300 years, the Mexicans shared a common history with Texas. Their influence can be recognized in the architecture, ranching, and cuisine of Texas. Many flavorful herbs and spices are indigenous to Mexico, and our own specialities are enhanced by the addition of comino or Mexican chocolate, to name just two.

Zann's Carrot Bread

1 cup whole wheat flour	1 teaspoon salt
1 cup flour	3 cups raw carrots, peeled
1 teaspoon baking soda	and sliced
2 teaspoons baking powder	1 cup corn oil
1⅓ cups sugar, or 1 cup honey	4 eggs
2 teaspoons cinnamon	

Preheat oven to 325°. Grease 1 large loaf pan or 2 smaller loaf pans. Mix flours, baking soda and baking powder in bowl. In large blender, combine corn oil and eggs. Add sugar or honey, cinnamon, salt, and carrots and blend until all carrots have gone through the blades. It may be necessary to turn the blender off, stir, and reblend to get all of the carrots blended. Pour blended mixture over dry ingredients. Mix well. Pour into pan and bake about 1 hour for the larger pan or 50 minutes or until done for the smaller.

Zann Shorey

 Texas was second in the nation in 1980 with the production of grapefruit, cantaloupes, carrots, and white corn.

Lemon Bread

Batter:

1 stick margarine	1 teaspoon baking powder
1 cup sugar	½ teaspoon salt
2 eggs, slightly beaten	½ cup milk
1½ cups flour	Grated rind of one lemon
	½ cup nuts, broken

Glaze:
½ cup sugar
Juice of one lemon

Cream margarine and sugar. Add rest of ingredients, mixing well. Bake in a greased 9 by 5 loaf pan at 325° for 50 to 60 minutes. Remove from oven and cool five minutes. Top with glaze that has been prepared while bread is baking. Cool thoroughly.

Mrs. D. D. Baker, Jr. (Agnes)

Honey Muffins

1¼ cups flour	1½ cups All Bran Cereal
3 teaspoons baking powder	1 egg
½ teaspoon salt	⅓ cup oil
1¼ cups milk	½ cup honey

Mix flour, baking powder and salt. In separate bowl, pour milk over cereal and let stand for 2 minutes or until milk is absorbed. Add egg and mix thoroughly. Pour in oil and honey and mix by hand. Combine bran mixture and dry ingredients. Stir only until combined. Spoon into greased muffin tins and bake at 400° for 25 minutes. Yields 1 dozen. *Recipe can be doubled easily. Freeze leftovers and pop them in your microwave for 30 to 45 seconds for a quick breakfast.*

Mrs. Randy Hagan (Robin)

Holiday Cranberry Muffins

1 cup raw cranberries, chopped	¼ teaspoon salt
½ cup sugar	¼ cup sugar
2 cups flour	1 egg, beaten
¾ teaspoon baking soda	¾ cup buttermilk
	¼ cup shortening, melted

Let cranberries stand overnight in ½ cup sugar. Combine dry ingredients. Add liquid ingredients all at once. Stir until moistened. Add cranberries and stir. Fill greased muffin pans two-thirds full. Bake in a 400° oven for 20 minutes. Yields 18 muffins.

Cookbook Committee

Cherry Brunch Muffins

1 egg	¼ cup chopped maraschino cherries
¾ cup milk	
¼ cup vegetable oil	3 teaspoons baking powder
3 tablespoons maraschino cherry syrup	1 teaspoon salt
	2 tablespoons sugar
2 cups all-purpose flour	2 tablespoons chopped almonds
¼ cup sugar	

Heat oven to 375°. Grease bottoms of 12 medium muffin cups or line with paper baking cups. Beat egg; stir in milk, oil and cherry syrup. Mix in flour, ¼ cup sugar, the cherries, baking powder and salt just until flour is moistened. Fill muffin cups ⅔ full. Mix 2 tablespoons sugar and the almonds; sprinkle over batter in cups. Bake 25 minutes. Makes 12 muffins. *If you want to serve at different times, muffins will hold in bun warmer or napkin-lined basket up to 1 hour. To reheat, wrap in aluminum foil and place in 350° oven 10 minutes.*

Marian Carlson Hidell

The present Capitol building in Austin was begun in 1882, after fire destroyed an earlier one. Advertisements were run in newspapers in Scotland, recruiting stone cutters to come to Texas. Sixty-five Scots responded and the building, with outside construction of native pink granite, was completed in 1888. Its interior and dome walls were finished in Texas limestone, and the dome, roofed with 85,000 square feet of copper, stands seven feet taller than the National Capitol. This impressive structure is surrounded by 46 acres of beautifully landscaped grounds, complete with 48 varieties of shade trees and a multitude of flowering gardens.

Desserts pictured: Kahlua Cake, Boccone Dolce, Toasted Pecan Ice Cream, and Pecan Pie Bars.

Desserts

Kahlua Cake

¾ cup butter, softened
2 cups sugar
¾ cup cocoa
4 eggs, separated
1 teaspoon baking soda
2 tablespoons cold water
½ cup cold coffee

½ cup Kahlua
1¾ cups cake flour
1 tablespoon vanilla extract
1 cup Kahlua
½ cup powdered sugar
Whipped cream to garnish
Strawberries to garnish

Cream butter and sugar well; add cocoa and one egg yolk at a time, beating well. Dissolve soda in water; combine soda, coffee and Kahlua. Add liquids to creamed mixture alternately with flour. Stir in vanilla. Fold in stiffly beaten egg whites. Pour into a greased and floured 10 inch bundt pan. Bake at 325° for 45 minutes or until done. Remove cake from pan while warm; pierce cake with fork.

For glaze, combine Kahlua and powdered sugar until smooth and pour over cake. Cover and store in refrigerator. Garnish with whipped cream and strawberries, if desired.

Nancy Young Moritz

Old Fashioned Chocolate Fudge Cake

2 cups flour
2 cups sugar
1½ teaspoons baking soda
¼ teaspoon salt
½ cup cocoa
1 cup oil
1 cup buttermilk
2 eggs, beaten
3 teaspoons vanilla

¾ cup hot water
4 tablespoons cocoa
6 tablespoons milk
1 stick butter
1 box (1 pound) powdered sugar
1 tablespoon vanilla
1 cup chopped pecans, optional

Sift together flour, sugar, soda, salt and cocoa. Add oil, buttermilk, eggs, vanilla and hot water; mix well. Bake in greased 9x13 inch pan at 350° for 30 to 40 minutes. For icing, make a paste of the cocoa and milk in a saucepan. Add butter and bring to a boil, stirring constantly. Remove from heat, and add powdered sugar and vanilla. Beat well; add pecans. Pour over still hot cake in baking pan.

Mrs. Don Bradford (Melinda)

Chocolate Kahlua Cake

1	box chocolate cake mix	4	eggs
½	cup oil	¾	cup strong coffee
1	small box instant chocolate pudding	¾	cup Kahlua and creme de cacao mixed

Glaze:

1	cup powdered sugar	2	tablespoons Kahlua
2	tablespoons strong coffee	2	tablespoons creme de cacao

Combine all cake ingredients at medium speed until well blended. Pour into greased and floured 9x13 inch pan; bake at 350° for 40 to 45 minutes. Cool in pan. Mix glaze ingredients together. Poke holes in cooled cake and glaze. *For a different cake, substitute white or yellow cake mix with instant vanilla pudding. Bake in three 8 or 9 inch layers at 350° for 30 to 40 minutes. Frost with whipped cream topping.*

Mrs. Clark Rector (Sue)

Whipped Cream Topping

½ pint whipping cream	1 teaspoon vanilla
1 to 2 tablespoons sugar	Slivered almonds to garnish
1 tablespoon Kahlua	Shaved chocolate to garnish

Whip cream, adding sugar, Kahlua, and vanilla. Frost cooled layers. Sprinkle with almonds and shaved chocolate. Refrigerate.

Mrs. Chris Williston (Janice)

Chocolate Chip Cake

1	box white cake mix	4	eggs
1	small box chocolate instant pudding	1	cup sour cream
½	cup oil	1	package (6 ounces) semisweet chocolate chips
½	cup water		Powdered sugar, optional

Combine all ingredients except chocolate chips and beat well. Add chocolate chips and stir. Pour into a greased and floured bundt pan. Bake at 350° for one hour or until done. If desired, sprinkle with powdered sugar.

Mrs. Joe Williams (Mary Margaret)

Chocolate Chiffon Cake

⅔ cup cocoa
¾ cup boiling water
1¾ cups sifted cake flour
1¾ cups sugar
1½ teaspoons baking soda
1   teaspoon salt

½ cup oil
8   eggs, separated, room temperature
2   teaspoons vanilla
½ teaspoon cream of tartar

Cocoa Frosting:
3   cups very cold whipping cream
1   cup sifted powdered sugar
½ cup sifted cocoa

1   teaspoon vanilla
⅛ teaspoon salt
1   cup chopped pecans, optional

Place cocoa in small bowl; add the boiling water and stir until smooth. In a large mixing bowl, sift flour, sugar, soda and salt. To the mixture, add the salad oil, egg yolks, vanilla and cooled cocoa. In another large bowl sprinkle cream of tartar over egg whites and beat until very stiff peaks form. Now, gently fold the cocoa mixture into the egg whites. Bake at 325° for 60 minutes in an ungreased 10 inch tube pan. Let cake cool completely and then carefully remove from pan and divide into three layers.

Mix frosting ingredients together at high speed until thick and stiff. Use approximately 1½ cups between layers and remaining icing to frost the top and sides of cake. If desired, sprinkle nuts on top and sides of cake. Refrigerate until serving time. *This is a fantastic cake if you find that you have an oversupply of eggs.*

Mrs. Denman Smith (Sandra)

Hershey Bar Cake

2   sticks margarine
2   cups sugar
4   eggs, well beaten
2   cans (5½ ounces each) Hershey's syrup
2½ cups flour

½ teaspoon baking soda
¼ teaspoon salt
1   cup buttermilk
2   teaspoons vanilla
7   small Hershey bars, melted

Cream margarine and sugar. Add eggs and chocolate syrup. In separate bowl, sift together flour, soda, and salt. Add flour mixture alternately with buttermilk to chocolate mixture. Add vanilla and melted candy bars. Pour into a large greased and floured bundt pan and bake at 350° for 1 hour. *Will stay moist for at least 7 days if you can keep it that long!*

Mrs. Larry Lerche (Gail)

Black Forest Chocolate Cake

5 eggs	2 tablespoons cornstarch
⅓ cup sugar	2 tablespoons cocoa
⅔ cup sifted cake flour	2 tablespoons butter, melted

Cream Filling:

1 quart heavy cream, divided	12 squares semisweet chocolate
½ cup powdered sugar	

Garnish:

4 squares semisweet chocolate	3 tablespoons Kirsch

Butter and flour a 9 inch springform pan. Combine eggs and sugar in a mixing bowl. Place bowl over a pan of hot water. Stir constantly for 3 minutes until the mixture reaches room temperature. Then, beat with electric mixer about 5 minutes until mixture becomes thick and creamy. Sift flour, cornstarch and cocoa together several times and fold into eggs. Slowly add hot melted butter, folding in thoroughly with a spatula. Pour into pan and bake at 350° for 30 minutes. Cool cake.

Whip cream; fold in sugar. Melt chocolate in double boiler. Add 2 cups of whipped cream. Heat briefly over low heat, blending the mixture with a beater until a creamy consistency is obtained. Add remaining whipped cream and fold in lightly.

To make chocolate curls, melt the 4 squares of semisweet chocolate in top of double boiler. Spread into a 4 inch square on a cold cookie sheet. Refrigerate 15 minutes, or just until chocolate sets. Pull a thin-bladed knife across the chocolate, letting the chocolate curl up in front of the knife.

Split cake into three layers. Sprinkle two layers with Kirsch and cover with cream filling. Add third layer and sprinkle with remaining Kirsch. Frost entire cake with cream filling. Put chocolate curls on top and chocolate sprinkles on sides. Chill well.

Mrs. Larry Hall (Jane)

Too slow an oven can coarsen a cake, as can too much shortening and sugar. A dry cake can come from too much flour, not enough shortening and sugar, overbeaten egg whites, or too-long baking. Too hot an oven can hump the cake up in the middle and crack the crust as well. A soggy streak through the cake can mean either too much liquid or not enough mixing to smoothly blend and integrate all ingredients. Too much sugar will make a sticky crust on the cake. Use the size of pan called for, because too-large a pan makes a thin, undersized layer.

Mocha Cream Cake Surprise

2 cups instant dissolving flour
2 cups sugar
1 teaspoon baking soda
1 teaspoon salt
½ teaspoon baking powder
¾ cup water
¾ cup buttermilk

½ cup shortening
2 eggs
1 teaspoon vanilla
4 squares unsweetened chocolate, melted and cooled

Filling:
3 ounces cream cheese, softened
About 1 tablespoon milk
1 tablespoon powdered instant coffee

1 teaspoon vanilla
2 cups powdered sugar

Frosting:
1 cup whipping cream
½ cup powdered sugar

¼ cup cocoa

Grease and flour three 8 inch baking pans, or two 9 inch baking pans. Beat all cake ingredients in a large mixer bowl on low speed, scraping bowl constantly, 30 seconds. Beat on high speed scraping bowl occasionally, 2 minutes. Pour into pans. Bake at 350° until wooden pick inserted in center comes out clean, 30 to 35 minutes; cool.

To prepare filling, mix cream cheese, milk, coffee, and vanilla. Gradually beat in powdered sugar until smooth and creamy. Spread about ⅔ cup between 8 inch layers, about 1 cup between 9 inch layers.

To prepare frosting, beat chilled whipping cream, powdered sugar and cocoa in chilled bowl until stiff. Frost sides and top of cake. Refrigerate until serving time. Store cake in refrigerator.

Nancy Young Moritz

Mock 7 Minute White Icing

1 cup powdered sugar
3½ tablespoons water
2 egg whites
¼ teaspoon cream of tartar

Pinch of salt
1 teaspoon vanilla or ¼ teaspoon almond extract

Bring sugar and water to boil. Combine remaining ingredients in a mixing bowl; add sugar mixture. Beat until fluffy. Frosts 1 cake.

Mrs. John Perkins (Sandy)

Mississippi Mud

2 sticks margarine	1 jar (8 ounces) marshmallow cream
2 cups sugar	
⅓ cup cocoa	1 stick melted margarine
4 eggs	½ cup evaporated milk
1 teaspoon vanilla	1 teaspoon vanilla
1½ cups flour	1 box powdered sugar
1 cup chopped pecans	½ cup cocoa
Dash salt	Chopped pecans, optional

Cream margarine, sugar and cocoa; add eggs and vanilla; mix. Add flour, nuts and salt; beat two minutes. Bake in a greased 9x13 inch pan at 350° for 35 minutes. Spread marshmallow cream on hot cake and cool. Melt one stick of margarine; add milk and vanilla. Stir in powdered sugar and cocoa until smooth. Spread on top of marshmallow cream. May be sprinkled with more chopped pecans, if desired.

Mrs. Larry Nau (Rose)

Chocolate Upside-Down Cake

1¼ cups flour	1 teaspoon vanilla
¾ cup sugar	½ cup chopped pecans
2 teaspoons baking powder	2 tablespoons cocoa
¼ teaspoon salt	½ cup brown sugar
1 square unsweetened chocolate	½ cup sugar
2 tablespoons butter	1 cup boiling water
½ cup milk	Sweetened whipped cream, optional

Sift and measure flour. Sift flour, sugar, baking powder and salt together. Melt the chocolate and butter; mix with the milk and vanilla. Stir into the dry ingredients; add nuts and blend thoroughly. Pour into a well greased 8 inch glass pan. Mix together the cocoa, brown sugar and granulated sugar. Sprinkle this mixture on top of the cake batter. Pour the boiling water over all. Bake at 250° for 1 hour. Serve warm topped with whipped cream.

Mrs. Larry Wisian (Kay)

Rum Cake

¼ pound butter, softened
½ cup shortening
2 cups sugar
4 eggs
3 cups flour
½ teaspoon baking soda

½ teaspoon baking powder
Pinch of salt
1 cup buttermilk
1 teaspoon rum flavoring
1 teaspoon vanilla

Glaze:
2 sticks butter
1 cup sugar

3 ounces rum

Cream butter, shortening and sugar. Add eggs one at a time. Combine flour, baking soda, baking powder and salt. Alternate adding flour mixture and buttermilk to creamed mixture beginning and ending with flour. Add vanilla and rum flavoring. Bake at 325° for 1 hour in a greased and floured bundt pan, tube pan or 2 loaf pans.

For glaze, melt butter with sugar over low heat; stir to melt sugar. Add rum. Pour over hot cake and leave in pan 2 hours. *This cake can be made ahead and frozen.*

Mrs. Jim Schultz (Mary Kay)

Harvey Wallbanger Cake

1 box yellow cake mix
1 small box vanilla instant pudding
½ cup oil
4 eggs

¼ cup vodka
¼ cup Galliano liqueur
¾ cup orange juice
Powdered sugar, optional

Glaze:
1 cup sifted powdered sugar
1 tablespoon orange juice

1 tablespoon vodka
1 tablespoon Galliano

Mix cake mix, pudding, oil, eggs, vodka, Galliano, orange juice and beat for 4 minutes. Pour batter into greased and floured tube pan. Bake at 350° for 45 to 50 minutes or until tests done. If desired, dust with powdered sugar or frost with glaze made from powdered sugar, orange juice, vodka, and Galliano.

Mrs. Tony Hall (Jane)

Sour Cream Pound Cake

3	cups flour	6	eggs
½	teaspoon baking soda	1	cup sour cream
2	sticks soft margarine	1	teaspoon lemon extract
3	cups sugar	1	teaspoon vanilla extract

Sift flour with soda. Set aside. Cream margarine; slowly add sugar, beating well. Add eggs, one at a time, beating after each addition. Stir in sour cream. Add flour mixture, ½ cup at a time, beating constantly. Add lemon and vanilla extracts. Pour batter into a greased 10 inch tube pan. Bake at 350° for 90 minutes or until done. *To make an Apricot Brandy Pound Cake add ½ cup apricot brandy.*

Mrs. Jack Bone (Joyce)

Marble Potato Cake

1	cup margarine	1	cup warm mashed potatoes
2	cups sugar	1	teaspoon vanilla
3	eggs	1	teaspoon cinnamon
3	cups flour	½	teaspoon nutmeg
3	teaspoons baking powder	¼	teaspoon cloves
¾	cup milk		

Cream margarine and sugar; add eggs. Add flour and baking powder to the egg mixture, alternately with milk, beating well after each addition. Add one cup warmed potatoes. For marble, take out 1 cup of batter and add vanilla, cinnamon, nutmeg, and cloves. Pour remaining batter into well greased tube pan. Spoon marbled batter onto batter in pan. Swirl through pan for marbling effect. Bake at 350° for 1 hour or until cake tests done. For chocolate cake, reduce flour to 2½ cups. Add 6 tablespoons cocoa and same amount of cinnamon and cloves. One cup chopped nuts may be added.

Mrs. Wilson Schuessler (Ruth)

Fresh Apple Cake

3   cups flour
1½ teaspoons baking soda
½   teaspoon salt
3   cups finely chopped pared
    apples

½   cup chopped walnuts or
    pecans
1   teaspoon grated lemon peel
2   cups sugar
1½ cups oil
2   eggs

Cream Cheese Frosting:
8   ounces cream cheese
1   tablespoon butter
1   teaspoon vanilla

1   box (1 pound) powdered
    sugar
1   cup walnuts

Grease and flour three 9 inch round layer cake pans. Sift flour with baking soda and salt. Mix apples, nuts and lemon peel. In large bowl, mix sugar, oil and eggs. Add sifted dry ingredients and mix until smooth. Add apples; mix well. Divide evenly between three pans and bake at 350° for 30 to 40 minutes. Cool in pans 10 minutes. Beat cheese, butter and vanilla until light and creamy. Add sugar and beat until spreading consistency. Fill and frost cake. Press chopped walnuts on sides of cake and refrigerate until serving time.

Mrs. Denman Smith (Sandra)

Alma Hamner's Diabetic Cake

2   cups flour
2   teaspoons baking soda
½   cup butter
1   egg
1½ cups applesauce, natural
    style

1   tablespoon Sucaryl
1   cup chopped dates
1   cup chopped pecans
1   teaspoon vanilla
1   teaspoon cinnamon

Mix flour and soda. Cream butter and add other ingredients one at a time, mixing after each addition. Turn into greased 9x5 inch loaf pan and bake at 350° for 1 hour or less.

Alma Hamner

Guter Kuchen Apple Cake

3 cups flour
2 cups sugar
3 teaspoons cinnamon
½ teaspoon baking soda
½ teaspoon salt
1 cup oil

3 whole eggs
2 teaspoons vanilla
½ to 1 cup hot water
3 cups chopped, unpeeled apples
1 cup pecans, in pieces

Mix dry ingredients in a large mixing bowl. Stir in oil, eggs, vanilla, and ½ cup hot water, mixing well. If batter is too thick, add ½ cup more hot water. Add apples and pecans to batter. Pour into greased tube or bundt pan. Bake at 325° for 1 hour and 20 minutes.

Cookbook Committee

Rum Sauce

1 stick margarine
1 cup water
1 cup sugar
2 tablespoons flour

⅛ teaspoon salt
2 teaspoons vanilla
¼ teaspoon butter flavoring
2 teaspoons rum flavoring

Melt margarine in water over medium heat. Stir together sugar, flour and salt; add to butter mixture. Add vanilla, butter and rum flavorings. Cook until bubbly. Poke holes in warm cake and pour sauce over.

Mrs. Jerry Hunt (Gail)

Holiday Apple Cake

4 eggs
2 cups sugar
1 cup oil
3 teaspoons vanilla
3 cups flour
3 teaspoons baking powder

1 teaspoon salt
½ cup orange juice
3 teaspoons cinnamon
½ cup sugar
5 to 6 apples, sliced or 1 can pie apples, drained

In a large bowl, combine eggs, sugar, oil and vanilla. In another bowl, combine flour, baking powder, and salt. Alternate adding flour mixture and orange juice into egg mixture. Mix well. Combine cinnamon and sugar. Grease and flour a tube pan. Pour ⅓ of batter into the tube pan. Follow with ⅓ of the apples and ⅓ of the cinnamon mixture. Repeat layers two more times. Bake at 325° for 1½ to 2 hours. *Good served as a coffee cake.*

Mrs. Ed Cornet (Kathi)

Gingerbread Apple Upside Down Cake

½ stick butter
½ cup brown sugar
Apple slices from one large
　apple
½ cup sugar
½ cup shortening
1 egg
½ cup molasses

½ teaspoon cinnamon
½ teaspoon ginger
¾ teaspoon salt
¾ teaspoon baking soda
1½ cups flour
½ cup boiling water
Ice cream or whipped cream

Melt butter in an 8 inch square pan. Sprinkle brown sugar over butter. Layer apples; set aside. Cream sugar and shortening. Add egg and molasses, beating thoroughly. Sift together dry ingredients. Add to creamed mixture alternately with boiling water, beating after each addition. Pour over apples and brown sugar; spread evenly. Bake in 350° oven for 30 to 35 minutes or until done. Remove from oven and invert on cake plate. Serve warm with vanilla ice cream or whipped cream.

Mrs. Larry Keith (Virginia)

Bill's Favorite Cherry Cake

1 egg
1¼ cups sugar
1 cup flour
¼ teaspoon salt
1 teaspoon cinnamon

1 tablespoon butter, melted
¾ teaspoon almond extract
1 can (16 ounces) sour red
　cherries, drained, reserve
　juice

Sauce:
1 tablespoon cornstarch
¼ cup sugar
1 cup cherry juice
Red food coloring

Dash salt
2 drops almond extract
Sweetened whipped cream

Beat egg; add sugar, beating until dissolved. Combine flour with salt. Add to sugar mixture along with cinnamon, butter and almond extract. Fold in drained cherries. Put in 8 inch square pan or pie plate. Bake at 350° for 45 minutes. For sauce, combine cornstarch, sugar and juice and cook until thick. Add food coloring, salt, and almond extract. To serve, layer sauce, whipped cream, and top with additional sauce.

Mrs. Wayne Davison (Cindi)

Strawberry Cake

1   small box strawberry gelatin
½   cup cold water
1   package white cake mix
4   eggs

1   cup salad oil
3   tablespoons flour
½   package (10 ounces) frozen strawberries

Strawberry Icing:
¾   stick margarine, softened
2   cups powdered sugar

½   package (10 ounces) frozen strawberries

Dissolve strawberry gelatin in cold water. Combine all cake ingredients including gelatin mixture and beat with mixer for 5 minutes. Bake in greased tube pan in 325° oven for 55 minutes. For icing, combine margarine, powdered sugar, and remaining strawberries and beat well. Pour over cooled cake.

Mrs. Dale Layton (Marilyn)

Orange Pineapple Pudding Cake

1   box butter cake mix
4   eggs
½   cup oil

1   can (11 ounces) mandarin oranges, undrained

Pineapple Frosting:
1   carton (9 ounces) whipped topping
1   can (20 ounces) crushed pineapple with liquid

1   large box instant vanilla pudding, dry
Few drops lemon juice

Mix all cake ingredients together and beat 4 minutes. Bake in two 9 inch layers in 350° oven for 25 minutes. Cool. Split each cake into 2 layers.

For frosting, combine all ingredients and spread between layers and over cake. Allow cake to cool in refrigerator several hours before serving.

Mrs. Charles Strong (Ginny)

Orange Cranberry Cake

1 cup sugar	2 orange rinds, grated
1 teaspoon baking powder	¾ cup oil
2¼ cups flour	2 eggs
1 teaspoon baking soda	1 cup buttermilk
¼ teaspoon salt	1 cup orange juice
1 cup chopped nuts	⅔ cup sugar
1 cup cranberries, chopped	

Sift all dry ingredients into a large bowl. Stir in nuts, cranberries and orange rind. Combine oil, eggs and buttermilk. Stir into first mixture, blending well. Pour into a well greased and floured 10 inch tube or bundt pan. Bake at 350° for 1 hour or until done. Cool in the pan for 30 minutes; remove to a wire rack. Combine orange juice and sugar. Stir until the sugar is dissolved and use as a basting sauce. When well basted, wrap in foil and refrigerate for 24 hours before serving. Serves 16 to 20.

Florence Batey

Orange Slice Cake

2 sticks butter	1 package (1 pound) candy orange slices, diced
2 cups sugar	
4 eggs	2 cups chopped nuts
½ cup buttermilk	½ cup orange juice
1 teaspoon baking soda	1 cup powdered sugar
3½ cups flour	
1 box (1 pound) pitted dates, diced	

Cream butter and sugar. Add eggs one at a time, beating after each addition. Mix buttermilk with soda. Add flour alternately with milk. Dust dates, candy and nuts with flour so they do not stick together. Add mixture to batter, and mix by hand. Bake in greased and floured tube pan at 250° for 2½ hours or until batter tests done. Mix together orange juice and powdered sugar and spoon over the top of the cake. Let stand in pan for at least 30 minutes. Hint: *Cut the orange slices with kitchen scissors that have been dipped in flour.*

Mrs. Milton E. Wilson (Allene)

Favorite Pineapple Cake

2   cups flour
2   cups sugar
1   teaspoon baking soda

Icing:
½ to ¾ box powdered sugar
½   cup margarine

2   eggs
1   can (20 ounces) crushed
    pineapple, undrained

8   ounces cream cheese,
    softened
1   teaspoon vanilla

Mix flour, sugar, soda, eggs, and pineapple. Pour into 9x13 inch pan. Bake at 350° for 40 or 45 minutes. Cool. Mix icing ingredients and spread on cooled cake.

Mrs. Wayne Davison (Cindi)

Lazy Daisy Oatmeal Cake

1¼ cups boiling water
1   cup uncooked oats
½   cup margarine, softened
1   cup sugar
1   cup brown sugar
2   eggs

Broiled Frosting:
¼   cup margarine, melted
3   tablespoons evaporated
    milk

1   teaspoon vanilla
1½ cups flour
1   teaspoon baking soda
½   teaspoon salt
¾   teaspoon cinnamon
¼   teaspoon nutmeg

½   cup brown sugar
⅓   cup chopped nuts
¾   cup coconut

Pour boiling water over oats; cover and let stand 20 minutes. Beat margarine until creamy; gradually add sugars and beat until fluffy. Blend in eggs and vanilla. Add oats mixture; mix well. Sift together flour, soda, salt, cinnamon, and nutmeg. Add to creamed mixture. Mix well. Pour into a greased and floured 9 inch square pan. Bake at 350° for 50 to 55 minutes. Leave in pan. Combine frosting ingredients. Spread over cake and broil until bubbly. Serve warm or cold.

Mrs. Larry Nau (Rose)

14 Karat Cake

2 cups flour	1 cup white sugar
2 teaspoons baking powder	2 cups grated carrots
1½ teaspoons baking soda	1 can (8 ounces) crushed
1½ teaspoons salt	pineapple, drained
2 teaspoons cinnamon	1½ cups chopped nuts
1 cup brown sugar	1 can (3½ ounces) coconut,
4 eggs	optional
1½ cups oil	

Orange Cream Cheese Frosting:

½ cup butter	1 teaspoon orange juice,
8 ounces cream cheese	optional
1 teaspoon vanilla	1 teaspoon orange rind,
1 pound powdered sugar	optional

Combine flour, baking powder, baking soda and salt. Add remaining ingredients, including coconut, if desired. Grease and flour three 9 inch pans. Bake at 350° for 35 to 40 minutes. Cool completely before frosting. To make frosting, cream butter, cream cheese, vanilla and powdered sugar together and spread on cake. *Variation: Spread buttermilk glaze over hot cakes while still in pans. When cool add Orange Frosting.*

Mrs. John Carrell (Jane)

Buttermilk Glaze

1 cup sugar	½ cup butter
½ teaspoon baking soda	1 tablespoon light corn syrup
½ cup buttermilk	1 teaspoon vanilla

Combine sugar, baking soda, buttermilk, butter and corn syrup in heavy saucepan. Bring to a boil; cook 4 minutes, stirring often. Remove from heat and add vanilla. Spread glaze over layers immediately after removing them from oven. Cool, remove from pans, and frost with cream cheese frosting on top of glaze.

Mrs. Jim Rado (Vicki)

How old are your eggs? Place one in the bottom of a bowl of cold water. If it lies on its side, it is fresh. If it stands at an angle, it is at least three days old, and ten days old if it stands on end.

Toasted Butter Pecan Cake

2	cups pecans, chopped	3	cups flour
¼	cup butter	2½	teaspoons baking powder
2	cups sugar	½	teaspoon salt
1	cup butter	1	cup milk
4	eggs	2	teaspoons vanilla

Icing:

½	cup butter	⅔	cup toasted pecans
2¼	cups sugar	1	teaspoon vanilla
1½	cups evaporated milk		

Toast pecans in ¼ cup butter in a 350° oven for 20 minutes. Set aside ⅔ cup. Cream sugar and 1 cup butter. Add eggs, beating well after each one. Sift the dry ingredients together and add to the creamed mixture, alternating with the milk. Add vanilla and 1⅓ cups toasted pecans. Pour into three 9 inch pans and bake at 350° for 20 to 25 minutes.

Mix butter, sugar and milk. Cook slowly and bring to a boil. Boil for 2 minutes, stirring constantly; add pecans and vanilla. Remove from heat and beat until creamy. Frost cool cake.

Mrs. Jack Bone (Joyce)

Olivia's Nut Cake

1	pound butter	¼	pound candied pineapple
2	cups sugar	5	cups broken pecans
6	eggs, separated	2	ounces lemon extract
3	cups cake flour, sifted		Bourbon or sherry
¾	pound candied cherries		

Cream butter and sugar. Add beaten yolks, flour, finely chopped fruit, nuts, and lemon extract. Beat egg whites until stiff, but not dry. Fold into batter. Bake in a greased bundt or tube pan at 325° for 1 hour or longer if necessary. Cake can be baked in 4 small pans. Saturate a cloth with bourbon or sherry and wrap until time to serve, keeping cloth moist.

Mrs. Richard Dorrell (Marianna)

Bûche de Noël

5   eggs, separated
1   cup powdered sugar, divided

3   plus tablespoons cocoa

Mocha Filling:
1   cup whipping cream
¼   cup powdered sugar

¼   cup cocoa
1   tablespoon instant coffee

Chocolate Butter Cream:
2   cups powdered sugar
4   tablespoons butter,
    softened
2   tablespoons milk

1   teaspoon vanilla
1   egg yolk
1   square unsweetened
    chocolate, melted

Grease 10½x15½ inch cookie sheet. Line bottom with well greased wax paper. In large bowl, beat egg whites until soft peaks form. Gradually add ½ cup powdered sugar and beat until stiff peaks form. In small bowl, beat egg yolks until thick. At low speed add ½ cup powdered sugar and 3 tablespoons cocoa. Scrape bowl often. Fold yolks into whites. Spread in pan and bake at 400° for 15 minutes or until top springs back when touched. Sprinkle clean kitchen towel with cocoa. Invert cake on towel and peel off paper. Roll cake like jelly roll. Put seam side down to cool.

For filling, combine cream, powdered sugar, cocoa, and instant coffee and beat at medium speed until stiff peaks form.

Make butter cream by mixing powdered sugar, butter, milk, vanilla, egg yolk, and melted chocolate to a spreading consistency.

Unroll cake. Spread with filling. Roll up. Put seam side down on platter and frost with butter cream. Mark frosting with knife to resemble tree bark. Refrigerate. Serves 8 to 10. *This is not as difficult as it looks! It can be made the day before and is beautiful for Christmas.*

Mrs. Jim Schultz (Mary Kay)

Yule Log, or Bûche de Noël, is the traditional end to the holiday meal in French homes on Christmas Eve. In 18th Century France a specially chosen spruce log was burned on Christmas Eve. The ashes were supposed to have magical qualities. Eventually the special log became the cake we know today.

To make the perfect Bûche, sprinkle cocoa evenly on the towel, using a fine meshed strainer. Be sure to roll the cake while it is still warm, otherwise it may crack. Roll tightly, but gently, to keep cake's light texture. Spread filling nearly to the edges so it won't ooze out when cake is rerolled. To keep platter clean while frosting, gently lift Bûche and insert two strips of waxed paper under roll. After icing carefully remove waxed paper. Bûche is best made one day ahead.

Italian Cream Cake and Cream Cheese Icing

1 stick margarine, softened	1 cup buttermilk
½ cup shortening	1 teaspoon vanilla
2 cups sugar	1 can (3½ ounces) flaked
5 eggs, separated	coconut
2 cups flour	1 cup chopped nuts
1 teaspoon baking soda	

Cream Cheese Icing:

8 ounces cream cheese, softened	1 box powdered sugar, sifted
	1 teaspoon vanilla
½ stick margarine, softened	Chopped nuts

Cream margarine and shortening. Add sugar; beat until mixture is smooth. Add egg yolks and beat. Combine flour and soda; add to creamed mixture, alternately with buttermilk. Stir in vanilla, coconut and nuts. Fold in stiffly beaten egg whites. Pour batter into well greased 9x13 inch sheet pan. Bake at 350° for 40 to 45 minutes.

Beat cream cheese until smooth. In separate bowl, combine sugar and margarine; mix well. Add to cream cheese. Stir in vanilla and beat until smooth. Frost cool cake in pan. Top with chopped pecans. Store in refrigerator.

Mrs. Ken Moyer (Bonnie)

Coconut Sour Cream Cake

1 box white cake mix, pudding type	1 carton (8 ounces) sour cream
1 cup oil	8 ounces cream of coconut
3 eggs	

Coconut Cream Cheese Icing:

1 teaspoon vanilla	2 tablespoons cream of coconut
8 ounces cream cheese, softened	
	1 package (3 ounces) frozen coconut
1 box powdered sugar	

Mix cake mix with oil, eggs, sour cream and 8 ounces cream of coconut. Pour into greased and floured 9x13 inch pan and bake at 350° for 30 to 45 minutes. Top with mixture of vanilla, cream cheese, powdered sugar, cream of coconut, and frozen coconut.

Mrs. Larry Nau (Rose)

Boccone Dolce (Sweet Mouthful)

4   egg whites
Pinch of salt
¼   teaspoon cream of tartar
1   cup sugar
6   ounces semisweet
    chocolate morsels

3   tablespoons water
1   pint whipping cream
⅓   cup sugar
1 or 2 pints fresh strawberries

Beat egg whites, salt and cream of tartar until stiff and glossy. Gradually beat in sugar; beat until very stiff.

Make three 8 inch circles out of parchment paper. (If none is available use wax paper). Place on baking sheet and spread the meringue evenly on the circles. It should be about ¼ inch thick. Bake for 25 minutes in a pre-heated 250° oven. Meringue should be slightly golden but still pliable. Remove from oven and very carefully peel the parchment paper off the back. Put on racks to cool and dry.

For chocolate layer, bring water to boil and put chocolate morsels into pan. Cover and set aside. The chocolate will melt while doing the next step. Stir to mix.

Stiffly whip cream, gradually adding sugar. Beat until very stiff.

Slice strawberries. Reserve some of the largest and prettiest berries to decorate the cake.

To assemble, put a meringue layer on a serving plate. (A footed cake stand really looks elegant.) Carefully spread a layer of melted chocolate using half the chocolate. Next spread a ½ inch layer of whipped cream, and half the sliced strawberries. Repeat with second meringue, chocolate, whipped cream, and strawberries. Place the last meringue on top. Frost with the remaining whipped cream, being sure to cover sides and top. Decorate the top with the reserved stawberries. Refrigerate for at least 2 hours. Serves 12. *Whipped cream rosettes and decorations, drizzled, melted chocolate, or chocolate curls add an elegant touch, but I think the strawberries are the prettiest. However you decorate it, get ready for raves. It is marvelous and sinfully rich. I first had this at Sardi's in New York about 20 years ago. It was heavenly. Several years later my sister-in-law, Gail, found a recipe for it and gave it to me. Now we don't have to go to New York for this special treat.*

Mrs. Dudley Baker (Kathy)

Praline Ice Cream Pie

1 cup flour
¼ cup brown sugar
½ cup margarine, melted
½ cup chopped pecans

½ gallon vanilla ice cream, softened
1 jar (12 ounces) caramel ice cream topping

Combine flour, brown sugar, margarine and nuts; spread in 9x13 inch pan. Bake at 350° for 20 minutes, stirring occasionally. Sprinkle ¾ of crust mixture in bottom of two 8 inch or one 10 inch pie pan. Spoon softened ice cream on top of crumbs. Freeze until firm. Top with caramel and return to freezer for several hours. Sprinkle the remaining crumb mixture on top. This pie can be made several days ahead of time. Serves 12 to 14.

Mrs. Wayne Davison (Cindi)

Jamoca Almond Fudge Pie

1 package (8½ ounces) chocolate wafers
3 to 4 tablespoons butter, melted
¼ cup sugar
1 quart jamoca almond fudge ice cream

3 egg whites
Dash of salt
1 jar (7 ounces) marshmallow creme
Chocolate syrup to garnish
Slivered almonds to garnish

Crush chocolate wafers and mix with butter and sugar. Pat into 2 pie plates. Refrigerate. Put slightly softened ice cream in the pie shells, using one pint for each pie. Freeze until firm. Top with mixture of stiffly beaten egg whites, salt, and marshmallow creme. Broil a very few minutes to brown meringue mixture. Decorate with chocolate syrup and almonds. Each pie serves 8. *May be frozen before browning. Chocolate mint ice cream makes an extra cool summer pie.*

Mrs. Charley Batey (Gail)

Amaretto Pie

1 cup whipping cream, whipped
1 can sweetened condensed milk
1 tablespoon Gran Marnier
1 tablespoon Amaretto
2 tablespoons Cream de Cacao
1 graham cracker crust, 9 inch

Mix filling ingredients and pour into pie crust. Freeze 4 hours. Serves 10. *For a different taste use other liqueur combinations and a chocolate crumb crust.*

Mrs. Steve Scheffe (Betsy)

Frozen Lime Pie

2 eggs
½ cup sugar
Green food coloring
1 cup half and half cream
⅓ cup lime juice
1 tablespoon grated lime peel
1½ cups graham cracker crumbs
⅓ cup powdered sugar
¼ cup butter, softened
2 pints vanilla ice cream

Beat eggs until thick and lemon colored. Gradually add sugar and continue beating until mixture is light and fluffy. Add a few drops of food coloring, cream, lime juice, and peel. Mix well. Pour into ice cube tray and freeze firm. Turn into chilled bowl and beat until smooth with electric mixer. Return to ice cube tray and partially freeze. Line a 9 inch pie plate with crust made from graham cracker crumbs, powdered sugar, and butter, reserving ¼ cup of mixture for top of pie. Soften vanilla ice cream and whip until smooth. Spread in pie crust. Top with frozen lime mixture and sprinkle with remaining crumbs. Freeze. Serves 8.

Mrs. Ron Garrick (Bonnie)

Lemon Meringue Pie

1½ cups sugar, divided
3 tablespoons flour
1½ cups hot milk
3 eggs, separated
Pinch of salt

½ teaspoon water
¼ teaspoon vanilla
3 tablespoons lemon juice
1 baked 9 inch pie crust

Mix 1 cup sugar and flour together. Add to hot milk, and cook over low heat until mixture has thickened. Beat egg yolks, salt and water with fork and add enough cooked custard to mix well. Return egg mixture to pan and simmer until egg is set, stirring constantly. Add vanilla, lemon juice, and lemon rind. Stir until mixture begins to bubble. Set aside. Make meringue by beating egg whites until fluffy. Add ½ cup sugar a little at a time until stiff. Remove one cup of meringue and stir into cooked custard. Blend until lumps disappear. Over beating causes mixture to lose its fluffiness. Pour into pie crust immediately. Spread remaining meringue over pie and brown in 425° oven, approximately 5 minutes.

Nancy Young Moritz

No Bake Fresh Peach Pie

4 to 6 fresh peaches
1 small package peach gelatin
¼ cup sherry
¼ cup sugar
¼ teaspoon cinnamon
2 tablespoons lemon juice

1 baked 9 inch pie shell, cooled
1 cup whipped cream, sweetened
Peach slices to garnish

Peel and purée peaches in blender. Measure 1¼ cups crushed peaches and heat just to boiling. Add gelatin, stirring to dissolve. Blend in sherry, sugar, cinnamon, and lemon juice. Chill until mixture starts to thicken. Pour into cooled shell. Garnish with whipped cream and peach slices. Serves 6 to 8. *This is an unusual peach pie with a really different taste, nice for the hot Texas summers.*

Mrs. Drue Denton (Jan)

Fresh Strawberry Pie

1 cup sugar	1 pint fresh strawberries,
2 tablespoons cornstarch	sliced
2 cups water	1 baked 9 inch pie shell
1 small package cherry	1 carton (4 ounces) whipped
gelatin	topping

Place sugar, cornstarch and water in saucepan. Cook over medium high heat until the mixture comes to a boil. Allow to boil until clear, stirring frequently. Add the gelatin and cook 2 to 3 minutes more. Cool. Place strawberries in pie crust and top with the gelatin mixture. Refrigerate several hours. To serve, place a dollop of whipped topping on each slice. Serves 6 to 8. *This pie does not keep well so eat up!*

Mrs. Ken Moyer (Bonnie)

Pumpkin-Lemon Cream Pie

2 eggs, slightly beaten	1 cup sour cream
1 can (16 ounces) pumpkin	2 tablespoons brown sugar
⅔ cup sugar	1 tablespoon lemon juice
1 teaspoon cinnamon	Grated peel of 1 lemon
½ teaspoon salt	¼ cup chopped pecans
½ teaspoon ginger	1 unbaked 9 inch pie shell
1⅓ cups half and half cream	

Combine eggs, pumpkin, sugar, cinnamon, salt, ginger, and cream and mix well. Pour into pie shell and bake at 425° for 15 minutes. Reduce heat to 350° and bake for 45 minutes more, or until knife inserted in center comes out clean. Cool 20 minutes. Blend together sour cream, brown sugar, lemon juice and peel, and spread evenly over baked filling. Bake at 350° for 10 minutes more. Sprinkle top with chopped pecans. Serves 6 to 8. *Good warm or cold.*

Mrs. Robert West (Linda)

1, 2, 3 Apple Pie

2   eggs
2   teaspoons baking powder
¼   teaspoon salt
1½ cups sugar

1   cup flour
1   cup diced, peeled apples
1   cup chopped nuts

Mix ingredients by hand until moist. Batter will be stiff. Place in buttered 10 inch pie plate, pressing dough against sides and bottom to form pie-crust. Bake at 350° for 25 to 30 minutes. Pie should still be moist. Serves 8 to 10. *Quick as 1, 2, 3 and delicious served warm with ice cream on top!*

Mrs. Robert West (Linda)

Edna's Apple Custard Pie

Crust:
1½ cups flour
½   teaspoon salt
1   stick butter

Filling:
3   apples, peeled and sliced
      thin
⅔   cup sugar
1   teaspoon cinnamon

1   egg
½   cup sugar
1   cup evaporated milk

For crust, mix flour, salt, and butter with fork until mixture resembles coarse meal. Press firmly on the bottom and sides of a buttered pie plate. Place sliced apples on crust. Sprinkle with ⅔ cup sugar and cinnamon. Bake at 375° for 20 minutes. Beat egg, ½ cup sugar, and milk. Pour over apples and return to oven to bake 30 minutes longer. Serves 6 to 8.

Florence Batey

Southern Pecan Pie

½   cup dark corn syrup
1   cup sugar
1   teaspoon flour
2   eggs
2   teaspoons milk

1   teaspoon vanilla
½   cup butter, melted
1¼ cups pecan halves
1   unbaked 9 inch pie crust

Combine all filling ingredients and pour into crust. Bake at 350° for one hour. Serves 6 to 8.

Mrs. Charles Cantwell (Winn)

Cheesecake Pecan Pie

8   ounces cream cheese,
     softened
1   egg
⅓   cup sugar
1   teaspoon vanilla
1   unbaked 9 inch pie shell

1½ cups pecan halves
2   slightly beaten eggs
¼   cup sugar
⅔   cup light corn syrup
½   teaspoon vanilla

Combine cream cheese, egg, ⅓ cup sugar, and 1 teaspoon vanilla. Beat until light and fluffy. Spread over bottom of pie shell. Arrange pecans on the cream cheese mixture. Mix the remaining eggs, sugar, corn syrup, and vanilla, stirring well. Carefully pour over the pecans. Bake at 375° for 40 to 45 minutes or until done. Serves 8.

Florence Batey

Pecan Pie Kahlua

¼   cup butter, softened
½   cup sugar
2   heaping tablespoons brown
     sugar
1   tablespoon vanilla
2   tablespoons flour
3   eggs

½   cup Kahlua
½   cup dark corn syrup
¾   cup evaporated milk
1   cup pecans
2   unbaked 9 inch pie shells
Whipped cream, to garnish

Combine butter, sugars, vanilla, and flour. Add eggs one at a time and continue to beat. Stir in Kahlua, corn syrup and milk, mixing well. Fold in pecans and bake at 400° for 10 minutes; reduce heat to 325° and cook 40 minutes until firm. Yields 2 pies.

Mrs. Denman Smith (Sandra)

The pecan tree is native to Texas and aptly chosen as the state tree. It has always been popular, but was brought to the state's attention when Governor James Hogg requested that a pecan tree be planted as a headstone for his grave.

Brownie Pecan Pie

⅔ cup sugar
⅛ teaspoon salt
1 cup light corn syrup
1 package (4 ounces) German sweet chocolate, broken in pieces
3 tablespoons margarine

3 eggs, slightly beaten
1 teaspoon vanilla
1 cup coarsely chopped pecans
1 unbaked 9 inch pie shell
Whipped cream to garnish

Combine sugar, salt and corn syrup in a saucepan. Bring to a boil over medium heat, stirring until sugar dissolves. Boil 2 minutes. Remove from heat. Add chocolate and butter and stir until melted. Cool. Gradually pour chocolate mixture over the eggs, mixing well. Add vanilla and pecans. Pour into pie crust and bake at 350° for 50 minutes. Cool. Serve topped with whipped cream. Serves 6 to 8.

Mrs. Joe Bowles (Mary)

Chocolate Cloud

3 egg whites
1 teaspoon vanilla
1 teaspoon baking powder
¾ cup sugar
1 package (4 ounces) German sweet chocolate, grated

1 cup Ritz cracker crumbs
½ cup chopped pecans
1 cup whipping cream
2 tablespoons sugar
1 teaspoon vanilla

Beat egg whites and vanilla to soft peaks. Combine baking powder and sugar and gradually add to whites, beating until stiff peaks form. Reserve 2 tablespoons chocolate and add remaining chocolate with crackers and pecans to egg white mixture. Spread in a 9 inch pie plate. Bake at 350° for 25 minutes. Cool thoroughly. Whip cream with sugar and vanilla and spread on top of pie. Garnish with reserved chocolate. Refrigerate at least 8 hours. Serves 8.

Mrs. Dan Ross (Lamonte)

Tipsy Chip Pie

¾ cup sugar
½ cup butter, melted and cooled
½ cup flour
2 eggs, lightly beaten
1 cup semisweet chocolate chips

1 cup pecans or walnuts
2 tablespoons bourbon or 1 teaspoon vanilla
1 baked 9 inch pie shell
Whipped cream or vanilla ice cream, to garnish

Combine sugar, butter, flour and eggs, and beat smooth. Add chocolate chips, nuts and bourbon. Pour into pie crust and bake at 350° for 30 to 35 minutes. Serve at room temperature topped with whipped cream or vanilla ice cream. Serves 6 to 8.

Mrs. Denman Smith (Sandra)

French Silk Chocolate Pie

¾ cup butter, softened
¾ cup plus ⅓ cup sugar
2 squares unsweetened chocolate, melted
1 teaspoon vanilla

3 eggs
1 baked 9 or 10 inch pie shell
Sweetened whipped cream to garnish
Shaved chocolate to garnish

Cream butter and sugar. Blend in melted and cooled chocolate and vanilla. Add eggs, one at a time, beating 5 minutes after each addition at medium speed. Pour into cooled crust and refrigerate overnight. Top with whipped cream and shaved chocolate before serving. Serves 6 to 8.

Mrs. Lorne Parks (Dephanie)

Chocolate Mint Pie

¾ cup chocolate mint liqueur
8 ounces cream cheese
4 ounces half and half cream
1 small package instant chocolate pudding

½ cup butter
1½ cups chocolate wafer crumbs
Whipped cream to garnish

Beat liqueur, cream cheese, cream and pudding until smooth. Make chocolate crust by combining butter and chocolate crumbs and pressing into pie plate. Spoon filling into pie shell. Serve chilled topped with whipped cream. Serves 6 to 8.

Mrs. Denman Smith (Sandra)

Old Fashioned Chocolate Pie

¾ cup sugar
2 heaping tablespoons flour
3 eggs, separated
1 cup milk
3 tablespoons cocoa or 1
   square unsweetened
   chocolate

⅛ teaspoon vanilla
1 tablespoon butter
1 baked 8 inch pie shell

Mix sugar, flour, egg yolks, milk, and chocolate in top of double boiler. Cook until thick. Using electric mixer, beat in vanilla and butter. Pour into baked crust. Top with meringue made by beating egg whites with an additional 6 tablespoons of sugar. Brown in 325° oven. Serves 8.

Mrs. Jim Smith (Jare)

Coffee Toffee Pie

Crust:
1 cup flour
1 cup chopped walnuts
1 ounce semisweet
   chocolate, ground

Dash salt
¼ pound cold butter
1 egg

Filling:
1 ounce unsweetened
   chocolate, melted
½ cup butter
¾ cup brown sugar
2 teaspoons instant coffee

2 eggs
1 cup whipping cream
2 tablespoons Kahlua
1 tablespoon powdered sugar

For crust, combine dry ingredients; cut in butter. Add egg and work in with hands. Press into a 9 inch pie plate. Prick several times with fork and bake at 375° for 12 minutes or until brown. Cool on wire rack. For filling, melt chocolate in top of double boiler or in microwave and set aside to cool. Cream butter and sugar together and beat for 2 minutes. Add cooled chocolate and instant coffee. Add eggs individually and beat until smooth. Pour into cooled crust and refrigerate at least 2 hours to set. Garnish with cream whipped with Kahlua and powdered sugar. Serves 8. *Freezes well.*

Mrs. Bill Odem (Joyce)

Barbara's Hershey Bar Pie

1	Almond Hershey bar (8 ounces)
2	tablespoons instant coffee
2	tablespoons water
1	carton (12 ounces) whipped topping, divided

1	graham cracker crust, 9 inch
2	Heath bars, crushed

Melt Hershey bar, instant coffee and water over low heat. Add whipped topping, reserving some for second layer. Stir and pour into pie crust. Freeze one hour; spread with remaining whipped topping. Sprinkle crushed Heath bars on top. Freeze for 2 more hours. Serves 6 to 8.

Mrs. Richard Dorrell (Mariana)

Chocolate Chess Pie

3	eggs, whipped lightly
1¾	cups sugar
1	tablespoon flour
1	tablespoon corn meal
¼	cup cocoa

1	stick margarine, melted
1	teaspoon vanilla
½	cup milk
1	unbaked 9 inch pie crust, optional

Combine all filling ingredients and pour into pie shell. Bake at 350° for 45 minutes. Serves 8. *This filling is equally as good baked without the pieshell.*

Mrs. Jim Smith (Jare)

Coconut Chess Pie

3	eggs, beaten
1½	cups sugar
½	cup butter, melted
4	teaspoons lemon juice

1	teaspoon vanilla
1	can (3½ ounces) flaked coconut
1	unbaked 9 inch pie shell

Combine ingredients in order given and pour into pie shell. Bake at 350° for 40 minutes or until set. Serves 6 to 8.

Mrs. Jerry Dow (Annette)

Buttermilk Pie

¼ cup flour
½ cup butter, melted
½ cup buttermilk
1½ cups sugar

½ teaspoon vanilla
3 eggs
1 unbaked 9 inch pie shell

Mix all ingredients together thoroughly and pour into pie shell. Bake at 350° for 1 hour. Serves 6 to 8.

Mrs. Glen Noble (Sharon)

Peanut Butter Pie

1 cup crunchy peanut butter
8 ounces cream cheese, softened
1 cup sugar
2 tablespoons butter, melted
1 cup whipped topping

1 tablespoon vanilla
1 graham cracker crust, 9 inch
Hershey's chocolate fudge topping, to garnish

Mix first six ingredients and pour into graham cracker crust. Chill overnight. Top with hot fudge. Serves 6 to 8. *Very, very rich!*

Mrs. Larry Morris (Diane)

Caramel Banana Pie

1 can sweetened condensed milk
1 graham cracker crust, 9 inch

3 bananas
1 cup whipping cream
¼ cup powdered sugar
2 small Heath bars, crushed

Pour condensed milk into an 8 inch glass pie plate; cover with foil. Set in shallow casserole filled with ¼ inch water. Bake at 425° for 1 hour and 20 minutes or until the condensed milk is thick and caramel colored. Add hot water to casserole as needed. Remove foil and set aside. Slice bananas and place in the bottom of the graham cracker crust. Spread carmelized milk over banana layer. Cool for at least 30 minutes. Combine whipping cream and powdered sugar and beat until stiff. Spread over caramel layer. Sprinkle with crushed candy. Chill at least 3 hours or overnight. Serves 8.

Mrs. Ron Garrick (Bonnie)

Pie Shell

1 cup unsifted all purpose flour	1 teaspoon sugar
	⅓ cup vegetable shortening
¼ teaspoon salt	3 level tablespoons ice water

Put flour, salt, and sugar in bowl. Mix with fork. Add shortening; stir until mixture is crumbly. Gradually sprinkle in ice water, stirring lightly with fork until dry ingredients hold together. Form into a ball and wrap in waxed paper. Place in refrigerator for 20 minutes. Roll out on lightly floured surface. Bake in 450° oven for 12 to 15 minutes. Yields 1 pie shell.

Nancy Young Moritz

Easy Mazola Pie Crust

½ cup Mazola corn oil	2 tablespoons sugar
1½ cups flour	2 tablespoons milk
½ teaspoon salt	

Mix all ingredients thoroughly and press onto bottom and sides of a 9 inch pie pan. Flute as you would any pie crust. Bake at 300° for 25 to 30 minutes.

Mrs. Ken Moyer (Bonnie)

Taria's Fudge Squares

1 stick butter	½ cup sifted flour
2 squares unsweetened chocolate	1 cup sugar
	1 cup broken nuts
2 eggs	1 teaspoon vanilla or whiskey

Mocha Frosting:

2 tablespoons butter, melted	3 tablespoons coffee
2 tablespoons cocoa	1 teaspoon flavoring, any kind
1½ cups powdered sugar	

Melt butter and chocolate in microwave or double boiler. Beat eggs; stir in flour and sugar. Add nuts, flavoring and chocolate mixture, stirring well. Bake in a greased 9 inch square pan at 350° for 25 minutes.

Prepare frosting by combining melted butter, cocoa, powdered sugar, coffee and flavoring. Ice and cut into squares while still warm. Yields 24.

Mrs. Adrian Piperi (Carole)

One Bowl Brownies

1 cup oil	1 teaspoon vanilla
6 tablespoons cocoa	1½ cups flour
4 eggs	1 teaspoon baking powder
2 cups sugar	1 teaspoon salt
2 tablespoons Karo syrup	1 cup chopped nuts, optional

Put oil in a bowl. Stir in cocoa, eggs, sugar, Karo and vanilla. Mix flour, baking powder and salt together; add to cocoa mixture. Stir in nuts. Pour into greased 8x12 pan and bake at 350° for 30 minutes. If a glass pan is used, bake at 325°. They are chewier if not overbeaten or overbaked. *These brownies have been the primary dessert addition to "cowboy" lunch boxes on the McBride ranch in Llano for some 30 years.*

Mrs. Heston McBride (Jean)

Caramel Fudge Bars

1 package German Chocolate cake mix	1 cup chopped nuts
¾ cup margarine, softened	1 package (14 ounces) caramels
⅔ cup evaporated milk, divided	1 cup semisweet chocolate chips

Stir cake mix, margarine, ⅓ cup evaporated milk, and nuts until well mixed. Pat one half of the mixture into a greased and floured 9x13 inch pan. Bake at 350° for 6 to 8 minutes. Melt caramels with ⅓ cup evaporated milk. Sprinkle chocolate chips on baked mixture, and carefully spread caramel mixture over the chips. Crumble remaining cake mixture over the top. Return to oven and bake 20 to 25 minutes. Yields 24 large squares.

Mrs. Wayne Davison (Cindi)

Seven Layer Cookies

½ stick butter	1 package (6 ounces) butterscotch chips
1 cup graham cracker crumbs	1 can sweetened condensed milk
1 can (7 ounce) flaked coconut	1 cup chopped pecans
1 package (6 ounces) semisweet chocolate chips	

Melt butter in a 9x13 inch baking pan. Add ingredients by layers, in order listed. Bake at 325° for 30 minutes. Let cool in pan, then cut into small squares. Yields 3 dozen.

Mrs. Tommy Love (Sherry)

Toffee Squares

1 cup butter	1 package (6 ounces)
1 cup brown sugar	semisweet chocolate chips
1 teaspoon vanilla	1 cup coarsely chopped
2 cups sifted flour	pecans

Cream butter, sugar, and vanilla until light and fluffy. Slowly add flour and mix well. Stir in chocolate chips and pecans. Spread evenly in a 15x10 inch greased and floured cookie sheet. Make sure dough covers the entire surface. Bake at 350° for 25 minutes. Cut into 2 inch squares, and leave in pan to cool. Yields 3 dozen squares.

Mrs. Ed Parker (Judy)

Forty-Niners

1 box (16 ounces) light brown	4 eggs, well beaten
sugar	2 cups chopped pecans
2 cups biscuit mix	Powdered sugar

Combine all ingredients except powdered sugar, blending well. Pour into greased and floured 9x13 inch pan. Bake at 325° for 35 minutes or until done. Remove from oven and cool thoroughly. Cut into bars and dust with powdered sugar. Yields 48 squares.

Mrs. B. L. Turlington (Jill)

Caramel Squares

2 sticks margarine	2 teaspoons baking powder
1 box (16 ounces) brown	1 scant teaspoon baking soda
sugar	4 tablespoons water
2 eggs	2 cups chopped pecans
2 cups flour	Powdered sugar

Melt margarine in saucepan and stir in brown sugar. Let cool; beat in eggs. Combine flour and baking powder; add to brown sugar mixture. Add soda dissolved in water. Stir in pecans. Bake in a greased and floured 9x13 inch pan at 375° for 30 minutes. Sprinkle generously with powdered sugar. Cool and cut into squares. Yields 3 dozen 2 inch squares.

Mrs. D. D. Baker, Jr. (Agnes)

O'Henry Bars

1½ sticks margarine
½ cup white sugar
½ cup brown sugar
½ cup dark corn syrup
1 tablespoon vanilla

4 cups quick cooking oatmeal
1 package (6 ounces) chocolate chips
⅔ cup crunchy peanut butter

Cream butter and sugars. Beat in corn syrup and vanilla. Stir in oatmeal. Pat mixture into a greased 9x13 inch pan. Moisten hands while spreading, as mixture is sticky. Bake at 350° for 15 to 18 minutes or until slightly brown. Melt chocolate chips and peanut butter in double boiler. When bar mixture is cooled slightly, spread the chocolate mixture evenly over the top. Chill. Cut into bars. Store in refrigerator. Yields 50 small bars.

Mrs. Jimmy Hall (Sue)

Citrus Coconut Squares

Crust:
½ cup butter
½ cup brown sugar

1 cup flour

Filling:
1 cup brown sugar
2 tablespoons flour
½ teaspoon baking powder
1 teaspoon salt

1 cup chopped pecans
1 cup coconut
2 eggs, beaten
1 teaspoon vanilla

Citrus Frosting:
1½ cups powdered sugar
2 tablespoons orange juice

1 tablespoon lemon juice
Grated rind of one lemon

To make crust, cream butter; add brown sugar and flour. Mix well; spread over botton of 9x13 inch greased pan. Bake at 350° for 15 minutes.

Mix brown sugar, flour, baking powder and salt. Add pecans, coconut, eggs and vanilla. Spread mixture over first layer and bake 30 minutes longer.

Combine powdered sugar, orange and lemon juices and rind and spread over hot layer. Cut into 2 inch squares. Yields 28 squares.

Mrs. Don Panter (Carolyn)

Praline Bars

12 unbroken graham crackers,
    4 squares to each
2 sticks unsalted butter

1 cup packed brown sugar
1 cup chopped pecans

Place graham crackers on a jelly roll pan with sides. Melt butter in sauce-pan; add sugar and pecans. Boil slowly for 2 minutes. Pour over graham crackers. Bake at 300° for 15 minutes. Cool 10 minutes, then cut into bars. Yields 3 dozen. *Very simple, good recipe for children to make, tastes like a Heath bar.*

Mrs. Don Harris (Nancy)

Pecan Pie Bars

1 package yellow cake mix
½ cup butter, melted
4 eggs, divided
½ cup firmly packed brown
    sugar

1 cup light corn syrup
½ cup dark corn syrup
1 teaspoon vanilla
1 cup chopped pecans

Set aside ⅔ cup cake mix. Combine remaining cake mix, butter, and one egg. Mix with fork until crumbly. Press mixture into a greased 9x13 inch baking dish. Bake at 350° for 15 to 20 minutes, or until light golden brown. Combine reserved cake mix, remaining eggs, brown sugar, corn syrups and vanilla in a mixing bowl. Beat at medium speed with mixer for 1 to 2 minutes. Pour over partially baked crust. Sprinkle with pecans. Bake at 350° for 30 to 35 minutes. Cool and cut into bars. Yields 24 bars.

Mrs. James Hurlbut (Marsha)

Cheese Cake Squares

⅔ cup brown sugar
2 cups sifted flour
⅔ cup butter, melted
8 ounces cream cheese,
    softened

¼ cup sugar
1 egg
1 cup sour cream
½ teaspoon vanilla

Combine brown sugar, flour, and butter; stir until light and crumbly. Press into an ungreased 9x13 inch pan. Bake at 350° for 15 minutes. Combine cream cheese, sugar, egg, sour cream and vanilla; beat until smooth. Pour over crust layer and bake at 350° for 30 minutes.

Mrs. Don Bradford (Melinda)

Congo Bars

3 cups brown sugar
⅔ cup shortening
3 eggs
1 teaspoon vanilla
2¾ cups flour
1½ teaspoons baking powder

½ teaspoon salt
1 small package chocolate
   chips
½ small package butterscotch
   chips (optional)
¾ to 1 cup chopped nuts

Cream sugar and shortening. Add eggs and vanilla. Add dry ingredients and mix. Stir in chips and nuts. Press in greased 9×13 inch pan. Bake at 350° for 30 to 40 minutes. Cut into bars when cool. *Can be frozen. Good when partially frozen.*

Marian Carlson Hidell

Loretta's Brownies

½ cup Hershey's syrup
⅓ cup butter
1 cup brown sugar
3 eggs

½ cup flour
¾ teaspoon baking powder
½ teaspoon vanilla
1 cup pecans, chopped

Blend syrup and butter; add sugar and eggs, beating thoroughly. Sift flour and baking powder together; then add to syrup mixture. Mix in vanilla and nuts. Pour into a greased 9×13 inch pan. Bake at 350° for 35 minutes. Yields 20 to 24 brownies.

Mrs. Edgar Bradford (Loretta)

Lemon Squares

¾ cup butter
⅓ cup powdered sugar
1½ cups flour
1½ cups sugar
3 eggs

3 tablespoons flour
¼ cup lemon juice
1 teaspoon lemon rind
Powdered sugar

Combine butter, powdered sugar and 1½ cups flour and pat into an 8 inch square greased pan. Bake at 350° for 20 to 30 minutes. Blend sugar, eggs, 3 tablespoons flour, lemon juice and rind and pour over hot crust. Bake at 350° for 20 to 30 minutes. When cooled, sprinkle with powdered sugar. Do not double recipe. Yields 1 dozen squares. *Recipe came from a great aunt. It won 1st prize at the Illinois State Fair.*

Mrs. Chris Williston (Janice)

Applesauce Bars

1½ cups sugar
½ cup margarine
2 eggs, beaten
2 cups flour
1½ teaspoons baking soda
½ teaspoon salt
½ teaspoon cinnamon

2 tablespoons cocoa
2 cups applesauce
2 tablespoons sugar
½ cup chopped nuts
1 package (6 ounces) semisweet chocolate chips

Cream 1½ cups sugar and margarine; add eggs beating well. Stir in flour, soda, salt, cinnamon, and cocoa. Add applesauce. Put in greased and floured 9x13 inch pan. Combine remaining sugar, nuts and chocolate chips; sprinkle over batter. Bake at 350° for 25 to 30 minutes. Cut into squares and serve. Yields 24 bars.

Mrs. Tim Bauerkemper (Pam)

Apricot Slices

1 stick butter, softened
½ cup sugar
1 tablespoon vanilla
3 eggs, separated
1½ cups flour

½ teaspoon baking powder
⅛ teaspoon baking soda
1 cup apricots, Solo brand
3 tablespoons sugar
1¼ cups chopped pecans

Cream butter and sugar. Add vanilla and egg yolks. Beat well. Add flour, baking powder and soda. Mix well or knead. Spread thinly in a jelly roll pan. Bake at 350° for 15 minutes. Cover with apricots. Make a meringue of egg whites and sugar by beating until stiff. Spread over fruit. Sprinkle with chopped nuts. Bake at 350° for 30 minutes. Cut into squares when cool. Yields 48 squares.

Mrs. Jim Schultz (Mary Kay)

Lemon Whippersnappers

1 box lemon cake mix, or any flavor but not with pudding
1 egg

1 carton (4 ounces) whipped topping
½ cup powdered sugar

Mix cake mix, egg, and whipped topping and roll into balls. Dip into powdered sugar and place on greased cookie sheet. Bake at 350° for 10 to 12 minutes. Yields: 3 to 4 dozen.

Mrs. Wayne Davison (Cindi)

Peanut Butter Cup Tarts

36 miniature Reese's peanut
    candies
1 roll (14 ounces) refrigerated
    slice and bake peanut butter
    cookies

Refrigerate candies. Spray miniature muffin tins with nonstick spray. Pull wrappers from cold candies. Follow directions for slicing cookies. Preheat oven to 350°. Drop a quarter slice of dough into each cup. Bake 8 to 10 minutes. Remove from oven and *immediately* push one candy into each muffin cup. When the candy presses down into the baked dough, the cookie rises up and nestles around the candy. The heat melts the chocolate candy topping. Let cool, then refrigerate until chocolate becomes dull. Gently lift each tart from pan. Yields 3 dozen. *These cookies are fun for the kids to make and easy enough that they can do them alone.*

Mrs. Jim Schultz (Mary Kay)

Coconut Meringues

3 egg whites
¼ teaspoon cream of tartar
⅔ cup sugar

½ teaspoon almond extract
6 tablespoons flour
1 can (3½ ounces) coconut

Place fluted paper cups in tiny muffin tins, 1¾ inch size. Combine egg whites and cream of tartar and beat with electric mixer until frothy. Gradually add sugar, continuing to beat until stiff peaks form and sugar is thoroughly blended. Add almond extract, then flour, sprinkling in a little at a time. Beat at low speed only until flour is blended. Fold in coconut; fill paper liners almost to the top. Bake at 325° for 15 minutes, or until golden brown. Yields 24 tiny cakes. *Freezes well.*

Mrs. Jim Kimbell (Ellen)

Almond Macaroons

1 can (8 ounces) almond
    paste

1 cup sugar
2 egg whites

Cut almond paste into small pieces in bowl; add sugar and egg whites. Mix until smooth, no lumps remaining. Use pastry gun with star tube; drop batter, in quarter size rounds, onto parchment lined sheets. Bake in 325° for about 30 minutes. Allow to cool; then wet back of paper with hot damp cloth to remove macaroons. Yields 2 dozen.

Mrs. Don Bradford (Melinda)

Almond Cookies

1 cup butter
1 cup sugar
1 egg, beaten
3 tablespoons almond extract

3 cups sifted flour
1½ teaspoons soda
¼ cup light corn syrup
1 cup blanched almonds

Cream butter and sugar until light and fluffy. Add beaten egg and almond extract; continue beating. Slowly stir in flour, baking soda, and corn syrup; mix until smooth. Form dough into 1 inch balls; place on greased or teflon baking sheet. Place an almond in the center of each cookie and gently press. Bake at 375° for 10 to 12 minutes, until golden brown. Yields 4 dozen. *This is a very good almond flavored cookie. It tastes very much like the almond cookies that Lung's Chinese Kitchen used to serve for desert.*

Mrs. Dudley Baker (Kathy)

Ranger Cookies

1 cup shortening
1 cup white sugar
1 cup brown sugar
2 eggs
1 teaspoon vanilla
2 cups flour

1 teaspoon baking soda
1 teaspoon baking powder
½ teaspoon salt
2 cups quick-cooking oatmeal
2 cups Rice Krispies
1 cup shredded coconut

Cream the shortening and sugars together. Add the eggs and vanilla; mix until smooth. Sift flour, soda, baking powder and salt together; add to creamed mixture. Mix well. Then add the oatmeal, rice cereal and coconut, and mix; dough will be quite crumbly. Mold with hands into balls the size of a walnut. Place on a greased cookie sheet and press slightly. Bake in 350° oven for 10 to 12 minutes. Yields 6 dozen. *One of my college roommates used to get these in her "care" package—it's probably the first recipe I ever asked anyone for!*

Mrs. Ken Moyer (Bonnie)

Oatmeal Cookies

1½ cups flour
1 teaspoon cinnamon
½ teaspoon baking soda
½ teaspoon salt
1¾ cups uncooked oatmeal
1 cup sugar

½ cup raisins, optional
½ cup chopped nuts
½ cup shortening, melted
1 egg
¼ cup milk
2 tablespoons molasses

In large bowl, combine first four ingredients. Stir in remaining ingredients. Drop by teaspoonfuls on ungreased cookie sheet. Bake at 350° for 10 to 12 minutes. Yields 5 dozen. *These are nourishing, easy to make and delicious!*

Mrs. Robert West (Linda)

Oats and Wheat Cookies

½ cup butter
1 cup packed light brown
  sugar
1 egg
2 teaspoons vanilla
1 cup whole wheat flour
½ teaspoon baking soda

½ teaspoon baking powder
½ teaspoon salt
1 cup rolled oats
1 cup chopped pecans
1 cup white raisins
1 cup dried apples, chopped

Cream butter and sugar. Add egg and vanilla; beat until fluffy. Add flour, baking soda, baking powder, and salt; mix well. Stir in oats, pecans, raisins and apples. Roll into balls and place on lightly greased cookie sheet. Bake at 350° for 12 to 15 minutes. Freezes nicely. Yields 3 to 4 dozen. *My daughter's brownie troop loves these for a healthy after school snack!*

Mrs. Marcus Bone (Beverly)

Sand Tarts

2 sticks margarine
2 cups flour
4 to 5 tablespoons sugar
Pinch of salt

1 cup finely chopped pecans
1 teaspoon vanilla
Granulated sugar

Melt butter in saucepan. Add flour, sugar, and salt; stir. Add nuts and vanilla; mix well. Form into balls. Place on ungreased cookie sheet. Bake at 300° for 30 minutes. Roll in granulated sugar while still warm. *Good and easy. Not much clean up!*

Mrs. Jim Schuessler (Liz)

Magic Window Cookies

¾ cup butter	2½ cups flour
1 cup sugar	1 teaspoon baking powder
2 eggs	½ teaspoon salt
½ teaspoon lemon extract	6 packages of Lifesavers

Mix together butter, sugar, eggs, and lemon extract. Blend in flour, baking powder, and salt. Cover and chill at least one hour. Roll dough ⅛ inch thick on a lightly floured board. Cut into desired shapes. Cut a small hole in center of each cookie with a sharp knife. Place cookies on foil covered baking sheet. Place a Lifesaver in the center of each cookie. Bake at 375° for 7 to 9 minutes until lightly browned or until candy is melted. Cool on baking sheet. Store in layers between waxed paper. These freeze nicely. Yields 6 dozen.

Marian Hidell

Crisp, thin cookies should be stored in a container with a loose-fitting cover. If they soften, recrisp by placing in 300° oven for 3 to 5 minutes. Soft cookies should be stored in a tightly covered container. A piece of bread or apple placed in the container helps keep the cookies soft if you change it frequently.

Teatime Tassies

3 ounces cream cheese	1 tablespoon soft butter or
½ cup butter or margarine	margarine
1 cup sifted enriched flour	1 teaspoon vanilla
1 egg	Dash salt
¾ cup brown sugar	⅔ cup coarsely broken pecans

For pastry, let cream cheese and ½ cup butter soften at room temperature; blend. Stir in flour. Chill slightly, about one hour. Shape in 2 dozen 1 inch balls; place in tiny ungreased 1¾ inch muffin cups. Press dough on bottom and sides of cups.

To make pecan filling, beat together egg, sugar, 1 tablespoon butter, vanilla, and salt just until smooth. Divide half the pecans among pastry-lined muffin cups; add egg mixture and top with remaining pecans. Bake in 325° oven for 25 minutes or until filling is set. Cool; remove from pans. Yields 24. *May be frozen.*

Mrs. Leon Melton (Vera)

Peanut Blossom Cookies

½ cup shortening
½ cup brown sugar
½ cup sugar
1   egg
1   teaspoon vanilla
½ cup peanut butter

2   tablespoons milk
1¾ cups flour
1   teaspoon baking soda
½ teaspoon salt
Granulated sugar
48 chocolate candy kisses

Cream shortening and sugars. Add egg, vanilla, peanut butter and milk; mix. Add dry ingredients and mix at lowest speed of mixer until dough forms. Shape dough into balls. Roll in sugar. Place on ungreased cookie sheet. Bake at 375° for 10 to 15 minutes. Top each cookie with a candy while hot from oven. Press firmly. Yields 48 cookies.

Mrs. Chris Williston (Janice)

Potato Chip Cookies

2   sticks butter, at room
    temperature
¾ cup sugar
1½ cups flour
1   teaspoon vanilla

¾ to 1 cup crushed potato
    chips
1   cup chopped pecans
Confectioners sugar

Cream butter and sugar until well blended. Add flour gradually. Stir in vanilla, potato chips, and pecans. Drop by spoonfuls on ungreased cookie sheet. Bake at 325° for 15 to 20 minutes. Sprinkle with confectioners sugar after baking. Cookies may be frozen before sprinkling with sugar, if desired. Yields 3 to 4 dozen.

Mrs. Robert Henderson (Dale)

Molasses Cookies

1   stick margarine
¾ cup sugar
1   egg
⅓ cup molasses

1½ cups flour
½ teaspoon salt
¾ teaspoon baking soda
½ cup chopped nuts

In large bowl, combine first four ingredients. Combine flour, salt and soda. Add to above mixture and mix well. Add nuts. Drop by teaspoonfuls on greased cookie sheet. Bake at 350° for 10 to 12 minutes. Yields 3 dozen.

Mrs. Jim Smith (Jare)

Snickerdoodles

1   cup shortening
1½ cups sugar
2   eggs
2¾ cups flour
1   teaspoon baking soda

½   teaspoon salt
¼   teaspoon cream of tartar
2   tablespoons sugar
2   teaspoons cinnamon

Cream shortening with sugar. Add eggs and beat well. Meanwhile, sift together the dry ingredients, except sugar and cinnamon. Stir them into the creamed mixture. Chill the dough for an hour. After chilling, roll the dough into small balls. Roll these balls in sugar-cinnamon mixture. Place about two inches apart on an ungreased cookie sheet and bake at 400° for 8 to 10 minutes. Yields 5 dozen. *This recipe has been passed through several generations in my family—it's always one of the favorites.*

Mrs. Ken Moyer (Bonnie)

Tea Cookies

3¼ cups flour
1   teaspoon baking soda
½   teaspoon salt
½   cup butter

1   cup sugar
1   egg
1   teaspoon vanilla
½   cup sour cream

Sift together flour, soda, salt. Mix butter with the sugar. Add the egg, vanilla, and sour cream; blend well. Add the sifted ingredients. Chill the dough. Roll out and cut into desired shapes. Bake at 425° for about 8 to 10 minutes. *This was a favorite recipe of my husband's grandmother.*

Mrs. Marcus Bone (Beverly)

Sugar Cookies

1   cup shortening
1   cup sugar
2   eggs
1   teaspoon vanilla

2¾ cups flour
¾   teaspoon salt
½   teaspoon baking powder
½   teaspoon baking soda

Cream shortening and sugar. Beat in eggs and vanilla. Gradually blend in dry ingredients. Chill 3 hours. Roll ⅛ to ¼" thickness. Cut out with cookie cutters. Bake at 375° for 8 to 10 minutes. Yields 2½ dozen. *I use this recipe at Christmas and ice the cookies with butter and powdered sugar icing—always popular. To make small round cookies I use the spout on a tupperware lid as a cutter.*

Mrs. John Perkins (Sandy)

Fruit Cake Cookies

1	cup whiskey or rum	1⅓	cups sugar
1	pound glazed pineapple, coarsely chopped	¾	pounds butter, softened
1	pound glazed red cherries, coarsely chopped	4	eggs
		4	teaspoons baking soda
		4	teaspoons milk
1	pound chopped dates	4	cups flour
1	box (16 ounces) white raisins	1¼	teaspoon cloves
		1¼	teaspoon allspice
2	pounds pecans, chopped	1¼	teaspoon cinnamon

In a large bowl, pour liquor over chopped fruits and nuts; marinate overnight. Cream sugar and butter. Add eggs, one at a time and mix well. Dissolve baking soda in milk and add to mixture. Sift together flour and spices; stir into liquid mixture. Mix batter with fruits and nuts. Drop by ½ teaspoonfuls onto greased cookie sheet. Bake at 375° for 12 minutes or until golden brown. Freezes well. Yields 18 dozen.

Mrs. Ron Bruney (Carol)

Date Cookies

1	cup sugar	1	teaspoon salt
1	cup brown sugar	1	teaspoon baking soda
1	cup shortening	1	teaspoon vanilla
3	eggs	2	cups chopped pecans
3	cups flour	2	cups chopped dates
1	teaspoon baking powder		

Cream sugars and shortening. Add eggs and continue beating. Sift dry ingredients and add to creamed mixture. Add vanilla, nuts, and dates. Drop by teaspoonfuls on greased cookie sheet. Bake at 350° for 8 to 10 minutes until golden. Do not overbake. Makes 6 to 8 dozen.

Mrs. Don Panter (Carolyn)

Milky Way Ice Cream

1	pound Milky Way candy bars		Milk to fill freezer
1	can sweetened condensed milk	1	can (5½ ounces) chocolate syrup, optional
1	pint half and half cream		

Chop Milky Way bars and melt with condensed milk. Add remaining ingredients. Put in ice cream freezer and freeze. Yields 1 gallon.

Mrs. Arthur Schroeder (Betty)

Lemon Milk Sherbet

2 quarts milk	1 can sweetened condensed
2 cups sugar	milk
	⅔ cup lemon juice

Combine milk and sugar in ice cream freezer until icy. Stop freezer, and add condensed milk and lemon juice. Finish freezing. Yields 3 quarts.

Judge O. E. Threlkeld

Mint Ice

2¾ cups water	Green food color
1 cup sugar	8 sprigs of mint, chopped
¼ cup lemon juice	Mint leaves to garnish

Put all ingredients into saucepan and bring to a boil. Remove from heat; cover and let steep 1 hour. Pour into 8x8 inch pan and freeze. Before serving, scrape mint ice with large spoon and put in stemmed glasses. Garnish with fresh mint leaf. Serves 6 to 8.

Mrs. Larry Wisian (Kay)

Berry Freeze

1 cup flour	1 package (10 ounces) frozen
¼ cup chopped pecans	strawberries or raspberries,
½ cup butter, melted	thawed
2 egg whites	1 carton (9 ounces) whipped
2 tablespoons lemon juice	topping
⅔ cup sugar	

Combine flour, pecans and melted butter in a 9x13 inch pan. Bake at 350° for 15 minutes, stirring every 5 minutes until brown. Mixture should be very crumbly. Press in bottom of pan, reserving ¼ cup mixture to sprinkle on top. Beat egg whites until fluffy; gradually add lemon juice and sugar. Next, add strawberries and beat until mixture peaks, about 15 minutes. Fold in whipped topping. Pour onto crust; top with remaining crumbs and freeze. Remove from freezer 15 minutes before serving. Yields 12 to 15 squares. *Super easy dessert to make ahead of time. Freeze and forget until ready to use.*

Mrs. David Armour (Betsy)

Chocolate Cinnamon Ice Cream

4 squares (1 ounce each) unsweetened chocolate
2 cans sweetened condensed milk
1 quart half and half cream
2 cups water

2 tablespoons vanilla
¼ teaspoon salt
2 teaspoons cinnamon
1 package (4 ounces) German sweet chocolate, crushed

Melt unsweetened chocolate in double boiler. Stir in milk and cook over water 5 minutes, stirring continuously. Pour into a large bowl to cool. Into cooled mixture, blend in the cream a little at a time. When smooth, add water, vanilla, salt and cinnamon. Place in ice cream freezer. After freezing about 15 minutes, add chocolate pieces; continue to freeze until firm. Yields 1 gallon.

Mrs. Dudley D. Baker (Kathy)

Cherry Nut Ice Cream

1 small envelope unflavored gelatin
¼ cup water
1 jar (6 ounces) Maraschino cherries, chopped, with juice
1 can sweetened condensed milk
1 cup chopped pecans

1 carton (12 ounces) whipped topping
1 pint half and half cream
1 teaspoon vanilla
Pinch of salt
1 cup sugar
Enough milk to fill freezer
Red food color to tint, as desired

Mix all ingredients and freeze in ice cream freezer. Yields 1 gallon.

Mrs. Norman Haertig (Doris)

Kahlua Ice Cream Cake

2 dozen ladyfingers, split
½ gallon vanilla ice cream, softened
1 quart chocolate ice cream, softened

¼ cup Kahlua
2 tablespoons coffee
9 Heath bars, crumbled
Whipped topping, optional

Butter 10 inch springform pan. Line sides and bottom with ladyfingers. Mix ice cream, Kahlua, coffee and candy. Pour into prepared pan. Freeze. Decorate top with whipped topping rosettes. Serves 12 to 15.

Mrs. Jim Schultz (Mary Kay)

Tropical Delight

Juice of 4 lemons	4 cups milk
Juice of 4 oranges	1 pint whipping cream
4 bananas, mashed	1 quart half and half cream
3 cups sugar	

Pour fruit juices over bananas, and add sugar. Let stand for 15 to 30 minutes. Add milk and cream; mix well. Freeze in ice cream freezer. Yields about 1 gallon. *This is my all time favorite ice cream. It is very simple to make and simply delicious. Some people call it sherbet because of the citrus fruits, but it is too velvety for sherbet.*

Mrs. Dudley D. Baker (Kathy)

Banana Ice Cream

2 eggs	1½ cups milk
1½ cups powdered sugar	1 cup mashed banana
1 envelope unflavored gelatin	1 tablespoon lemon juice
2 tablespoons cold water	2 cups whipping cream,
⅛ teaspoon salt	whipped
⅛ teaspoon nutmeg	

Beat eggs and sugar until light. Soften gelatin in water and dissolve over pan of hot water. Add gelatin, salt, nutmeg, and milk to egg mixture. Stir lemon juice into mashed bananas and add to egg mixture. Add whipped cream and freeze in ice cream freezer. Yields 2 quarts.

Mrs. B. L. Turlington (Jill)

Butter Pecan Ice Cream

1 cup chopped pecans	2 teaspoons butter flavoring
1 tablespoon butter	¼ teaspoon maple flavoring
5 eggs	Dash of salt
1¼ cups sugar	1 small package instant
1 can sweetened condensed milk	vanilla pudding
1 teaspoon vanilla	Milk or cream

Toast pecans in butter in oven at 300° for 10 minutes, no longer. Beat eggs and sugar together. Add other ingredients. Put in 1 gallon ice cream freezer bucket and add enough milk or cream to make one gallon. Freeze until firm. Yields 1 gallon.

Mrs. Charles Cantwell (Winn)

Homemade Vanilla Ice Cream

4 eggs	3 cups milk
2 cups sugar	1 pint whipping cream
⅛ teaspoon salt	1 tablespoon vanilla
4 teaspoons flour	2 to 3 cups milk

Combine eggs, sugar and salt in large bowl. Add flour and blend well. Stir in 3 cups milk. Pour mixture into a double boiler and cook until slightly thickened. Cool. Whip the cream and add vanilla. Fold into cooled custard. Before pouring into freezer container, the mixture may need to be strained to eliminate lumps. Place in freezer container and add remaining milk to within 3 inches of top. Freeze according to manufacturer's directions. Yields 1 gallon.

Mrs. Ken Moyer (Bonnie)

Kelly's No Cook Ice Cream

5 eggs	4 cups evaporated milk
2½ cups sugar	1½ teaspoons vanilla
6 cups milk	½ teaspoon salt

Beat eggs until light. Add sugar, gradually beating until mixture thickens. Stir in remaining ingredients and mix thoroughly. Place in ice cream freezer and freeze. Yields 1 gallon.

Mrs. John Perkins (Sandy)

Cheesecake Ice Cream

2 egg yolks	½ teaspoon grated orange rind
1 cup sugar, divided	1 tablespoon lemon juice
1 cup half and half cream	½ teaspoon vanilla
16 ounces cream cheese	1 pint plain yogurt
½ teaspoon grated lemon rind	

Beat egg yolks with ½ cup sugar; add cream. Cook over low heat, stirring constantly until thick enough to coat spoon. Remove from heat; chill thoroughly. Beat cream cheese until light. Add remaining sugar, fruit rinds, lemon juice and vanilla, continuing to beat until smooth. Add yogurt and chilled egg yolk mixture, beating until smooth. Freeze in ice cream freezer or in flat trays. If freezing in trays, beat before serving. Yields 2 quarts.

Mrs. Jim Rado (Vicki)

Aunt Sadie's Frozen Eggnog Dessert

4 eggs, separated	½ pint whipping cream
½ cup sugar	Nutmeg
4 tablespoons whiskey	

Combine egg yolks, sugar and whiskey in top of double boiler. Beat and cook until slightly thickened, about 3 to 5 minutes. Remove from heat; add to well beaten egg whites; beat well and add whipping cream. Beat until well blended. Pour into 2 ice cube trays and freeze. *This is a favorite family recipe. My great aunt always kept several trays ready in her freezer and served in crystal champagne glasses with homemade cookies. A wonderful dessert any time of year.*

Mrs. Don Bradford (Melinda)

Frozen Mocha Cream Jelly Roll

5 eggs, separated, at room temperature	Dash salt
	⅓ cup light brown sugar
1 cup powdered sugar, divided	2 tablespoons instant coffee
3 tablespoons cocoa	2 pints whipping cream

Grease jelly roll pan; line with waxed paper; grease and flour paper. Beat egg whites until soft peaks form, beating at high speed. Gradually sprinkle in ½ cup powdered sugar. Beat until sugar is dissolved; set aside. Do not scrape sides of bowl during beating. In small bowl, beat egg yolks at high speed until thick and lemon colored; at low speed beat in ½ cup powdered sugar, 3 tablespoons cocoa, and salt, occasionally scraping bowl. With whisk, gently fold yolk mixture into beaten egg whites until blended. Spread batter evenly in pan and bake 15 minutes or until top springs back when lightly touched. Loosen edges; immediately invert cake onto cloth towel that has been sprinkled with cocoa. Remove waxed paper. Roll towel with cake from narrow end. Cool completely seam side down on wire rack. When cool, unroll from towel. To make mocha cream, mix brown sugar, instant coffee, and cream at medium speed. Spread onto cake. Starting at narrow end, roll cake without towel. Place seam side down on platter. Wrap and freeze. Remove from freezer 15 minutes before serving. Serves 8.

Mrs. Ronald Davidson (Jackie)

Chocolate Mint Tarts

1 cup margarine
2 cups sifted powdered sugar
4 squares (1 ounce each) unsweetened chocolate, melted
4 eggs
1 teaspoon peppermint extract
2 teaspoons vanilla
18 vanilla wafers
1 pint whipping cream, whipped
Chopped nuts
Maraschino cherries
18 cupcake liners

Cream margarine and sugar. Blend in melted chocolate and eggs. Beat well. Add flavorings. Place a vanilla wafer in each cupcake liner. Fill ¾ full with chocolate mixture. Freeze in muffin tins to keep shape. After freezing, tarts may be stored in plastic bags. Before serving top with whipped cream, nuts and a cherry. Yields 18. *These are just enough to satisfy that sweet craving after a big dinner.*

Mrs. Jim Schultz (Mary Kay)

Blitz Torte

½ cup shortening
½ cup sugar
⅛ teaspoon salt
1 cup sifted cake flour
4 eggs, slightly beaten
3 tablespoons milk
1 teaspoon baking powder
4 egg whites
½ cup sliced blanched almonds
½ teaspoon cinnamon
1 tablespoon sugar
¾ cup sugar

Cream Filling:
⅓ cup sugar
3 tablespoons cornstarch
1 teaspoon vanilla
¼ teaspoon salt
2 egg yolks
2 tablespoons butter
2 cups milk, scalded

Cream shortening; beat in ½ cup sugar, salt, eggs, vanilla, milk and flour sifted with baking powder. Spread mixture in 2 greased 9 inch cake pans. Beat egg whites until very light; add ¾ cup sugar gradually and spread mixture in both pans. Sprinkle with almonds, 1 tablespoon sugar and cinnamon. Bake at 350° for 30 minutes. Cool and put together with cream filling in the middle. For filling, combine sugar, cornstarch, eggs, and salt. Beat thoroughly, add butter and enough milk to make a smooth paste. Add paste to remaining hot milk and cook over boiling water, stirring constantly until mixture is thickened. Cool. Add vanilla.

Mrs. Marcus Bone (Beverly)

Brownie Almond Torte

4 squares (1 ounce each)
   unsweetened chocolate
1¼ cups sifted flour
½ teaspoon baking powder
¼ teaspoon salt
1 cup butter
1½ cups sugar

4 eggs
1 teaspoon vanilla
1 cup blanched almonds,
   finely chopped
3 packages (2 or 2⅛ ounces
   each) whipped topping mix
Chocolate curls to garnish

Melt chocolate in microwave or double boiler. Cut eight 9 inch circles from wax paper. On another sheet of wax paper, sift flour with baking powder and salt. In large bowl, with electric mixer at medium speed, cream butter with sugar until fluffy. Add eggs, one at a time, until light and fluffy. At low speed, beat in melted chocolate, vanilla, flour mixture, and chopped almonds. Grease a large cookie sheet; on it place two wax paper circles; grease circles. With a broad spatula, spread ½ cup of chocolate mixture on each circle. Bake at 350° for 10 to 12 minutes. Let cool on cookie sheet about 5 minutes; then carefully remove to wire rack to cool completely. Remove wax paper. Continue baking until all dough is used, making 8 layers in all. Brownie layers may need to be trimmed to obtain uniformity.

Prepare whipped topping mix as label directs, one package at a time, and refrigerate. Reserve about ¾ cup whipped topping for garnish; spread the rest between seven layers; top with last layer. For garnish, drop spoonfuls of whipped topping on top layer and add a chocolate curl on top. Refrigerate. Serve chilled. Serves 15 to 18. *May be prepared up to one week before serving. Freezer wrap after the torte is completely finished and freeze. About 2 hours before serving, remove from freezer to thaw.*

Mrs. Joe Bowles (Mary)

Ice Box Graham Cracker Roll

8 ounces graham crackers,
   crushed
8 ounces marshmallows, cut
   fine

8 ounces chopped dates
½ cup half and half cream
20 cherries, chopped

Mix together and roll on wax paper; add a few additional cracker crumbs. Let stand in refrigerator until nearly ready to serve. Garnish with colored candies or cherries and serve with or without whipped cream. *Rich, but delicious. The best fruit cake I've ever eaten.*

Mrs. Larry Morris (Diane)

Pecan Torte

6   eggs, separated
½   teaspoon cream of tartar
3   cups pecans, ground,
    reserving some for garnish
1   tablespoon flour

1   teaspoon baking powder
1½ cups sugar
½   cup tart jelly
Sweetened whipped cream to
garnish

Beat egg whites and cream of tartar until stiff. Fold pecans, reserving ¼ cup, flour and baking powder into egg whites. Beat egg yolks, gradually adding sugar, until mixture is stiff. Fold into egg white mixture. Line two 9 inch pans with wax paper. Do not grease. Pour mixture into pans and cook at 350° for 20 minutes. Let cool in pan for 20 minutes. When cooled, spread tart jelly between layers and top with sweetened whipped cream and ground pecans. Serves 12 to 15.

Mrs. D. D. Baker, Jr. (Agnes)

Cheese Blintzes

3   eggs
1   tablespoon sugar
¼   teaspoon salt
1½ cups flour
1   cup milk

1   cup 7-Up
1   teaspoon vanilla
¼   teaspoon baking powder
1   tablespoon oil

Filling:
8   ounces cream cheese,
    softened
1   carton (12 ounces) small
    curd cottage cheese or
    ricotta

1   egg yolk
4   tablespoons sugar
1   teaspoon grated orange rind
½   teaspoon vanilla
Dash cinnamon

For pancakes, place all ingredients in blender and mix well. Put oil in small skillet and heat until hot. Remove the oil; return skillet to medium high and cook pancakes. Use approximately 2 to 3 tablespoons batter for each pancake, swirling the pan above the heat so that the batter totally covers the bottom. Return to burner and cook until the bottom is browned. Loosen edges and flip to brown the other side for a few seconds. Remove from pan and stack.

Combine all filling ingredients. Use 2 to 3 tablespoons filling per blintz. Roll up and keep in pyrex dish in warm oven. Serve warm. Yields 15 to 18. *This traditional Jewish favorite is also quite versatile. Served in the morning with preserves, it is nice for breakfast or brunch. It makes a great dessert covered with fruit, sour cream, whipped cream, or sprinkled generously with powdered sugar.*

Mrs. Jim Rado (Vicki)

Apple Kuchen

½ cup margarine, softened
1 package (18½ ounces)
   yellow cake mix
1 can (21 ounces) apple pie
   filling

½ cup sugar
1 teaspoon cinnamon
1 cup sour cream
2 egg yolks or 1 egg

Cut margarine into cake mix until crumbly. Pat mixture lightly into ungreased 9x13 pan, building up slightly on edges. Bake at 350° for 10 minutes. Arrange apple pie filling on warm crust. Mix sugar and cinnamon and sprinkle on apples. Blend sour cream and egg yolk. Drizzle over apples. (Topping should not completely cover apples). Bake at 350° for 20 to 25 minutes or until edges are brown. Serve warm. Yields 12 servings.

Mrs. John Perkins (Sandy)

Apple Crisp

1 can (20 ounces) pie sliced
   apples, mostly drained
1 can (16 ounces) applesauce
½ cup raisins
½ cup sugar
1 teaspoon cinnamon

1 teaspoon nutmeg
½ teaspoon salt
1 cup brown sugar
¾ cup rolled oats
¾ cup flour
½ cup margarine, softened

Combine apples, applesauce, raisins, sugar and spices. Place in 1 quart baking dish. For topping, mix brown sugar, oats, flour, and margarine until crumbly. Sprinkle over apple mixture and bake at 350° for 35 minutes. Serves 8.

Mrs. Wayne Davison (Cindi)

Fruit Party Pizza

1 package (16 ounces) sugar
   cookie dough
8 ounces cream cheese,
   softened
½ cup powdered sugar

Fresh fruits to cover
1 cup apricot or peach
   preserves
6 tablespoons water

Press cookie dough into a 15 inch pizza pan and bake at 350° for 10 minutes. Cool. Sweeten cream cheese with powdered sugar and spread over baked cookie dough. Place fruits on crust. Use bananas, strawberries, pineapple, grapes, mandarin oranges, or any fruit to make a colorful assortment. Thin preserves with water and cook until a glaze forms. Drizzle glaze over fruit. Serves 8 to 10. *This is a beautiful dessert and is really good for a brunch or luncheon.*

Mrs. Linden Welsch (Phyllis)

Carmon's LBJ Cake

1	cup flour	2	small packages instant
1	stick margarine, melted		pudding mix, vanilla or
1	cup chopped pecans		chocolate or 1 of each
8	ounces cream cheese,	3	cups milk
	softened	1	carton (12 ounces) whipped
1	cup powdered sugar		topping
		1	cup toasted coconut

Mix flour and melted margarine. Add pecans and pat mixture in bottom of 9x13 inch pan. Bake at 350° for 20 minutes. Cool. Mix cream cheese and powdered sugar; spread over flour mixture. Mix pudding and milk and when thick fold in one cup topping. Spread on top of cheese mixture. Top with remaining whipped topping and sprinkle with toasted coconut. Refrigerate 4 hours. Serves 12.

Mrs. Lee Dickerson (Carol)

Pineapple Crunch Pie

Butter Nut Crust:

2	cups flour	1	cup butter
½	teaspoon salt	1	cup chopped pecans

Filling:

8	ounces cream cheese	1	can (20 ounces) crushed
1	cup powdered sugar		pineapple
2	tablespoons milk	1¼	cups sugar
1	carton (8 ounces) whipped	2	tablespoons cornstarch
	topping		Pecans to garnish, optional

Mix flour and salt. Cut in butter; add chopped pecans. Press into 9x13 inch pan. Bake at 350° until light brown, about 10 minutes. Cool. Combine cream cheese, powdered sugar and milk. Spread over crust. Spread with whipped topping. Mix pineapple, sugar and cornstarch and cook until thick. Cool and spread over topping. If desired, sprinkle with pecans. Serves 16 to 20.

Mrs. John C. Waller (Elsie)

Meringues

4   egg whites
Pinch of salt
¼   teaspoon cream of tartar

1   cup sugar
Vanilla or creme de menthe

Combine egg whites with salt and cream of tartar and beat until stiff but not dry. Gradually add sugar, beating well after each addition until meringue is no longer grainy. Add flavoring. Shape meringue as desired. For tart shells cut 3½ to 4 inch circles out of parchment or wax paper. Use rose tip of cake decorator. Make rings until base is covered. Then add a ring to the outside to form a cup. Meringue swans can be shaped by making oval cups peaked at one end. On a separate paper, spread meringue in 2 inch lengths to make swan necks. Bake in 275° oven for 10 minutes; lower heat to 250° and bake 20 to 25 minutes longer. Yields 12 tarts or 1 large pie shell. *These are delicious filled with fresh fruit and whipped cream. For an easy and pretty dessert, fill shells with ice cream and fresh berry sauce.*

Mrs. Don Bradford (Melinda)

Cheesecake

Crust:
1   cup graham cracker crumbs
½   teaspoon cinnamon

1   tablespoon sugar
4   tablespoons butter, melted

Filling:
40 ounces cream cheese,
     softened
1¾ cups sugar
3   tablespoons flour

5   eggs
2   egg yolks
¾   cup milk
1   teaspoon vanilla

For crust, mix crumbs, cinnamon, sugar and butter and press in a 9 inch springform pan. Chill before filling. Blend cream cheese, sugar and flour and beat well. Add eggs and yolks one at a time, beating after each addition. Stir in milk. Pour over crust and bake at 475° for 10 minutes. Lower temperature to 200° and bake 1 hour longer. Leave cake in oven until cool. Serves 12. *This is best when made the day before and allowed to cool in refrigerator.*

Mrs. Jim Rado (Vicki)

Pineapple Cheesecake

Crust:

2 cups graham cracker crumbs
¼ cup sugar

1 teaspoon cinnamon
1 stick margarine, melted

Filling:

16 ounces cream cheese, softened
1 cup sugar
2 eggs
Salt to taste

1 teaspoon vanilla
1 pint sour cream
1 can (15 ounces) crushed pineapple, well drained

Mix graham cracker crumbs, ¼ cup sugar and cinnamon. Add melted margarine and stir. Press mixture into a 10 inch springform pan and bake at 350° for 8 minutes; cool.

For filling, beat cheese, 1 cup sugar, eggs, salt and vanilla until smooth. Add sour cream and beat well. Stir in pineapple. Pour filling into crust. Bake at 350° for 1 hour, or until a knife inserted in center comes out clean. Do not overcook. Serves 12. *This cheesecake is also delicious without the pineapple, served plain or with fruit topping.*

Mrs. Terry Arndt (Barbara)

Flan Cheesecake

12 tablespoons sugar, divided
8 ounces cream cheese, softened
5 egg yolks, beaten
1 can (13 ounces) evaporated milk

1 can sweetened condensed milk
1 can water measured in condensed milk can
1 teaspoon vanilla
Pinch of salt

Place 10 tablespoons sugar in a heavy skillet. Stir over medium heat until sugar dissolves into a light brown syrup. Pour immediately in flan pan or shallow dish and let cool and harden. In mixing bowl, place cream cheese; add beaten egg yolks. Stir in both milks, water, vanilla, remaining sugar and salt. Blend with caramelized sugar and set in pan of hot water. Bake at 350° for 1½ to 1¾ hours. Serves 12. *Flan will look soft, but hardens in refrigerator. Be sure it chills thoroughly; it is better if it can be refrigerated overnight. When ready to serve, invert on a flat plate, and the flan will come out easily with the caramel sauce on top. Do not freeze.*

Mrs. Rush McGinty (Carol)

Mini-Cheesecakes

¾ cup graham cracker crumbs
2 tablespoons soft butter
8 ounces cream cheese, softened
1 egg

¼ cup sugar
½ teaspoon vanilla
1 can (16 ounces) cherry pie filling, optional

Set small cupcake liners in miniature muffin pans. Mix cracker crumbs with butter and press one teaspoon of mixture in bottom of each paper cup. Combine cheese, egg, sugar and vanilla. Beat until smooth. Fill cups ¾ full. Bake at 350° for 10 to 12 minutes. Store in refrigerator. If desired, top each cheesecake with a dollop of cherry pie filling. Yields 32 to 34. *These are pretty for teas and coffees and are very festive at Christmas.*

Mrs. Ken Moyer (Bonnie)

Natural Ingredients Cheesecake

8 ounces finely ground pecans
½ cup honey
2 tablespoons melted butter
24 ounces cream cheese, softened

⅔ cup honey
1 teaspoon vanilla
4 egg whites beaten rather dry

Mix pecans, ½ cup honey and butter; spread with wet hands over bottom of 10 inch spring form pan. Combine cream cheese, ⅔ cup honey and vanilla; fold into egg whites until smooth. Bake at 350° for exactly 25 minutes. Chill 2 hours before serving. Loosen edges of cake before removing outer ring.

Mrs. Charles Strong (Ginny)

Danish Pudding

2 packages (10 ounces each) frozen strawberries, thawed
2 packages (10 ounces each) frozen raspberries, thawed
1 cup sugar

4 teaspoons arrowroot
Red food coloring, optional
½ pint whipped cream to garnish
Slivered almonds to garnish

Mix berries, sugar and arrowroot. Stir and cook until thick. Add a few drops of red food coloring if desired. Chill and serve in compotes, topped with whipped cream and slivered almonds. Serves 10 to 12. *A very nice and colorful dessert that is light enough to follow a heavy meal.*

Mrs. D. D. Baker, Jr. (Agnes)

Cherry Pudding

1 can (16½ ounces) water packed red sour cherries	½ teaspoon salt
	¾ cup sugar
1 cup flour	½ cup chopped nuts
1 teaspoon baking soda	1 egg
1 teaspoon cinnamon	1 tablespoon butter, melted

Cherry Sauce:

¼ cup sugar	1 tablespoon butter
1 tablespoon cornstarch	Whipped cream to garnish
1 cup cherry juice	

Drain cherries, reserving juice. Mix flour, soda, cinnamon, salt, sugar, and nuts. Beat egg and add to butter. Add to dry mixture, along with cherries, and mix until moist. Spread into greased 1½ quart casserole. Bake at 375° for 30 minutes. Cut in squares and serve warm with whipped cream and cherry sauce.

To make sauce, mix sugar and cornstarch in a saucepan. Add 1 cup cherry juice, or juice plus water to make 1 cup. Cook, stirring, until smooth and thick. Add butter. Serve hot. Makes 8 servings.

Mrs. Ron Garrick (Bonnie)

Brandied Caramel Flan

¾ cup sugar	½ cup sugar
2 cups milk	½ teaspoon salt
2 cups half and half cream	2 teaspoons vanilla
6 eggs	⅓ cup brandy

Place ¾ cup sugar in large, heavy skillet. Cook and stir over medium heat until sugar melts and forms light brown syrup. Immediately pour syrup into heated shallow glass baking dish or flan pan. Holding dish with pot holder, quickly rotate to cover bottom and sides completely. Set aside. To make custard, heat milk and cream until bubbles form around edge. In large bowl beat eggs slightly. Add sugar, salt and vanilla. Gradually stir in the hot milk mixture and brandy. Pour into prepared dish. Set dish in shallow pan; pour boiling water to ½ inch level of flan. Bake at 325° for 35 to 40 minutes, or until silver knife inserted comes out clean. Let custard cool; refrigerate 4 hours or overnight. To serve, run small spatula around edge of dish to loosen. Invert on serving dish; shake gently to release. Serves 6 to 8.

Mrs. Lee Provinse (Dottie)

Heavenly Hash

1 can sweetened condensed
  milk
1 carton (12 ounces) whipped
  topping
1 can (21 ounces) cherry pie
  filling
1 can (11 ounces) mandarin
  oranges, drained

1 can (20 ounces) pineapple
  tidbits, drained
1 cup pecans
1 cup miniature
  marshmallows
1 cup coconut

Mix condensed milk and whipped topping together and place in refrigerator overnight, or in freezer until cold. Add remaining ingredients and mix well. Leave in refrigerator until well chilled. Serves 12 to 15. *Fantastic as a salad or dessert.*

Mrs. Charles Strong (Ginny)

Banana Rum Fruit Dip

1 banana
1 cup sour cream
2 tablespoons light rum
2 tablespoons brown sugar

¼ teaspoon ginger
⅛ teaspoon salt
2 teaspoons lime juice

Mash banana and add remaining ingredients. Mix well and refrigerate, covered, until well chilled. Serve over fresh fruit for a light dessert. Yields 1 cup sauce. For a variation, substitute 1 tablespoon fruit liqueur for the banana. *This recipe can double as a refreshing dip on a hot afternoon!*

Mrs. Marcus Bone (Beverly)

Fruit Medley

⅓ cup Port wine
¼ cup orange juice
1 tablespoon lemon juice
1 cup peeled and sliced fresh
  peaches

1 cup sliced fresh
  strawberries
6 pear halves, canned or fresh
1 large banana, sliced

Combine and toss all of the ingredients. Chill 3 to 6 hours. Serves 6. *A refreshingly different fruit salad that's pretty for brunch.*

Mrs. Bernard Vise (Marion)

Apples in Amaretto

8   apples, peeled and very   1½ cups Amaretto liqueur
    thinly sliced

Marinate apples in Amaretto overnight. About one hour before serving, place apples on a serving tray. Put in freezer. Remove just prior to serving. Use party toothpicks for serving. Serves 20.

Marian Hidell

White Chocolate Surprises

2   pounds white chocolate   2   cups small pretzel sticks,
2   cups Spanish peanuts   broken

Melt chocolate in a double boiler; stir in peanuts and pretzels. Drop by spoonfuls on wax paper. Work fast, as mixture hardens quickly. Yields 5 dozen. *This is especially nice to give for a Christmas gift.*

Mrs. David Armour (Betsy)

After Dinner Mints

8   ounces cream cheese,   2   teaspoons mint flavoring
    softened   Food color as desired
2   boxes (16 ounces each)   Granulated sugar
    powdered sugar

Blend cream cheese until smooth. Add powdered sugar, mint flavoring and color. Knead as pie dough. Pinch a bit of dough and dip one side in granulated sugar. Press into candy mold, until edges are even. Unmold immediately on wax paper. If firmer texture is wanted, add more powdered sugar. Keeps well and may be frozen. For variation, try other flavors such as lemon, rum, maple or vanilla. For chocolate mints, add 3 teaspoons cocoa. Yields 100 mints.

Mrs. Tom Tullos (Mary)

Pecan Pralines

1½ cups brown sugar   2   tablespoons butter
1½ cups white sugar   2   cups pecans
1   cup evaporated milk   1   teaspoon vanilla

Cook sugars and evaporated milk until soft ball forms in cold water. Remove from heat and add butter. Beat until creamy. Add pecans and vanilla. Drop on waxed paper. Yields 30 pieces.

Mrs. Ron Garrick (Bonnie)

Toffee Candy

1 cup chopped pecans	4 plain chocolate Hershey
½ cup butter	bars, regular size
¾ cup brown sugar	

Butter an 8 inch square pan generously. Cover the bottom of the pan with the chopped pecans. Melt the butter and brown sugar on medium heat. Bring to a boil and boil for 6 minutes, stirring continuously. Remove from heat and pour over the pecans. While still hot, lay the Hershey bars on top. As they melt, spread them evenly over mixture. Cool completely. Break into uneven pieces with a table knife. Yields 12 to 16 pieces. *This easy recipe tastes exactly like Heath candy bars.*

Mrs. David Armour (Betsy)

English Toffee

2 cups sugar	Pinch salt
2 tablespoons light corn syrup	1 cup whole pecans
6 tablespoons water	1 package (6 ounces)
½ pound butter	semisweet chocolate chips,
½ pound margarine	melted
Vanilla	1 cup chopped pecans

Cook sugar, corn syrup, water, butter, margarine, vanilla and salt to 290°; continue cooking two minutes longer. Line buttered cookie sheet with whole pecans. Pour mixture over pecans. Spread melted chocolate over this layer. Sprinkle with chopped pecans. Break into pieces when cool.

Mrs. Don Panter (Carolyn)

Graham Cracker Roll

1 can sweetened condensed milk	1 cup chopped pecans
1½ squares sweet chocolate, grated	1 cup coconut
1¼ cups graham cracker crumbs	Large marshmallows

In a saucepan, cook the milk and chocolate until thick. Remove from heat and add the graham cracker crumbs and pecans; mix well. Sprinkle coconut on a board and pour mixture over and pat out in rectangle form. Line with one row of marshmallows and roll up jelly-roll fashion. Wrap in wax paper and freeze. Cut into slices before serving.

Mrs. Larry Wisian (Kay)

Yummy Pecan Rolls

1	jar (7 ounces) marshmallow cream	1	package (14 ounces) assorted vanilla and chocolate caramels
1	package (16 ounces) powdered sugar	3	tablespoons water
1	teaspoon vanilla	1	cup chopped pecans

Combine marshmallow, powdered sugar and vanilla; mix well with hands. Shape mixture into 5 rolls, each 1x4 inches. Chill 3 hours. Melt caramels and water in top of double boiler or in microwave. Dip rolls in melted caramel and roll each in pecans. Chill 1 hour and cut into slices to serve. Yields 5 rolls.

Mrs. Robert West (Linda)

Kookie Brittle

1	cup margarine	2	cups flour
1½	teaspoons vanilla	1	package (6 ounces) semisweet chocolate chips
1	teaspoon salt	½	cup chopped nuts
1	cup sugar		

Combine margarine, vanilla, and salt. Add sugar, flour, and chocolate chips. Mix well. Press into a 10x15 inch cookie sheet. Sprinkle with chopped nuts and press into dough. Bake at 375° for 25 minutes. Cool and break into pieces.

Mrs. Jerry Dow (Annette)

Peanut Butter Candy

1	cup butter	1½	cups graham cracker crumbs
1	cup crunchy peanut butter		
1	box (16 ounces) powdered sugar, sifted	1	package (12 ounces) semisweet chocolate chips

Blend butter and peanut butter in a large bowl. Work in the powdered sugar and cracker crumbs with a wooden spoon until combined thoroughly. Press into a 9x13 inch pan. Set aside. Melt chocolate pieces in microwave or double boiler, watching carefully to make sure the chocolate does not get too hot. Quickly spread melted chocolate over the top of the peanut butter mixture. Chill until firm, but not too cold. Cut into small squares. These may be stored in air tight container once they are made. Yields 60 pieces. *Tastes like Reese's candy!*

Mrs. Ken Moyer (Bonnie)

Fudge

2 cups sugar
⅔ cup evaporated milk
10 marshmallows
1 stick margarine

1 package (6 ounces)
semisweet chocolate chips
¾ cup chopped pecans

Mix sugar, evaporated milk, marshmallows and margarine in saucepan. Boil 6 minutes and remove from heat. When cool, add chocolate chips and nuts. Beat well by hand and pour into buttered 8 inch square dish. Yields about 50 squares. *This candy has made a hit around Muleshoe, Texas for a long time.*

Mrs. Charles Cantwell (Winn)

Martha Washington Candy

1 stick margarine, softened
2 boxes (16 ounces each)
powdered sugar
1 can sweetened condensed
milk
1 teaspoon vanilla

2 cups chopped pecans
2 cups coconut
1 package (12 ounces)
semisweet chocolate chips
2 ounces paraffin bar

Mix margarine, powdered sugar, milk, and vanilla. Stir well. Divide in half. Put nuts in one half and coconut in the other. Form into balls. Put in tray in freezer for thirty minutes. Melt chocolate chips with paraffin in a double boiler. Using toothpicks, dip chilled balls into chocolate. Place on buttered wax paper to dry. Store in air tight container. Freezes well. *This is a really good candy to serve at Christmas.*

Mrs. Jim Rado (Vicki)

Divinity

2½ cups sugar
½ cup white corn syrup
½ cup water

2 egg whites, beaten until stiff
1 teaspoon vanilla
1 cup chopped pecans

Mix sugar, syrup, and water; cook until mixture reaches 240° on candy thermometer. Pour ½ of the mixture over the beaten egg whites, and stir well. Cook the remaining ½ of the sugar mixture until it reaches 290° on candy thermometer. Pour into egg white mixture. Beat until thick and creamy. Add vanilla and pecans. Drop by spoonfuls onto waxed paper. This mixture hardens rapidly so it has to be finished quickly. *This is a family recipe and my grandmother said divinity will never "set up" properly on a cloudy or rainy day, so only make this divinity on a clear, sunny day.*

Mrs. Larry Keith (Virginia)

Date Balls

2 cups chopped dates
1 stick margarine
2 egg yolks
⅔ cup sugar

1 teaspoon vanilla
2 cups Rice Krispies
1 cup chopped pecans
Powdered sugar

Cook dates, margarine, egg yolks, sugar and vanilla in heavy skillet, stirring until mixture boils. Simmer 2 to 3 minutes. Add Rice Krispies and nuts. Shape into bite size balls and roll in powdered sugar. Keep hands buttered when handling hot dates. Yields 5 dozen. *For a special effect, these can be formed into strawberry shapes, rolled in red sugar, and topped with leaves, using green decorator icing.*

Mrs. Robert West (Linda)

Date Pinwheels

Cookie Dough:
4½ cups sifted all purpose flour
1 teapoon salt
1 teaspoon baking powder
1 teaspoon cinnamon
1 cup margarine or butter

2 cups brown sugar, firmly
packed
½ cup granulated sugar
3 eggs

Filling:
1½ cups ground dates, and/or
raisins, or figs
1 cup sugar

1 cup water
½ cup chopped nuts

Sift flour, salt, baking powder, and cinnamon together. Cream butter until soft. Then gradually work in both sugars until smooth. Add unbeaten eggs; mix until thoroughly blended. Mix dry ingredients into creamed mixture. Chill in refrigerator several hours while you make the filling. For filling, cook fruit, sugar, and water over low heat until mixture is thick, stirring constantly. Remove from heat, stir in nuts. Cool completely. Divide dough in half and roll ¼ inch thick on lightly floured board. Spread with an even layer of filling. Both dough and filling should be very cold to roll neatly. Roll dough into jelly roll and carefully wrap in wax paper. Store overnight in refrigerator. Cut in ⅛ inch slices, place one inch apart on a greased cookie sheet and bake in a 375° oven for 10 to 15 minutes. Yields 6 dozen.

Mrs. C. Z. Leonard (Marcia)

Bourbon or Rum Balls

2   tablespoons cocoa
1   cup powdered sugar
¼ cup bourbon or rum

2   tablespoons light corn syrup
2   cups crushed vanilla wafers
1   cup finely chopped nuts

Sift cocoa and powdered sugar into bowl. Stir in liquor, which has been combined with syrup; mix well. Add vanilla wafers and nuts; mix well. Form into ¾ inch balls and roll in powdered sugar. Dry several hours. Freezes well. Yields 3 dozen.

Mrs. Wayne Davison (Cindi)

Orange Balls

1   box (12 ounces) vanilla
    wafers
1   stick margarine
1   box (1 pound) powdered
    sugar

1   can (6 ounces) orange juice
1   cup chopped pecans
1   can (3½ ounces) flaked
    coconut

Crush vanilla wafers. Cream margarine and sugar together; add orange juice, wafers, and pecans. Form into balls and roll in flaked coconut. Yields 5 dozen.

Mrs. Jim Smith (Jare)

Sugared Peanuts

1   cup water
1   cup sugar

4   cups raw, unblanched
    peanuts

Combine water and sugar in large saucepan. Cook over medium heat until sugar dissolves. Add peanuts and continue cooking, stirring frequently, until all syrup has been absorbed by peanuts. This takes about 30 minutes. Spread on greased baking sheet. Bake in 300° oven for one hour, stirring about 4 times. Watch carefully. Do not double recipe. Yields 4 cups.

Mrs. Jim Schultz (Mary Kay)

 Vanilla flavor evaporates when it is boiled. Add vanilla extract to candies and desserts after they have been removed from heat.

Spiced Nuts

1 cup sugar
½ teaspoon cinnamon
⅓ cup evaporated milk

1½ cups pecans
½ teaspoon vanilla

Mix sugar and cinnamon. Stir in evaporated milk. Cook to soft ball stage. Add pecans and vanilla; stir until hard. Turn out on waxed paper and separate. Serves 4 or 5.

Mrs. Don Panter (Carolyn)

Caramel Popcorn

1 cup margarine
2 cups brown sugar
½ cup corn syrup, dark or light
1 teaspoon salt

½ teaspoon baking soda
1 teaspoon vanilla
6 quarts popped corn

Melt margarine in large saucepan. Stir in brown sugar, syrup, and salt. Bring to a boil, stirring constantly. Boil without stirring for 5 more minutes. Remove from heat and stir in baking soda and vanilla. Gradually pour mixture over popped corn in large pan and mix well. Bake at 250° for 1 hour, stirring every 15 minutes. Remove from oven, cool completely. Break and store in sealed container. Yields 6 quarts.

Mrs. Larry Wisian (Kay)

Popcorn Balls

1 cup sugar
⅓ cup water
⅓ cup light corn syrup
1 teaspoon salt

½ cup butter
1 teaspoon vanilla
7 cups warm popcorn

Boil sugar, water, corn syrup, salt and butter until the soft ball stage is reached. Add vanilla and pour over popcorn. Form into balls. *These make quite a hit with children.*

Mrs. Charles Cantwell (Winn)

The Highland Lakes of Central Texas, a chain of sparkling jewels, stretching 100 miles northwest of Austin, attract thousands of Texans each weekend. There is so much to do and to see, so much everchanging beauty and restful atmosphere to enjoy, that a Texan can return again and again without ever tiring of the lakes. With more square miles of inland water than any state except Alaska, water sports are favorites of all Texans. Whether water skiing, sailing, fishing, scuba diving, or just sunning, Austinites and all Texans flock to "the Lake" to enjoy their favorite outdoor activities. On weekends the lakes are dotted with brightly colored sail boats, while the parks along the shores are filled with campers. It can be said with certainty that in this land of the cowboy there are more boats than horses.

Microwave dishes pictured: Spicy Hot Fruit, Speedy Split Pea Soup, New England Chowder, Mexican Soup, Garlic Cheese Brussels Sprouts, Deviled Cauliflower, Stuffed Green Peppers, Beef Strips with Tomatoes, Calico Salad, and Grasshopper Pie.

Microwave

The microwave recipes are included for those busy days when there is no time to spend an afternoon in the kitchen. Whether we work, play tennis, drive carpools, or just loaf, these recipes can all be prepared in minutes. Many of the recipes in this section have been adapted from conventional recipes usually prepared in the oven. Besides saving time, using the microwave makes for cooler cooking in the hot Texas summers. From appetizers to desserts, these recipes have been selected for the woman on the go. This section was lovingly compiled and tested by cookbook committee members who very often resorted to "last minute" meals.

Apricot Glow

3 cups apricot nectar
1 cup orange juice
2 cinnamon sticks, broken

1 teaspoon whole cloves
Orange slices for garnish
optional

Combine all ingredients except orange slices in a 4 cup glass container and heat on HIGH for 7 to 8 minutes. Stir, heat 5 to 6 more minutes on MEDIUM-LOW. Strain into mugs and garnish with orange slices. Yields 4 servings. *For a variation add ½ to one tablespoon rum to each mug.*

Mrs. Jack Baker (Cooki)

Café Caribe

Lime wedge
Brown sugar
1 tablespoon Kahlua
1 ounce brandy

1 cup boiling water
1¼ teaspoons instant coffee
Whipped topping or cream to
garnish

Moisten the top of a stemmed glass by running a lime wedge around the rim. Frost rim with brown sugar. Add Kahlua and brandy to each glass. Microwave water on HIGH for 2½ to 3 minutes until boiling. Stir in coffee. Add coffee to liqueur mixture, stirring and filling glass ¾ full. Top with whipped topping or cream, and sprinkle with brown sugar. Serves 1.

Cookbook Committee

Irish Coffee

1½ ounces Irish whiskey
1   teaspoon sugar
2   teaspoons instant coffee

Water
Whipped cream

Combine whiskey and sugar in mug. Add coffee and water to make ¾ full. Microwave on HIGH 1½ minutes, until mixture is hot but not boiling. Stir well. Top with whipped cream. Do not stir. Serves 1.

Clark Rector

Mulled Cider

1   quart apple cider
2   whole allspice
2   whole cloves
1 to 2 cinnamon sticks

5   tablespoons brown sugar
½   orange, unpeeled, thinly sliced

In a 2 quart glass container, combine cider, allspice, cloves, cinnamon sticks and brown sugar; float orange slices on top. Cover with wax paper and cook on HIGH 8 to 10 minutes. Stir halfway through cooking time. Serve hot. Serves 4 to 5.

Dudley Baker

Easy Hot Buttered Rum

1 to 2 teaspoons packed brown
    sugar
¼   cup rum
Water

Butter
Nutmeg
Cinnamon stick

In a tall mug place sugar and rum. Add water to ⅔ full. Microwave on HIGH 1½ to 2 minutes, until very hot but not boiling. Add about a ¼ inch thick slice of butter. Sprinkle with nutmeg and serve with cinnamon stick for stirring. Serves 1.

Jim Schultz

 Warm liqueurs for flaming at HIGH; allow about 15 seconds for 2 tablespoons to ¼ cup.

Really Different Hors D'oeuvres

4 ounces cream cheese	1 tablespoon dry Hidden
1 package (6 ounces) frozen	Valley salad dressing mix
crab meat or shrimp,	1 tablespoon mayonnaise
thawed and drained	2 zucchini, thinly sliced
2 tablespoons fresh lemon	Paprika to garnish
juice	

Heat cheese in 1 quart bowl on HIGH 30 seconds to 1 minute to soften. Add all ingredients but zucchini and paprika. Arrange zucchini slices on microwave proof serving dishes. Top each slice with a teaspoonful of crab mixture. Sprinkle with paprika. Cook on HIGH until zucchini is crisp-tender, about 1 to 2 minutes. Let cool slightly. Chill before serving. Yields about 40.

Mrs. Larry Hall (Jane)

Before refrigerating appetizers prepared in advance, place them on serving platters that are microwave safe. This will eliminate the need to transfer them after microwaving.

Cheese Savories

½ cup butter	4 green onions, finely
1½ cups flour	chopped
½ pound extra sharp Cheddar	1 teaspoon salt
cheese, grated	Paprika

Cut butter into flour with pastry blender or in food processor. Add grated cheese, chopped onions and salt and blend until mix can be formed into balls about the size of a walnut. Place in plastic bags and chill overnight in refrigerator. When ready to serve, place 8 to 10 savories on lightly greased pie plate and microwave on HIGH for 2 to 2½ minutes. Do not over-cook. While hot, sprinkle with paprika. Serve warm. Can be frozen, but if so, cook 3 to 3½ minutes. Yields 4 to 5 dozen. *For extra zing, add a few drops of Tabasco sauce.*

Mrs. Don Bradford (Melinda)

Blackeyed Pea Dip

4   cups blackeyed peas,
    cooked and drained
5   canned jalapeños, chopped
1   tablespoon jalapeño juice
½   medium onion, chopped
1   can (4 ounces) green chilies,
    chopped

1   clove garlic, minced
½   pound sharp Cheddar
    cheese, grated
½   pound margarine

Blend peas, jalapeños, juice, onion, chilies and garlic in blender. Heat cheese and margarine in microwave until melted and combine with black-eyed pea mixture. Serve hot from chafing dish with corn chips. Serves 16 to 20. *This is a New Year's Day version of refried beans!*

Cookbook Committee

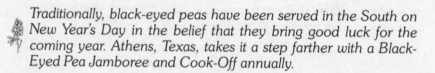

Traditionally, black-eyed peas have been served in the South on New Year's Day in the belief that they bring good luck for the coming year. Athens, Texas, takes it a step farther with a Black-Eyed Pea Jamboree and Cook-Off annually.

Chili Con Queso

1   large onion, chopped
1   green pepper, chopped
2   tablespoons olive oil
4   jalapeños
1   can (10 ounces) tomatoes
    with green chilies

2   pounds pasteurized process
    cheese spread, cubed
1   can (2 ounces) chopped
    pimiento, drained

Sauté onion and green pepper in oil on HIGH for 2 to 3 minutes. Chop jalapeños with tomatoes in blender or seed jalapeños and chop. Add to onion and pepper. Add cubed cheese and pimiento. Cover with wax paper and microwave on MEDIUM-HIGH for 10 to 12 minutes, stirring halfway through, or until cheese is melted. Serve with crisp tortillas. Serves 8.

Mrs. Jim Schultz (Mary Kay)

Speedy Split Pea Soup

5 cups water	½ cup chopped celery
1 package (6 ounces) split pea soup mix	2 parsley sprigs
	1 garlic clove, minced
1 potato, peeled and finely chopped	1 bay leaf
	2 teaspoons chicken stock base
1 carrot, finely chopped	
1 large onion, finely chopped	⅛ teaspoon dried dill

Combine all ingredients in 3 quart covered bowl and blend well. Cover and cook on HIGH 20 minutes. Stir several times. Cover and cook on MEDIUM 50 minutes. Stir well. Cover and let stand 15 minutes before serving. Thin with additional water if desired. Serves 4 to 6.

Mrs. Ron Garrick (Bonnie)

Onion Soup

½ cup butter	1 egg yolk
2 cups thinly sliced white onions, about ¾ pound	2 tablespoons milk
	Grated Parmesan cheese to garnish
¼ cup flour	
5 cups beef consommé	Buttered bread crumbs to garnish
¼ teaspoon cayenne pepper	
1 teaspoon salt	

In a 2 quart bowl melt butter for 1½ minutes on HIGH. Add onions and cook for 6 minutes on HIGH, stirring halfway through cooking. Add flour and cook for 2½ to 3 minutes on HIGH, or until mixture turns slightly golden. Add consomme, pepper and salt; stir well and cover. Cook for 6 minutes on HIGH; then 13 to 15 minutes on MEDIUM. Beat together egg yolk and milk, add a little of the soup and mix quickly, then add to soup mixture. Garnish with Parmesan and buttered crumbs. Yields 1 quart.

Ann Steiner & **CiCi Williamson** of Houston, Texas
from their copyrighted column, **MicroScope**

To absorb grease from the top of soup, drop a leaf of lettuce into the pot. Remove and throw away when it has served its purpose.

Mexican Soup

3 tablespoons margarine
1 large onion, minced
1 can (28 ounces) peeled tomatoes, diced (save liquid)
1 can (4 ounces) diced green chilies

1 jar (2 ounces) chopped pimientos
Salt and pepper
½ pound Cheddar cheese, grated
¼ pound Monterey Jack cheese, grated

Combine margarine and onion in 2 quart casserole. Cover and cook on HIGH for 7 minutes, stirring once. Add tomatoes and liquid, chilies, pimientos, salt and pepper and stir well. Cover and cook on HIGH until mixture comes to full boil, about 9 or 10 minutes. Stir in cheeses. Continue cooking on HIGH until cheeses are melted, stirring often, about 2 to 3 minutes. Serves 4 to 6.

Cookbook Committee

√ New England Clam Chowder

2 slices bacon, diced
1 medium onion, chopped
2 medium potatoes, peeled and chopped
2 cans (7½ ounces each) minced clams, drained, reserving liquid

Water to make 2 cups liquid, including clam liquid
¼ cup butter, melted
¼ cup flour
3 cups milk
¾ teaspoon salt
⅛ teaspoon pepper

In 3 quart casserole, cook bacon on HIGH for 3 minutes. Add onion and potatoes. Cover and cook on HIGH 5 minutes. Add clam juice and water. Cook on HIGH 8 to 10 minutes or until potatoes are tender. Melt butter. Stir in flour and add to potato mixture, mixing well. Add clams, milk, salt and pepper. Cook on HIGH 4 to 5 minutes or until hot. Serves 4 to 6.

Mrs. Clark Rector (Sue)

Zucchini Soup

1½ pounds zucchini
1⅓ cups water
⅔ cup beef consommé
¼ cup chopped onion
2 slices bacon, cooked and crumbled
1 small clove garlic
2 tablespoons chopped parsley

½ teaspoon basil
½ teaspoon salt
½ teaspoon Lawry's seasoning salt
⅛ teaspoon pepper
Grated Parmesan cheese

Cut zucchini into 1 inch chunks, making enough for 3 cups. Place in 2 quart casserole. Add remaining ingredients except cheese and cover and cook on HIGH 13 to 15 minutes, stirring midway. Cool slightly. Process zucchini mixture in blender until smooth. Garnish each serving with grated Parmesan. Yields 5 cups.

Mrs. Ken Moyer (Bonnie)

...w

p sugar
aspoon salt
aspoon dry mustard
aspoon celery seeds
p cider vinegar
p oil

to very fine pieces. Place in
mustard and celery seeds in 4
g to boil on HIGH. Stir until
toss well. Cool to room temperature, cov... Serves 6 to 8.

Mrs. Larry Lerche (Gail)

Spinach Salad

6 to 12 slices bacon, diced
3 scallions, cut up
4 tablespoons brown sugar
3 teaspoons dry mustard
½ teaspoon curry powder
1 tablespoon soy sauce
½ teaspoon garlic powder
4 ounces white vinegar

½ teaspoon black pepper
1 pound fresh spinach, washed, trimmed and drained
½ pound mushrooms, sliced
1 or 2 hard cooked eggs, minced, optional

Place bacon in 4 cup measure and cover with paper towel. Cook on HIGH until bacon is crisp. Remove with slotted spoon and drain on towel. Add scallions, brown sugar, dry mustard, curry powder, soy sauce, garlic powder, vinegar and pepper and stir. Cook on HIGH until mixture boils, about 1 to 2 minutes. Put spinach in salad bowl with sliced mushrooms. Pour hot dressing over and serve immediately. If desired, sprinkle with eggs to garnish. Serves 6.

Cookbook Committee

Calico Salad

2 large cooked carrots, thinly sliced
1 cup cooked small shell macaroni
1 tablespoon oil
1 teaspoon salt
1 can (4 ounces) sliced mushrooms, drained
1 can (6 ounces) whole pitted black olives, drained

1 can (1 pound) green peas, drained
1 medium tomato, diced
1 cup cubed cheese (American, Cheddar, or Swiss) or any combination
½ cup sweet green pickle relish
¼ cup horseradish
½ cup Hellman's mayonnaise

Slice carrots into shallow casserole. Add 1 tablespoon water. Cover with plastic wrap and cook on HIGH 2 to 3 minutes or until tender crisp. To cook shell macaroni in microwave, put 6 cups very hot tap water in large casserole. Cover and cook on HIGH until water boils, about 8 minutes. Add oil, salt and macaroni; stir. Cover and microwave on HIGH 6 to 8 minutes or until done. Place all salad ingredients in bowl; stir in dressing made of relish, horseradish, and mayonnaise. Serves 8. *This keeps very well and is better made at least a day ahead of time. Do use the very small shell macaroni.*

Mrs. John Beeson (Cleo)

Spicy Hot Fruit

1	can (29 ounces) pear halves, drained	1	can (11 ounces) mandarin orange segments, drained
1	can (20 ounces) sliced pineapple, drained	½	cup butter
1	can (16 ounces) apricot halves, drained	1	cup packed brown sugar
		1	teaspoon ground cinnamon
		⅛	teaspoon ground cloves

Drain fruit and pat dry on paper towels. Place in oblong casserole. Put margarine in small bowl and microwave on HIGH 1 minute or until melted. Stir in brown sugar, cinnamon and cloves and spoon over fruit. Cook on HIGH 5 minutes. Rotate dish one quarter turn and microwave 5 more minutes or until bubbling. Serves 8.

Mrs. Charles Tupa (Sidney)

Meal in One Baked Potatoes

4	medium baking potatoes	1	carton (8 ounces) sour cream
3	tablespoons margarine		
½	cup diced ham	½	teaspoon celery salt
½	cup grated Monterey Jack cheese with jalapeño peppers	½	teaspoon pepper

Rinse and dry potatoes. Prick once with fork. Arrange in a circle on paper towels in microwave. Cook on HIGH 12 to 14 minutes, rearranging once. Let potatoes cool to touch. Slice away top of each potato and carefully scoop out pulp, leaving shells whole. Mash pulp. Place margarine in 1 cup measure and cook on HIGH 30 to 45 seconds until melted. Combine margarine, mashed potato, ham, cheese, sour cream, celery salt and pepper. Mix well and stuff into potato shells. Microwave on HIGH 5 to 6 minutes until heated through, giving dish one half turn during cooking time. Serves 4.

Mrs. Ken Moyer (Bonnie)

Select potatoes for baking that are uniform in shape and size. Pierce only once. Place potatoes on a rack to aid in more even cooking. Potatoes continue to cook after microwaving time is completed, so let them stand 5 minutes before checking for doneness.

Potatoes Parmesan

4 tablespoons butter
4 medium potatoes, unpeeled, sliced ¼ inch thick
⅔ cup chopped onion
2 garlic cloves, minced

1 green pepper, cut into 1 inch chunks
½ teaspoon salt
¼ teaspoon pepper
½ cup grated Parmesan cheese
Paprika

Melt butter in shallow casserole in microwave. Add potatoes, onion, and garlic. Stir. Cover loosely with plastic wrap and microwave on HIGH for 8 to 10 minutes. Stir in green pepper, salt and pepper. Cover and microwave on HIGH 4 minutes. Toss gently and dust with cheese and paprika. Microwave on HIGH, uncovered 3 minutes. Let rest 5 minutes. Serves 4 to 6.

Mrs. Jim Rado (Vicki)

Deviled Cauliflower

1 head cauliflower
1 tablespoon water
½ cup finely chopped onion
½ cup mayonnaise

½ cup grated Cheddar cheese
3 tablespoons mustard
Salt and pepper to taste
Paprika

Place cauliflower stem side down in a covered casserole dish with water and cook for 6 minutes on HIGH. Mix remaining ingredients, except paprika; spread over top of cauliflower. Replace cover and cook on HIGH for 3 more minutes. Sprinkle with paprika. On very large heads a few extra minutes may be necessary to insure tenderness. Serves 4.

Mrs. Jette Campbell (Sally)

Garlic Cheese Brussels Sprouts

1 pound fresh Brussels sprouts
¼ cup water
2 tablespoons margarine

1 garlic clove, minced
Salt and pepper
¼ cup Parmesan cheese

Wash and clean Brussels sprouts. Trim any outside leaves and stems. Put in shallow 1 quart casserole with water. Cover and cook on HIGH 7 minutes or until sprouts are tender. Rest covered 3 to 4 minutes. Combine margarine and garlic in small measuring cup and cook on HIGH 1 to 2 minutes; to this add salt, pepper and Parmesan cheese and mix well. Drain Brussels sprouts, add cheese sauce and serve warm. Serves 6.

Mrs. Robert Henderson (Dale)

Spicy Baked Beans

½ pound bacon, diced
½ pound bulk hot sausage, cut into patties
2 large onions, chopped
2 medium green peppers, chopped
6 cloves garlic, peeled and chopped
3 cans (16 ounces each) pork and beans
2 tablespoons Worcestershire sauce
1 tablespoon liquid hickory sauce
¼ teaspoon cayenne pepper
¼ teaspoon black pepper
2 tablespoons prepared mustard
1 teaspoon dry mustard
¼ cup molasses
3 ounces tomato paste, ½ of a small can

Place bacon in 4 cup measure and cover with paper towel. Microwave on HIGH until bacon is crisp; save drippings. Microwave sausage patties 3 minutes on HIGH, covered with wax paper. Remove sausage and crumble. Combine bacon and sausage drippings and sauté onion, green pepper and garlic in the grease about 5 minutes on HIGH. Add all other ingredients and microwave 5 minutes on HIGH and then 5 minutes on MEDIUM, stirring twice. Serves 12 to 15.

Ann Steiner & **CiCi Williamson** of Houston, Texas
from their copyrighted column, **MicroScope**

Peas Pagoda

½ cup water
1 chicken bouillon cube
¼ teaspoon ground ginger
½ teaspoon sugar
1 tablespoon oil
1½ teaspoons cornstarch
1 tablespoon soy sauce
1 package (10 ounces) frozen peas
1 can (8 ounces) sliced water chestnuts, drained
1 can (4 ounces) mushrooms, drained

Microwave water, bouillon, ginger, sugar, oil, cornstarch and soy sauce on HIGH for 2 to 3 minutes until mixture is smooth. Cook peas until tender, 5 minutes. Add water chestnuts, mushrooms and sauce and cook on MEDIUM for 10 minutes. Serves 4 to 6.

Mrs. Roger Borgelt (Cindy)

Do not salt vegetables prior to microwaving. Salt tends to toughen vegetables and causes brown freckles if put directly on them.

Ann Steiner & **CiCi Williamson** of Houston, Texas
from their copyrighted column, **MicroScope**

Jiffy Tomato Stack Ups

1   package (10 ounces) frozen
    chopped broccoli
1   cup grated Swiss cheese

2   tablespoons finely chopped
    onion
4   large tomatoes

Make two knife slits on top of broccoli package. Cook on HIGH for 6 minutes. Drain. Combine cheese, onion and broccoli. Cut tomatoes into 1 inch slices and place in flat casserole. Spoon broccoli mixture onto each slice. Cook on HIGH for 4 minutes. Serves 4 to 6.

Mrs. Jim Schultz (Mary Kay)

Ratatouille

1   large eggplant, peeled and
    diced
½   cup sliced onion
1   clove garlic, minced
3   tablespoons olive oil
1   medium green pepper, cut
    into strips

1   cup thinly sliced zucchini
1   can (14½ ounces) stewed
    tomatoes
1   teaspoon salt
¼   teaspoon thyme
¼   teaspoon oregano
2   teaspoons dried parsley

Combine eggplant, onion, garlic and olive oil in 2 quart casserole. Cover and cook on HIGH for 5 minutes. Add pepper and zucchini; mix well. Mix tomatoes and seasonings; pour over other vegetables. Microwave covered on HIGH 8 to 10 minutes or until vegetables are tender. Let stand covered 5 minutes before serving. May serve hot or cold. Serves 6.

Mrs. Don Bradford (Melinda)

Orange Glazed Sweet Potatoes

1   can (40 ounces) yams,
    drained or 3 large fresh
    yams, cooked, peeled and
    cut into chunks
¼   cup packed brown sugar
¼   cup sugar

1   tablespoon cornstarch
⅛   teaspoon salt
1   cup orange juice
1   teaspoon grated orange peel
2   tablespoons margarine

Arrange yams in 1½ quart dish. Combine sugars, cornstarch and salt in glass bowl; add orange juice and peel. Cook on HIGH 2 minutes. Stir several times. Cook 2 minutes more. Add margarine, stirring until melted. Pour over yams and cook on HIGH about 3 minutes or until hot. Serves 6 to 8.

Mrs. Jim Schultz (Mary Kay)

Zucchini Custard

5 cups grated zucchini
1 teaspoon salt
2 cups grated Monterey Jack cheese
¼ cup biscuit mix

¼ cup chopped parsley
2 garlic cloves, minced
⅛ teaspoon freshly ground pepper
4 eggs, beaten

Sprinkle zucchini with salt and let drain one hour. Press out liquid. Coat 1½ quart casserole with melted butter. Combine all ingredients except eggs and blend well. Mix in eggs. Spoon into casserole and cook uncovered on HIGH until set around the edges, about 8 to 10 minutes. Let stand 5 minutes before serving. Serves 6. *Note: 2 packages (10 ounces each) frozen broccoli may be substituted for zucchini.*

Mrs. Jim Schultz (Mary Kay)

Spinach Cheese Soufflé

1 package (10 ounces) frozen chopped spinach
1½ tablespoons margarine
Salt and pepper to taste
2 tablespoons chopped onion

2 eggs, beaten
⅛ cup milk
½ cup grated Cheddar cheese
½ cup buttered crumbs

Make 2 knife slits in spinach box and microwave on HIGH 6 minutes or until thawed. Drain well. Combine spinach, margarine, salt and pepper; cook on HIGH 3 minutes. Combine remaining ingredients except crumbs and put in 1 quart greased casserole. Microwave on MEDIUM-HIGH about 5 to 7 minutes, rotating at 3 minute intervals. Add crumbs before final cooking. Center will be soft but will firm after standing. Serves 4.

Mrs. Jim Schultz (Mary Kay)

All pie crusts, whether flaky or crumb, need to be microwaved before adding any filling. If using a frozen pastry shell, pop it out of the foil pan while still frozen and place in a glass pie plate. When defrosted, mold pastry to shape the pie plate with your fingers. For a sweet pie, brush pie shell with vanilla before baking. For a quiche, brush with beaten egg yolk before baking. These treatments will give the pie shell a brownish appearance. A microwaved pastry shell should look dry, opaque and blistered in appearance when done.

Ann Steiner & **CiCi Williamson** of Houston, Texas
from their copyrighted column, **MicroScope**

Monterey Quiche

2 cups grated Monterey Jack
cheese
9 strips bacon, cooked and
crumbled
1 can (4 ounces) chopped
green chilies, drained

3 green onions, thinly sliced
1 baked deep dish pie shell, 9
inch
1 can (13 ounces) evaporated
milk
4 eggs

Combine cheese, bacon, chilies and onions in bowl and toss lightly. Sprinkle about ¾ mixture over pie shell. Heat milk in measuring cup on HIGH 2½ minutes. Beat eggs in separate bowl. Add milk to eggs and beat again. Pour over cheese in pie shell. Sprinkle with remaining cheese mixture. Cook on MEDIUM until center is just set, about 12 to 15 minutes, rotating one quarter turn every 3 minutes. Let stand 5 minutes before serving. Serves 6.

Mrs. Ron Garrick (Bonnie)

Fish Provençale

2 pounds fresh or frozen fish
filets, thawed
4 green onions, chopped
1 cup sliced fresh mushrooms
2 tomatoes, peeled and cut
into eighths

1 teaspoon salt
1 teaspoon lemon pepper
seasoning
⅓ cup dry white wine
1 tablespoon lemon juice
3 tablespoons butter

Sauce:
¼ cup water
2 tablespoons cornstarch

1 tablespoon chopped parsley
1 cup poaching liquid

Arrange filets in 3 quart glass baking dish with thick edges toward outside of dish. Sprinkle with remaining ingredients, except butter. Dot top with butter; cover with wax paper. Microwave for 15 to 17 minutes on MEDIUM, or until fish flakes easily. Drain, reserving 1 cup poaching liquid for sauce. Let fish stand covered 5 minutes before serving. For sauce, combine water, cornstarch and parsley in 4 cup glass measuring cup; beat with rotary beater until smooth. Beat in 1 cup reserved poaching liquid, or ¾ cup liquid and ¼ cup wine. Microwave for about 3 minutes on HIGH or until thickened. Beat lightly and pour sauce over fish and vegetables to serve. Serves 6 to 8.

Mrs. Don Bradford (Melinda)

Shrimp Penelope

½ cup margarine, divided
1 pound shrimp, peeled and deveined
6 tablespoons flour
1 teaspoon onion salt
2 cups milk
½ cup vermouth or light dry white wine

Dash of Tabasco
1 jar (4 ounces) artichoke hearts, drained and cut in fourths
1 can (4 ounces) sliced mushrooms, drained
Hot cooked rice

Melt ¼ cup margarine in a 2 quart casserole 1 minute on HIGH. Add shrimp and microwave 3 minutes on HIGH, stirring twice, until shrimp are pink and tender. Remove shrimp and set aside. In same dish, add remaining ¼ cup of margarine and melt 1 minute on HIGH. Stir in flour and onion salt. Add milk gradually and stir with wire whisk until blended. Cook 4 minutes on HIGH, stirring twice. When smooth and thickened, stir in vermouth, Tabasco, artichoke hearts, mushrooms and shrimp. Heat 2 to 3 minutes on MEDIUM-HIGH until hot. Spoon over rice. Serves 4 to 6.

Ann Steiner & **CiCi Williamson** of Houston, Texas
from their copyrighted column, **MicroScope**

Corn and Ham Casserole

3 eggs, slightly beaten
1 can (17 ounces) creamed style corn
⅛ cup milk
¼ cup chopped onion

⅛ teaspoon pepper
1½ cups cooked rice
1½ cups cooked ham
4 ounces Cheddar cheese, grated

Combine all ingredients in an ungreased 6x10 inch casserole. Stir twice during cooking. Cook on MEDIUM 12 to 15 minutes or until center is barely firm. Let stand 5 minutes before serving. Serves 6.

Mrs. Ken Moyer (Bonnie)

The Indians of East Texas grew corn long before Anglos and Europeans came here, but it wasn't until the 1830's that corn was grown commercially. Today, it is Texas' second largest cash crop.

Oriental Chicken

4 to 6 chicken breasts, split,
  skinned and boned
1 tablespoon cornstarch
2 tablespoons brown sugar
¼ teaspoon oregano
1 clove garlic, crushed

2 tablespoons cooking oil
¼ cup soy sauce
1 cup rosé wine
½ cup teriyaki marinade sauce
Pepper to taste

Pierce chicken with a fork. Arrange in 3 quart casserole dish. In a small bowl combine remaining ingredients. Pour over chicken, cover with plastic wrap pierced several times, and cook on HIGH 20 minutes rotating dish several times. Check for doneness and cook additional time as needed. Serves 4 to 6.

Mrs. Larry Ruggiano (Gay)

Enchiladas Verde

2 whole chicken breasts, cut
  in halves
1 package (10 ounces) frozen
  spinach
1 dozen corn tortillas
½ cup chopped onion
2 medium tomatoes, chopped

1½ cups grated Monterey Jack
  cheese
1 can cream of chicken soup
1 can (4 ounces) chopped
  green chilies, drained
1 cup sour cream

Microwave chicken breasts covered with waxed paper on HIGH for 6 minutes. Let cool slightly; debone and chop. Microwave frozen spinach in package 5 minutes on HIGH. Press out liquid. Reserve half of liquid for sauce. Soften tortillas in microwave. Wrap 6 tortillas at a time in a damp paper towel and place between two plates. Cook 45 seconds on HIGH. To assemble enchiladas, sprinkle tortillas with chopped chicken, onion, tomatoes, spinach and 1 cup grated cheese. Save ½ cup cheese for top of casserole. Roll up and place in a 2 quart rectangular casserole. To make sauce, combine reserved spinach liquid, soup, chilies and sour cream in blender or food processor. Blend until smooth. Pour over enchiladas and top with cheese. Microwave 13 minutes on MEDIUM-HIGH, or until heated through. Serves 4.

Ann Steiner & **CiCi Williamson** of Houston, Texas
from their copyrighted column, **MicroScope**

Micro-Meatloaf

1 pound lean ground beef	¼ teaspoon pepper
1 egg, beaten	1 garlic clove, crushed
¼ cup dry bread crumbs	¼ cup chopped green pepper
1 onion, minced	¼ cup chopped celery
1 tablespoon minced parsley	½ cup tomato juice
¾ teaspoon salt	¼ cup catsup

Mix all ingredients except catsup. Pack lightly into 9 inch glass dish making well in center and placing an empty glass right side up in center of dish. Cook uncovered 6 minutes on HIGH, rotating ¼ turn halfway through cooking time. Drizzle catsup over top and cook 5 minutes longer, rotating ¼ turn halfway through cooking time. Let stand 5 minutes. Remove glass and spoon off drippings. Serves 5 to 6. *Children like this if the vegetables are grated. They get the nutrition, but don't know it!*

Mrs. Dan Steakley (Susan)

Meat Loaf Teriyaki

2 pounds lean ground beef	2 tablespoons brown sugar
2 eggs, slightly beaten	2 tablespoons fresh lemon
2 slices bread, soaked in	juice
water and squeezed dry	1 tablespoon chopped fresh
½ cup chopped green pepper	parsley
1 medium onion, finely	¾ teaspoon ground ginger
chopped	1 tablespoon brown sugar
1 garlic clove, crushed	1 tablespoon soy sauce
2 tablespoons soy sauce	

Combine all ingredients except 1 tablespoon each brown sugar and soy sauce and mix well. Spoon into microwave-proof 6 cup ring mold. Cook on HIGH 15 minutes, rotating dish once if loaf seems to be cooking unevenly. Meat loaf will be done when it begins to pull away from sides of dish. Let stand 5 minutes. Pour off juices and invert on serving platter. For topping combine remaining brown sugar and soy sauce. Heat on HIGH 30 seconds. Spread over hot meat loaf. Serves 6 to 8.

Mrs. Ken McConchie (Paulette)

Zucchini Lasagne

5 to 6 zucchini cut lengthwise into ¼ inch strips
¼ cup water
1 pound lean ground beef
¼ cup finely chopped onion
1 can (16 ounces) tomato purée
1 teaspoon garlic salt
1 teaspoon oregano
⅛ teaspoon freshly ground pepper
12 ounces dry cottage cheese
¼ cup grated Parmesan cheese
1 egg
2 tablespoons flour
4 ounces Mozzarella cheese, sliced
¼ cup grated Romano cheese

Put zucchini in 1½ quart pyrex dish; add water. Cover and cook on HIGH 6 to 7 minutes or until zucchini are tender. Drain well. Be sure to drain well or casserole will be runny! Combine beef and onion in 1½ quart pyrex dish and cook on HIGH for 3 minutes, stirring to break up meat. Continue to cook 1 to 2 minutes more, until meat is no longer pink. Drain well. Stir in tomato puree, garlic salt, oregano and pepper. Cook uncovered on HIGH for 5 minutes. Stir. Combine cottage cheese, Parmesan and egg and blend well. Arrange half of zucchini slices in oblong pyrex dish. Sprinkle with one tablespoon flour. Layer with half of cottage cheese mixture, then meat sauce and Mozzarella. Repeat layers. Sprinkle with remaining cheese. Cook on HIGH until heated through, about 8 to 10 minutes. Serves 8 to 10.

Mrs. Jim Rado (Vicki)

Saucy Beef Brisket

½ cup catsup
1 medium onion, chopped
3 tablespoons brown sugar
2 tablespoons vinegar
1 teaspoon basil
½ teaspoon garlic salt
¼ teaspoon thyme
½ teaspoon salt
⅛ teaspoon pepper
3 pound brisket

Combine all sauce ingredients in a small bowl. Place brisket in an oblong casserole and cover with half of sauce. Seal with plastic wrap, turning back one corner to vent. Microwave on HIGH for 15 minutes; lower to MEDIUM for 45 minutes. Turn brisket over and add other half of sauce. Microwave at MEDIUM 45 to 60 minutes, until tender. Let stand 10 minutes. Carve in thin slices and serve with sauce. Serves 6 to 8.

Mrs. Jim Schultz (Mary Kay)

Beef Strips with Tomatoes

⅓ cup soy sauce
⅓ cup white wine
1 teaspoon sugar
1¼ pound flank steak, cut into thin strips
2 tablespoons cornstarch

1 medium onion, sliced thin
8 ounces fresh mushrooms, sliced
1 small green pepper, sliced
1 pint cherry tomatoes

Combine soy sauce, wine and sugar and pour over meat. Stir to coat well and marinate at least 2 hours or overnight in refrigerator. Stir in cornstarch and mix well. Put in 2 quart casserole and add onions and mushrooms. Cover with waxed paper and cook 8 minutes on HIGH, stirring halfway through. Add green pepper and cook on HIGH 3 to 4 minutes until thickened. Add tomatoes, cover and cook 1½ minutes on HIGH until tomatoes are heated through. Let stand 5 minutes. Serves 6.

Ann Steiner & **CiCi Williamson** of Houston, Texas
from their copyrighted column, **MicroScope**

Stuffed Green Peppers

4 large green peppers, tops removed and seeded
¼ cup water
1 pound lean ground beef
¼ cup chopped onion
1½ cups cooked rice
1 can (8 ounces) tomato sauce
1 large garlic clove, finely chopped

2 tablespoons chopped celery
1 tablespoon Worcestershire sauce
2 teaspoons minced parsley
½ teaspoon salt
⅛ teaspoon pepper
4 tablespoons catsup

Place peppers upright in deep casserole. Add water. Cover and cook on HIGH 3 minutes. Let stand without draining while preparing filling. Combine beef and onion in bowl and cook on HIGH 3 minutes. Stir to crumble beef. Add remaining ingredients except catsup and blend well. Divide among peppers. Cover and cook on HIGH 10 minutes. Spread 1 tablespoon catsup over top of each and cover; let stand 2 to 3 minutes to soften. Serves 4.

Mrs. Don Bradford (Melinda)

Hot Reuben Sandwiches

1 cup shredded corned beef	½ cup Thousand Island
2 cups grated Swiss cheese	dressing
1 cup sauerkraut, drained well	8 to 12 slices rye bread, toasted
¾ teaspoon dill weed	

In small bowl combine all ingredients except bread. Mix well. Spoon filling on 4 to 6 slices of toasted bread. Microwave on MEDIUM about 3 to 4 minutes or until cheese starts to melt. Top with remaining slices of bread and heat on MEDIUM about ½ minute or until bread is warm. Serves 4 to 6.

Larry Lerche

Spiced Pecans

4 tablespoons butter flavored oil	½ teaspoon ground ginger
	5 or 6 drops Tabasco sauce
1½ tablespoons Worcestershire sauce	2 cups pecan halves
	Salt to taste
2 teaspoons soy sauce	

In 2 quart glass casserole mix oil and seasonings. Add pecans and stir well to coat. Microwave on HIGH for 6 to 8 minutes or until light brown, stirring after 4 minutes. Watch carefully. Do not burn! Drain on paper towels. Store in air tight container. Yields 2 cups.

Mrs. Denman Smith (Sandra)

Microwave Pecan Brittle

1 cup pecan halves	1 teaspoon butter
1 cup sugar	1 teaspoon vanilla
½ cup light corn syrup	1 teaspoon baking soda
⅛ teaspoon salt	

Stir pecans, sugar, syrup, and salt together in a 1½ quart glass bowl. Microwave on HIGH 7 to 8 minutes, stirring well after 4 minutes. At the end of 8 minutes, add butter and vanilla. Blend well. Return to microwave and cook on HIGH 1 to 2 minutes more. Remove and add baking soda and gently stir until mixture is light and foamy. Pour onto lightly greased cookie sheet and let cool 30 minutes to 1 hour. Break into pieces and store in airtight container.

Mrs. Robert West (Linda)

Microwave Pralines

1 **pound light brown sugar**	2 **tablespoons butter**
1 **cup whipping cream**	2 **cups pecan pieces**

Combine sugar and cream in large bowl, mixing well. Microwave on HIGH 14 minutes, stirring after 7 minutes. Add butter and pecans. Microwave on HIGH 1 to 2 minutes or until a few drops form a soft ball in a cup of cold water. Working quickly, drop by large tablespoonfuls onto wax paper. If necessary, return to microwave for a few minutes to soften the mixture. Do not beat after the soft ball test shows the consistency is correct. Spoon out immediately. Yields about 30.

Mrs. Jim Schultz (Mary Kay)

Carrot Cake

3 **eggs**	1¼ **teaspoons baking soda**
1½ **cups sugar**	1¼ **teaspoons cloves**
1 **cup oil**	¾ **teaspoon salt**
1 **teaspoon vanilla**	2½ **cups grated carrots (4 to 6**
1½ **cups flour**	**carrots)**
2½ **teaspoons cinnamon**	¼ **cup chopped pecans**

Icing:

1½ **cups powdered sugar**	1½ **tablespoons butter,**
2 **ounces cream cheese,**	**softened**
softened	½ **teaspoon vanilla**

Combine eggs, sugar, oil and vanilla in large bowl and stir well. Stir in flour, cinnamon, soda, cloves and salt, mixing well. Add carrots and nuts. Pour into ungreased 10 to 12 cup bundt pan and microwave on HIGH 14 to 18 minutes, rotating ¼ turn every 4 minutes. Cake can also be baked in an oblong pyrex dish, cooking about 11 to 13 minutes on HIGH, turning about 4 times. Remove cake from pan onto platter and drizzle with icing.

For icing, blend powdered sugar, cream cheese, butter and vanilla until smooth and fluffy. Microwave on HIGH about 30 seconds. Stir well and pour over cake. Serves 8 to 10. *This is a very moist cake and is good without icing.*

Cookbook Committee

Chocolate Wafer Crust

6 tablespoons margarine

1½ cups chocolate wafer
   crumbs

Microwave margarine in 9 inch pie plate on HIGH one minute. Add crumbs and press evenly around plate. Chill.

Cookbook Committee

Chocolate Bars

¾ cup butter, melted
3 eggs
1½ cups sugar
¾ teaspoon salt

1½ teaspoons vanilla
1 cup plus 2 tablespoons flour
¾ cup cocoa
1 cup chopped nuts, optional

Melt butter in microwave on HIGH, about 1½ minutes. Beat eggs, sugar, salt and vanilla together with electric mixer about 1 minute. Pour in melted butter and beat until butter is mixed in. Beat in flour and cocoa. Stir in nuts by hand. Pour into greased 7½x11¾ inch flat glass casserole. Microwave on HIGH 8 minutes, rotating dish a quarter turn every 2 minutes. Brownies are done when they pull away from sides of dish slightly. There will be moist spots on top, but they continue to cook after they are removed from microwave. Cool and cut into 24 pieces. *These are easy enough for children to do. Also, they can be cut into larger squares and served with vanilla ice cream and chocolate sauce on top.*

Mrs. Clark Rector (Sue)

Baked Apples

6 medium cooking apples
6 tablespoons brown sugar
3 tablespoons margarine
½ cup cinnamon red hots
   (candy)

3 ounces cream cheese,
   softened
¼ cup chopped pecans
6 large marshmallows

Core apples. Cut a strip of peel from around center of each apple. Put in glass pie plate. Distribute brown sugar, margarine, cinnamon candies among apples. Cook on LOW 5 minutes. Turn one half. Cook on MEDIUM for 5 minutes. Combine cream cheese and pecans. Stuff apples. Top each apple with marshmallow. Microwave on MEDIUM 1 minute or until marshmallow is melted. Serves 6.

Mrs. Ken Moyer (Bonnie)

Grasshopper Pie

¼ cup margarine
16 to 18 Oreo cookies, crushed
35 large marshmallows
½ cup milk
¼ cup creme de menthe

¼ cup white creme de cacao
2 cups whipped topping
Chocolate curls to garnish
Whipped topping to garnish

Melt margarine in 9 inch pie plate for 30 seconds on HIGH. Add crushed Oreos and press to cover bottom and sides of plate. Cook on HIGH 1½ to 2 minutes. Cool. In 2 quart bowl, heat marshmallows and milk on HIGH for 2 to 2½ minutes or until marshmallows begin to melt. Stir until completely melted. Cool 5 minutes. Add liqueurs. Refrigerate until partially thickened. Fold in whipped topping. Spoon into pie plate and freeze. Garnish with additional topping and chocolate curls. Serves 6 to 8.

Mrs. Larry Hall (Jane)

Mexican Chocolate Pie

24 large marshmallows
½ cup milk
1 package (6 ounces)
  semisweet chocolate chips
2 tablespoons creme de cacao

2 tablespoons Kahlua
1 cup whipping cream
1 chocolate wafer crust,
  9 inch (see Index)

Combine marshmallows, milk, and chocolate chips in 3 quart casserole and cook on MEDIUM 3 to 4 minutes. Stir. Cool slightly. Add liqueurs. Chill at least 30 minutes. Whip cream until stiff. Fold into chocolate mixture. Pour into crust and freeze. Remove at least 5 to 10 minutes before serving. Serves 6 to 8.

Mrs. Jim Rado (Vicki)

Tipsy Pecan Pie

¼ cup butter
1 cup light corn syrup
1 cup dark brown sugar
1 tablespoon flour
¼ teaspoon salt
1 teaspoon vanilla

1 teaspoon brandy extract
1 teaspoon rum extract
3 eggs, beaten
1 cup pecan halves
1 baked pie shell, 9 inch

In a large glass bowl, microwave butter on HIGH for 45 seconds. Add remaining ingredients. Stir well. Put in pie shell and bake 15 to 17 minutes on MEDIUM, just until center is set. Serves 8.

Cookbook Committee

Microwave Hot Fudge Sauce

2 cups sugar
Dash salt
2 squares unsweetened
 chocolate

1 cup half and half cream
2 tablespoons butter
2 teaspoons vanilla

Cook all ingredients except vanilla 5 minutes on LOW. Take out and whip. Cook another 5 minutes. Set in cold water until just warm. Add vanilla and beat until smooth. Yields 3 cups. *This is also a good chocolate fondue sauce.*

Mrs. Larry Keith (Virginia)

Microwave Butterscotch Sauce

1¼ cups brown sugar
1 cup evaporated milk
2 tablespoons white corn
 syrup

¼ cup margarine
⅛ teaspoon salt
1 teaspoon vanilla

Combine brown sugar, milk, corn syrup, margarine and salt in a 1 quart casserole. Cook on HIGH 4 minutes. Stir. Cook 4 minutes more. Add vanilla. Stir until smooth. Serve warm. Yields 2 cups. Store in refrigerator and reheat before serving.

Mrs. Larry Lerche (Gail)

Cherries Jubilee

1 can (17 ounces) pitted Bing
 cherries
½ cup sugar

1½ tablespoons cornstarch
¼ cup brandy
Vanilla ice cream

Drain cherries, reserving one cup liquid. In medium glass bowl combine sugar and cornstarch. Stir in cherry syrup. Heat on HIGH 3 to 4 minutes, stirring twice, until sauce is thickened. Just before serving, add cherries to sauce and heat one minute. In 1 cup measure heat brandy ½ to ¾ minute on HIGH. Pour over cherries and ignite. Serve over vanilla ice cream. Serves 6.

Mrs. Jim Schultz (Mary Kay)

To soften store bought sauces, transfer to microwave-proof cup. For refrigerated hot fudge or butterscotch sauce, heat on HIGH about 1½ minutes.

Luckenbach, Texas, is unique and, at the same time, representative of the many small towns dotted throughout Texas. Consisting of a general store and an open-air dance hall, it has been eulogized in song by country singers, Waylon Jennings and Willie Nelson. Luckenbach stands as a reminder to us of the relaxed lifestyle of yesteryear. Giant shade trees beckon you to lounge beneath them, and a table already set with dominoes invites you to "set a spell" and let the world go by.

This table of pickled, marinated, dried and assorted goodies are typical of home preserving done by young and old Texas homemakers. These and many more recipes can be found in our Serendipity Chapter.

Serendipity

A Texas "Pit" Bar-B-Que

Dig a pit three feet deep, four feet wide, and 40 feet long. Place a layer of wood across bottom of pit and start fire. Keep fire at the same height for about 5 hours and then let die down to coals. (Any type of hardwood is suitable—pecan, oak, or any other hardwood available.)

Place iron pipe across pit every three feet and cover with heavy wire mesh and make sure that mesh is tied securely so that the meat will not be dumped into the fire. Make a one-foot opening under wire at intervals through which additional coals may be added. Start another fire to one side so that additional coals will be available to add to the trench as needed. Start fire at least six hours before meat is put on. *Do not have any blaze after meat is put on*—only coals.

Have meat cut into heavy pieces of six to eight pounds each. Salt and pepper meat generously before putting on to cook. Do not let pieces overlap—allow room for smoke to come up around the pieces.

Pieces with adequate fat will be self-basting. For leaner portions, baste with cooking oil or melted margarine to which a small amount of vinegar has been added. Turn the meat frequently so that it will cook evenly and allow at least 18 hours of cooking time.

LBJ Ranch

Mueller's Muldoon Mustang Wine

Get mustang grapes, mash them up and put them in a large wooden barrel, with hole on bottom to drain the juice off, leave in this barrel for five days, then drain and put in large crock and keep three days, while you wait for the second batch to ferment, then mix all the juice together, measure your kegs to see how much each keg will hold, then pour about 60 percent of capacity in keg, then take 2¾ or 3 pounds sugar to the capacity of your keg, and dissolve it in warm water, use as little water as possible to dissolve it then if you have any space left add good clean rain water if you can get it, then set in a place where you can leave it until it has gotten thru fermenting, which will take all the way from two to three months, be sure to put a screen wire over the bung hole while it is fermenting otherwise rats or mice may get in it. Save some, ½ gallon, of the second batch and save it to fill the keg everyday or so, then after a week or two just use water to fill.

Leo Mueller, Jr.

Blueberry Liqueur

1 quart fresh or frozen
  blueberries
½ cup water
1 teaspoon cinnamon

1 teaspoon whole cloves
Strips of peel from one lemon
2 cups sugar
1 cup vodka

Simmer blueberries, water, cinnamon, cloves, lemon peel for 25 minutes. Strain through cheesecloth. Pour about 1¼ cups liquid into saucepan. Add sugar and simmer 10 minutes, stirring occasionally. To make liqueur, combine 1 cup blueberry syrup and 1 cup vodka. Refrigerate for 4 weeks. Makes approximately one pint.

Mrs. Hank Howard (Sandy)

Hot Buttered Rum Mix

1 pound butter
1 teaspoon cinnamon
1 teaspoon cloves
1 teaspoon allspice

1 teaspoon nutmeg
2 pounds light brown sugar
3 beaten eggs
Rum

Melt butter; add all spices. Pour over sugar and add well beaten eggs. Pour into jars. Refrigerate at least 24 hours before using. For each mug use 2 large tablespoons of mix, a jigger of rum and hot water. Yields approximately 4½ pints.

Mrs. Lee Provinse (Dottie)

Kahlua

1 quart water
2½ cups sugar
4 tablespoons instant coffee

1 teaspoon vanilla
2½ cups vodka

Bring first three ingredients to a boil. Barely simmer for 3 hours. Cool to near room temperature. Add vanilla and vodka. Stir. Refrigerate for one week before serving. Makes approximately 1 quart. Store in the refrigerator.

Mrs. Johnny Johnson (Marcy)

 In the area surrounding Del Rio, the Val Verde Winery can be found. A fourth-generation enterprise, grapes from several nations are grown and bottled here.

French Chocolate

5   squares unsweetened
    chocolate
1   cup cold water
1½ cups sugar

Dash salt
1   cup whipping cream,
    whipped

Melt chocolate with water. Beat until smooth. Add sugar and salt. Return to stove and cook a little longer to blend flavors. When cool, fold in whipped cream. Store in freezer. When ready to serve as hot chocolate, heat milk until boiling. Place 1 tablespoon of chocolate mixture in cup. Pour hot milk over and stir. This makes a lovely after dinner coffee. Mix 1 tablespoon chocolate mix and 1 jigger of Kahlua with a cup of coffee. Top with whipped cream and enjoy! Yields about 3 cups of chocolate mix.

Mrs. Dan Steakley (Susan)

Dry Hot Chocolate Mix

1   box (8 quarts) powdered
    milk
1   box (16 ounces) Nestle's
    Quik

¾   cup powdered sugar
16 ounces non-dairy creamer

Mix all ingredients in large covered container for storage. Use ⅓ cup mixture to one cup of boiling water for each cup of hot chocolate. Add marshmallows, if desired.

Mrs. Charles Cantwell (Winn)

International Coffees

¼   cup powdered non-dairy
    coffee creamer

⅓   cup sugar
¼   cup instant coffee

Mix ingredients well and store in a covered container. Use this basic recipe to make the variations.

Cafe Vienna: Add ½ teaspoon ground cinnamon to basic recipe.

Bavarian Mint: Add 2 tablespoons cocoa and 2 pieces of hard candy peppermints crushed in a blender to basic recipe.

Suisse Mocha: Add 2 tablespoons cocoa to basic recipe.

Orange Cappuccino: Add 1 piece of hard orange candy crushed in a blender to the basic recipe.

A set of these coffees would make an excellent gift at Christmas time.

Mrs. Don Panter (Carolyn)

Spiced Tea Mix

1 jar (9 ounces) Tang	1 cup instant tea
½ cup instant lemonade mix	2 teaspoons cinnamon
1½ cups sugar	1 teaspoon cloves

Combine all ingredients in a large bowl with a lid. Shake. To serve, add three teaspoons mix to 1 cup hot water. *This mixture can be stored and used up to 8 months. Just shake before using.*

Mrs. Charles Cantwell (Winn)

Discovered Valley Ranch Mix

1½ tablespoons salt	1 teaspoon pepper
2 teaspoons monosodium glutamate	½ teaspoon onion powder
	1 cup mayonnaise
2 teaspoons dry parsley flakes	1 cup buttermilk
1 teaspoon garlic powder	

Mix salt, monosodium glutamate, parsley, garlic powder, pepper, and onion powder. Store this dry mixture in airtight container in refrigerator until ready to use. Yields about 4 pints of dressing. To make 1 pint of dressing, combine mayonnaise and buttermilk with 3⅛ teaspoons dry mix. Store this dressing in the refrigerator for 24 hours prior to use. Stir well before using.

Creamy Herb Dressing: To one pint of basic dressing add 1 tablespoon chopped chives, ½ teaspoon dried, crushed tarragon leaves.

Bleu Cheese: To one pint of basic salad dressing, add ¼ to ½ cup Bleu Cheese.

Creamy Italian: To one pint basic salad dressing add dash of cayenne pepper, 1 teaspoon crushed, dried Italian seasoning.

Bet you can't tell the difference between this mix and the real ranch salad mix, and this one is definitely cheaper, once you've invested in the basic ingredients.

Mrs. Paul Shull (Sandy)

Salad Cheese Mix

1 teaspoon freshly ground pepper	1½ teaspoons garlic powder
1 teaspoon sugar	2 teaspoons powdered oregano
1 teaspoon dry mustard	2¾ teaspoons salt
1 teaspoon monosodium glutamate	1 cup grated Parmesan cheese

Combine all ingredients; store in refrigerator. Sprinkle small amount over green salad. Then add vinegar and oil. *This is equally good on baked squash and broiled tomatoes, and as a garnish to liven up everyday vegetables.*

Mrs. Bob Edgecomb (Mary)

Jalapeño Pepper Jelly

3 large green peppers, seeded and diced	5 pounds sugar
6 or 7 fresh jalapeño peppers, seeded and chopped	3 cups cider vinegar
⅓ cup water	3 pouches (3 ounces each) Certo
	Green food coloring

Process peppers in blender with water. Wear rubber gloves while handling jalapeños. In large saucepan, combine pepper mixture, sugar and vinegar; boil 4 minutes. Watch carefully because mixture boils over easily. Remove from heat and add Certo and food coloring. Stir well. Pour into sterilized jars and seal with paraffin. Yields 8 to 10 pints.

Mrs. Jim Schultz (Mary Kay)

Jalapeño jelly is quite a versatile condiment. It can be used as an accompaniment to pork, beef, or game. For a colorful holiday hors d'oeuvre spoon the bright green jelly over cream cheese and serve with crackers.

Pickled Okra

6   cloves garlic
6   teaspoons celery seed
6   small hot red peppers
6   teaspoons dill seed
3   pounds small okra

½   cup salt, not iodized
1   cup sugar
1   quart water
1   quart white vinegar

Divide garlic, celery seed, red peppers and dill seed evenly among 6 pint jars. Pack okra in jars. Combine salt, sugar, water and vinegar and bring to boil. Fill jars and seal. Process in hot water bath for 5 minutes.

Mrs. Henry Boedeker (Stasie)

Dill Pickles

3 to 4 small dry red hot peppers
3 to 4 cloves garlic
3 to 4 tablespoons dill seed or
    fresh dill weed

1   gallon cucumbers
6   cups water
2   cups white vinegar
½   cup salt, not iodized

Distribute seasonings evenly among 3 to 4 quart jars. Pack pickles in jars. Bring water, vinegar and salt to boil. Pour over pickles in jars. Seal and immerse in hot water bath about 5 minutes. Remove from water immediately. Yields 3 to 4 quarts.

Mrs. Henry Boedeker (Stasie)

Bread and Butter Pickles

1   gallon sliced cucumbers
1   quart ice cubes
4   small onions, sliced
2   green peppers, sliced
1   teaspoon alum
1   teaspoon salt

5   cups vinegar
5   cups sugar
2   teaspoons turmeric
2   teaspoons mustard seed
1   tablespoon celery seed

Mix cucumbers, ice, onions, green peppers, alum and salt; let sit 3 hours, stirring occasionally. Drain and put in large pan. Add vinegar, sugar, turmeric, mustard seed and celery seed. Bring to a boil on high heat. Remove from heat. Put into sterilized jars and seal quickly. Yields 8 pints.

Mrs. Larry Morris (Diane)

Martha Ellen's Sweet Pickles

2 cups household lime
7½ pounds cucumbers, sliced
8 cups sugar
1 teaspoon whole pickling
   spices

8 cups white vinegar
1 tablespoon salt
1 tablespoon turmeric

Sprinkle lime over cucumbers. Cover with ice water for 20 hours. Rinse well. Cover with cold water. Let stand 3 hours. Make brine by heating sugar, pickling spices, vinegar, salt and turmeric to boiling. Pour hot brine over cucumbers and soak 12 hours. Simmer until pickle center starts to clear. Then spoon pickles into sterilized jars and pour liquid to top. Seal. After 30 minutes tighten lids. Turn upside down. Next day tighten again and check for leaks. Pickles can be eaten after four weeks.

Mrs. Johnny Johnson (Marcy)

Chow-Chow

2 quarts green tomatoes,
   chopped
4 quarts cabbage, shredded
6 green peppers, chopped
6 onions, chopped
1 bunch celery, chopped

2 quarts apple cider vinegar
4 tablespoons salt
1 teaspoon turmeric
4 cups sugar
2 ounces mustard seed

Combine all ingredients and cook on high heat until boiling. Cut heat to simmer and cook 1 hour. Can in sterilized jars and seal.

Mrs. Larry Morris (Diane)

Summer Corn Relish

2 cups sugar
2 cups vinegar
1½ teaspoons salt
1½ teaspoons celery seed
½ teaspoon turmeric

2 cups chopped onion
2 cups chopped tomato
2 cups chopped cucumber
2 cups corn cut from cob
2 cups chopped cabbage

In large Dutch oven combine sugar, vinegar, salt, celery seed, and turmeric and bring to a boil. Add onion, tomato, cucumber, corn, and cabbage; cook uncovered for 25 minutes, stirring occasionally. Pack in hot, sterilized jars and seal. Yields 3 pints.

Mrs. Thomas Schwartz (Ellana)

Cousin Mattie's Relish

20 pounds cabbage	4 pounds sugar
7 pounds onions	2 heaping tablespoons
Salt	turmeric
1 gallon and 1 quart brown	½ box (1½ ounces) celery seed
vinegar	1 box (1½ ounces) white
1 handful each wholespices,	mustard seed
allspice, cinnamon, cloves	Salt, optional

Grind cabbage and onions together with a coarse grinder, and salt thoroughly. Let sit overnight; squeeze dry. Mix vinegar, wholespices, allspice, cinnamon and cloves; bring to a boil. Add sugar and turmeric, and return to stove and boil for a few minutes. Strain. Put strained liquid back on stove and add cabbage mixture, celery seed, mustard seed, and salt. Bring to a boil. Pour into sterilized jars and seal. Yields 26 pints. *This is a very, very old family recipe, a delicious accompaniment to meats. It is a family tradition to serve it with Spiced Round (see Index) during the Christmas holidays. The recipe can be halved for a smaller quantity.*

D. D. Baker, Jr.

Chutney

2 packages (6 ounces each) dried apricots	2 cups vinegar
	1 onion, chopped
2 cans (20 ounces each) pineapple chunks, drained	2 cloves garlic, chopped
	4 slices fresh ginger, chopped
1 package (6 ounces) golden raisins	or 1 tablespoon ground
	1 tablespoon cloves
1 cup currants	1 tablespoon cinnamon
4 green pears, unpeeled and chopped	½ teaspoon cayenne pepper
	1 teaspoon dry mustard
1 cup sugar	¼ teaspoon salt
1 cup brown sugar	

Cut apricots in bite-size pieces and mix with pineapple, raisins, and currants; set aside. Cook pears with sugars, vinegar, onion, garlic, ginger and spices for 1½ to 2 hours. While hot, pour over the apricot mixture, and toss to mix all ingredients. Refrigerate at least 24 hours before serving to allow flavors to blend. Seasonings may be varied to your personal tastes.

Mrs. Denman Smith (Sandra)

Mango Chutney

1 pint cider vinegar
3½ cups brown sugar, firmly packed
2 medium onions, chopped
1 lemon, sliced thin
1 clove fresh garlic, minced
1½ cups seedless raisins or currants
¼ teaspoon cayenne pepper
1½ teaspoons salt
1 tablespoon mustard seed
4 ounces fresh ginger, thinly sliced

6 tomatoes, peeled and cut into eighths
1 green pepper, chopped
6 whole cloves
¼ teaspoon nutmeg
6 medium apples, peeled, cored and sliced, or 3 apples and 3 hard pears
4 large mangoes, peeled and sliced

Combine all ingredients, except apples and mangoes, in a large kettle. Cook 1 hour or until liquid is clear and syrupy. Add apples and mangoes; continue cooking until fruit is tender. Fill sterilized jars, leaving ½ inch head space. Seal, place in boiling water bath for 10 minutes. Yields about 5 pints. *This is the king of the chutneys; it's great with curry.*

Mrs. Jim Shorey (Zann)

Pickled Serrano or Jalapeño Peppers

3 pounds peppers
¼ cup salt

3 cups white (5%) vinegar
3 cups water

Pack peppers in canning jars. Bring remaining ingredients to a boil and pour over peppers to ¼ inch of the top. Seal. Cook 10 minutes in a hot water bath. Yields 3 quarts.

Mrs. Jim Shorey (Zann)

Chili Pequin or Tabasco Peppers

1 glass cruet
Chili pequins to fill

Hot vinegar to cover

Chili pequins are those decorative little fire balls that you occasionally end up with from the nursery instead of the bell peppers you thought you were buying. The vinegar from these is wonderful on hot, cooked green or pinto beans, etc. Don't eat the peppers!

Cookbook Committee

Pickled Lima Beans

2 pounds frozen lima beans	¼ teaspoon cayenne pepper
½ cup pimiento	2 cloves garlic, crushed
1 cup vinegar	2 to 3 cups water
2 tablespoons dillweed	

Defrost lima beans, toss with pimiento and pack in a 2 quart jar. Bring remaining ingredients to simmer and cook for 5 minutes. Pour over limas and store in refrigerator up to 30 days. Yields 2 quarts. *These are a wonderful addition to any tossed salad, macaroni or vegetable medley.*

Mrs. Denman Smith (Sandra)

Pickled Beets

3 cups sliced or whole beets	1 teaspoon whole allspice
2 cups vinegar	6 whole cloves
1 cup water	3 sticks cinnamon
½ cup sugar	

Put beets into quart jar. Boil remaining ingredients for 5 minutes, cool slightly and pour over beets. Cover and store in refrigerator and use to garnish any salad.

Mrs. Denman Smith (Sandra)

Spiced Pears

1 part sugar	Food coloring, optional
2 parts water	Cloves
Pears, peeled, cored and quartered	

Mix sugar and water. Put pears in covered saucepan and cook in syrup until tender. Test with fork. Add red or green food coloring, if desired. Seal in sterilized jars. Cloves add a nice spicy flavor; add 3 cloves to pint jars and 4 to 6 for quart jars.

Mrs. Jack Dempsey (Estelle)

Spiced Peach Jam

4 cups peaches (3 pounds)	2 teaspoons cinnamon
¼ cup lemon juice	1 teaspoon powdered cloves
7½ cups sugar	½ teaspoon allspice
1 pouch (3 ounces) Certo	

Peel and pit ripe peaches; chop in blender or mash. Put fruit in large pan; add sugar. Mix well. Over high heat bring to full boil and boil hard one minute, stirring constantly. Remove from heat; immediately stir in Certo. Skim off foam with metal spoon. Stir and skim for 5 minutes. Add spices and mix well. Put into sterilized jars and cover at once with ⅛ inch hot paraffin.

Mrs. Don Bradford (Melinda)

Sun Cooked Strawberry Preserves

6 cups sugar	3 pounds large strawberries, hulled and washed, about 5 quarts
¾ cups water	

Combine sugar and water. Cook until mixture just starts to bubble; syrup will be thick and white. Turn heat to high and add strawberries. Mix gently, being careful to coat each berry, but do not crush. Stir until sugar dissolves, about 5 minutes. Pour in one layer into large aluminum roasting pan, so fruit lies flat in syrup; cover with cheesecloth. Place in sun 4 to 5 days, about 36 hours of full sunlight; stir occasionally to expose all surfaces of berries and syrup to sun. Bring in at night. If rainy or cloudy weather should interfere, bring berries inside; they will keep safely several days if fruit has had 4 to 5 hours of sun. Continue cooking as soon as weather clears. When fully cooked, syrup will have evaporated to about half its original amount and berries will be plumped. Place berries in sterilized jars and cover with syrup. Seal with paraffin and lid. Any remaining syrup may be stored in refrigerator. *Add a bit of raspberry liqueur and use as a delightful ice cream topping.*

Mrs. Don Panter (Carolyn)

Marinated Mushrooms

4 cups chopped mushrooms
4 cups chopped olives
2 cups chopped carrots
1 cup chopped onion
½ cup chopped pimiento

2 tablespoons dry tarragon
2 cups vinegar
½ cup olive oil
1 tablespoon salt

Toss mushrooms, olives, carrots, onions and pimientos gently together and pack into jar. Bring remaining ingredients to a boil and pour over vegetables. Keep refrigerated up to 30 days. *These mushrooms just get better and better. Serve over any tossed salad or in the center of an aspic.*

Mrs. Denman Smith (Sandra)

Pickled Eggs

12 hard boiled eggs, peeled
    and pricked
1 medium onion, sliced
1 cup beet juice

1 cup vinegar
1 teaspoon salt
1 teaspoon mixed pickling
    spice

Pack eggs in a jar, alternating with onion slices. Heat juice, vinegar, salt and spices to boiling point. Pour hot solution over eggs. Store in refrigerator for 36 hours before serving.

Mrs. Clark Rector (Sue)

Sweet Banana Peppers

2 pounds banana peppers
2 cups sugar
2 cups tarragon vinegar
2 cups water

½ teaspoon celery seed
1 teaspoon mustard seed
2 cloves garlic, crushed
1 teaspoon salt

Cook peppers 3 to 5 minutes in boiling water, drain and pack in jars. Bring remaining ingredients to boil and simmer 5 minutes. Cool slightly and pour over peppers. Store in refrigerator up to 30 days and serve as accompaniment for burgers and sandwiches.

Mrs. Denman Smith (Sandra)

Schutzenfests (shooting fests), saengerfests (singing fests), and wurstfests (sausage fests) are an integral part of the German culture. All are equally enjoyed throughout the state.

Barbecued Onions Diablo

1 cup catsup	1 tablespoon sugar
¾ cup boiling water	1 teaspoon salt
¼ cup cider vinegar	1 teaspoon celery seed
1 tablespoon Worcestershire sauce	¼ teaspoon Tabasco
	3 cups sliced onions

Combine all ingredients except onions in medium saucepan. Heat to boiling. Reduce heat to medium. Cover and cook 4 minutes. Stir in onions. Cook an additional 3 minutes. Cover and chill.

Mrs. Denman Smith (Sandra)

Pickled Onion Relish

1 tablespoon mixed pickling spices	¾ teaspoon salt
⅓ cup water	¼ teaspoon pepper
⅓ cup cider vinegar	1 cup chopped tomato
2 tablespoons sugar	1 cup chopped green pepper
	2 cups sliced onions

Tie pickling spices in cheesecloth. In medium saucepan, heat spice bag and remaining ingredients, except onions, to boiling. Reduce heat to medium. Cover and cook 3 minutes. Stir in onions. Cook an additional 3 minutes. Remove spice bag. Cover and refrigerate. Makes 8 to 10 servings.

Mrs. Denman Smith (Sandra)

Jezebel Sauce

1 jar (6 ounces) prepared mustard	1 jar (8 or 10 ounces) apple jelly
1 jar (6 ounces) prepared horseradish	1 jar (8 or 10 ounces) pineapple preserves

Combine all ingredients. Serve as sauce with ham or pour over cream cheese and serve with crackers. Also good as an egg roll sauce.

Mrs. Jim Schultz (Mary Kay)

 Texas' second largest cash crop, corn, has grown here for more than four hundred years.

Sweet and Sour Sauce

½ cup peach preserves
1 whole pimiento, drained
and finely chopped

2 to 3 tablespoons white
vinegar

Blend all ingredients well. Serve with egg rolls.

Mrs. Larry Nau (Rose)

Cocktail Sauce

½ cup chili sauce
⅓ cup catsup
2 tablespoons horseradish
1½ teaspoons Worcestershire
sauce

¼ teaspoon salt
2 tablespoons lemon juice
Dash pepper
Tabasco to taste

Combine all ingredients and chill. Serve with seafood.

Mrs. Larry Nau (Rose)

Remoulade Sauce

4 green onions, chopped
1 medium onion, chopped
1 green pepper, chopped
½ cup chopped celery
1 teaspoon garlic powder
1 teaspoon chopped parsley
1 tablespoon capers
3 hardboiled eggs, chopped

1 quart Hellman's mayonnaise
1 tablespoon Worcestershire
sauce
2 tablespoons creole mustard
1 tablespoon French mustard
½ teaspoon Tabasco
Salt and pepper to taste

Mix onions, green pepper, celery, garlic powder, parsley, capers and eggs.
Add mayonnaise, Worcestershire, mustard, Tabasco, salt and pepper;
blend together. Mix ingredients the day before serving. Yields 1 quart.
*Serve as dip for raw vegetables, or as dipping sauce for cold, boiled
shrimp. It can also be mixed with shrimp for shrimp salad.*

Mrs. K. L. McConchie (Katherine)

 *To correct curdled mayonnaise or hollandaise, put an egg yolk
into a clean pan. Beat until thick. Gradually beat in curdled sauce
until it becomes smooth again.*

Blender Hollandaise Sauce

3 egg yolks
2 teaspoons lemon juice
¼ teaspoon salt

2 drops Tabasco
½ cup butter, melted

In blender, mix yolks, lemon juice, salt, and Tabasco. Slowly pour melted butter into blender while mixing on low speed. Refrigerate if not using immediately. Yields 1 cup.

Mrs. Ken Moyer (Bonnie)

 To adapt Hollandaise sauce to a Bernaise sauce, add 1 tablespoon minced parsley, 1 tablespoon tarragon vinegar, and ½ teaspoon tarragon.

Mustard Sauce

1 pint half and half cream
½ cup sugar
4 tablespoons dry mustard

2 egg yolks
1½ tablespoons cornstarch
1 cup vinegar
Salt to taste

Mix together cream, sugar, mustard, yolks and cornstarch; cook until thick. When thick, add vinegar and salt. Cook about 5 more minutes. Great with cold ham or on sandwiches. Yields about 2 pints. *Keeps for a long time.*

Mrs. George Wade (June)

Cuisinart Mayonnaise

2 egg yolks
½ teaspoon dry mustard
½ teaspoon salt

2 tablespoons vinegar or lemon juice
1½ cups vegetable oil

Place yolks, mustard, salt, and vinegar in Cuisinart; mix briefly. Add ½ cup of oil, mix briefly and then add remaining oil in a steady stream while mixing. When all oil has been added, turn Cuisinart off. If mixture seems thick, dilute with 1 teaspoon hot water. Yields approximately 1½ pints. *Better than store bought and will last in refrigerator for 4 to 5 weeks in covered plastic container. Use one-half vegetable oil and one-half olive oil for a different flavor.*

Mrs. Marcus Bone (Beverly)

Honey Mayonnaise

1 egg	1 teaspoon honey
2 tablespoons white wine vinegar	½ teaspoon salt
	¼ teaspoon white pepper
½ teaspoon dry mustard	1¼ cups corn oil

Combine egg, vinegar, mustard, honey, salt and pepper in blender. Blend until smooth. With machine running, add oil very slowly. Blend until thickened and emulsified. Store in refrigerator for up to 10 days. Yields about 1¾ cups.

Nancy Young Moritz

Avocado Butter

1 large ripe avocado, peeled and cubed	½ pound sweet butter, softened
2 tablespoons fresh lime juice	⅛ teaspoon ground ginger

Put avocado in the blender with lime juice. Blend until creamy. Blend in butter and ginger. Chill. Yields about 1½ cups. *This is a good spread with tostados, crackers or fresh vegetables and also as the butter on any kind of sandwich. It makes an excellent dunk for beef fondue and it can be frozen.*

Mrs. James Hurlbut (Marsha)

Almond Butter

½ cup butter	1 clove garlic, optional
½ cup sliced almonds	Salt to taste

Melt butter in a heavy skillet. Add almonds and garlic. Cook over low heat until almonds are golden. Nuts will burn easily, so do not rush. Season with salt. Discard garlic clove. Yields about ½ cup. *Delicious over fish or vegetables.*

Nancy Young Moritz

In the small town of Taylor, they hold an annual International Barbecue Cook-Off. However, unlike the traditional use of beef, their motto is, "You can cook whatever will stand still long enough."

Spicy Venison Sauce

1   cup margarine
½   cup fresh lemon juice
1   teaspoon salt
1   teaspoon pepper

2   tablespoons Worcestershire
     sauce
2   jalapeños, diced with seeds

Bring all ingredients to a boil and simmer 10 minutes. This sauce can be used to reheat venison. Place venison in aluminum foil; add sauce. Seal and put in oven until warm. Sauce can also be used for marinating venison overnight, or as a basting sauce for meat on barbecue grill.

Mrs. Robert West (Linda)

Beef Marinade

1½ cups salad oil
¾   cup soy sauce
¼   cup Worcestershire sauce
2   tablespoons dry mustard
2¼ teaspoons salt

1   tablespoon pepper
½   cup red wine vinegar
1½ teaspoons parsley flakes
2   cloves crushed garlic
⅓   cup lemon juice

Put all ingredients in blender and mix well. Sauce is good for basting on grilled roast or brisket, but is best for shish kebabs. Marinate meat as long as possible. The vegetables for shish kebab are good marinated with the meat, but might need to be parboiled first if the meat is cooked rare to medium rare. *Keeps indefinitely in freezer or 1 week in refrigerator. May be used and refrozen.*

Mrs. Jim Rado (Vicki)

Hot Barbeque Sauce

1   large onion, chopped
¼   cup butter
1½ cups catsup
1   cup meat stock or 1 cup
     chicken bouillon
⅓   cup lemon juice

¼   cup Worcestershire sauce
2   tablespoons vinegar
1   teaspoon celery seed
¼   teaspoon cayenne pepper
¼   cup brown sugar, when used
     for pork

Sauté chopped onion in butter until clear. Add the remaining ingredients. Cook over low heat for 20 minutes, stirring frequently. Yields 2½ cups sauce. *This is a good sauce for beef, chicken, leg of lamb, cabrito or pork. If using pork, add brown sugar to sauce.*

Mrs. Daniel O'Donnell (Sharon)

Bar-B-Q Sauce

½ cup vinegar
1 cup catsup
½ cup chopped onion
½ to 1 teaspoon cayenne
   pepper
2 tablespoons Liquid Smoke,
   optional

¼ cup brown sugar
2 teaspoons dry mustard
2 tablespoons Worcestershire
   sauce
½ cup butter
Salt to taste

Combine in saucepan and simmer slowly for 30 minutes to blend flavors. Brush on any meat or chicken as it grills and serve with cooked meat also. Yields 2 cups.

Denman Smith

Cajun Barbeque Sauce

1 pint oil
2 medium onions, finely
   chopped
1 or 2 green peppers, finely
   chopped
4 or 5 ribs of celery, finely
   chopped
2 cloves garlic, minced
1 can (8 ounces) tomato
   sauce

1 can (6 ounces) tomato paste
½ cup catsup
3 tablespoons Worcestershire
   sauce
3 tablespoons mustard
Juice of one lemon
Salt, red and black pepper to
   taste

Heat oil in Dutch oven; add onions, green pepper, celery and garlic. Cook until onions are soft. Add remaining ingredients and simmer until vegetables are tender. Add water if too thick. Sauce will separate; do not stir. Baste meat, chickens, ribs, etc., with the oil on top of sauce as it cooks on grill. Thirty minutes before serving baste with the thick part of the sauce on the bottom. Serve a big bowl of the heated sauce with your meal. It is delicious on French bread. It will keep up to six weeks in the refrigerator and indefinitely in the freezer. Yields about 6 cups. *This recipe has been in my family for about 35 years.*

Mrs. John Baker (Jo)

 Sausage and beer—no wurstfest in Texas would be complete without these delicious go-togethers. English, Polish, German—each is a little different, but all are guaranteed to tempt the palate.

Basic Gravy

2 tablespoons flour
2 tablespoons margarine, melted, or fat skimmed from meat stock

1 cup meat stock
½ teaspoon salt
Pepper to taste

Prepare roux by blending melted margarine and flour in hot frying pan, stirring constantly until dark brown in color. Reduce heat; slowly add liquid, stirring constantly to avoid lumps. Add salt and pepper. Extra roux may be prepared in advance with equal quantities of flour and fat or margarine, then sealed and refrigerated or frozen to be used as required. Do not add liquid and salt until ready to use. Meat stock may be obtained from roast drippings, or chicken broth from stewed chicken. Also soup bone may be cooked, stock strained and chilled overnight to remove excess fat.

Mrs. Bob Bluntzer (Jo)

Home Cured Jerky

1½ to 2 pounds lean, boneless meat
¼ cup soy sauce
1 tablespoon Worcestershire
¼ teaspoon pepper

¼ teaspoon garlic powder
½ teaspoon onion powder
1 teaspoon hickory smoke flavored salt
Hot sauce or Tabasco, optional

Trim and discard all fat from meat. Cut meat into ⅛ to ¼ inch thick slices. In a bowl, combine soy sauce, Worcestershire, pepper, garlic powder, onion powder and smoke flavored salt. Stir until seasonings are dissolved. Add all the meat strips and work them thoroughly into the mix until all surfaces are well coated. The meat will absorb most, if not all, of the liquid. Cover tightly and let stand overnight in the refrigerator. Shake off any excess liquid, sprinkle coarse ground black pepper on both sides. Arrange strips of meat close together, but not overlapping, directly on oven racks or cake racks set in shallow, rimmed pans. Dry meat in oven at the lowest possible oven setting, 150° to 200°, until it turns brown, feels hard and is dry to the touch. This will take 5 hours for chicken and turkey, 4 to 7 hours for beef and venison. Pat off any beads of oil. Cool and store in airtight plastic bags or in jars with tight fitting lids. Keeps in refrigerator or at room temperature indefinitely. *Men love to make this! This particular jerky can be made from beef flank, brisket or top round steak, venison or the white meat from chicken or turkey. Partially freezing meat makes it easier to slice evenly. Cut with the grain for chewy jerky, across the grain for more tender, brittle jerky.*

Don Bradford

Salami

5   **pounds lean ground meat**
¼   **cup Morton's Tender Quick Curing Salt, no substitute**
3   **teaspoons Liquid Smoke**
3   **teaspoons mustard seed**
5   **teaspoons black pepper**
2   **teaspoons poultry seasoning**

3   **teaspoons dry garlic salad dressing mix**
2   **cloves garlic, pressed**
1   **teaspoon red pepper**
2   **teaspoons Italian herb seasoning mix**

Place all ingredients in a large bowl. Using both hands, blend thoroughly, being particularly careful that the curing salt is well mixed. Cover and refrigerate for 24 hours. Mix again, and refrigerate another 24 hours. Divide the meat into 5 portions. Roll each into a log shaped roll, 2½ to 3 inches in diameter, and 6 to 8 inches long. Press meat firmly together to eliminate air pockets. Bake at 250° on a rack, rolling each roll back and forth so that it does not flatten out on one side. Bake for 30 minutes at 250°, and then reduce heat to 200°; continue baking for 6 hours. When done, drain on paper towels. These rolls will keep in the refrigerator wrapped in foil for 3 weeks and up to 6 months in the freezer.

D. D. Baker, Jr.

Salsa Fresca

1   **large tomato, seeded and chopped**
½   **cup finely chopped onion**
2   **jalapeños, seeded and chopped**

¼   **cup tomato sauce**
1   **teaspoon salt**
2   **teaspoons cilantro, chopped**

Mix all ingredients together and store in refrigerator for 30 minutes before serving to allow flavors to blend together. Yields about one pint. *This is an excellent side dish for any Mexican food or a good dip. Keeps for a couple of days in refrigerator but not much longer.*

Mrs. Jim Rado (Vicki)

Popcorn Herb Butter

½ pound soft whipped
    margarine
1 pinch each of any 5 herbs
2 pinches curry powder
1 tablespoon paprika
6 cups popped popcorn

1 tablespoon sesame seed
1 tablespoon Parmesan
    cheese
1 clove garlic, mashed
1 teaspoon onion powder

Combine all ingredients, except popcorn, in saucepan and cook or microwave until margarine is melted. Pour over popcorn. *A pinch is what you pick up with two fingers and your thumb!*

Cookbook Committee

Granola

½ to 1 cup oil
½ to 1 cup honey
4 cups rolled oats
1 cup wheat germ
1 cup shredded coconut
1 cup chopped nuts

½ cup sesame seeds
½ cup bran
1 cup sunflower seeds,
    optional
Dried fruits

Heat oil and honey and mix with dry ingredients. Toast in oven on large cookie sheet, stirring frequently. Any combination of ingredients is fine. To this basic recipe may be added dried fruits such as raisins, dates, apples, pears, apricots, or pineapple. Add fruit after mixture has cooled. Store in covered containers. Keeps well.

Mrs. Steve Scheffe (Betsy)

Play Dough

1 cup flour
½ cup salt

⅓ cup water
Food coloring, optional

Mix all ingredients together and knead until smooth. Store in covered container. *It's just like the real thing!*

Mrs. Don Panter (Carolyn)

Fingerpaint

⅔ cup elastic dry starch
1 cup cold water
3 cups boiling water
1 cup Ivory Soap Flakes

3 drops oil of cloves, as a
   preservative
Food coloring

Dissolve elastic starch in cold water. Smooth lumps and add boiling water. Stir constantly and cook to thicken but do not boil more than one minute. Add remaining ingredients. *This is fun entertainment for your children to use on butcher paper, newsprint, or wrapping paper.*

Mrs. Jim Rado (Vicki)

Potter's Clay

3¾ cups boiling water
1 cup salt

6½ to 8 cups flour, divided
½ cup cornstarch

Boil water and salt until salt dissolves. Blend ½ cup flour and cornstarch with enough water to make a smooth paste. Add to salt and water and cook until clear. Cool overnight and then add 6 to 8 cups flour and knead until you have the consistency for molding. *This is a good molding clay for children. It may be painted when dry.*

Mrs. Jim Rado (Vicki)

Iridescent Soap Bubbles

4 cups of water
8 tablespoons liquid
   detergent
4 tablespoons glycerine,
   optional

1 small bottle commercial
   bubbles
2 teaspoons sugar

Mix all ingredients. *This inexpensive homemade version is good to refill the purchased bubbles all children love.*

Spicewood Country School

Equivalents

Ingredient	Equivalent
3 medium apples	3 cups sliced apples
3 medium bananas	2½ cups sliced, 2 cups mashed banana
1 medium lemon	2 to 3 tablespoons juice and 2 teaspoons grated rind
1 medium lime	1½ to 2 tablespoons juice
1 medium orange	⅓ cup juice and 2 tablespoons grated rind
4 medium peaches	2 cups sliced peaches
4 medium pears	2 cups sliced pears
1 quart strawberries	4 cups sliced strawberries
1 pound head cabbage	4½ cups shredded cabbage
1 pound carrots	3 cups shredded carrots
2 medium corn ears	1 cup whole kernel corn
1 large green pepper	1 cup diced green pepper
1 pound head lettuce	6¼ cups torn lettuce
8 ounces raw mushrooms	1 cup sliced cooked mushrooms
1 medium onion	½ cup chopped onion
3 medium white potatoes	2 cups cubed cooked or 1¾ cups mashed white potatoes
3 medium sweet potatoes	3 cups sliced sweet potatoes
8 slices cooked bacon	½ cup crumbled bacon
1 pound American or Cheddar cheese	4 to 5 cups shredded cheese
4 ounces cheese	1 cup shredded cheese
5 large whole eggs	1 cup eggs
6 to 7 large eggs	1 cup egg whites
11 to 12 large eggs	1 cup egg yolks
1 cup quick-cooking oats	1¾ cups cooked oats
1 cup uncooked long grain rice	3 to 4 cups cooked rice
1 cup pre-cooked rice	2 cups cooked rice
1 pound coffee	40 cups perked coffee
1 pound pitted dates	2 to 3 cups chopped dates
1 pound all-purpose flour	4 cups flour
1 pound granulated sugar	2 cups sugar
1 pound powdered sugar	3½ cups powdered sugar
1 pound brown sugar	2¼ cups firmly packed brown sugar
1 cup (4 ounces) uncooked macaroni	2¼ cups cooked macaroni
4 ounces uncooked noodles	2 cups cooked noodles
7 ounces uncooked spaghetti	4 cups cooked spaghetti
1 pound shelled nuts	4 cups chopped nuts

1 cup whipping cream	2 cups whipped cream
1 cup soft bread crumbs	2 slices fresh bread
1 pound crab in shell	¾ to 1 cup flaked crab
1½ pounds fresh, unpeeled shrimp	2 cups cooked, peeled deveined shrimp
1 pound fresh small shrimp . . .	35 or more shrimp
1 pound fresh medium shrimp .	26 to 35 shrimp
1 pound fresh large shrimp	21 to 25 shrimp
1 pound fresh jumbo shrimp . .	less than 20 shrimp

Crackers

19 chocolate wafers	1 cup crumbs
14 graham cracker squares	1 cup fine crumbs
28 saltines	1 cup finely crushed crumbs
22 vanilla wafers	1 cup finely crushed crumbs

Substitutions

Recipe Ingredients	Substitution
1 cup sour or buttermilk	1 tablespoon vinegar or lemon juice plus sweet milk to make 1 cup
1 cup commercial sour cream .	1 tablespoon lemon juice plus evaporated milk to equal 1 cup
1 cup yogurt	1 cup sour or buttermilk
1 whole egg	2 egg yolks plus 1 tablespoon water
1 tablespoon cornstarch	2 tablespoons all-purpose flour
1 teaspoon baking powder	½ teaspoon cream of tartar plus ¼ teaspoon soda
1 cup cake flour	1 cup all-purpose flour minus 2 tablespoons
1 cup self-rising flour	1 cup all-purpose flour plus 1 teaspoon baking powder and ½ teaspoon salt
1 cup honey	1¼ cups sugar plus ¼ cup liquid
1 ounce unsweetened chocolate	3 tablespoons cocoa plus 1 tablespoon butter or margarine
1 pound fresh mushrooms	6 ounces canned mushrooms
1 tablespoon fresh herbs	1 teaspoon ground or crushed dry herbs
1 teaspoon onion powder	2 teaspoons minced onion
1 clove fresh garlic	1 teaspoon garlic salt or ⅛ teaspoon garlic powder

Measurements to Remember

3 teaspoons	=	1 tablespoon
4 tablespoons	=	¼ cup
8 tablespoons	=	½ cup
16 tablespoons	=	1 cup
5 tablespoons plus		
1 teaspoon	=	⅓ cup
4 ounces	=	½ cup
8 ounces	=	1 cup
16 ounces	=	1 pound
1 ounce	=	2 tablespoons fat or liquid
2 cups fat	=	1 pound
2 cups	=	1 pint
1 pound butter	=	2 cups or 4 sticks
2 pints	=	1 quart
4 cups	=	1 quart

The Metric System

2 cups	=	473 milliliters
1 cup	=	237 milliliters
¾ cup	=	177 milliliters
⅔ cup	=	157 milliliters
½ cup	=	118 milliliters
⅓ cup	=	79 milliliters
¼ cup	=	59 milliliters
1 tablespoon	=	15 milliliters
1 teaspoon	=	5 milliliters
1 fluid ounce	=	30 milliliters

How to Convert:

liters x 2.1 = pints	kilograms x 2.2 = pounds
liters x 1.06 = quarts	grams x .035 = ounces
cups x .24 = liters	pounds x .45 = kilograms
gallons x 3.8 = liters	ounces x 28 = grams

Temperatures:

250 degrees Fahrenheit = 121 degrees Celsius
300 degrees Fahrenheit = 149 degrees Celsius
350 degrees Fahrenheit = 177 degrees Celsius
400 degrees Fahrenheit = 205 degrees Celsius
450 degrees Fahrenheit = 232 degrees Celsius

Index

A

C

CAKES

CANDY

MEXICAN DISHES

P

T

V

Austin Junior Forum Publications
P.O. Box 26628
Austin, Texas 78755-0628

Please send me _____ copies of *Lone Star Legacy*   @ $14.95 each_____
Please send me _____ copies of *Lone Star Legacy II*   @   14.95 each_____
Texas residents add 6¼% sales tax (1-1-87 to 8-31-87)   @   .93 each_____
Texas residents add 5⅛% sales tax (after 8-31-87)   @   .77 each_____
Postage and handling   @   2.00 each_____
Gift wrap   @   2.00 each_____
                                                           Total Enclosed_____

Name _____
Address _____
City _____ State _____ Zip _____

Make checks payable to *Lone Star Legacy*.

Austin Junior Forum Publications
P.O. Box 26628
Austin, Texas 78755-0628

Please send me _____ copies of *Lone Star Legacy*   @ $14.95 each_____
Please send me _____ copies of *Lone Star Legacy II*   @   14.95 each_____
Texas residents add 6¼% sales tax (1-1-87 to 8-31-87)   @   .93 each_____
Texas residents add 5⅛% sales tax (after 8-31-87)   @   .77 each_____
Postage and handling   @   2.00 each_____
Gift wrap   @   2.00 each_____
                                                           Total Enclosed_____

Name _____
Address _____
City _____ State _____ Zip _____

Make checks payable to *Lone Star Legacy*.

Austin Junior Forum Publications
P.O. Box 26628
Austin, Texas 78755-0628

Please send me _____ copies of *Lone Star Legacy*   @ $14.95 each_____
Please send me _____ copies of *Lone Star Legacy II*   @   14.95 each_____
Texas residents add 6¼% sales tax (1-1-87 to 8-31-87)   @   .93 each_____
Texas residents add 5⅛% sales tax (after 8-31-87)   @   .77 each_____
Postage and handling   @   2.00 each_____
Gift wrap   @   2.00 each_____
                                                           Total Enclosed_____

Name _____
Address _____
City _____ State _____ Zip _____

Make checks payable to *Lone Star Legacy*.

If you would like to see *Lone Star Legacy* in your area, please send the names and addresses of your local gift or book stores.

If you would like to see *Lone Star Legacy* in your area, please send the names and addresses of your local gift or book stores.

If you would like to see *Lone Star Legacy* in your area, please send the names and addresses of your local gift or book stores.

Austin Junior Forum Publications
P.O. Box 26628
Austin, Texas 78755-0628

Please send me _____ copies of *Lone Star Legacy*   @ $14.95 each_____

Please send me _____ copies of *Lone Star Legacy II* @   14.95 each_____

Texas residents add 6¼% sales tax (1-1-87 to 8-31-87)   @   .93 each_____

Texas residents add 5⅛% sales tax (after 8-31-87)   @   .77 each_____

Postage and handling   @   2.00 each_____

Gift wrap   @   2.00 each_____

Total Enclosed_____

Name _____

Address _____

City _____ State _____ Zip _____

Make checks payable to *Lone Star Legacy.*

Austin Junior Forum Publications
P.O. Box 26628
Austin, Texas 78755-0628

Please send me _____ copies of *Lone Star Legacy*   @ $14.95 each_____

Please send me _____ copies of *Lone Star Legacy II* @   14.95 each_____

Texas residents add 6¼% sales tax (1-1-87 to 8-31-87)   @   .93 each_____

Texas residents add 5⅛% sales tax (after 8-31-87)   @   .77 each_____

Postage and handling   @   2.00 each_____

Gift wrap   @   2.00 each_____

Total Enclosed_____

Name _____

Address _____

City _____ State _____ Zip _____

Make checks payable to *Lone Star Legacy.*

If you would like to see *Lone Star Legacy* in your area, please send the names and addresses of your local gift or book stores.

If you would like to see *Lone Star Legacy* in your area, please send the names and addresses of your local gift or book stores.

If you would like to see *Lone Star Legacy* in your area, please send the names and addresses of your local gift or book stores.